ANDERSON'S
Law School Publications

Administrative Law Anthology
Thomas O. Sargentich

Administrative Law: Cases and Materials
Daniel J. Gifford

Alternative Dispute Resolution: Strategies for Law and Busine
E. Wendy Trachte-Huber and Stephen K. Huber

American Legal Systems: A Resource and Reference Guide
Toni M. Fine

An Admiralty Law Anthology
Robert M. Jarvis

Analytic Jurisprudence Anthology
Anthony D'Amato

An Antitrust Anthology
Andrew I. Gavil

Appellate Advocacy: Principles and Practice, Second Edition
Ursula Bentele and Eve Cary

Basic Accounting Principles for Lawyers: With Present Value and Expected Value
C. Steven Bradford and Gary A. Ames

A Capital Punishment Anthology (and Electronic Caselaw Appendix)
Victor L. Streib

Cases and Problems in Criminal Law, Third Edition
Myron Moskovitz

The Citation Workbook: How to Beat the Citation Blues, Second Edition
Maria L. Ciampi, Rivka Widerman, and Vicki Lutz

Civil Procedure: Cases, Materials, and Questions, Second Edition
Richard D. Freer and Wendy Collins Perdue

Clinical Anthology: Readings for Live-Client Clinics
Alex J. Hurder, Frank S. Bloch, Susan L. Brooks, and Susan L. Kay

Commercial Transactions Series: Problems and Materials
Louis F. Del Duca, Egon Guttman, Alphonse M. Squillante, Fred H. Miller, Linda Rusch, and Peter Winship
    Vol. 1: Secured Transactions Under the UCC
    Vol. 2: Sales Under the UCC and the CISG
    Vol. 3: Negotiable Instruments Under the UCC and the CIBN

Communications Law: Media, Entertainment, and Regulation
Donald E. Lively, Allen S. Hammond, Blake D. Morant, and Russell L. Weaver

A Conflict-of-Laws Anthology
Gene R. Shreve

A Constitutional Law Anthology, Second Edition
Michael J. Glennon, Donald E. Lively, Phoebe A. Haddon, Dorothy E. Roberts, and Russell L. Weaver

Constitutional Conflicts, Parts I & II
Derrick A. Bell, Jr.

Constitutional Law: Cases, History, and Dialogues
Donald E. Lively, Phoebe A. Haddon, Dorothy E. Roberts, and Russell L. Weaver

The Constitutional Law of the European Union
James D. Dinnage and John F. Murphy

The Constitutional Law of the European Union: Documentary Supplement
James D. Dinnage and John F. Murphy

Constitutional Torts
Sheldon H. Nahmod, Michael L. Wells, and Thomas A. Eaton

Contracts: Contemporary Cases, Comments, and Problems
Michael L. Closen, Richard M. Perlmutter, and Jeffrey D. Wittenberg

X **A Contracts Anthology, Second Edition** *59 Col*
Peter Linzer

X **A Corporate Law Anthology** *47 Cal @ Berf*
Franklin A. Gevurtz

Corporate and White Collar Crime: An Anthology
Leonard Orland

X **A Criminal Law Anthology** *58 Boston*
Arnold H. Loewy

Criminal Law: Cases and Materials
Arnold H. Loewy

X **A Criminal Procedure Anthology** *?*
Silas J. Wasserstrom and Christie L. Snyder
56 - Yale

Criminal Procedure: Arrest and Investigation
Arnold H. Loewy and Arthur B. LaFrance

Criminal Procedure: Trial and Sentencing
Arthur B. LaFrance and Arnold H. Loewy

Economic Regulation: Cases and Materials
Richard J. Pierce, Jr.

Elements of Law
Eva H. Hanks, Michael E. Herz, and Steven S. Nemerson

Ending It: Dispute Resolution in America
   Descriptions, Examples, Cases and Questions
Susan M. Leeson and Bryan M. Johnston

Environmental Law Series
Jackson B. Battle, Robert L. Fischman, Maxine I. Lipeles, and Mark S. Squillace
      Vol. 1: Environmental Decisionmaking: NEPA and the Endangered Species Act, Second Edition
      Vol. 2: Water Pollution, Second Edition
      Vol. 3: Air Pollution, Second Edition
      Vol. 4: Hazardous Waste, Third Edition

X **An Environmental Law Anthology**
Robert L. Fischman, Maxine I. Lipeles, and Mark S. Squillace
56 - MICH   45 - Naru   46 - UTAH

Environmental Protection and Justice
   Readings and Commentary on Environmental Law and Practice
Kenneth A. Manaster

An Evidence Anthology
Edward J. Imwinkelried and Glen Weissenberger

Federal Evidence Courtroom Manual
Glen Weissenberger

Federal Income Tax Anthology
Paul L. Caron, Karen C. Burke, and Grayson M.P. McCouch

Federal Rules of Evidence Rules, Legislative History, Commentary and Authority
   1997-98 Edition
Glen Weissenberger

Federal Rules of Evidence Handbook, 1997-98 Edition
Publisher's Staff

First Amendment Anthology
Donald E. Lively, Dorothy E. Roberts, and Russell L. Weaver

International Environmental Law Anthology
Anthony D'Amato and Kirsten Engel

International Human Rights: Law, Policy, and Process, Second Edition
Frank C. Newman and David Weissbrodt

Selected International Human Rights Instruments and
   Bibliography For Research on International Human Rights Law, Second Edition
Frank C. Newman and David Weissbrodt

X **International Intellectual Property Anthology** *— 43 — Cornell*
Anthony D'Amato and Doris Estelle Long *61 — Harv*

X **International Law Anthology** *— above*
Anthony D'Amato

International Law Coursebook
Anthony D'Amato

Introduction to the Study of Law: Cases and Materials
John Makdisi

Judicial Externships: The Clinic Inside the Courthouse
Rebecca A. Cochran

Justice and the Legal System: A Coursebook
Anthony D'Amato and Arthur J. Jacobson

A Land Use Anthology
Jon W. Bruce

The Law of Disability Discrimination
Ruth Colker

ADA Handbook: Statutes, Regulations and Related Materials
Publisher's Staff

The Law of Modern Payment Systems and Notes, Second Edition
Fred H. Miller and Alvin C. Harrell

Lawyers and Fundamental Moral Responsibility
Daniel R. Coquillette

Microeconomic Predicates to Law and Economics
Mark Seidenfeld

Patients, Psychiatrists and Lawyers: Law and the Mental Health System, Second Edition
Raymond L. Spring, Roy B. Lacoursiere, and Glen Weissenberger

Preventive Law: Materials on a Non Adversarial Legal Process
Robert M. Hardaway

Principles of Evidence, Third Edition
Irving Younger, Michael Goldsmith, and David A. Sonenshein

Problems and Simulations in Evidence, Second Edition
Thomas F. Guernsey

X **A Products Liability Anthology**
Anita Bernstein *37 — Yale*

Professional Responsibility Anthology
Thomas B. Metzloff 44 – Harv

A Property Anthology, Second Edition
Richard H. Chused

Public Choice and Public Law: Readings and Commentary
Maxwell L. Stearns

The Regulation of Banking
  Cases and Materials on Depository Institutions and Their Regulators
Michael P. Malloy

Science in Evidence
D.H. Kaye

A Section 1983 Civil Rights Anthology
Sheldon H. Nahmod 58 – Harv

Sports Law: Cases and Materials, Third Edition
Ray L. Yasser, James R. McCurdy, and C. Peter Goplerud

A Torts Anthology
Lawrence C. Levine, Julie A. Davies, and Edward J. Kionka 59 – Ill
  (42 – UCLA

Trial Practice
Lawrence A. Dubin and Thomas F. Guernsey

Unincorporated Business Entities
Larry E. Ribstein

FORTHCOMING PUBLICATIONS

A Civil Procedure Anthology
David I. Levine, Donald L. Doernberg, and Melissa L. Nelken
  (45 – Penn

Contract Law and Practice: Cases and Materials
Michael L. Closen, Gerald E. Berendt, Doris Estelle Long, Marie A. Monahan, Robert J. Nye, and John H. Scheid

Environmental Law: Air Pollution, Third Edition
Mark S. Squillace and David R. Wooley

European Union Law Anthology
Karen V. Kole and Anthony D'Amato
  (44 Northwestern

Federal Antitrust Law: Cases and Materials
Daniel J. Gifford and Leo J. Raskind

Federal Wealth Transfer Tax Anthology
Paul L. Caron, Grayson M.P. McCouch, Karen C. Burke

Law and Economics Anthology
Kenneth G. Dau-Schmidt and Thomas S. Ulen – 52 phd Stanford
  (42 mich

Readings in Criminal Law: An Anthology
Russell L. Weaver, John M. Burkoff, Catherine Hancock, Alan Reed, and Peter Seago

Natural Resources: Cases and Materials
Barlow Burke, Jr.

International Taxation: Cases, Materials, and Problems
Philip F. Postlewaite

International Civil Procedure Anthology
David S. Clark and Anthony D'Amato
  '54 Stanford

Copyright Law Anthology
Richard H. Chused 55 Chicago

A LAND USE
ANTHOLOGY

A LAND USE ANTHOLOGY

EDITED BY

JON W. BRUCE

PROFESSOR OF LAW
VANDERBILT UNIVERSITY
SCHOOL OF LAW

ANDERSON PUBLISHING CO.
CINCINNATI, OHIO

A LAND USE ANTHOLOGY
EDITED BY JON W. BRUCE

Anderson Publishing Co.
2035 Reading Road / Cincinnati, Ohio 45202
800-582-7295 / e-mail andpubco@aol.com / Fax 513-562-5430

ISBN: 0-87084-023-1

To

B.J.B.

Contents

Preface

The articles included in this volume examine the complex and dynamic nature of land use law. These works consider both private restriction and public control. The focus is on governmental activity, particularly zoning and regulatory takings.

The land use field has produced abundant commentary. The articles excerpted in this anthology deal with legal issues arising across the land use spectrum. These works were selected to provide diverse insights regarding the law governing land use.

An ellipsis signals material omitted from an article. Brackets surround material added. However, an ellipsis or bracketed material found in a quotation is that of the author of the article. Corrections of a de minimus nature have been made without notice. Likewise, summaries, tables of contents, outlines, and the like that appear at the beginning of certain articles have been omitted without signal, as have footnotes. Remaining footnotes are numbered as they were originally.

I thank my wife, Barbara, for her support throughout my work on this anthology. Other individuals also deserve recognition. James W. Ely, Jr. made numerous thoughtful comments; William L. Phillips III, Corrie R. Seagroves, and Ross G. Shank were excellent research assistants; Lillian G. Ray provided superior secretarial assistance; and Sean M. Caldwell was a most helpful Managing Editor.

Jon W. Bruce
Vanderbilt University
September, 1997

PART I

PRIVATE RESTRICTION—COVENANTS CONSTRAINING LAND USE

Often ignored in the ongoing land use debate over the appropriate scope of governmental activity, privately-crafted constraints have become an increasingly significant mode of land use control. Private land use restrictions of various types provide the adhesive for many real estate developments. The articles that follow analyze problems stemming from the utilization of real covenants to restrict land use and the evolution of the homeowners' association as an institution designed to implement these restrictions. The authors of the following four articles are from diverse backgrounds—judicial (Armand Arabian), academic (Clayton P. Gillette and James L. Winokur), and practice (co-authors Wayne S. Hyatt and Jo Anne P. Stubblefield). They offer an array of perspectives.

THE MIXED BLESSINGS OF PROMISSORY SERVITUDES: TOWARD OPTIMIZING ECONOMIC UTILITY, INDIVIDUAL LIBERTY, AND PERSONAL IDENTITY

James L. Winokur
1989 Wis. L. Rev. 1[*]

I. INTRODUCTION

Over dinner with a friend recently, I touched a sensitive nerve by asking about the new house he had just contracted to purchase. My friend was moving to Denver and had invested several days in house hunting. He was disappointed to find no inner-city homes suited to his family's needs within his price range, and had reluctantly settled on a home in the suburban sprawl southeast of town. My friend seemed almost embarrassed describing the homogeneity of his new neighborhood . . . .

Like other suburban neighborhoods, the one my friend described is in a low-density subdivision of all single-family residences built in a virtually uniform design. The lots are of uniform size and shape. The homogeneity of the houses matches the socio-economic homogeneity of their residents. Neighborhood uniformity is preserved by a complex battery of restrictions on everything from permitted uses to permissible colors of garden accessories to storage of personal belongings visible from other lots or the street. Even minor aesthetic changes are often prohibited without advance approval of a neighborhood architectural review committee.

Often called conditions, covenants, and restrictions ("CC&R's"), such residential restrictions typically take the form of real covenants and equitable servitudes that bind for several decades, or even permanently, not only the original creating parties but their successors in interest. They are usually reciprocally enforceable among residence owners within a subdivision or condominium project and also by the homeowners or condominium association.

These restrictions serve the significant salutory purpose of maintaining a desirable character and quality in many residential areas. Reciprocally enforceable promissory servitudes preserve neighborhood characteristics important to residents who value quiet, privacy, and status; who prefer car transportation to walking or public transit; and who favor supermarkets and shopping center department stores over ethnic or esoteric neighborhood shops. Consistency of aesthetic design throughout a neighborhood can produce residential areas of striking beauty. Servitudes often mandate continuing resident financing of owner association common area maintenance, thereby alleviating residents' individual maintenance burdens.

However, reciprocal residential promissory servitudes confer decidedly mixed blessings on our neighborhoods and on our society as a whole. By so strictly segregating land uses, these servitudes often exclude not only all nonresidential uses, but also residential uses which vary in density, in cost, or in caliber of improvements. Neighborhood servitude restrictions can effectively segregate social classes, isolating residents of one neighborhood from outsiders who neither live, shop nor work with residents of these exclusive districts. In contrast to some uniquely beautiful servitude-restricted neighborhoods, much of the suburban sprawl controlled by association-administered servitude regimes has become aesthetically undifferentiated and culturally desolate. Servitude regimes have generated growing resident dissatisfaction with "strait jacket" restrictions which invade aspects of home life previously left to personal choice. Conflict among neighbors is often sharp, and litigation between servitude regime residents and their owners associations has mushroomed.

My friend's dilemma as a home buyer is far from unique. Restrictions similar to those in his new neighborhood bind a substantial and growing percentage of new and used residential properties in this country. Though imposed by separate developers in markets largely free from monopolist control, these servitude regimes are increasingly uniform from development to development, progressively eliminating a homebuyer's option to purchase in nonrestricted or distinctively restricted areas. Developers often draft reciprocal residential promissory servitudes to bind lots

either permanently or with renewal available indefinitely by vote of some majority of neighborhood residents. Relief from controversial, obsolete, or unpopular
restrictions often requires prohibitive expenditures.

Both the substantial benefits and the significant burdens created by promissory
servitudes are by-products of a growing judicial willingness to enforce these servitudes against successors to the creating parties. Until the nineteenth century, real
covenants were rarely used outside of the landlord-tenant setting. But as the Industrial Revolution completed the great transformation of feudal society into modern
industrial capitalism, courts began to see promissory servitudes as efficiently allocating resources and enhancing individual liberty. Since the mid-nineteenth century,
courts have liberalized doctrines that had once limited the enforceability of promissory servitudes between successors. More recently, commentators have urged further liberalization and simplification.

Liberalized enforcement of promissory servitudes has, on the whole, served
substantial social interests and helped to create and maintain many desirable residential neighborhoods. But the domination of housing markets by potentially perpetual, uniform servitude regimes has begun to undercut both the economic
efficiency of these servitudes and the personal liberties of existing residents and
potential buyers. Enforcement of all restrictions imposed by servitude regimes, limiting neither the duration nor the content of servitudes, can also undermine the
availability of neighborhoods conducive to human flourishing, where each individual's identity can be based on personal control of a unique place in the residential environment.

Reciprocal residential restrictions are among a growing variety of promissory
servitudes which modern courts enforce between successors to the creating parties.
Promissory servitudes in large-scale, association-administered regimes raise particularly serious policy questions because the servitude regimes have become so
common and are typically impervious to individual control. However, the liberalized
doctrines governing enforcement of servitude regimes also control enforcement of
promissory servitudes generally. In suggesting drawbacks and proposing limits for
enforceability of large-scale servitude regimes, this Article distinguishes them from
servitudes enforceable by only a small number of adjacent landowners . . . . The perpetual persistence of obsolete servitudes is less likely where potential enforcers are
few and consensual adjustment of servitudes can be realistically accomplished.

The mixed blessings of promissory servitudes—blessings which vary depending on the number of potential enforcers and on the age, substantive content, and
possible obsolescence of particular servitudes—call for moderation in enforcement.
Optimizing promissory servitudes requires coherent, predictable doctrines which
include clear restriction on enforcement of older servitudes. In reforming promissory servitude doctrines, reformers should first emphasize structural changes in the
relationship among parties to servitudes, providing them with greater opportunity
and responsibility for adjusting servitude impacts over time. Second, reform should
aim to decrease recourse to courts for substantive review of individual servitude
controversies.

Accordingly, beyond a statutory initial term of a few decades, large scale promissory servitude regimes should remain enforceable against any given lot by, at most, an enforcement group much smaller than the entire development. Legislative enactment of such a reform would facilitate consensual modification of obsolete servitudes, thus decreasing growing pressures for costly discretionary judicial supervision of servitudes. With modification of older servitudes realistically attainable by the parties themselves, termination of servitudes under the "changed circumstances" doctrine could then be decreed only where unanticipated changes wholly frustrate the servitudes' purposes. The "touch and concern" doctrine restricting servitude subject matter might be narrowed to avoid comparing each servitude's benefits and burdens; this doctrine would then focus exclusively on whether the covenant serves a land planning function. Legislation should bar private, quasi-governmental servitude regimes from impinging on several specific individual rights already constitutionally protected from infringement by public governments. Courts should less readily infer an intention that servitudes bind successors and give reasonable notice to those bound. One unified body of doctrine should control both injunctive enforcement of "equitable servitudes" and enforcement by damages of "real covenants" at law. Doctrines currently associated with equitable servitudes should apply to permit enforcement regardless of the type of relief sought.

. . . .

IV. POLICY IMPLICATIONS FOR PROMISSORY SERVITUDE DOCTRINE

A. The Mixed Desirability of Promissory Servitudes: General Implications

The significant economic inefficiencies of promissory servitudes, and their adverse impacts on individual liberty and personal identity, demonstrate that these servitudes confer decidedly mixed blessings.

While promissory servitudes have been thought to enhance land values by segregating land uses, universal segregation of single-family residential uses from all other uses may be unwise. Such segregation may actually threaten the neighborhood safety it was intended to promote, force reliance on car transportation for even basic needs, sap neighborhood vitality, and encourage blight. The available empirical evidence establishes no clear correlation between segregation of land uses and land values.

Promissory servitudes can promote efficient allocation and re-allocation of land resources. But the efficiencies become questionable in housing markets overwhelmingly dominated by association-administered regimes based on incomprehensible, standardized forms; housing consumers retain little choice as to the restrictions under which they will live. As a servitude regime ages, obsolescence of restrictions becomes more likely. But where a regime of obsolete servitudes includes a large number of parcels, negotiation costs and potential holdout distortions dim the prospect of free market adjustment of restrictions to meet current needs, unless the original servitudes expressly provided for an adjustment mechanism.

When home buyers purchase properties in servitude regimes, they may well be oblivious to the highly technical servitude documentation imposing servitude regimes—documentation which need not be called to a purchaser's attention or even be recorded in order to remain binding. This purchaser ignorance undercuts the assertion that ready salability of homes in servitude regimes demonstrates the servitudes' market desirability or reflects the autonomous will of those bound by the restrictions.

Important limits on the desirability of servitude regimes are borne out by studies finding great resident dissatisfaction with these regimes. The recent dramatic increases in litigation challenging association enforcement of servitudes further challenge the desirability of servitude regimes. Home purchasers requiring family-sized houses face increasingly limited alternatives to buying homes within servitude regimes. Whether or not these buyers are even aware of applicable servitudes at the time of purchase, the increased dissatisfaction and conflict suggest that some who remain do so despite the servitudes rather than because of them. Purchasers aware of the existence and meaning of applicable servitudes may be seeking the security of highly structured neighborhoods and thus consciously trading their own future autonomy for regimentation which progressively undercuts personal identity. Widespread resident dissatisfaction and burgeoning litigation call into question idealized projections of community consensus, of homebuyers who anticipate their own agreement with future application of servitude restrictions.

Among the impacts of servitude regimes is acceleration of abstraction and standardization of societal components which, in an earlier age, differentiated place from place and highlighted the uniqueness of each person's character and style. Some coordination of uses and aesthetic styles on a neighborhood-wide scale can undoubtedly generate substantial economies and strikingly beautiful visual effects. However, these come at a real cost, especially when individuals are barred from controlling even the details of styling and improving their own homes. Significant components of the sense of self, and of the personal identity necessary for human flourishing, are at stake when neighbors have control over each others' homes.

These negative impacts of promissory servitudes should by no means undercut enforcement of all servitudes. Some servitude drawbacks appear primarily in particular settings. For example, the advisability of enforcing promissory servitudes is more doubtful after a significant period of time than in the years immediately after imposition of the restrictions. Servitude impacts on personal autonomy and identity are most severe where the use of one's own home is curtailed in large scale servitude regimes. Servitude burdens are less justified when no substantial externality is imposed on the use of neighboring lands. Enforcement of servitudes between successors to the original parties is less justifiable when creating parties did not intend to bind successors or when a successor did not have reasonable notice of the servitudes.

Servitude impacts also depend heavily on the substance and enforcement context of each restriction. Yet reform which relies heavily upon case-by-case review of servitude enforcement would be ill advised. Recourse to courts is often prohibitively expensive. Doctrinal, interpretive, or factual uncertainties in servitude application hinder the allocative efficiency of otherwise useful servitudes, imposing risks on parties evaluating which uses will be permitted on land they may acquire. Such uncertainty saddles servitudes with transaction costs ranging from attorney fees to unquantified fear that a valid servitude cannot be created. Even if these costs do not block transfers of land restricted by servitudes, they may distort the pricing of such transfers or discourage later servitude enforcement.

To optimize promissory servitudes, any reform of servitude doctrines should aim to simplify application of the rules governing enforcement. Distinctions between enforceability and unenforceability need to be more easily understandable and predictable. Inherently unpredictable discretionary doctrines are to be avoided or, where substantively important to foster servitude policies, circumscribed to the degree possible consistent with those policies.

   . . . .

B. Limiting Enforcement of Older Promissory Servitudes

Shifting the burden of addressing servitude obsolescence from the discretionary changed circumstances doctrine to statutory limitations on enforcement beyond a fixed durational limit is the most urgently needed doctrinal servitude reform. Limitations on the enforcement of servitudes beyond a fixed initial term can be structured to allow neighbors' ongoing responsible reexamination of older servitudes. Those whose properties are within the servitude arrangement could then bargain under circumstances which encourage good-faith reevaluation relatively free from the holdout problem. Limitations structured to allow small areas within a larger development to alter their own restrictions may also counter the standardization of restrictions which has limited homebuyers' options in recent years.

   . . . .

Although many observers have recommended some form of fixed, legislative durational limit on promissory servitudes, there is very little legislation to this effect. Prominent among the designs proposed thus far are an automatic expiration of servitudes after some fixed period (i.e., reimposition requires unanimity) or a vote on the servitude's continuance by all owners within the servitude regime. Under such schemes, the results tend toward all or none; the initial servitude term will be followed either by preservation of the regime unchanged or by elimination of all private restrictions. All lots will be similarly restricted or nonrestricted, and differences by degree in the definitions of permitted versus restricted uses will be almost impossible to negotiate.

A more useful enforcement limit on older promissory servitudes would provide that servitudes binding any lot would remain enforceable beyond twenty years only if the parcels thereafter entitled to enforcement against that lot were fewer than eleven. Servitudes mutually enforceable between all lot owners in a larger development would be affected only after their initial twenty-year term—at which point the servitudes would become unenforceable if the servitudes themselves failed to limit potential enforcers. Servitudes would remain in force according to their terms where the original servitude documents identified, for each lot, a group or "pod" of no more than twelve lots for which enforcement would be ordered beyond the initial twenty-year term. Thereafter, any servitude modification would be decided and applied only within a given enforcement pod, and only by unanimous agreement of all its constituents. An owners' association could enforce servitudes beyond the initial term, but only if requested to do so by at least one owner within the enforcement pod.

. . . .

As part of the original servitude documentation, the developer will have designated which homes will be permitted to enforce restrictions against which other homes after the initial twenty-year term. These enforcement designations would presumably be based on location; homes located adjacent to each other, and thus likely to be most affected by the externalities of each other's use, would usually be grouped in the same pod.

While externalities of some uses violative of the original servitudes could potentially affect lots across pod boundaries, the continuing power of each pod member to enforce the original restrictions throughout the pod should allow servitude proponents to retain broad coverage of reasonable restrictions within the servitude regime. Threatened use externalities that would affect lots beyond the pod would also usually affect at least some homes within the user's pod; any one of these pod owners could protect the interests shared with the broader community. Even in the unusual cases where burdens of a proposed change threaten only a property outside the user's pod, the neighbor outside the pod favoring adherence to a currently reasonable restriction should be able to persuade at least one pod member to either request its enforcement or exchange enforcement group memberships with the threatened lot owner. Where a servitude restriction commands no support within an enforcement group, that group of lot owners could elect to remove or modify its restrictions without necessarily undermining the restrictions binding other enforcement groups. As a by-product of such group-by-group decisions, housing markets presently dominated by increasingly uniform servitude restrictions could offer home buyers a widening range of servitude options.

. . . .

As an alternative to limiting the number of enforcers for older servitudes, restricting enforcement beyond the initial twenty-year term to damages rather than injunctive relief might also promote adjustments among neighbors. The impact of limiting enforcers to damage remedies will depend on judicial accuracy in quantifying externalities of any violation, as well as the parties' skill in anticipating court awards. Merely withholding injunctive relief does not, however, fully address the overwhelming transaction costs facing an owner whose proposed use will be vulnerable to suit by any of hundreds of neighbors. . . .

. . . .

The adoption of the enforcement pod reform should neither eliminate nor broaden the changed circumstances doctrine as a means of terminating obsolete servitude restrictions. Rather, the durational legislation should expressly narrow the focus of the changed circumstances doctrine so that it applies only where changes, unanticipated by the creating parties, have wholly frustrated a servitude's purpose. . . .

C. Limits on the Subject Matter of Promissory Servitudes

1. THE "TOUCH AND CONCERN" REQUIREMENT
AND RELATED DOCTRINES

The prerequisite that promissory servitudes enforceable between successors must "touch and concern" the land has been so amorphously interpreted over the past four centuries that it has now become an available justification for denying servitude enforcement on any of several distinct concerns. . . .

. . . If the touch and concern doctrine is retained, it is important that its application be more focused. . . . A more focused touch and concern doctrine would require that the primary value to any enforcer of the servitude obligation depend on the enforcer's ownership of particular land. Where performance of a servitude obligation would retain its value regardless of the enforcer's land ownership, the obligation would "touch" the enforcer rather than his land, and would fail the touch and concern test.

Retention of a more focused touch and concern doctrine would keep land ownership—and particularly possession—free from servitudes binding successors to obligations which are essentially personal. Such a touch and concern doctrine would still deny enforcement against successors of promises mandating ideological or religious conformity involving no land-related externalities, or binding land ownership with obligations to purchase future supplies from a named seller or to perform personal labor away from the burdened land. By insulating possessory land interests from a predecessor's personal commitments, the doctrine recognizes land ownership and possession as crucial in advancing the social values of individual liberty and personal identity. As such, land ownership and possession should not be compromised into a mere lever for securing performance of obligations inherently unrelated to enriching land possession.

2. CIVIL RIGHTS IN ASSOCIATION-ADMINISTERED SERVITUDE REGIMES:
ANALOGIZING TO CONSTITUTIONAL SAFEGUARDS

Protection of fundamental civil rights within association-administered servitude regimes is critical to the goals of participatory democracy within these regimes. Although these rights are waivable, the fact that servitudes are rarely comprehended or even read by home purchasers should belie the assertion that the residents have consented to relinquishing their civil rights to free participation in association governance. Nonetheless, blanket extension of constitutional protections to association-administered servitude regimes raises a host of problems. The delineation of appropriate constitutional protections is beyond the scope of this Article. As a general matter, however, the uncertainties raised by the extension of constitutional principles to association-administered servitude regimes can be limited by legislation. This legislation would expressly select and assure only those protections constitutionally accorded in connection with public government which are most crucial in assuring a participatory democracy appropriate to private ownership in residential subdivisions.

D. Consent to Servitudes: The Intent and Notice Requirements

By reciting the intent and notice requirements, promissory servitude doctrine pays lip service to the importance of private volition in enforcing servitudes between successors to the original covenanting parties. Considering the ease of both expressing the intention that a covenant run with the land and of providing reasonable record notice of servitude burdens, these doctrines should be strengthened to require more realistic consent to promissory servitudes.

1. EXPRESSED INTENTION TO BIND OR BENEFIT SUCCESSORS

Under the usual formulations of the intent requirement, neither the burden of a promissory servitude nor its enforcement power is to run with land unless the original parties intended it to run. Such intention can easily be manifested by express provision that the servitude shall bind the promisors' heirs, successors, and assigns, or benefit the promisees' heirs, successors, and assigns. Nonetheless, even in the absence of any language expressing an intention that the covenant run, modern American courts readily infer such intention from the nature of the covenant. . . .

. . . .

. . . [T]he likelihood that purchasers of servitude regime homes unwittingly accept uncomprehended boilerplate or possess little bargaining power to alter restrictions, calls for judicial hesitancy in inferring facts to satisfy all servitude prerequisites. While the presence of "assigns" or similar language cannot assure the parties' actual intention, the absence of any express intention that a covenant is to run calls such intention into question. Some explicit language of intention that a covenant run should be a prerequisite for enforcement by or against successors.

2. REASONABLE NOTICE OF SERVITUDE BURDENS TO LATER POSSESSORS

Many courts stretch doctrines of constructive notice to infer the consent of successors to servitudes burdening the land they buy. . . .

. . . .

In addition to the modern tendency favoring servitude enforcement generally, dilution of notice requirements . . . also reflects the legitimate concern that earlier purchasers not be deprived of servitude protection because of the developer's or other predecessor's failure to document and record previously imposed servitudes. As in many priority disputes, both competing claimants—the earlier and later purchasers—often merit protection. Whichever claim is recognized in these cases of flawed documentation, fairness requires that the wrongdoer—the developer or other predecessor who failed to keep his or her earlier servitude commitments—bear the burden of this failing by compensating residents for their losses. More fundamentally, the vulnerability of consent to servitudes underscores the importance of allowing owners to reevaluate and modify restrictions over time.

E. Privity of Estate Requirements and Elimination of Distinctions Between Legal and Equitable Enforcement

Promissory servitude privity of estate refers to two distinct categories of required relations: the relationship between the original covenanting parties (known as "horizontal" privity), and the relationship between a present owner of a parcel either burdened or benefited by the servitude and the original covenantor or covenantee (known as "vertical" privity). Doctrines establishing technical privity of estate as a prerequisite to enforcement of real covenants have generated controversy, confusion, and judicial reform. The peculiar course of these privity controversies has resulted not only in privity requirements which are themselves questionable, but also in distinctions between legal and equitable enforcement—between availability of damage remedies and injunctive relief—which are currently indefensible.

1. THE REQUIREMENT OF "HORIZONTAL PRIVITY" BETWEEN THE ORIGINAL COVENANTING PARTIES

Prior to the recognition of equitable servitudes in 1848, English courts defined horizontal privity of estate to require that a real covenant, enforceable between the original parties' successors, be made part of the tenurial relation of a landlord and a tenant. As a result, covenants between owners of fee interests could be enforced only between the original covenanting parties, unless a successor voluntarily assumed the obligation of performance.

Two related developments loosened this strict English position. First, the Chancery in *Tulk v. Moxhay*[399] declared real covenant doctrine irrelevant to enforcement of the "equity" created by an earlier use agreement against a successor with notice of the agreement. Second, during the nineteenth century, American courts still applying the horizontal privity requirement progressively loosened its definition, first accepting the ownership of mutual or simultaneous interests in a parcel of land touched and concerned by the covenant. These courts have followed England's lead in applying the horizontal privity requirement only in suits for damages at law. Even in suits for damages, the further loosened American horizontal privity requirement is now satisfied wherever the covenant has been created as part of a larger land transaction involving land affected by the covenant. Some states have simply abolished the requirement in all enforcement settings.

Recent commentary explains horizontal privity requirements as designed to avoid binding successors without notice. . . .

If horizontal privity were merely a vehicle for addressing notice issues, the requirement today would be pointless because modern recording systems are available to provide notice. Beginning with such a perspective, modern critics have

---

[399] 41 Eng. Rep. 1143 (Ch. 1848). . . .

D. Perspective and Bias

As attorneys who have practiced exclusively in the area of community associations for years, the authors support the community association concept. . . .

. . . .

II. THE NATURE OF COMMUNITY ASSOCIATIONS

. . . .

. . . [C]ommunity associations depend on a system of covenants imposed on the property, which ensures that every owner contributes a pro rata share to the cost of maintaining the common areas and amenities. Typically, these covenants also ensure that standards of conduct and architecture are maintained throughout the community. The entity charged with enforcing these standards, the community association, provides the vehicle by which the home owners within the community govern themselves, furthering the common interest of the entire community.

. . . .

Community associations have special roles and functions. Certainly, the association has responsibility for the preservation and maintenance of the property itself. Condominium associations, which may not own common property[25] but are responsible for it on behalf of association members, and home owners associations, which have title to common property, have maintenance responsibilities. Depending on how the developer drafts the documents and implements the general plan of development, maintenance responsibility may be great or minimal.

Another community association function is enforcement. The developer initially creates a regulatory scheme, with which each purchaser agrees to comply when taking title to a unit. The community association is vested, through community association documentation and through various principles of law, with the power to perform this regulatory function. These roles—maintenance and operation on the one hand and regulation on the other—set the community association apart from mere voluntary, civic organizations and give rise to the discussions prompting this article.

. . . .

Because community associations have the power to levy assessments against members for common expenses and to impose sanctions for violations of the declaration, a number of commentators have suggested that the community association should be characterized as a "mini-government."[31] A few have suggested that some activities of the community association could be[32] or should be characterized

---

[25] . . . [M]any large condominium associations do own property, such as recreational facilities and streets, other than that held by the unit owners as tenants-in-common.

[31] *See, e.g.,* Wayne S. Hyatt & James B. Rhoads, *Concepts of Liability in the Development and Administration of Condominiums and Home Owners Associations,* 12 WAKE FOREST L. REV. 915 (1976) [hereinafter *Concepts of Liability*].

[32] *See* Katharine Rosenberry, *The Application of the Federal and State Constitutions to Condominiums, Cooperatives and Planned Developments,* 19 REAL PROP. PROB. & TR. J. 1, 5 (1984).

as "state action," requiring that the association extend to property owners the protections guaranteed by the Fourteenth Amendment to the United States Constitution.

Other commentators have taken the position that application of constitutional principles to community association activities could have far-reaching, undesirable consequences from the perspective of community association administration and judicial and legislative economy. The result of this application could be an impairment of the ability of the community association to operate as intended and to accomplish the purposes for which it was created.

Some commentators have suggested that in attempting to protect the constitutional rights of a minority of the property owners within a common interest community, the courts would infringe upon the constitutional rights of the majority. These commentators have recommended either limiting the application of state action concepts to community associations[36] or rejecting the application of constitutional principles. They argue that the common law of servitudes[37] or the well-established bodies of corporate,[38] trust,[39] or municipal[40] law provide a more appropriate framework for reviewing the validity of a community association's actions.

. . . .

Community associations are no longer, however, just home owner residential operations. Community association law has a substantial impact in commercial developments and mixed-use developments, as well as developments seeking to go "back to the future" and return to non-automotive-drive, small-town planning concepts. . . .

. . . .

Community association law is relatively new, without the "Massachusetts Rule," "New York Rule," "California Rule," or other well-recognized rules that law students confront in so many other areas of practice. Each state has its own approach, but interestingly, in both statutory law and case law, the states follow the same general paths. This is true for several reasons. First, the courts have looked to jurisdictions with substantial community association experience as the jumping off point for their analyses of community association issues and have borrowed from that experience.

---

[36] *See, e.g.,* Gerald Korngold, *Single Family Use Covenants: For Achieving a Balance Between Traditional Family Life and Individual Autonomy,* 22 U.C. DAVIS L. REV. 951 (1989); James L. Winokur, *The Mixed Blessings of Promissory Servitudes: Toward Optimizing Economic Utility, Individual Liberty, and Personal Identity,* 1989 WIS. L. REV. 1.

[37] *See* Richard A. Epstein, *Covenants & Constitution,* 73 CORNELL L. REV. 906 (1988).

[38] *See* Curtis C. Sproul, *Is California's Mutual Benefit Corporation Law the Appropriate Domicile for Community Associations?,* 18 U.S.F. L. REV. 695 (1984).

[39] *See* Uriel Reichman, *Residential Private Governments: An Introductory Survey,* 43 U. CHI. L. REV. 253 (1976).

[40] *See* Robert C. Ellickson, *Cities and Homeowners Associations,* 130 U. PA. L. REV. 1519 (1982).

Another reason is the profound effect that the NCCUSL has had through the promulgation of the Uniform Condominium Act, the Uniform Planned Community Act, and the Uniform Common Interest Ownership Act. These acts have served as predicates for legislatures in the creation of statutory law.

. . . .

IV. DESCRIBING COMMUNITY ASSOCIATIONS: THE SEARCH FOR AN APPROPRIATE ANALOGY

A. The Perceived Models

. . . .

1. *The Corporate Model*

Most community associations created today are incorporated under the not-for-profit corporation law of the state in which they operate. This may be due in part to statutory requirements, a desire to limit liability, a desire to make the established body of corporate law applicable to the administrative operations of the community association, or a combination of these factors. Yet regardless of whether a community association is incorporated, one perceived option for analyzing and "caging" it is by analogy to corporate law.

Those who advocate applying corporate principles first look at what a community association is, how it is structured, and how it is intended to operate. . . . [C]ommunity association activities and corporate activities are similar. Moreover, a compelling common-sense argument favors use of corporate law as a significant resource to assist in, if not totally dispose of, community association law questions. Indeed, some have long asserted that community associations should always be incorporated if for no other reason than to dispose of legal questions.[126] . . .

. . . .

Comparing corporate law and documentation to that of the community association shows that corporate law addresses a wide array of community association activities. However, many community association activities are totally foreign to corporations. Nevertheless, the corporate analogy is quite helpful on the business side of the community association, particularly with the duties and responsibilities of officers and directors because of the valuable practical and case law experience to guide such individuals.

Whether one characterizes the governing role of a community association as municipal, municipal-like, quasi-governmental, or purely corporate, the body of statutory and case law dealing with corporations does not square with all of the issues faced by community associations.

---

[126] *See, e.g.,* Wayne S. Hyatt, *Condominium and Home Owner Associations: Formation and Development,* 24 EMORY L.J. 978 (1975); *see also* F. Scott Jackson, *Non-profit Homeowners' Associations: Should They Incorporate?,* 49 L.A. BAR BULL. 509, 511 n.12 (1974).

2. *The Trust Model*

. . . .

After control of the community association has passed from the developer to the property owners, the law of trusts generally is not applicable to the conduct of the community association's officers and directors. The officers and directors do not hold title to any of the association's property and are subject to the control of the property owners. In addition, state law on the form of the association generally covers association governance adequately, including the duties and liabilities of association officers and directors.

. . . .

When the developer controls the community association, however, the stricter scrutiny of trust law rather than the business judgment rule may be appropriately applied to the developer-appointed officers and directors and their employees to the extent the employees are acting within the scope of their employment. The association has all the features of a trust while the developer controls it. The developer has dominion and control over the association (the trust property) to carry out the general plan of development (the settlor's instructions) for the benefit of the association's present and future members (the beneficiaries).

The association's creator is also its controller and is not subject to any direction from the members. Because the developer and its appointed officers and directors could easily take advantage of the members, the courts may apply to them the same rigidly defined duties, high standards of conduct, and strict scrutiny applied to trustees under the general principles of trust law. Some courts have applied this higher standard of conduct, which is consistent with the UCIOA.

. . . .

In one case not dealing with community associations but highly analogous to the community association context, the court specifically examined trust law while analyzing the conduct of officers and directors of a charitable corporation and held that trust law was inapplicable.[171] This is a better reasoned approach to the issues and relevance of trust law within the community association context.

3. *The Municipal Model*

Countless pages have been devoted to discussing the similarities between community associations and municipal governments.[172] Most commentators agree that the resemblance is undeniable, but it is only resemblance. Equating the community association with a municipality fuels the argument favoring the application of principles of public law, with constitutional ramifications. There is sufficient

---

[171] Stern v. Lucy Webb Hayes Nat'l Training Sch. for Deaconesses and Missionaries, 381 F. Supp. 1003, 1013 (D.D.C. 1974).

[172] *See, e.g., Concepts of Liability, supra* note 31, at 916-44.

basis, however, to argue that the community association is, at some level, a quasi-government, paralleling the powers, duties and responsibilities of a municipal government.[173]

A community association provides its members with services, such as road maintenance, street and common area lighting, utilities, security, and snow and refuse removal. Furthermore, community associations and municipalities both have power to levy assessments. The assessment power is loosely equated with the municipal taxing power.

Both community associations and municipalities elect representatives, offer at least limited immunity for acts within the scope of authority, and have architectural control over the construction standards of the community. Architectural restrictions are analogous to the municipal power to issue building permits or grant a zoning variance.

However, the municipal analogy is neither intended nor sufficient to elevate the community association's activities to the precise equivalent of municipalities, thus giving rise to the full scope of municipal law and constitutional regulation. The municipal analogy is incomplete though some process is due in community association governance. Commentators agree that this analogous use of some principles is not equivalent to the acceptance of all principles.

. . . .

4. *The Statutory Model: UCIOA*

The level of community association development greatly increased in the 1970s and 1980s, as did the diversity of residential, commercial, and resort products using community associations. Lawyers naturally began to see the need for laws, and a movement toward the preparation of uniform acts through the auspices of the NCCUSL resulted. . . .

. . . .

The process began with the adoption of the Uniform Condominium Act in 1977.[209] Next, the NCCUSL adopted the Uniform Planned Community Act at its 1980 annual meeting.[210] . . .

. . . .

The NCCUSL believed that the states should have available a uniform approach reflecting the same policy considerations for planned communities as it did for condominiums. This would extend the protections and certainty contained in the Uniform Condominium Act to other forms of common interest communities. The commendable result was the UCIOA.

---

[173] *See, e.g., id.;* Katharine Rosenberry, *Actions of Community Association Boards: When Are They Valid and When Do They Create Liability?*, 13 REAL EST. L.J. 315, 329-33 (1985); Brian L. Weakland, *Condominium Associations: Living Under the Due Process Shadow,* 13 PEPP. L. REV. 297 (1986).

[209] . . . *See* UCA, 7 U.L.A. 421 (1985).

[210] UCIOA, Prefatory Note, 7 U.L.A. 231 (1982).

Prior to the completion of the UCIOA, however, there was an intermediate step that dealt with cooperatives and resulted in the adoption, in 1981, of the Model Real Estate Cooperative Act. . . .

The basic goal of the UCIOA is uniformity and balance among all three forms of ownership. As the Act itself acknowledges, it achieves this goal "simply by consolidating the three prior Acts of the Conference and adding a very few generic definitions. The principal new definition is 'common interest community.'"[217] . . .

. . . .

5. *The Constitutional Model: External Controls on the Models*

a. *Introduction*

Both courts and commentators recognize that the nature of community association life makes it necessary to intrude upon unit owners' rights more than usually necessary under traditional forms of property ownership. Consequently, several writers have concluded that constitutional safeguards are necessary to protect property owners in common interest communities and that the appropriate standard for both describing and controlling the relevant model is constitutional.[233]

In truth, the state action approach is not a fifth model, but is more appropriately characterized as a dark shadow over all other options. If the concept that community association activities constitute state action is accepted, all of the models are affected. The concept of state action must be considered with the effect of this application in mind.

Commentators have diverse points of view on the applicability of constitutional law to community associations, partially because of their personal biases, intellectual foundations, and previous experiences. Some are concerned about unfettered community association activities, because associations are often administered by amateurs who are not familiar with, do not understand, or are otherwise inept at enforcement of association rules.[234] Other commentators stress that management of a community's common property requires the routing of a significant amount of money through the association and thus the individual owners have a large stake in association decision-making, which should be protected.[235] Some have raised the concern that the quality of association management can have a substantial impact on the value of a property owner's investment in the community, which cannot be liquidated as readily as corporate stock.[236] Moreover, one commentator supports his

---

[217] *Id.* at 235.

[233] Sharmeen C. Bomarni, Comment, *Residential Associations and the Concept of Consensual Governance*, 9 GEO. MASON U. L. REV. 91 (1986); James M. Grippando, Note, *Condominium Rule-making—Presumptions, Burdens and Abuses: A Call for Substantive Judicial Review in Florida*, 34 U. FLA. L. REV. 219 (1982); Weakland, *supra* note 173.

[234] *See, e.g.,* Winokur, *supra* note 36, at 64-65.

[235] *See, e.g.,* [Robert G.] Natelson, [*Keeping Faith: Fiduciary Obligations in Property Owners Associations*, 11 VT. L. REV. 421 (1986)] . . . , at 427.

[236] *See, e.g., id.* at 435.

call for greater protection of property owners by arguing that the property owner cannot walk away from the investment as can a shareholder in a corporation because assessments for common expenses of the association are generally the property owner's personal obligation as well as a lien against the property.[237]

Although management of the community association can have a significant impact on property values and quality of life within a common interest community, the authors' experience shows that these concerns are somewhat exaggerated. Although volunteer boards of directors administer many associations, a large majority employ professional managers to provide advice and assistance in handling day-to-day management of the community. This is particularly true in non-residential or mixed-use developments.

Management contracts often are written for a one-year term and with provisions allowing termination with or without cause on ninety days' notice or less. Thus, if the property owners decide the professional management is inadequate, incompetent, or otherwise mismanaging the community, they can pressure the directors to make a change. Similarly, if a majority of the property owners feel the board of the community association is not responding to their complaints or otherwise mismanages the association, the property owners are usually empowered, under the bylaws, to remove the entire board and replace them with directors who are responsive. It is not easy, but the remedy is available.

Although a property owner's investment may not be as liquid as corporate stock, an owner is not irretrievably locked into the investment. In fact, property owners in common interest communities and other developments sometimes tender deeds in lieu of foreclosure to their lenders when unable to fulfill their financial obligations. The property owner ceases to be obligated for any assessments levied by the community association once title to the property is transferred, whether by foreclosure or otherwise. Although abandoning an investment in this manner may be costly, especially if substantial equity exists in the property or significant outstanding assessment debt must be satisfied, the nature of the loss is no different than an equivalent bad investment in stock.

Other commentators have focused on a lack of informed consent by purchasers of property in a common interest community as the basis for suggesting a need for greater limitations on community association power.[244] James L. Winokur asserts that home buyers do not intelligently review or understand the covenants that the developer imposes on a non-negotiable basis before deciding to purchase property.[245] He adds that the process of drafting covenants excludes participation by the future property owners and that a purchaser's only real option is to take them or leave them.[246] Winokur concludes that consent is a "purely theoretical

---

[237] *Id.*

[244] *See, e.g.,* Winokur, *supra* note 36, at 56-62; *see also* Note, *The Rule of Law in Residential Associations*, 99 HARV. L. REV. 472 (1985) (discussing government enforcement of residential agreements contrary to the American concept of association rights).

[245] Winokur, *supra* note 36, at 59-60.

[246] *Id.* at 57-59.

premise."[247] Presumably, the protected property owner's consent should not be relied upon to determine whether judicial or legislative intervention is appropriate to protect property owners in a common interest community. The authors' experience indicates the contrary.

Market forces play a significant role in shaping the covenants that govern common interest communities. Most developers are acutely aware of the lifestyles and desires of the people to whom they are marketing property and of their degree of sophistication and understanding of common interest communities. In many cases, the developer has conducted an extensive market analysis prior to acquiring the property, has lived in the general community, and has dealt with the press, local government, and abutting property owners for years during the feasibility, permitting, and infrastructure stages of development.

. . . .

Because the developer usually does not record the documents in the land records until immediately before the closing of the first lot, the first group of prospective purchasers generally has ample opportunity to ask questions and take issue with the legal documents. Prospective purchasers often take advantage of this chance.

Although the purchasers of lots in later phases have much less of an opportunity to raise issues, often the concerns raised by the initial purchasers clear the way and set the tone for the development's documents, establishing what the market is willing to accept for that particular community. If not, community association documents usually provide for amendment if the property owners subsequently decide that certain covenants established during the development period are unacceptable. Amendments usually require supermajority approval to protect the interests of those who buy in reliance upon them. Nevertheless, amendments often pass, which demonstrates that the rules for common interest communities in fact reflect the will of a large majority of the property owners.

. . . .

In light of the consensual nature of a community association and the ability of members to invoke change if willed by the majority, none of the foregoing allegations justifies characterization of community association activities as state action nor application of the strict principles inherent in such an analysis. Current judicial standards, market forces, and state legislative powers adequately address these concerns while preserving the vital flexibility to accommodate the unique characteristics of each common interest community and the people living in them.

In contrast, state action analysis severely limits the rights of property owners to choose the rules under which they wish to live and to associate with other property owners. Community associations would be so limited in their ability to accommodate the desires of the property owners in their communities that use of the community association concept likely would be abandoned altogether.

. . . .

---

[247] *Id.* at 61-62.

c. *Legal Theories for Finding State Action*

Three theories explain when community associations might be exercising state action. First, "judicial enforcement" of community association "laws" may be state action. Second, "state involvement" in community association activities may constitute state action. Third, the community association may be performing a "public function."

(1) *Judicial Enforcement Theory*

The Supreme Court held in *Shelley v. Kraemer*[270] that the attempt of a private group of property owners to obtain judicial enforcement of racially restrictive covenants constituted state action. The rationale was that the discriminatory purposes of the covenant could be achieved only through intervention of the court. . . .

The applicability of *Shelley* to community association covenant enforcement is debatable. Some courts view *Shelley* as limited to cases of racial discrimination. Other courts read *Shelley* as applicable to all discriminatory covenants. This interpretation could result in a finding of state action in various contexts, including community association attempts to enforce age restrictive covenants, occupancy restrictions, and other common restrictions. . . .

(2) *State Involvement Theory*

State action concepts arguably may be applied to community associations by virtue of the state involvement in creating and regulating community associations. Under this theory, state action is present whenever there is a significant degree of state involvement in the conduct causing injury, and the state aids or encourages this conduct. This analysis requires weighing the facts and circumstances on a case-by-case basis to determine how significant the state's involvement has been.

States are increasingly involved in the creation of common interest communities. All fifty states have statutes regulating the creation of condominiums, and a number have statutes addressing other forms of common interest ownership developments. These statutes frequently grant the associations greater powers than they would have at common law. For example, many state statutes give community associations the right to create, perfect, and enforce liens for assessments and fines. In at least one unreported case,[283] the existence of an automatically perfected statutory lien led the court to conclude that state action was present. Other courts, however, have concluded that associations' "maintenance, assessment, and collection activities are not sufficiently connected to the State to warrant a finding of state

---

[270] 334 U.S. 1 (1948).

[283] Surfside 84 Condominium Council of Unit Owners v. Mullen, No. 495 (Ct. of Sp. App. of Md., Sept. 1984).

action,"[284] and that the state is not implicated in association activity merely because the association is subject to state law.[285]

(3) *Public Function Theory*

A third theory for finding state action in the community association context, and perhaps the theory favored by proponents of constitutional constraints on community association activities,[286] is the "public function" doctrine articulated by the United States Supreme Court in *Marsh v. Alabama*.[287] In *Marsh* a company town was held to exercise state action because it had "all the characteristics of any other American town."[288] Furthermore, in *Evans v. Newton*,[289] the Court stated that "when private individuals or groups are endowed by the State with powers or functions governmental in nature, they become agencies or instrumentalities of the State and subject to its constitutional limitations."[290]

Although there are some exceptionally large mixed-use community associations that might satisfy the public function test, the overwhelming majority of community associations do not have the characteristics necessary to constitute the functional equivalent of a municipality. At least one court that has addressed the issue of state action in an association's activities has rejected the public function theory, viewing the association as "a supplement to, rather than a replacement for, . . . local government."[293]

. . . .

V. THE CASE FOR COMMUNITY ASSOCIATIONS— REMOVING THE BLINDERS

A. Which Rules Apply?

Paradoxically, all of the options work, and none of the options works. The clear message from the application of the various models to the illustrative issues is that each model has viability on some issues and limited or no viability on others. The dif-

---

[284] Brock v. Watergate Mobile Homes Park Ass'n, Inc., 502 So. 2d 1380, 1382 (Fla. Dist. Ct. App. 1987); *see* Owens v. Tiber Island Condominium Ass'n, 373 A.2d 890 (D.C. 1977); Parnell Woods Ass'n v. Schreider, No. 156-639 (Wis. Cir. Ct. 1982).

[285] *Brock*, 502 So. 2d at 1380. . . . *See generally* Reichman, *supra* note 39, at 275-76 (discussing problems in applying constitutional restrictions to private community associations).

[286] *See, e.g.,* Gerald Frug, *The City as a Legal Concept*, 93 HARV. L. REV. 1057 (1980); Note, *Democracy in the New Towns: The Limits of Private Government*, 36 U. CHI. L. REV. 379 (1969); *The Rule of Law in Residential Associations, supra* note 244.

[287] 326 U.S. 501 (1946).

[288] *Marsh*, 326 U.S. at 502.

[289] 382 U.S. 296 (1966).

[290] *Id.* at 299.

[293] Brock v. Watergate Mobile Home Park Ass'n, Inc., 502 So. 2d 1380, 1382 (Fla. Dist. Ct. App. 1987).

ficulty arises from attempting to find a single source of law to be the definitive answer to a complex web of interests, structures, and management and legal challenges. Perhaps the best approach is to make the candid admission that community association law is indeed something special, comprising multiple areas of legal endeavor.

. . . .

B.   The Case for *Sui Generis*

Viewing the degree of possible control over community association activities as a continuum, with one end representing total absence of controls and the other end representing a strict application of state action principles, it becomes clear that many sources of and controls upon community association activities and community association law already exist. Almost all of the commentators have recognized that a community association does not fit neatly within the framework of any of the models to which community associations historically have been compared.

Neither corporate law nor trust law is flexible enough or broad enough to provide a suitable framework for regulating community association activities. When combined with the law of covenants and servitudes, the growing body of community association case law, existing and proposed legislation dealing with common interest communities, and market forces, however, it becomes evident that there are already in existence sufficient controls with sufficient flexibility to accommodate the unique characteristics of common interest communities. The combined effect of these controls is to permit community associations to function in the manner and for the purposes for which they are established, while ensuring that community associations do not unreasonably interfere with personal rights in the process.

An expanding body of case law applies the reasonableness standard and the business judgment rule to community association activities. This growing application provides a certain level of predictability. In addition the commentators and the courts have shown great willingness to draw analogies to the well-established body of corporate law as a basis for setting standards for community association boards of directors. To some extent, analogies can also be drawn from trust law. Furthermore, basic principles of the law of covenants and servitudes should continue to be applied. The combination of these common law and statutory principles provide at least as much certainty and predictability as application of state action analysis to the operation and administration of community associations.

The reasonableness standards currently used by most courts in judging the validity of association rulemaking and enforcement activities embody many of the same analytical issues addressed by the courts in undertaking a state action analysis. Yet the reasonableness standard permits the court to judge those activities within the context of the particular community involved, rather than in the context of the broader society which has not chosen to live by that community's standards or to be subject to that community's covenants. Although application of the reasonableness standard does involve a case-by-case analysis and a certain degree of uncertainty, this is no more of a problem than application of state action analysis.

A finding of state action does not immediately make available to the court a definitive list of standards by which to judge action. As the court recognized in

Reitman v. Mulkey,[504] "formulating an infallible test" of state action is an impossible task.[505] Professor Charles Black long ago concluded that the state action cases are "a conceptual disaster area."[506] As Justice Harlan recognized in his dissenting opinion in *Poe v. Ullman*,[507] "the full scope of the liberty guaranteed by the Due Process Clause cannot be found in or limited by the precise terms of the specific guarantees elsewhere provided in the Constitution."[508]

Application of state action analysis to community association activities will not provide any greater degree of predictability or certainty than is presently available through application of the reasonableness standard and the business judgment rule. In fact, it may provide a lesser degree of predictability for property owners than the reasonableness standard because reasonableness, to a great extent, is a matter of common sense and fairness in light of the standards of a particular community. A state action analysis, on the other hand, does not guarantee that one will not be deprived of those rights that are inherent in liberty but only that one will not be deprived of such rights without due process of law.

The underlying assumption of state action proponents is that, because states are prohibited from engaging in certain activities by the Constitution, private citizens should be prohibited from engaging in those activities as well. Neither the language of the Constitution nor the history of judicial decisions interpreting it supports such a premise. To the extent that Congress and state legislatures feel that additional protection from private conduct is needed to preserve basic rights, they are more than capable of providing such guidance, and they have not hesitated to do so in the past.

The courts should not be called upon to implement constitutional protections where, as in the community association context, it would require a blurring of the distinction between governmental and private actors, between traditional local, state, and federal governmental entities and groups of private individuals exercising their freedom to choose between living in unrestricted communities or restricted ones. If the courts take that step, it will essentially destroy the freedom of the latter to choose. This will result in an abandonment of the community association concept and the societal benefits of that lifestyle. The better alternative would be a recognition of the unique character of common interest communities and the community association concept and continuation of the current trend toward defining a unique set of standards and body of law to deal with that concept. This alternative will preserve what has become a desirable and popular form of property ownership capable of accommodating the unique interests and desires of the people who choose to participate in it.

. . . .

---

[504] 387 U.S. 369 (1967).

[505] *Id.* at 378.

[506] Charles L. Black, Jr., *The Supreme Court, 1966 Term — Foreword: "State Action," Equal Protection, and California's Proposition 14*, 81 HARV. L. REV. 69, 95 (1967).

[507] 367 U.S. 497 (1961).

[508] *Id.* at 543.

Condos, Cats, and CC&Rs: Invasion of the Castle Common

Armand Arabian
23 Pepp. L. Rev. 1 (1995)[*]

I. Introduction

The American dream of owning a home usually brings with it the assurance of a peaceful retreat from the demands of the outer world, including its constraints on many lifestyle choices. For those who purchase a condominium or similar residence in a planned development community, however, the expectation of protective insulation is often not realized. Such individuals are subject to the covenants, conditions, and restrictions (CC&Rs) contained in the development's declaration or in the bylaws of its homeowners association (HOA). These restrictions not only impose limitations on conduct in common and publicly visible areas but they also often dictate basic aspects of a resident's mode of living within the privacy of his or her own unit.

A development's rules and regulations are commonly enforced by the association's board of directors, which holds substantial sway over the financial and property interests of residents. Many owners may be completely unaware of such a possibility when purchasing their units. Only after they have moved in and settled down do they discover that the development declaration contains a host of intrusive restrictions affecting their daily lives, including, quite possibly, the prohibition of household animals. Even when pets are confined entirely to an owner's unit and do not impair the quiet enjoyment of others, the board, on behalf of the association, can institute enforcement proceedings and impose substantial fines pending capitulation. In most states, the legal system will uphold such actions in all but the most egregious of circumstances.

In *Nahrstedt v. Lakeside Village Condominium Ass'n, Inc.*,[1] I took exception to the California Supreme Court's determination that a virtual ban on pets was not unreasonable and could be enforced against the owner of three cats when the animals remained inside her unit at all times, did not make noise or generate odor, and did not create a nuisance for other residents. Although the authority aggressively wielded by development associations was not at issue in the case, I became convinced that the authority—unrestrained by basic principles of due process or even rationality— threatens fundamental interests heretofore assumed as sacrosanct incidents of home ownership. Given the growing popularity of multi-unit developments and the presumption of reasonableness the law accords recorded restrictions, vast numbers

---

[1] 878 P.2d 1275, 1278-79 (Cal. 1994) (en banc).

of people are vulnerable to significant limitations on their conduct enforced by their neighbors without accountability or independent review.

In this article, I extrapolate from my dissent in *Nahrstedt* and discuss some of the critical concerns implicated in its holding. I also proffer model legislation designed to protect individual property owners from the specter of unbridled majoritarian domination and to restore a measure of balance in the enforcement of CC&Rs applicable to condominiums and other planned community developments. Such a curative effort may promote harmonious communal living, prevent judicial enmeshment into this emotionally charged area of law, and instigate a national scholarly and legislative debate on the subject.

II. *NAHRSTEDT V. LAKESIDE VILLAGE CONDOMINIUM ASS'N, INC.*

A. *Factual and Procedural Background*

In January 1988, Natore Nahrstedt purchased a condominium in Lakeside Village, a large development in Culver City, in Los Angeles. Lakeside Village consists of 530 units in twelve separate three-story buildings. Residents share many common facilities including lobbies, hallways, laundry, and trash services.

As with most common interest communities, ownership interests in Lakeside Village are subject to certain CC&Rs set forth in the developer's declaration. Upon purchasing a unit, each owner automatically becomes a member of the development's homeowners association, the Lakeside Village Association, which enforces the CC&Rs as well as other regulations contained in the bylaws. Lakeside Village maintains a pet restriction that provides in relevant part: "No animals (which shall mean dogs and cats), livestock, reptiles or poultry shall be kept in any unit."[7] When Nahrstedt moved into her condominium, she brought along her three cats, which she had owned for many years and which she considered to be her family. After learning of the cats' presence, the Association demanded Nahrstedt remove them and imposed a fine for each month she remained in violation of the prohibition, for a total in excess of $6,000.

Nahrstedt denied any prior knowledge of the pet restriction and initiated a lawsuit against the Association for damages and injunctive relief. She contended the restriction was unreasonable as applied because the cats did not penetrate the common areas or otherwise create a nuisance for others. The Association demurred, maintaining the pet restriction was enforceable because it furthered the "collective health, happiness and peace of mind" of those living in the development.[12] The trial court sustained the demurrer and dismissed the action on that basis. The court of appeal reversed, concluding the test of reasonableness depended on the facts of each case. In the majority's view, the pet restriction was not reasonable when measured against the allegations in Nahrstedt's complaint. . . .

---

[7] *Id.* The CC&Rs permit residents to keep domestic fish and birds. *Id.* at 1278 n.3.

[12] *Id.* [at 1279.]

B. *California Supreme Court Majority Opinion*

The California Supreme Court's majority categorically rejected the court of appeal's "as applied" approach and held that under the provisions of Civil Code section 1354, CC&Rs are presumptively valid and not subject to challenge on the basis of individual considerations. Citing the recent dramatic increase in the number of condominiums, cooperatives, and planned unit developments with HOAs, the majority noted that common interest developments (CIDs) have become a widely accepted form of real property ownership. Owners enjoy many advantages associated with having their own residence while also acquiring "an interest in the amenities and facilities included in the project."[21] This dual aspect of ownership accounts in large measure for their popularity.

The creation of many severable interests in one property development requires the preparation of a declaration setting forth the CC&Rs that will eventually govern residents and that may limit and control their use of both the common and individually owned areas. This document is recorded prior to the sale of any individual unit. Because the intended purpose of CC&Rs is to promote the health and happiness of the majority of unit owners, they are "an inherent part of any common interest development and are crucial to the stable, planned environment of any shared ownership arrangement."[25] Mandatory membership in a HOA is typically incident to common interest property ownership. Acting on the association's behalf, an elected board of directors enforces property use restrictions and other regulations. Because their function allows these boards to exercise considerable control over many aspects of everyday life, they "must guard against the potential for the abuse of that power."[27] Nevertheless, in the majority's view, anyone purchasing a unit in a CID with knowledge of the HOA's enforcement authority accepts the possibility it may be exercised for the purported benefit of the community, even if it is to the detriment of the individual. In addition to affordability, this mutual enforceability of CC&Rs against future as well as current homeowners is a primary advantage of common interest property ownership and accounts for the recent increase in popularity of CIDs.

The majority next turned to California's governing law, the Davis-Stirling Common Interest Development Act (the Act), which addresses various aspects of CIDs, including CC&Rs. Pursuant to the Act, "[t]he covenants and restrictions in the declaration [of a CID] shall be enforceable equitable servitudes, unless unreasonable."[31] Under the majority's interpretation, this language manifests a legislative intent in favor of enforceability, according recorded use restrictions the same effect as equitable servitudes by making them binding against current and subse-

---

[21] *Nahrstedt*, 878 P.2d at 1279. . . .

[25] *Id.* at 1275.

[27] *Nahrstedt*, 878 P.2d at 1281-82. . . .

[31] *Nahrstedt*, 878 P.2d at 1284-85 (citing Cal. Civ. Code § 1354(a) (West 1982 & Supp. 1995)). . . .

quent purchasers without actual notice. Such deference to broad applicability reinforces and enhances stability and predictability in CIDs since it both conforms to owners' expectations as to the use of their property and protects them from unexpected fee increases. In construing Civil Code section 1354, the majority placed the burden on the individual to establish unreasonableness and declined to permit challenges on a case-by-case basis; only the validity of a particular restriction in the abstract is subject to attack. This interpretation avoids the financial drain on HOA resources and other disadvantages that might arise from frequent litigation over the enforceability of CC&Rs. The court did acknowledge, however, that covenants violating public policy or causing harm disproportionate to their benefit are unreasonable within the meaning of the statute.

. . . .

Applying the standard to the Lakeside Village prohibition of household animals, the court denied Nahrstedt relief because "[a]s a matter of law, . . . the recorded pet restriction . . . is not arbitrary, but is rationally related to health, sanitation and noise concerns legitimately held by residents."[43] The court noted the pet restriction may have attracted many purchasers to the community. Moreover, since residents could change the restriction, their inaction manifested a desire to maintain its enforcement.

C. The Dissent

Although I did not quarrel with the majority's construction of Civil Code section 1354 in the abstract, I took exception to its conclusions as to the enforceability of the Lakeside Village pet restriction, which I found patently arbitrary and unreasonable. The analysis failed to consider the integral role household animals have come to play in the lives of human beings regardless of age, economic status, or any other distinguishing factor. In imposing a total prohibition even for pets like Nahrstedt's that created no nuisance for other residents, the CC&Rs substantially burdened those many individuals deprived of their valued companionship without a corresponding benefit to the community as a whole. Liberally construing the pleadings "with a view to substantial justice between the parties,"[46] the complaint sufficiently alleged the unreasonableness of the pet restriction to allow the action to go forward.

. . . In my view, the majority's failure to consider the significant and substantial role household animals play in the larger context of human affairs fatally undermined the conclusion that the restriction did not impose an undue burden imposed on some condominium owners while providing a minimal benefit to the community at large. It appeared obvious that prohibiting animals cannot in any respect foster the "health, happiness [or] peace of mind" of others who do not see, hear or smell them. I found this absence of a nexus between burden and benefit to

---

[43] *Id.* at 1290. . . .
[46] *Id.* at 1293 (Arabian, J., dissenting) . . . .

be the essence of unreasonableness under Civil Code section 1354, as construed by the majority.

Moreover, the pet restriction itself, with an exception for domestic birds and fish, was inherently inconsistent and even contradictory as to the Association's proffered justification. Birds are capable of making noises resulting in the kind of disturbance the restriction presumably is intended to prevent. Bird droppings may create a health hazard when placed in common trash areas. Similarly, maintenance of fish may lead to problems, such as tank leakage, that cause damage both to other units and the common areas. Thus, when applied to Nahrstedt's ownership of three household cats, the rationale that the pet restriction must be enforced for "the health, sanitation and noise concerns of other unit owners" cannot be reconciled with the express exceptions the majority impliedly recognized as permissible under Lakeside Village's CC&Rs.[58]

Witnessing the majority cloak essentially all CC&Rs in a presumption of validity and concomitantly accord virtual sovereignty to the HOAs that enforce them, I realized the individual unit owner in any CID in this state had little, if any, control over many intimate aspects of personal lifestyles most homeowners take for granted. Not only is virtually every development declaration created by a business enterprise that may have no residential interest in the property and primarily seeks to maximize its financial return, but actual notice is irrelevant to enforceability. In my estimation, the reasoning and result in *Nahrstedt* illustrated a matter of increasing concern both for those who choose and those who have no choice but to purchase their residential property in a CID. Their individual rights and interests may be sharply curtailed by CC&Rs they have little ability to modify. At the same time, they may find themselves at the mercy of their HOAs, which have the authority pursuant to the majority's construction of Civil Code section 1354 articulated in *Nahrstedt* to intrude into many everyday activities in the guise of enforcing CC&Rs, with little accountability, much less due process. This realization prompted my research into possible means for striking a balance between the governing power accorded these HOAs and the individual freedoms of their members.

III. STANDARDS OF ENFORCEABILITY

Most courts assessing the enforceability of CC&Rs found in CID declarations have adopted a standard of reasonableness. While often formulated in similar terms, application of the test can differ depending in part on whether the source is statutory or judicial. Alternatively, some courts utilize a corporate analogy, applying the business judgment rule to HOA enforcement actions, either exclusively or in conjunction with a variant of the reasonableness standard. Regardless of the test used, however, the decisions most commonly uphold the restriction against the individual owner.

---

[58] *Id.* at 1295-96 (Arabian, J., dissenting).

A. The Reasonableness Standard

As noted, review under the reasonableness standard follows either statutory mandate or decisional authority. Depending upon its origins, the test may vary in three respects: (1) how the court defines reasonableness; (2) which party has the burden of proof on the issue; and (3) whether any presumption of validity prevails.

. . . .

B. The Business Judgment Standard

New York has rejected the reasonableness standard and has become the leading proponent of the business judgment rule. Pursuant to this standard, courts do not inquire into the reasonableness of a CC&R or decision by the HOA board of directors, but instead apply the same measure used for evaluating corporate board decisions. Rather than focusing on the interests of the individual or the larger CID community, this standard looks to any advantage afforded the board. Thus, not only are personal interests subject to serious restriction, judicial validation of the board's enforcement actions does not even depend upon a finding they benefit the community as a whole. "If the corporate directors' conduct is authorized, a showing must be made of fraud, self-dealing or unconscionable conduct to justify judicial review."[89] Consequently, courts will uphold restrictions unless they are "the result of fraud, dishonesty or incompetence."[90]

. . . .

To its advantage, the business judgment standard preserves board authority and deters lawsuits that the reasonableness standard might otherwise permit or at least encourage. Concomitantly, the narrow scope of judicial review obviously disadvantages the individual owner to the extent it permits infringement of rights and interests with little or no recourse but to relocate.

C. Combined Reasonableness/Business Judgment Standard

In yet another alternative, some courts have combined elements of the reasonableness standard and business judgment rule when evaluating CC&R enforcement actions. . . .

. . . .

D. All Review Standards Substantially Limit Individual Challenges

Regardless of their analytical perspective, all standards of review are, for the most part, indulgent of the exercise of authority by HOAs and their governing boards. The reasonableness standard, whether or not in combination with the busi-

---

[89] Papalexiou v. Tower W. Condominium, 401 A.2d 280, 286 (N.J. Super. Ct. Ch. Div. 1979).
[90] *Id.* . . . .

ness judgment rule, may vary somewhat in its formulation, but, in the majority of cases, it substantially burdens the individual's ability to challenge a particular restriction. Either the standard itself weights the equation wholly in favor of enforceability or the burden as to unreasonableness lies with the unit owner. In California, the individual must overcome both judicial obstacles. Thus, courts are unlikely to overturn a board decision except in extreme circumstances.

The business judgment rule is even more limiting because HOA decisions, regardless of their impact on daily life, are subject to judicial review only upon a showing of wrongdoing by the board. As long as the action is taken in good faith, the courts will decline to consider the matter further. Thus, where the business judgment rule prevails, the individual is equally at the mercy of HOAs, if not more so, than where the rule of reasonableness governs. In addition, since business "judgment" includes both good and bad decision-making, unit owners have virtually no legal alternative in the case of poor judgment despite the negative consequences.

. . . .

IV. IMPACT OF CC&RS AND HOA ENFORCEMENT

Individuals purchasing units in a CID acquire the property subject to CC&Rs contained in the developer's declaration, which must be prepared and recorded prior to any sale. The developer thus has tremendous, and disproportionate, impact on the eventual quality of lifestyle in the development, with owners concomitantly losing control over many everyday matters, such as maintenance of their units. The imbalance of power relative to the interests at stake is manifest: the developer, whose primary concern is to maximize financial gain, makes the initial and sole determination of which restrictions and limitations on personal activities to include in the declaration. To the extent multiple restrictions make units more salable to certain people, the developer has an incentive to include as many as the market will bear. At the same time, protection of individual interests has little economic value; hence, those who may desire a less restrictive living situation can expect little accommodation. Since amendment or modification of the CC&Rs is difficult, the original restrictions usually remain intact long after the developer has departed.

Once CC&Rs are in place, HOAs have the responsibility of enforcing them. In that capacity, these organizations exert considerable influence over the bundle of rights normally considered integral to home ownership. To effectuate their enforcement functions, HOAs may levy fines, impose liens on property, and even foreclose on individual mortgages. . . .

. . . .

The HOA exercises its power through a board of directors, a small group of individuals selected from among the unit owners. In this respect, the organizational system of CIDs is consistent with the oligarchic structure usually found in private governments. . . .

. . . .

The CID governing structure deprives owners of a substantial measure of independence traditionally associated with home ownership not only because it controls so many details of daily life, but also because it remains inflexible and essentially immutable. This circumstance has prompted legal scholars, commentators, and members of the public to suggest the need for some curative action, possibly in the drafting of more generalized CC&Rs or provision of a review mechanism to determine if restrictions continue to serve their intended purpose. Currently, although an owner may theoretically challenge the HOA in a lawsuit, the disparity in the parties' relative financial resources and legal positions renders this alternative unavailing in all but the most egregious cases. . . .

V. PROPOSED MODEL LEGISLATION

Common interest developments are the fastest growing form of housing in the United States, in part due to the rise in housing costs relative to income. The mandatory HOAs managing and controlling CIDs operate, in many instances, like city councils, collecting assessments, providing public services, enforcing CC&Rs and bylaws through fines and liens on unit property. Because these associations are not governments, their actions are subject to scant judicial review and do not have to meet any constitutional standards of reasonableness or fairness. Neither equal protection nor due process guarantees apply to the CC&Rs governing CID owners or the proceedings by which HOAs enforce them. As CIDs increase in popularity, so too does the need for some type of check on the power of HOAs to restrict individual interests.

The legislature is the most logical institution to provide this necessary restraint and protection. Although some states have already enacted statutory schemes governing some of the issues related to CIDs, they focus principally on interpretation of CC&Rs and do not address the question of specifically enumerated individual rights. . . .

. . . .

Complementing my criticism of the majority's application of Civil Code section 1354 in *Nahrstedt*, I am now proposing model language that will address the serious and legitimate concerns that HOA enforcement of CC&Rs has occasioned.[157]

. . . .

1   **SECTION 1.** BE IT ENACTED BY THE STATE OF
2   CALIFORNIA, that the Laws of California read as follows:
3   **ARTICLE — REAL PROPERTY**
4   A recorded covenant, condition or restriction, a provision in a
5   declaration, or a provision of the bylaws or rules of a common
6   interest development may not restrict the use or maintenance of a
7   unit or the common elements:

---

[157] This language derives from similar legislation now pending in the Maryland General Assembly. *See* H.B. 651, 1995 Md. Leg. Sess.

8   (1) Without reasonable justification, based on economic,
9   aesthetic, health, or safety considerations; or
10   (2) In a manner that denies a civil right granted or guaranteed
11   under the United States Constitution, the California Constitution, or
12   a federal, state, county, or local statute, ordinance or regulation.

If similar legislation had been enacted when Natore Nahrstedt moved into Lakeside Village with her three cats, her battle with the Association would most likely have taken a different turn. The proviso that CC&Rs and bylaws "may not restrict the use or maintenance of a condominium unit . . . without reasonable justification" places the burden on the HOA to demonstrate reasonableness based on economic, aesthetic, health or safety considerations. Moreover, even if the HOA can defend a restriction as reasonable in the abstract, this legislation does not prevent the unit owner from challenging it based on individual circumstances. Since Nahrstedt's cats created no nuisance, did not threaten the quiet enjoyment of other residents, and did not otherwise impair community interests of Lakeside Village, the Association could not have justified their exclusion as reasonable.

VI. CONCLUSION

The burgeoning popularity of common interest developments in recent decades has placed personal freedoms and lifestyle interests on the endangered species list. Because the developer, who has only an economic motivation, controls the content of the declaration and the specifics in the CC&Rs, both those who are attracted to CIDs for their amenities and those who purchase for financial reasons are extremely limited in their capacity to negotiate changes or otherwise alter burdensome restrictions. The threat to individual interests arises first from the relatively lenient standards for determining the validity of CC&Rs and second from the virtually unrestrained power of HOAs to enforce compliance. While HOAs function like self-contained governments, they remain largely unaccountable for the manner in which they discharge their authority.

In the *Nahrstedt* decision, the California Supreme Court divined a legislative intent to elevate uniformity of application over consideration of whether the owner's "transgression" actually impaired the viability of community life. By rejecting an "as applied" standard, the court not only tipped the scales in favor of stability and predictability of enforceable common interests, it created a major imbalance between those interests and the personal freedoms considered an integral part of residential property ownership. The court in *Nahrstedt* thus enhanced and augmented the substantial power HOAs already enjoy with no countervailing check on the exercise of that power.

The model legislation I propose is intended to address these concerns by establishing some semblance of balance between community and individual interests. While the stability of CIDs both in terms of quiet enjoyment and economic investment remains an important and worthy consideration, it should not come at the expense of the personal freedoms Americans traditionally expect to enjoy in their own homes. If enacted into law, such legislation will provide a minimal level of protection for those expectations and ensure an adequate measure of consideration for lifestyle choices.

Balkanization of owners and tenants is a risk now reasonably foreseen under empowered bureaucratic regimes that suffocate liberty, moving dynamically from tranquility to threat to compulsion. As custodians of tradition entering the millennium, our duty in avoidance is to encourage instead a hymn to harmony and a paean to peaceful coexistence.

COURTS, COVENANTS, AND COMMUNITIES

Clayton P. Gillette
61 U. Chi. L. Rev. 1375 (1994)*

The dramatic rise of residential associations gives reason to believe that both the blessing and the curse of decentralization can be realized more fully within these communities than through more traditional local governments. Both consequences follow from the fact that associations allow individuals with common preferences to gravitate to a common location where they can pursue their conception of the good life. The blessing of this possibility is illustrated by Chief Justice Burger's dissent in *Schad v Borough of Mount Ephraim*.[2] The majority in that case invalidated, on First Amendment grounds, a zoning ordinance that prohibited live entertainment and that was directed specifically at nude dancing. But to the Chief Justice, First Amendment interests had no clear priority over the desires of residents within a small community who wished to be "masters of their own environment."[3] Hence, the borough's exercise of its zoning power "to provide a setting of tranquility" was nothing more than a legitimate attempt "to preserve the basic character of [the] community."[4] Refusal to permit residents "to shape their community so that it embodies their conception of the 'decent life'" would, in Burger's view, destroy the diversity of local communities and force all localities into "a mold cast by this Court."[5] Perhaps it is imputing too much to Burger's sympathetic view of small-town life, but his appeals to mastery and to diversity seem to incorporate many of the more academic justifications of decentralization: the creation of opportunities for self-government, the opportunity to generate a mutually respectful heterogeneity within the larger society,[6] and—perhaps most relevant for current

---

*   © 1994. Reprinted by permission.

[2]   452 US 61, 85 (1981).

[3]   Id at 85.

[4]   Id at 85-86.

[5]   Id at 87.

[6]   See Jerry Frug, *Decentering Decentralization*, 60 U Chi L Rev 253 (1993). . . .

purposes—the creation of an institution that the individual can identify more closely with than an impersonal and distant centralized state.

The curse that confronts this idyllic view of small communities is evident in those critiques of localism that view the pursuit of a common vision of the good life as inherently exclusionary. Moreover, they contend, the bases of exclusion tend to reflect selfishness, wealth, or ethnicity rather than a unique preference for particular local public goods or an idiosyncratic, but benign, lifestyle.[7] . . .

Thus, we suffer, in the words of one commentator, from the "instincts of inclusion and exclusion."[10] Because both the blessing of a participatory, communal system in which individuals can pursue their goals and the curse of irresponsible isolation from needy neighbors are entrenched in the way we think of our society, we face substantial ambivalence about attempts to carve out enclaves that depart from majoritarian norms. . . .

  . . . .

I. The Promise of Residential Associations

A. The Structure of Residential Associations

Residential associations range from condominium, cooperative, or homeowners associations with fewer than ten residents to city-sized developments with tens of thousands of residents. While cooperative and condominium associations share most of the features of homeowners associations that I discuss,[24] these associations are most like local governments in that they encompass significant geographical areas rather than a single building or series of buildings. Like municipalities, associations frequently hold property in common for their resident members, and either provide or contract out for the provision of services that benefit members. Associations supply goods and services ranging from the most common municipal functions, such as security patrols and street maintenance, to more exotic but still common municipal services, such as maintaining golf courses or community centers. Like municipalities, associations have the authority to impose exactions on residents (annual dues or assessments for the maintenance of association property) and to enforce that power by imposing liens on the property of nonpayors.

  . . . .

---

[7] See Gary J. Miller, *Cities by Contract: The Politics of Municipal Incorporation* 37-41, 63 (MIT, 1981); Richard Briffault, *Our Localism: Part I—The Structure of Local Government Law*, 90 Colum L Rev 1 (1990); Richard Briffault, *Our Localism: Part II—Localism and Legal Theory*, 90 Colum L Rev 346 (1990); Lawrence Gene Sager, *Tight Little Islands: Exclusionary Zoning, Equal Protection, and the Indigent*, 21 Stan L Rev 767 (1969).

[10] Frug, 60 U Chi L Rev at 291 (cited in note 6).

[24] Condominium associations typically govern single buildings, whose residents own their residences individually and their common areas (such as hallways and dividing walls) in common. Cooperative associations own and maintain their buildings, while residents own shares in the corporation and have a leasehold interest in their residence. Homeowners associations typically consist of residents who own separate plats and improvements within a development, while the association owns and manages common property such as lakes, streets, and gateways. . . .

Regulation by an association typically takes the form of conditions, covenants, and restrictions (which I will refer to collectively as "covenants") that constitute servitudes imposed on the lots within the association's boundaries. The covenants are initially drafted by the developer of the area before individual units are sold to the public. In addition, it is routine for voting control over amendment or enforcement of covenants to remain with the developer until a certain number or percentage of units within the development are sold. At that point, the developer transfers control to the association, or more specifically, to its board of directors. The developer will also create the governance structure of the association by drafting bylaws or articles of incorporation that allocate voting rights within the association and that typically delegate interpretive and enforcement authority over covenants to the board.

Regulatory covenants may be quite lengthy and detailed. They typically purport to regulate such issues as architectural design, fencing, use of structures, use of common property, and subdivision of lots. They may restrict the activities of residents far more than would be expected as a matter of common law or by local ordinance. Although they no longer control the ethnicity of residents, covenants may regulate at a microlevel, so that they address such issues as the kinds of pets that can be kept within the association, numbers of guests that can be accommodated, the erection of a satellite dish, the size of a mailbox, exterior colors, and types of vehicles maintained on the premises. In short, it is largely through the explication and enforcement of these covenants that the association signals its vision of the good life to current and prospective homeowners.

Even for those within the association, covenants, which are intended to bind current owners and their successors for decades, necessarily contain ambiguities. The passage of time can only exacerbate these ambiguities as technologies develop and social norms change.[44] The original purposes for restrictions on fencing, perhaps intended to ensure unimpaired vistas, may have little application to electronically controlled "invisible" fencing that keeps pets from wandering; limitations on uses to "single-family" residences may have uncertain application in an age when group homes challenge traditional concepts of what it means to be a "family." Efforts to resolve these ambiguities have caused both courts and commentators difficulty in determining how rigorously and by what standard to review the application of association covenants.

One approach has been to incorporate rules drawn from seemingly analogous areas. Most commonly, covenants are subsumed within the law of servitudes, even though covenants governing many associational concerns will have difficulty satisfying the technical requirements of servitude law, such as the prerequisite to enforcement that the servitude "touch and concern" the land. Incorporating these covenants within traditional servitude law loads the dice against the party seeking

---

[44] The passage of time may also lead to a problem of obsolescence for some covenants. See Glen O. Robinson, *Explaining Contingent Rights: The Puzzle of "Obsolete" Covenants*, 91 Colum L Rev 546 (1991). My concern here is more with ambiguity than with obsolescence, although to the degree that courts would ultimately determine whether a covenant has become obsolete, the same analysis about the proper scope of judicial intervention would apply.

enforcement of the covenant; property law has a long history of disfavoring restraints on alienation.[46] The legal doctrine that has evolved from this disfavor insists on strict construction against limitations on the contested use. In myriad rulings on association covenants, courts explicitly invoke the rule of strict construction with reference to little other than historical disapproval.

Other courts, and several commentators, rely on the contractual nature of association membership to justify a different approach. They purport to invoke the intent of the parties, or the volitional nature of the undertaking, in spite of evidence that association residents tend to be ignorant of the covenants by which they are governed. Hence, much of the debate about the enforcement of covenants simply reflects broader debates about the scope and meaning of freedom of contract. Landlord-tenant law, local government law, and the law of private corporations have also been impressed into service to explain the scope of association decision making and the proper scope of judicial review. In addition, regardless of the specific analogy used, courts frequently examine the "reasonableness" of the restriction and its application. Commentators have found this reasonableness test to be more stringent than the test that courts apply to the regulations imposed by the entities to which associations are compared.

While these analogies provide some context by which to measure the role and autonomy of associations, none of them reaches the issue most relevant to judicial intervention into associations' affairs: the core question of institutional competence. The level of associations' autonomy to govern the relationships among their members or between members and nonmembers should depend on the threshold questions of what roles associations play and the extent to which, left to their own devices, covenants will fulfill those roles. It is to these threshold questions that I next turn.

B. Models of Residential Associations

1. The public goods model.

a) Associations as providers. For those who consider a primary value of local governments to be their capacity to provide local public goods efficiently, the ability of residential associations to achieve that same objective underlies much of their appeal. . . .

. . . .

A discrete group that prefers a good not desired (or more of a good than is desired) by others within the community . . . will be successful in obtaining it only if the group can secure the support of the local decision-making body. Legal doctrine as well as political concerns usually mean that the group faces an uphill battle. . . .

---

[46] See James L. Winokur, *The Mixed Blessings of Promissory Servitudes: Toward Optimizing Economic Utility, Individual Liberty, and Personal Identity,* 1989 Wis L Rev 1, 7-16. Winokur suggests that courts took a still less charitable view of servitudes before the nineteenth century, when economic development suggested a need for controls on private land use.

Thus, residents who desire a service not preferred by a majority within the locality may be better off if they can bind themselves to pay for the service through private funds. Associations provide just such an opportunity for those with similar preferences to gravitate to a common area and bind each other to make payments for the goods that they find most attractive, but that cannot be easily obtained through political processes. It is important to note, since I will return to this theme, that those joining the association thereby evince a desire for private ordering rather than for politics. At the same time, provision of the service by the association may be socially desirable, since it reduces the incentives of the group to seek subsidies through the public treasury for goods and services that the majority would prefer not to provide. In these circumstances, the further decentralization of provision requires those who idiosyncratically prefer a different good or more of a good than the majority to pay something closer to its full cost. Individuals who, for instance, desire more police services than the average resident of the municipality may find it easier to coalesce in a section of the municipality and hire private security forces rather than to lobby for more police services citywide. . . .
. . . .

Finally, private provision of services may actually have a positive distributional effect on nonmembers. Members who make payments to associations for services that would otherwise be provided in whole or in part by the locality are typically not permitted to offset those payments against local taxes. The locality, therefore, can either reduce tax payments for all residents or expend additional funds for locality-wide services. In either case, payments for private services that reduce the need for municipal services within the association increase the ability of the locality to address the needs of nonmember residents.

The distributional effects of associations and the justifications for them, therefore, are more ambiguous than might be thought from simplistic initial reactions that view these entities either as mechanisms of escape for the privileged or as social benefactors that limit wasteful cross-subsidies. . . .

 b) Covenants as proxy and as common plan. . . .
 . . . [T]he goods that associations provide tend to be impure public goods beyond a limited geographical range. At some point, congestion will threaten the ability to take advantage of roads, lakes, golf courses, or other common areas typically administered by localities or associations. Hence, some sorting mechanism is necessary to separate those who are and are not entitled to the good. Explicit pricing, first come/first served, or auctions may all be used for such separation; association covenants provide an alternative: selection on the basis of homogeneity. While we do not necessarily value homogeneity where it is based on invidious forms of discrimination, association covenants (at least those that courts will be willing to enforce) typically discriminate on more mundane characteristics of lifestyle. Covenants that indicate socially acceptable, if not universally commended, lifestyles permit individuals who seek to live among those with similar tastes a relatively costless means of identifying each other. At the same time, covenants allow individuals to define characteristics of the favored lifestyle. As

indicated above, lifestyle choices may be reflected in a desire for differential levels of service, such as security; but lifestyles may also be reflected in an aversion to certain activities or land uses to which a segment of the population is uniquely averse. The legal effects that we give to covenants, effectively making them operative in perpetuity, provide the added assurance that homogeneity of preferences will remain. The same stability cannot be attributed to zoning ordinances, which are susceptible to political shifts.

. . . .

My claim, then, is that covenants may play multiple roles in the allocation of local public goods. They permit individuals whose preferences to encourage or discourage discrete activities are sufficiently common to serve as a coordination point, but not so robust as to warrant supervision by a governmental body, to enact regulations that supplement those of the state. For those who consider any competing lifestyle to be an externality imposed on them, covenants produce a tranquil homogeneity. And for those who seek security in the status quo, covenants also provide a mechanism that binds both themselves and others against radical change in those desires.

But covenants do not simply regulate the specific activity they address. The preferences that motivate individuals to migrate to a particular location or association may not be readily susceptible to precise description. Covenants may serve as rough, but appropriate, surrogates, providing signals of sufficient salience to allow coordination among individuals with vague, but similar, lifestyle preferences. In this sense, covenants are indicators of a way of life, rather than simply restrictions on specific land uses.

. . . .

Finally, the concern for the use of covenants as proxies for discrimination on the basis of wealth may make sense against a background in which most associations are seen as weapons of the wealthy. But there are reasons to believe that the same tools may be used by those less advantaged. Recent press accounts indicate that residents of low-income housing units have attempted to bar certain undesirable activities, and those efforts would presumably be simplified if they could be embodied in covenants that bound all tenants. . . .

c) Associations as enforcers of covenants. Even where covenants among private actors capture the benefits of homogeneity, stability, and more appropriate levels of service, homeowners associations might still be superfluous. The covenant, not the governing body, gives expression to a common perspective of the good life. The terms of the covenant make violations of this perspective apparent to, and enforceable by, individual residents. Individual enforcement of covenants, however, is costly both in terms of the effort (including financial effort) that must be expended to remedy an alleged violation, and in terms of the injury to neighborly relations that one must risk by "snitching" on the defector. For any one resident, each of these costs can be avoided if some other resident undertakes the enforcement action. The expected result is that individual residents, even those who object to a violation, will underenforce the community's norm.

. . . .

In all cases that affect the collective rights of association members, whether those members have grievances against the initial developer, against other association members, or against external activity that threatens the autonomy of the group, the association, as the members' representative, is capable of overcoming the obstacles to collective action. In fact, at least one court has found that a homeowners association could be liable to its members for failure to enforce its covenants.[86] The presence of the association reduces enforcement costs by creating a repeat player who is charged with monitoring compliance and designating the association as the party who must seek redress. The association's interests may even coincide with those of its nonmember neighbors, each of whom similarly suffers from inducements to free riding, but none of whom has a surrogate similar to the association. In such a case—for example, where an association seeks to enforce a zoning ordinance that applies both within and without the association's boundaries—the association's activity may produce spillover benefits for nonmembers.

. . . .

2. The civic community model.

To this point, I have suggested that associations may facilitate the formation of homogeneous communities by encouraging those with similar tastes to gravitate to a hospitable area in which they can pursue their vision of the good life. I have also suggested that associations may improve the allocation of goods within the broader society by allowing those who desire a particular package of local public goods to obtain them without either subsidizing or being subsidized by others with different tastes. Defenses of community, however, often rely on loftier virtues than mere preferences for homogeneity of tastes or lifestyles. For many, these preferences are related to participatory values that render associations susceptible to treatment as little democracies and potential fountainheads of civic virtue. . . .

Attractive as this model may be, its practical applications are dubious. If disputes involving homeowners associations centered on issues that indicated robust debate or civic virtue, we might infer that associations foster these values. For the most part, however, these disputes, at least as reflected in the reported cases, center on more mundane issues: satellite dishes, trailer homes, or architectural styles. Many, concerning efforts to collect assessments for financing collective goods after residents refused to make payments, reflect the *failure* of civic virtue. . . .

. . . .

Even if we reject this application of the civic communitarian model, however, pieces of that model may explain much of the appeal of at least some associations. For instance, consider that legal doctrines that facilitate condominium conversions, urban gentrification, or economic development have been claimed to disturb long-

---

[86] See *Cohen v Kite Hill Community Ass'n,* 142 Cal App 3d 652, 191 Cal Rptr 209, 215-16 (1983). See also *Duffey v Superior Court*, 3 Cal App 4th 425, 4 Cal Rptr 2d 334, 338 (1992).

standing neighborhoods in which established groups form homogeneous communities. These claims rest on an assumption that neighborhood stability is a positive good that fosters useful relationships among individuals. The Supreme Court has invoked similar claims about the desirability of neighborhood stability to uphold property tax schemes that discriminate in favor of longstanding residents.[98] The stability of neighborhoods is vulnerable both to political processes, because zoning or changes in political boundaries may alter the scope of local activities, and to market processes, because demand for particular land uses may dictate the character of a neighborhood. Covenants, which have a permanence less susceptible to the vicissitudes of politics or markets, permit those who are particularly averse to neighborhood instability to contract with neighbors for an additional level of assurance. Thus, those drawn to associations may be those least confident that they will succeed in political disputes that affect the character of their neighborhood, a factor that, I will argue, may influence the extent to which we are willing to permit associations to impose on outsiders.

3. Summary.

To this point, I have tried to suggest the variety of explanations for associations and the covenants by which those institutions bind themselves. This discussion shows that associations do not perform a monolithic function, but offer different residents different advantages, ranging from service provision more consistent with resident preferences, to private lawmaking that embodies a lifestyle defined by residents, to community stability. Each of these objectives permits those who speak for the association to restrict the activities of members or the activities of outsiders that affect members. Thus, enforcement of association covenants creates the potential for conflict, and some of those conflicts are likely to require final resolution outside of the decision-making structures created by the association. When this happens, courts must address the issue of how much deference to grant to actions taken by the association. I next address the extent to which the functions and structure of association decision making affect this issue.

II. IMPLICATIONS FOR JUDICIAL CONSTRUCTION OF COVENANTS

A. Some False Starts—Voluntariness and the Analogy to Local Governments

. . . .

The extent to which associations provide benefits could, in theory, be advanced by allowing external review of their regulations. There is no a fortiori reason to sug-

---

[98] In *Nordlinger v Hahn*, 112 S Ct 2326 (1992), the Court upheld a California property tax scheme that was based on the acquisition value of property rather than the fair market value of the property at the time the tax was levied. The Court concluded that the state's desire to preserve neighborhood stability and the reliance interest of purchasers against significant increases in taxes were sufficient to overcome Equal Protection Clause objections. Id at 2333.

gest that associations should be able to escape a level of scrutiny that applies to local governments providing similar services. Nevertheless, associations are not governments, and the analysis above suggests that some of their benefits emerge from the very fact that they are not governments. Hence, it remains unclear whether associations should share the level of deference that is granted to local governments when associations purport to interpret and enforce the regulations that I have suggested define their character.

A common argument in favor of granting autonomy to associations is that relationships among members are voluntary, or at least more so than relationships among neighbors in municipalities. On this theory, the covenants of an association constitute a volitional contract, the terms of which are entitled to all the consideration that courts traditionally afford to contracting parties. Ambiguity in the meaning of covenants, on this view, should be resolved only by reference to the intent of the parties rather than to the reasonableness of their agreement. Decisions in which courts find explicit prohibitions on above-ground swimming pools or satellite dishes to be unreasonable independent of what the parties intended by inclusion of those prohibitions would, on this view, constitute unwarranted judicial interference with contract.

While the decision to live in an association can certainly be understood as a "voluntary" one, buyers' initial ignorance of the attendant covenants and their legal effects may give pause to any effort to rest too much on the parties' subjective volition. James Winokur contends that "[m]ost prospective owners do not intelligently review the restrictions to which they subject themselves upon acceptance of a deed to land burdened by servitudes."[104] But ignorance does not translate into allowing purchasers to escape the effects of covenants. Especially in a legal regime that requires disclosure of covenants before the buyer enters a binding purchase contract, when the buyer *could* reasonably have investigated their terms, alone or with legal advice, it does not follow that we should reward those who fail to make more inquiries. In ordinary contract law, the absence of perfect information does not, of itself, render a decision "involuntary," if we mean by that conclusory term that courts need not enforce the agreement.

I do not assert the converse claim that all covenants are voluntary. Rather, my claim is that, even where homeowners lack knowledge or understanding of their covenants, little is to be gained by reducing the debate about association autonomy to one about "choice and choicelessness" for residents.[106] Similarly, analysis of the scope of association autonomy is not much advanced by recognizing that even those who are aware of covenants may prefer only some of them, but are locked into a "coercive," all-or-nothing regime.[107] As Glen Robinson has suggested, the dichotomy between fully free choice and coercion obscures the complicated ques-

[104] Winokur, 1989 Wis L Rev at 59 (cited in note 46).

[106] See Gregory S. Alexander, *Freedom, Coercion, and the Law of Servitudes*, 73 Cornell L Rev 883, 888 (1988).

[107] See id; Winokur, 1989 Wis L Rev at 57 (cited in note 46).

tion of when market failures become so severe that the buyers of bundled goods are acting under duress.[108]

Instead of seeking a single factor to separate coerced choices (subject to judicial rescission) from voluntary, binding choices, it may be more fruitful to consider whether purchasers can limit the enforcement of covenant restraints or obtain concessions in exchange for accepting them. Our reaction to constraints on choice may be very different if homeowners are exposed to arbitrary sanctions that they can neither control nor escape than if those same homeowners could reduce their exposure by exercising control over the conditions that might lead them to regret their decision.

Consider residents of municipalities, who similarly must purchase bundled municipal services; they cannot, for example, decrease their property taxes by choosing private schools or contracting for private garbage collection. They presumably are able to use the political marketplace, augmented by judicial review of political decisions, to compensate for the "involuntary" choices to which they are subject. If associations that serve the same functions as municipalities provide similar opportunities for resident participation in decisions about what goods to provide and what characteristics to enforce, then one would imagine that we could afford private covenants the same deference that we grant to local officials without invoking the quandary of voluntariness. Thus, it may be worthwhile to explore the degree of latitude that courts grant to municipal decision makers.

. . . .

B. Association Politics

1. The relational setting.

I suggested above that judicial deference to associations might follow the scope of judicial review of municipal regulation. Unfortunately, any effort to discover that scope must confront the doctrinal fact that no single standard of judicial review governs all local regulations. In the absence of some constitutional or statutory provision to the contrary, the traditional rule of local government powers, Dillon's Rule, provides that local governments possess only those powers that have been explicitly delegated to them, or that are necessarily implied from express legislative grants.[110] Doubts about the exercise of a power are to be resolved against the locality. Courts, therefore, play a substantial role in defining the scope of municipal autonomy and construing the meaning of state enabling statutes without necessarily acceding to the interpretations of municipal officials. Any analogy from ordinances to covenants based on Dillon's Rule similarly suggests that associations should have limited autonomy from judges.

. . . .

---

[108] Robinson, 91 Colum L Rev at 577-78 (cited in note 44).

[110] John F. Dillon, 1 *Commentaries on the Law of Municipal Corporations* § 237 at 448-49 (Little, Brown, 5th ed 1911). . . .

The better way to resolve the issue of the judicial role is to ask why we might want substantial review of local decisions, and whether those same concerns affect decision making by associations. I have previously argued that Dillon's Rule is best understood as a mechanism for controlling interest group domination of parochial activity.[115] The Rule allows courts to monitor decisions that appear to have been made at the behest of an influential local minority, or without representation of a disadvantaged minority. . . .

. . . .

The costs of judicial intervention may be worth incurring, for instance, if we believe that residents would otherwise be vulnerable to strategic behavior by the association or by a nonrepresentative subgroup of residents that had captured association decision making. These defects in the political process, I have suggested above, are just the factors that validate judicial scrutiny of municipal decision making. On the other hand, we would take more comfort in relying on associations to construe and administer covenants free from judicial intervention if we were confident that association decisions systematically represented the consensus of members' views rather than a failed political process within the association.

I think that there are reasons to believe that these latter conditions will hold, so that association autonomy should be favored over strict construction and scrutiny of covenants. The basis for my conclusion lies in the very homogeneity of associations that frequently serves as a basis for their being criticized. Homogeneity implies that, within the association, the sources of friction within municipalities—selection of goods or services that are to be provided, the definition of permissible activities, and the avoidance of externalities—have already been resolved. . . .

The conditions necessary to this conclusion should be familiar to students of relational contract. Principles of relational contract suggest that self-policing may be superior to judicial policing against chiseling on the relationship in settings characterized by continuous interactions among parties who are bound to each other either voluntarily (for example, through contract) or by circumstance (for example, by virtue of being neighbors), who cannot exit the relationship easily (primarily because of investment in transaction-specific assets[121]), and who depend on reputation for benefits from others (a function of being members of the same decentralized community).[122] This proposition holds in contractual settings, because the terms of the agreement that generate disputes are likely to revolve around vague principles not readily susceptible to judicial measurement. Hence, even though we might be able to articulate a general standard, such as "best efforts," to which relational parties should aspire,[123] judicial attempts to determine when that standard has

---

[115] Clayton P. Gillette, *In Partial Praise of Dillon's Rule, or, Can Public Choice Theory Justify Local Government Law?*, 67 Chi Kent L Rev 959, 983-85 (1991).

[121] See Oliver E. Williamson, *Transaction-Cost Economics: The Governance of Contractual Relations*, 22 J L & Econ 233, 239 (1979).

[122] Charles J. Goetz and Robert E. Scott, *Principles of Relational Contracts*, 67 Va L Rev 1089, 1149-50 (1981).

[123] Id at 1111-19.

been satisfied are vulnerable to significant error. Those who participate in the practice defined by such standards, however, are likely to be capable both of defining
them and of detecting defections from the cooperative norm.

Relationalism explains how neighbors may evolve a set of mutually beneficial
norms that govern their unique circumstances, even when those norms contravene
positive law that applies to the broader society.[124] Norms have the feature of being
sustained by the approval or disapproval of those who share them. . . .

The purchase of a residence within an association bears the characteristics of
a classic relational contract. The transaction constitutes an investment in specialized resources, as the residence will likely be inappropriate for other uses, and even
transformation of the property into a rental property may be difficult. Exit from the
transaction (selling and moving to a different home) is difficult given the costs (fiscal and emotional) of uprooting. This difficulty of exit suggests that the purchaser
expects to remain in the property for a substantial period of time. Since other purchasers within the association face similar constraints, each resident expects repetitive interactions with neighbors. "Misbehavior" by violation of the association's
norms, therefore, is open to substantial opportunities for punishment through
informal mechanisms of gossip, shunning, or infliction of other reputational
injury.[127]

Thus, the transaction by which a homeowner becomes subject to covenants is
a contractual one, regardless of whether one wishes to append the additional
description of "voluntary." But it is a contract of a particular type, and a type that
has been misunderstood by those who criticize the contractual approach to the question of covenants. . . .

. . . .

2. Courts and associations as interpreters of covenants.

An association's covenants may be thought to vary in one important respect
from the relational theory that I have described above. One indicium of a relational
contract is the unwillingness or inability of the parties to reduce the nature of their
relationship to precise terms. The fact that the relationship will unfold over a substantial period of uncertainty means that parties will not want to allocate contractual risks based on current circumstances. Instead, relational parties may wish to
deal with uncertainty by defining standards for performance in "unusually general
terms."[137] . . .

Unlike traditional relational contracts, however, covenants tend to be quite specific. Relationalism is inherent in a contractual clause that requires "best efforts."

---

[124] The classic article for this proposition is Stewart Macaulay, *Non-Contractual Relations in
Business: A Preliminary Study*, 28 Am Soc Rev 55 (1963). A more recent and wide-ranging appli-
cation is found in Robert C. Ellickson, *Order without Law: How Neighbors Settle Disputes* 141-44
(Harvard, 1991).

[127] See Ellickson, *Order without Law* at 56-60 (cited in note 124).

[137] Goetz and Scott, 67 Va L Rev at 1092 (cited in note 122).

But "no dogs" means "no dogs" *simpliciter*; relationalism, one might claim, is irrelevant to a proper construction of the term. . . .

Specificity of covenants, however, does not necessarily mean that the parties do not recognize their relational situation or do not rely on norms of reciprocity to enforce it. Other explanations may suffice. First, it may be that property regimes historically require greater specificity than commercial regimes. The relaxation of requirements of definiteness in commercial contracts, such as the ability to have an enforceable contract with an open price term, does not appear to have spilled over into the traditional insistence in real property contracts on specificity and detail. Thus, specific clauses standing alone do not betoken a lack of cooperative intent.

Second, specific covenants may establish the parameters of the relationship without exhausting the details. Just as covenants provide strong signals about the lifestyle of association members, so do they provide a basis from which to extrapolate when the association attempts to advance that lifestyle in ways that are not explicit in the covenants themselves. . . .

Once we recognize the force of relationalism, judicial intervention may still be useful to enforce the implicit norms of cooperation when inevitable disputes arise. Legal review of the enforcement of covenants may avoid spiteful actions against an outlier within the community or may clarify ambiguities where the meaning of a covenant is substantially in doubt even among members. . . .

As a general matter, the setting in which disputes over covenants arise does not inspire confidence that courts have an advantage over the informal interpretive processes of associations. The relational nature of the community provides a reason for believing that when cooperation breaks down sufficiently to require a lawsuit, the association's interpretation of the covenant is likely to represent the common understanding of its members. Courts, on the other hand, are likely to miss any gap between the association's understanding and the understanding outside the association. . . .

From this perspective, it is important that it is the association that is enforcing the covenants. Consider, for instance, the situation in which one resident of the association brings an action against another for violation of a covenant. After entering into the association, it may be in the interest of each member to retain maximum individual autonomy for himself or herself while restricting the autonomy of others. In this manner, residents who seek the refuge of covenants to prevent others from imposing externalities on them may still attempt to impose externalities on those others; the fact that I do not want to look at your ranch-style home in our federalist-style neighborhood does not mean that I do not want to require you to look at the commercial vehicle that I park in my driveway.

. . . .

An action by the association, however, is more likely to involve a complaint against an actual defector from the relationship. A board of directors is unlikely to bring a costly and time-consuming action in the association's name until it has heard multiple complaints against a neighbor, made an independent investigation, and attempted informal resolution of the matter. Where the association decides to proceed, therefore, it is unlikely that the complainers have been idiosyncratic. Since the association acts on behalf of all members (while the individual complainant speaks only for himself or herself), its interpretation is more likely to reflect the common understanding of members than an interpretation of any one party. Given the relationship among members, it is unclear why a court, left to its own devices, should attempt to do anything more than comprehend that same understanding.

This analysis implies that presentation of the same issue—interpretation of a covenant—in two different judicial proceedings, one initiated by the association and one initiated by an individual member of the association, may properly carry different presumptions. The action by the association can be presumed to reflect the current understanding of its members as to the meaning of the contested covenant. The same action, initiated by an individual member, carries no such cachet. Courts that treat interpretation of all covenants the same, regardless of the identities of the disputing parties, fail to make this distinction.

. . . .

Finally, note that, when based on the cooperative relationship among association members, judicial deference to the association's construction of its covenants is actually more consistent with the policies that disfavor restrictions on land uses than is the traditional doctrine of strict judicial construction of covenants. The doctrine of strict construction emerges from antipathy to restraints on the alienation of land and a fear that future productive uses of property will be prohibited by outdated limitations. Reliance on relationalism, however, serves the very goal of retaining flexibility of land use by permitting the association to interpret covenants dynamically to reflect the changing preferences of the community. Courts that stand outside the community will have a more difficult time discerning shifts in those preferences, and failure to accede to the interpretation of the association may bind courts to a more rigid interpretation of covenants than the association itself would endorse. Assume, for instance, that a covenant bars "fences" higher than six feet during a period when wooden fencing is a primary mechanism for marking boundaries on lots within the association. A homeowner now plants a row of saplings on her boundary and allows them to grow in excess of six feet. A court applying the traditional rule would have difficulty enjoining the maintenance of the "fence," notwithstanding that the function of the covenant was to ensure unimpeded views for all residents at a time when traditional fencing posed the primary threat.

. . . .

C. Agency Costs in Residential Associations

To this point, my argument has been that judicial deference to association interpretation of covenants is appropriate because the very commencement or defense of a lawsuit signals courts that a violation of the community norm has occurred. This conclusion, however, is predicated on an assumption that those who make decisions that bind associations, typically the board of directors, are representative of the association's members. To the extent that this is not true, the relationship between the parties provides little reason for the court to favor one interpretation of the covenant over another. Hence, competing policies, such as the traditional policy of construing servitudes narrowly, may trump any appeal to association autonomy. It is necessary, therefore, to examine whether there are reasons to believe that governors of an association will tend to reflect or not to reflect the common understanding of its members.

. . . .

I cannot readily conclude . . . that either the association or the developer will necessarily interpret covenants in a manner consistent with the consensus of association members. Divergence in the views of association officials, however, does not necessarily invite more intrusive judicial scrutiny of covenants. If we believed that courts were adept at identifying those cases in which decision makers had interests that deviated from those of association members, we might direct courts to intervene more readily in those cases. But if courts have no greater ability than association members to discern rent-seeking activity by association officials, there seems little reason to rely on those outside the community to define the scope of community norms as embodied in covenants.

III. Associations and Nonresidents

The assertion that cooperative norms will emerge within the association and are more readily identifiable and enforceable by members than by courts does not entail that these norms will serve the welfare of those outside the association. Thus, one negative implication of my argument to this point is that judges should be far more interventionist where associations impose costs on nonresidents. The problem is that this principle, without more, swallows up the argument for judicial restraint. All covenants affect those outside the association, in that they restrict access to prospective home purchasers who prefer the same lifestyle as association residents, except for one (or more) of the covenants. At the same time, there are few situations in which decisions of associations are specifically aimed at nonresidents. We return, then, to the problem with which we began: determining the latitude that we are willing to confer on groups that seek some degree of isolation, notwithstanding that their private arrangements affect nonmembers.

The polar case for judicial intervention exists where the association seeks to engage in conduct that could not constitutionally be enforced with the participation of state actors. Here, the externality may take the rather intangible form of affecting even those who are not directly excluded, because the basis of exclusion makes them uncomfortable about living in a society where such exclusions are practiced. Less clear is which outcome is preferable when the association seeks to enforce a covenant that does not offend constitutional principles, but that is inconsistent with other social norms. In these cases, our willingness to allow the association to set itself up against the broader society reflects our reaction to the kind of diversity that I suggested at the outset underlies Chief Justice Burger's opinion in *Schad*. The desire for heterogeneity implicit in those remarks finds resonance in the sociological literature that urges the development of community by allowing greater autonomy for localities . . . . Some courts that have rejected intrusive interpretations of covenants, notwithstanding that enforcement creates adverse effects for nonresidents, appear at least implicitly to endorse the same view. Other courts, however, appear to seize on the conflict between covenants and conflicting social policies either explicitly to abrogate the private covenants or to entertain narrow constructions of them.

Analysis of these cases may provide some hints toward a theory of when association activity generates sufficient effects on nonresidents as to require intervention. Consider, for instance, the issue of whether prohibitions in covenants on the operation of businesses within the association or limitations of occupancy to "single-family" residences can be enforced to prohibit group homes. Several courts have recognized that a restrictive definition of residence or family that requires blood or marital relationships between the occupants is inconsistent with state policies in favor of the creation of group homes, where individuals live together and either care for each other or are cared for by a common supervisor. Other courts have upheld the association's restrictive definition of residence or family to more traditional forms.

. . . .

One way to sort out when the adverse effects are sufficiently substantial to warrant intervention is to ask whether we are confident that the conflicting social policy actually reflects a consensus of the broader society. Principles that reach constitutional proportions do so in large part because they reflect the deeply held views of a substantial segment of the population. Thus, when we reject private arrangements that conflict with constitutional principles, we may feel comfortable that we are properly imposing a majoritarian conception of what is necessary to pursue the good life for society as a whole. Statutory embodiments of public policy may be more suspect. . . .

. . . [E]xemptions might make sense only in those cases where judges detect a reasonable likelihood that the conflicting legislation resulted from capture. It should not be surprising, therefore, if courts reject claims that associations are exempt from municipality-wide zoning plans, because such an exemption cannot easily be explained by capture.

More commonly, however, covenants involve efforts by an association to create restrictions that are not directly addressed one way or the other by the locality or the state. We would expect this type of case to arise frequently if I am correct that a primary function of associations is to allow privatized regulatory schemes that are more tailored to residents' preferences than municipal regulation. Even if we are willing to recognize some value in this objective, we would expect some nonconstitutional limits on its pursuit, given the consequences for nonresidents and the fact that even municipal corporations have only limited ability to impose adverse effects on nonresidents. While the permissible level of these externalities is hard to define, one might infer from judicial reaction to the group-home cases that the limitations on association autonomy depend on whether enforcement of the covenant at issue excludes in a manner that substantially impairs the mobility of those excluded.

. . . .

Focus on the extent of the exclusion may be seen as a corollary to the Lockean proviso that permits individuals to retain the fruits of their labor as long as there remains "enough and as good left in common for others."[187] Exclusion from an idiosyncratic community permits the members of that community to realize their interests without significantly penalizing those who are excluded. As the number of communities who endorse the same exclusion multiplies, however, the mobility of the excluded may become so constrained as to trump the interests in upholding the exclusion. . . .

This distinction between permissible and impermissible exclusions provides a justification for allowing a community to impose its preferences on outsiders where the basis for exclusion does not substantially constrain the mobility of those excluded. . . .

. . . .

CONCLUSION

Residential associations may be easy targets. Their attraction is frequently based on mundane aspects of the good life rather than on the creation of robust communities. They tend to exclude those worst off in the society. They impose costs on their members who seek to avoid restrictions and on outsiders who may have to bear a greater level of undesirable activities and land uses that are excluded from the associations. Nevertheless, I have suggested that they may fulfill important functions and do so in a manner that entitles their decisions to substantial deference in a wide range of cases. Whether associations realize this potential depends on such issues as their ability to signal a common lifestyle to potential members and the susceptibility of their officials to interests inconsistent with those of their members. On some of these issues, I remain agnostic. But the overall picture I have attempted to paint is of a mechanism for sorting that is no more invidious than we allow through the creation of more formal jurisdictions (municipal corporations) and that is more responsive than those institutions to the desires of residents. That these smaller jurisdictions may engage in activities that set them apart from others in society is undeniable. But that is a source for further analysis, not a conclusion that necessarily leads to denigration of these institutions.

Note

For the argument that many homeowners' associations engage in state action and thus, constitutional standards should be employed to evaluate association activities that affect outlanders, see David J. Kennedy, Note, *Residential Associations as State Actors: Regulating the Impact of Gated Communities on Nonmembers*, 105 Yale L.J. 761 (1995).

---

[187] John Locke, *Second Treatise on Government* § 27 at 19 (Hackett, 1980) (C.B. Macpherson, ed).

PART II

ZONING—BEDROCK OF PUBLIC CONTROL

Zoning, although frequently maligned, is at the core of governmental efforts to control land use. The articles in this part examine multifarious facets of zoning.

A. Perspective: Historic and Modern Considerations

PRESERVING PROPERTY VALUES? PRESERVING PROPER HOMES? PRESERVING PRIVILEGE?: THE PRE-*EUCLID* DEBATE OVER ZONING FOR EXCLUSIVELY PRIVATE RESIDENTIAL AREAS, 1916-1926

Martha A. Lees
56 U. Pitt. L. Rev. 367 (1994)[*]

I. INTRODUCTION

The phenomenon of exclusionary zoning and its inequitable effects have been well documented in recent commentary. Some scholars have recognized the roots of exclusionary zoning in the early part of this century, when laws barring industry, businesses, and multiple dwellings from private residential areas were first enacted and later definitively upheld by the Supreme Court in *Village of Euclid v. Ambler Realty Company*.[3] They have noted that early twentieth-century proponents of laws protecting private residential districts were motivated by class, racial, and ethnic bias and by economic interests such as the desire to protect property values. . . .

---

[*] Copyright © 1994. Reprinted by permission.
[3] 272 U.S. 365 (1926).

While scholars have focused on the economic and social incentives underlying pre-*Euclid* support for protecting private residence districts through zoning, few have examined the influence of ideology on early zoning advocates. Although supporters of private residential zoning in the early 1900s were strongly swayed by economic considerations and by prejudice, they were also influenced by the domesticity, pastoral, and public health ideologies prevalent at the time.

This article attempts to provide a more complete account of the complicated web of motivations that underlay both sides of the zoning debate between 1916, when the first "modern" zoning law was passed, and 1926, when *Euclid* was decided. . . .

. . . .

II. Historical and Legal Background

A. *The Genesis of Exclusively Private Residential Zoning*

> Zoning may be defined, in general, as action by the state, or by a city under authority of the state, to control, under the police power: (a) The heights to which buildings may be erected; (b) The area of lots that must be left unbuilt upon; and (c) The uses to which buildings and lots may be put.[9]

Although the Boston City Planning Board wrote these words in 1924, conventional accounts deem 1926 the year when zoning began. In that year the United States Supreme Court upheld the constitutionality of comprehensive zoning in *Village of Euclid v. Ambler Realty Co.*, and since then zoning has played a prominent role in American land-use planning.

Yet the story of zoning begins long before *Euclid*. The common law of nuisance, which serves to separate noxious land uses from nonoffensive ones, and restrictive covenants, deed provisions limiting or prohibiting certain land uses, were used to control development throughout the nineteenth century. Moreover, zoning's immediate parent, the city planning movement, took hold before 1900.[13] While in its early days city planning had focused on municipal art and the architecture of public buildings, by 1911 city planners began to concentrate on the "promotion of an orderly and attractive development of a city and its environs."[14] Zoning—the systematic regulation of land-use—was an outgrowth of planners' efforts to order the urban environment.

---

[9]   City Planning Board, Boston, Mass., Zoning for Boston: A Survey and A Comprehensive Plan 12 (1924) [hereinafter Zoning for Boston].

[13]   Seymour I. Toll, Zoned American 117 (1969) (noting that while city planning may be traced as far back as Greek and Roman times, city planning "as a self-conscious movement with its own literature" began in the late nineteenth century).

[14]   M. Christine Boyer, Dreaming the Rational City: The Myth of American City Planning 84 (1983).

It is difficult to point to a "first" zoning law. By the turn of the century, some cities had enacted ordinances limiting building heights; under the Boston City Planning Board definition, these could be considered zoning ordinances. A 1909 Los Angeles ordinance was one of the first laws to establish use districts. The regulation established 25 industrial districts in the city and reserved the rest of the land for residential use. . . . While the Los Angeles ordinance fits the Boston City Planning Board's definition of "zoning," it is sometimes considered simply an extension or codification of nuisance law, since its primary object was to remove offensive industries from residential areas.

New York City's 1916 ordinance is traditionally seen as the first modern zoning law. Unlike the somewhat piecemeal Los Angeles ordinance, New York's law was comprehensive, systematically regulating the height, bulk, and use of every building in the city. . . .

Following the passage of New York's ordinance in 1916, zoning became very popular in the United States. . . . The rapid proliferation of zoning legislation was encouraged in part by the issuance in 1922 of a Standard State Zoning Enabling Act by a committee within Herbert Hoover's Commerce Department. The standard act made it simpler for legislatures to initiate zoning in their states.

The arrival of zoning legislation on the statute books of American municipalities was not frictionless, however. Between 1916, the date of the first comprehensive zoning law, and 1926, when the Supreme Court upheld the constitutionality of comprehensive zoning, there was great disagreement in state courts over the constitutionality of zoning. According to constitutional doctrine, states could regulate property pursuant to the police power—that is, for the purpose of preserving the public health, safety, welfare, and morals—but were subject to the strictures of the Fourteenth Amendment, which forbade states to deprive any person of life, liberty, or property without due process of law. Thus, the constitutional problem was to determine whether zoning was within the police power or whether it was a deprivation of property without due process. The cases focused less on whether industrial facilities could constitutionally be kept out of business and residential areas than on whether businesses and apartments could be excluded from private residential areas. The reason for this was that until 1926 it was not fully established whether the police power extended just to the exclusion of nuisances, or whether it was broader. It was relatively simple to classify industries as traditional nuisances, but more difficult to see businesses or apartments as such, since they were not obviously offensive in the way that industries often were.

A number of state courts between 1916 and 1926 held that barring businesses and apartments from private residential areas was within the police power. . . .

Some state courts during the period, however, held that neither businesses nor apartments could constitutionally be excluded from private residential areas. . . .

By the time *Euclid* was decided, the trend in state courts was towards favoring the constitutionality of comprehensive zoning regulations, including those with provisions that excluded businesses and apartments from private residential areas. By 1926, more state courts favored such zoning than opposed it. . . . Nonetheless, the constitutionality of comprehensive zoning was by no means clearly established when *Euclid* came before the Supreme Court in 1926.

Although the case was close, the Court upheld the entire ordinance challenged in *Euclid* as within the police power, thereby establishing conclusively the constitutionality of comprehensive zoning. Significantly, *Euclid* resolved the debate over the constitutionality of excluding businesses and apartments from private residential districts. Such exclusion was constitutional, the Court held, even though businesses and apartments were not traditional nuisances.

B. The Class-Segregating Effect of Exclusively Private Residential Zoning

While the Supreme Court's *Euclid* decision expanded municipal planning power, it also legitimized a form of zoning that reinforced socioeconomic class segregation. Euclidean zoning promoted class segregation for the simple and self-evident reason that the ability to afford different types of housing varies with income. Many working-class people in the first quarter of this century could not afford to buy or even rent single-family homes. Thus, ordinances excluding all but single-family dwellings from certain neighborhoods created districts where few working-class people could afford to live.

Housing probably became somewhat more affordable for poorer people than it had previously been over the course of the first quarter of this century. . . . After World War I, factors such as the fall of building costs due to more efficient production methods and the increased availability of credit at moderate interest rates enabled more working people to purchase single-family homes. The advent of the automobile also increased housing affordability between the World Wars. Having a car allowed people formerly confined to the city center for job accessibility reasons to seek homes farther away, where the supply of land was more abundant. The greater supply lowered housing costs and made detached homes more affordable, while the automobile allowed quick and easy access to jobs in the city.

Single-family homes were by no means available to everyone between 1916 and 1926, however. In the early 1920s, shortages of labor, materials, and capital resulting from World War I caused housing construction costs to increase. At the same time, until after World War II most workers could not afford to buy even the relatively cheap Model T Ford cars that might have rendered accessible areas where housing costs were more moderate. For reasons like these, significant numbers of people still could not afford single-family or even two-family homes between 1916 and 1926. Thus, comprehensive zoning ordinances obviously contributed to class segregation. An ordinance that excluded two-family homes and apartments from single-family districts and apartments from single-family and two-family districts would have reinforced the existence of separate upper middle-class, central/lower middle-class, and working-class neighborhoods.

. . . .

While comprehensive zoning did not initiate class segregation, it did intensify such separation. At the very least, by codifying into public law patterns generated by private factors, ordinances excluding multiple dwellings constituted an unprecedented governmental endorsement of pre-existing class-segregated configurations.

Furthermore, such ordinances undoubtedly reinforced economic separation more efficiently than their predecessor forces did; unlike the relatively piecemeal restrictive covenants,[60] single-family-only provisions applied to entire neighborhoods or even municipalities, and unlike market and social forces, zoning ordinances demanded compliance. . . .

. . . .

III. Motivations Driving the Criticism of Exclusively Private Residential Zoning and Zoning Proponents' Responses

A. *The Criticism*

Between 1916 and 1926, a number of judges, attorneys, and commentators expressed their opposition—in opinions, briefs, and periodicals—to the use of zoning to preserve exclusively private residential districts. These early twentieth-century writers, like present day critics, tended to focus on the invidious motivations behind zoning and the inequitable effects it fostered. Conservative critics voiced concern not only that zoning was detrimental to property rights and constituted excessive regulation, but also that it tended to discriminate in favor of the wealthy. Progressive writers criticized the use of zoning to maintain exclusively private residential areas because they felt that it harmed poorer people by reinforcing the prejudices of the wealthy and by strengthening class and ethnic segregation. Unlike conservative critics, however, progressives objected to this use of zoning only to the extent they perceived it as hindering the interests of the less fortunate; to the extent they found zoning to favor the less wealthy at the expense of the more wealthy, progressive critics endorsed it.

. . . .

B. *Zoning Proponents' Responses*

Zoning advocates strenuously disputed the critics' claim that ordinances maintaining exclusively private residential districts harmed the interests of any class, arguing instead that such regulations actually advanced the welfare of all. Planners and attorneys who supported such ordinances were understandably careful not to portray them as favoring the relatively wealthy, or as detrimental to the interests of the less wealthy; instead, these advocates praised the tendency of such laws to serve

---

[60] Until the 1920s, it was rare to find restrictive covenants covering more than one parcel or subdivision at a time. GWENDOLYN WRIGHT, BUILDING THE DREAM: A SOCIAL HISTORY OF HOUSING IN AMERICA 212 (1981). During the 1920s, developers did begin applying covenants to neighborhood-sized areas, but tended not to have control of entire municipalities. *Id.; see also* WILLIAM TUCKER, ZONING, RENT CONTROL AND AFFORDABLE HOUSING 11 (1991) (arguing that in Houston, Texas, the nation's largest unzoned city, restrictive covenants protect wealthy neighborhoods but do not exclude low income people from the entire municipality).

the needs of the entire community. For example, in its report on Boston's zoning plan, the basis for Boston's zoning law, the Boston City Planning Board continually emphasized the democratic, egalitarian nature of the legislation, which excluded industry from business and residence districts, industry and businesses from general and single residence districts, and any use but single-family homes from single residence districts. . . . In fact, the Board explained, if the zoning law helped anyone, it helped the less fortunate:

> Zoning is protection for the poor man. It gives by law to the citizen of modest means, both in his home and in his business, the protection the citizen of larger means is able to secure by litigation or by private restrictions. The rich man can often protect himself against various forms of nuisances by legal action. The poor man cannot indulge in the luxury of a law suit[.][131]

. . .

. . . .

Most likely planners like . . . the Boston City Planning Board recognized that protecting private residential districts tended to benefit the wealthy more than the poor. However, they undoubtedly understood the prudence of portraying zoning ordinances as egalitarian in order to ensure that judges upheld the laws. To be constitutional, a zoning regulation had to be within the police power, which required that the law bear a "reasonable relationship" to promoting the health, safety, morals, and welfare of the general public. The Boston City Planning Board's contention that the Boston zoning law constituted a "reasonable invocation of the police power not for personal preferences or private gain, but in the interest of the health, safety, morals and general welfare of the entire community,"[155] phrased as it was precisely in the correct doctrinal language, seems like an overt attempt to justify the law's constitutionality to the courts. In making the statement, it appears the Board members knowingly sacrificed accuracy in the interest of upholding the law in court.

. . . .

Planners had another tool at their disposal to persuade judges to uphold zoning ordinances besides egalitarian rhetoric or an emphasis on property values: scientific methodology. A faith in scientific and bureaucratic management techniques as the route to solving social problems was a characteristic typical of Progressive reformers. Thus, it is not surprising that city planners approached zoning in a systematic fashion, using trained experts and performing comprehensive factual investigations. . . .

. . . .

While city planners probably would have used scientific methods regardless of how they felt these methods would affect judges' acceptance of zoning, their use of scientific methodology was motivated to some degree by their belief that it would command judicial respect. . . .

. . . .

---

[131] . . . [ZONING FOR BOSTON, *supra* note 9,] at 13.
[155] ZONING FOR BOSTON, *supra* note 9, at 14 . . . .

IV. Motivations Driving the Advocacy of Exclusively
Private Residential Zoning

The willingness of early twentieth-century zoning proponents to shade the truth to ensure the upholding of ordinances protecting exclusively private residential areas might suggest that these advocates were motivated by nothing more than economic concerns and prejudice. Certainly, their use of somewhat instrumentalist argumentation suggests not only that they were pragmatists but also that some sort of offensive views may have underlain their somewhat obfuscatory rhetoric. Yet to focus solely on economic and social forces, as contemporary scholars usually have, is to overlook the complexity of zoning supporters' motivations. Their writings suggest that zoning advocates were influenced not only by the concrete forces of economics and class/ethnic/racial prejudice but also, more abstractly, by their desire to preserve neighborhoods that were consistent with domesticity, pastoral, and health ideologies.

The argument that ideology, as well as economics and prejudice, influenced zoning supporters requires some explanation of what is meant by the term "ideology." For the word, as a number of sociologists have recently noted, has no one discernible meaning.[174] This article uses the term to refer to the concept of a world view, or, in sociologist Terry Eagleton's words, to the "ideas and beliefs . . . [that] symbolize the conditions and life-experiences of a specific, socially significant group or class."[175] The "socially significant group or class" that typically held the domesticity, pastoral, and health beliefs discussed in this Part was the class that included city planners, judges, and attorneys: the middle class. Thus, the article argues that support for zoning was influenced not only by economics and social forces, but also by a systematic set of middle-class beliefs.

A. *Minimizing Net Social Annoyance*

Zoning advocates' writings do suggest that they wished to maintain exclusively private residential districts at least in part for economic reasons: to minimize net social annoyance, and to stabilize property values and tax rates. For instance, one reason Judge Kramer of the Cuyahoga County, Ohio Court of Common Pleas upheld East Cleveland's zoning ordinance, which excluded apartments from single and two-family residence districts, was his belief that confining apartments to their own areas would result in the least loss to the community. According to Judge Kramer, "the apartment house, or tenement, in a section of private residences, is a nuisance to those in its immediate vicinity," for among other things it reduced the light and air reaching adjoining residences, and reduced the quiet and privacy of the

---

[174] *See, e.g.*, John B. Thompson, Ideology and Modern Culture 5 (1990) (noting the "ambiguity of the concept of ideology" due to the term's "many different uses and shades of meaning"); Terry Eagleton, Ideology 1 (1991) (stating that "the term 'ideology' has a whole range of useful meanings, not all of which are compatible with each other").

[175] Eagleton, *supra* note 174, at 29.

neighborhood.[177] However, banning apartments from the city altogether would result in a loss to those who wished to inhabit them. The best way to minimize the loss occasioned either to private home dwellers or to apartment residents was to use zoning to confine apartments to certain districts . . . .

. . . .

B. Preserving Property Values

Another apparent reason zoning advocates wished to exclude industry, businesses, and apartments from private residential areas was that they wished to protect the investments of residential property owners. A number of judges argued that the arrival of a manufactory, store, or apartment building in a private residential area reduced the values of the residences. They seemed to believe that a zoning ordinance that excluded industry, businesses, and apartments from residential districts would prevent such depreciation. Thus, they urged zoning's adoption in part to capitalize on its value-stabilizing effect. . . .

. . . .

C. Minimizing Taxes

The desire to protect city dwellers from excessive taxes also apparently motivated zoning advocates to push for the exclusion of industry, businesses, and apartments from private residential areas. City planners noted that industries, businesses, and residences placed different demands on public utilities and services. For example, according to the Boston City Planning Board, lightly-traveled residential areas did not need wide, heavily paved streets, while business areas did need such streets to cope with the greater amount of traffic to which they were subject. . . .

. . . .

. . . [T]he argument as stated by the Boston City Planning Board did not provide any rationale for excluding apartments from private residential areas. The Board did not argue that apartments required a different level of public utility service from that needed by private residences. Attorneys, however, extended the argument to apartments, claiming that apartments required a greater level of public services than did private residences, and then used the argument as a rationale for excluding apartments from private residential areas. . . .

. . . .

D. Venting Class, Ethnic, and Racial Bias

It seems clear that other motivations besides a concern for taxpayer investments and pocketbooks led judges, attorneys, and planners to advocate the use of zoning to preserve exclusively private residential areas in the ten years before *Euclid*. Non-

---

[177] State *ex rel.* Morris v. Osborn, 22 Ohio N.P. (n.s.) 549, 554 (1920).

economic motivations such as class, ethnic, and racial bias certainly influenced zoning proponents as well.

It would not be surprising to find undercurrents of class bias in writings between 1916 and 1926, since by that time there had long been wide differentiations in income in the United States. Moreover, one might expect ethnic bias to have influenced the advocacy of exclusively private residential zoning between 1916 and 1926, since it was during those years that middle-class Americans reacted particularly strongly against the acceleration of immigration that had begun at the turn of the century. . . .

. . . .

In addition to nativism and class bias, one would expect racism to have influenced the debate over private residential zoning between 1916 and 1926, since just before that period American cities had passed a flurry of facially racist residential segregation ordinances. These regulations, which established separate residence districts for blacks and whites, were implemented by racist whites in a number of northern and southern cities in reaction to the migration of numerous black people from the rural south to urban areas, both northern and southern, during and after World War I. After Baltimore passed the first racial zoning ordinance in 1910, racial zoning persisted for some time, even after the Supreme Court invalidated the practice in 1917.[212]

While the use-oriented ordinances this article discusses were not facially discriminatory, it is hard to imagine that their passage was not influenced to some degree by the same racial fear and hatred that spawned their patently racist counterparts. The acceptance of private residential zoning was also most likely influenced by the same bias against the poor and the foreign-born that led to immigration restrictions. . . .

. . . .

While zoning supporters were undoubtedly motivated by unfair prejudice against "undesirables," however, such a motivation does not completely explain why they advocated the use of zoning to preserve exclusively private residential areas. For in arguing for the exclusion of what they feared, zoning advocates were simultaneously revealing what they valued, however bourgeois their values might be. . . . If the desire to exclude the unwanted was a driving force behind zoning, then its converse—the desire to realize certain ideals or values—would logically be an equally important motivation.

E. Realizing the Single-Family Home Ideal

That the desire to realize certain ideals was an important force motivating judges, attorneys, and planners to support exclusively private residential zoning raises the question of what ideals these writers wished to realize. A simple answer is that zoning advocates placed great value on the single-family home with a yard

---

[212] *See* Buchanan v. Warley, 245 U.S. 60 (1917) . . . .

in a neighborhood of similar homes as the ideal home environment, and apparently wished to use zoning to preserve and foster this environment. . . .

. . . .

F. Preserving a Home Environment That Conformed to Domesticity, Pastoral, and Health Ideals

Simply to state that zoning advocates were trying to foster their ideal of the proper home environment—a neighborhood of single-family homes—fails to uncover fully their motivations, for it does not explain why they valued the single-family home with a yard, nor what made the exclusion of industry, businesses, and apartments so essential to effectuate their values. A more complete explanation is that the desire to preserve a home environment that conformed to domesticity, pastoral, and health ideologies appeared to be an important motivation leading judges, attorneys, and planners to advocate the use of zoning to maintain exclusively private residential areas. . . .

1. Zoning Advocates' Acceptance of Domesticity Ideology

Zoning advocates appeared to believe that the ideal home should be a private sanctuary from the supposedly "public" world of industry, businesses, and apartments, a conception that was rooted in domesticity ideology. This ideology arose in the early nineteenth century and matured towards the end of the century. While domesticity ideology is typically associated with the nineteenth century, the mindset did persist in some form into the early twentieth century, and to some degree may affect thinking even today.

. . . .

That zoning advocates portrayed the ideal home as a "separate sphere" from the "public" world of business, industry, and apartments, as a private sanctuary of comfort, quiet, and cleanliness where the focus was on family life and child-rearing rather than on the pursuit of profit, reflects the extent to which aspects of nineteenth-century domesticity ideology persisted into the early twentieth century. . . .

. . . .

2. Zoning Advocates' Acceptance of the Pastoral Ideal

Zoning supporters also pictured the ideal home as surrounded by lawns, trees and gardens, a vision that was grounded in the American tradition of idealizing the natural environment. Americans have long possessed, and still entertain, a romanticized view of nature; the "pastoral ideal," as Leo Marx terms this view, "has been used to define the meaning of America ever since the age of discovery, and it has not yet lost its hold upon the native imagination."[262] . . .

. . . .

---

[262] LEO MARX, THE MACHINE IN THE GARDEN: TECHNOLOGY AND THE PASTORAL IDEAL IN AMERICA 3 (1964) . . . .

The persistence of the pastoral ideal in the American psyche has always been the product both of a positive attraction to natural surroundings and a negative reaction against the complications of city life. Thus, it is not surprising that, as the forces of urbanization and industrialization intensified in the late nineteenth century, bringing with them increased central city congestion and increasing numbers of immigrants, middle class Americans experienced a heightened affinity for the pastoral ideal, a preference they expressed physically by moving in large numbers from city row houses to detached suburban homes on grassy lots between 1870 and 1900. . . .

Similarly, as urban congestion and immigration reached their highest levels yet in the early twentieth century, the middle class affinity for the pastoral ideal endured, as evidenced by the fact that more and more of those who could afford to do so moved to the suburbs.

Zoning advocates apparently shared the pastoral ideal's emphasis on the desirability of withdrawing from business and industrial areas, the epitome of civilization, and of having homes surrounded by domesticated green spaces. . . .
 . . . .

3. Zoning Advocates' Emphasis on the Healthiness of the Home

Zoning advocates felt that the ideal home environment should be not only a semi-rural sanctuary of privacy, comfort, and morality, but also a place preservative of good health. . . .

Zoning advocates' beliefs about the requirements for a healthy home were consistent with the views of public health and housing reformers of the period. One major concern of early twentieth-century housing reformers was ensuring that dwellings received adequate light and air, for dark, unventilated conditions were believed to be unhealthy. . . .
 . . . .

4. Preserving the Ideal Home Environment Through Zoning

A complex web of beliefs shaped zoning advocates' perceptions of the conditions necessary to constitute the ideal home environment. Pursuant to their domesticity beliefs, they felt the ideal home should be a quiet, comfortable, private sanctuary conducive to child-rearing. Their acceptance of pastoral ideology led them to see the ideal home as situated in the aesthetically pleasing, peaceful, semi-natural setting of lawns, trees, and gardens. Their beliefs about health led them to prefer homes that received ample light and air and that avoided overcrowding and exposure to excessive amounts of auto exhaust. Viewing judges', attorneys', and planners' advocacy of zoning in light of their beliefs about the proper home environment leads to a better understanding of their position. One reason they favored the single-family home and wished to use zoning to preserve and expand single-family neighborhoods was that they believed detached dwellings to possess ideal home conditions. One reason they wished to exclude industry, business, and apartments from private residential areas was that they believed the presence of these uses was destructive of the ideal home environment, one that they wished to preserve, at least for the wealthier citizens who were most able to afford it.

. . . .

Zoning advocates feared that apartments, like industries and businesses, frustrated ideal home conditions; their desire that dwellings conform to their vision of the ideal home environment explains in part why these writers wished to exclude apartments from private residence districts. . . .

. . . .

Some zoning advocates even went so far as to argue that two-family houses were nearly as antithetical to proper home conditions as apartments. . . .

V. RHETORIC AND REALITY

The claim that zoning advocates were influenced by what were in some sense idealistic beliefs may seem inconsistent with the reality that zoning for exclusively private residential districts was motivated to some extent by class bias, nativism, and racism, that it promoted class segregation, that zoning advocates were aware of this segregatory effect, and that zoning advocates were willing, nonetheless, to claim that zoning served all classes equally in order to ensure that it was upheld as within the police power. There are at least two aspects to the argument that the presence of ideological motivations cannot be squared with the economic and social causes and effects of zoning. First, since one of my premises is that zoning proponents were to some degree rhetorical instrumentalists, insofar as they claimed that private residential zoning served the interests of all when they knew that in some ways it did not, one might argue that it is naive to believe that zoning advocates were sincere to any appreciable extent in their apparent adherence to domesticity, pastoral, and health ideologies.

Second, it could be argued that ideological motivations are in some sense "honorable" in a way that economic, racist, nativist, or classist motivations are not. Racism, nativism, and class bias are obviously invidious, and economic interests are essentially selfish. The term "ideology," as it is used in this article, on the other hand, refers to a set of shared beliefs about the world, and thus to something by definition greater than the self. One might view adherence to such tenets as in some sense altruistic. Therefore, it might appear that I am inconsistently claiming that, while zoning proponents were self-interested bigots, they were simultaneously altruistic visionaries.

In regards to the first argument, it would be undeniably simplistic to take at face value the types of materials I consult here—legal briefs, planners' writings, and judicial opinions—in attempting to uncover the various motivations of early twentieth-century participants in the zoning debate. The goal of pro-zoning attorneys was to convince courts that zoning ordinances that protected exclusively private residential areas were within the police power, and not to voice their personal feelings regarding those ordinances. Thus, it is never clear that the arguments in a given legal brief reflect the writer's sincere beliefs rather than what the writer felt would best convince the judge that private residential zoning advanced the public health, safety, welfare, and morals. . . .

Likewise, as the "scientists" responsible for devising most zoning ordinances, planners obviously had an interest in ensuring that their creations were upheld by courts. It would not be surprising if much of their rhetoric were geared to this purpose rather than to expressing their "true" feelings about zoning. . . .

Finally, even judges were faced with the need to persuade colleagues and to legitimize to the public their positions on zoning. In upholding an ordinance permitting the exclusion of apartments from single-family residence areas, a judge would presumably prefer extolling the values of family and nature to admitting that prejudice against the working class influenced his decision. . . .

Undoubtedly zoning advocates to some extent employed ideological rhetoric because it legitimized exclusive private residential zoning as within the police power better than arguments based on property values or class bias, rather than because they truly believed such rhetoric. Yet to explain the apparent influence of ideology on zoning proponents' writings by suggesting that zoning advocates never meant what they said, that they used domesticity, pastoral, and health rhetoric only because they felt that it was more persuasive than their "real" reasons for supporting zoning, is unsatisfying. As discussed above, it is difficult to understand zoning proponents' motivations without accepting the proposition that ideology influenced them to some extent. For example, one typical explanation for why single-family homeowners desired to zone stores and multiple dwellings out of their neighborhoods was that they wished to preserve the values of their homes. Yet the property values explanation simply raises the question of why apartments and stores were seen as damaging to neighborhoods. If single-family homeowners disliked the noise created by stores and the lack of privacy and decreased view caused by large apartment buildings, presumably they valued privacy, quiet, and attractive surroundings. These preferences suggest that such homeowners were influenced by domesticity and pastoral ideology as well as by a concern for their pocketbooks. . . .

As for the second inconsistency argument, to discount altogether the possibility that ideology motivated zoning proponents, on the grounds that prejudiced pragmatists whose chosen form of land-use planning had unquestionably inequitable effects could not simultaneously have been influenced by what were to some extent idealistic notions, is to misunderstand my argument regarding domesticity, pastoral, and health ideologies. I am not claiming that zoning advocates' acceptance of these ideologies rendered them unassailably "altruistic visionaries," and it would be inaccurate to do so. First of all, while these world views had their valuable aspects, they were simultaneously closely intertwined with class bias, nativism, and racism. The bourgeois embrace of domestic morality became more fervent just as middle-class city dwellers were increasingly confronted with immigrants forced to live in overcrowded and purportedly "improper" conditions. The middle-class pursuit of pastoral surroundings was simultaneously a prejudice-fueled flight from cities that were becoming increasingly poor and non-Anglo-

Saxon. And the middle-class emphasis on healthy homes was reinforced by middle-class horror at the higher infection rates of poor slum dwellers.

Furthermore, to the extent these ideologies possessed worthwhile elements, the wealthier powerholders who formulated them tended to ignore the fact that most poorer citizens could not conform to them even if they wished to. Domesticity, pastoral, and health ideologies were always pursued predominantly by the middle and upper classes, because only they tended to be able to afford to realize such ideals. To the extent that working class families wished to maintain their homes as havens from the market and as safe, "moral" nurseries for children, the financial necessity of working and of living in crowded urban apartments precluded many of them from achieving the domesticity ideal. . . .

Were they unimpeachably altruistic, middle-class zoning proponents might have concentrated on finding a way to make the conditions they so valued more accessible to poorer citizens. Instead, however, they often acted selfishly, tending to focus on ensuring that they and their fellow middle-class citizens achieved their ideals, rather than on the extent to which that process at best failed to address working class problems and at worst actively exacerbated them. . . .

VI. CONCLUSION

It is undeniable that zoning for exclusively private residential areas between 1916 and 1926 did not benefit all Americans equally, and contemporary critics tended to focus on this problem. . . .

. . . While zoning advocates were unquestionably affected by economics and bias, they were also motivated to some extent by the desire to actualize their middle-class world view. Zoning advocates accepted domesticity ideology and pastoral ideology, and greatly valued the healthiness of the home. To exclude industry, businesses, and apartments from private residential areas (and to exclude two-family homes from single-family districts) through zoning was a way for them to ensure that middle-class homes (particularly single-family homes) conformed to these typically bourgeois ideologies. That zoning advocates were motivated by principle as well as by pragmatism and bias in no way excuses the fact that zoning to protect exclusively private residential areas legally reinforced preexisting class segregation and planted the seed for the exclusionary zoning practices from which the nation presently suffers. However, a full recognition of the wide range of influences that led to the acceptance of exclusively private residential zoning between 1916 and 1926 is essential to counteract effectively the inequities that are its legacy today.

LOCAL KNOWLEDGE, LEGAL KNOWLEDGE, AND ZONING LAW

Lea S. VanderVelde

75 Iowa L. Rev. 1057 (1990) (reprinted with permission)

. . . .

It has always struck me as odd that legal scholars and legal education have paid so little attention to the field of local government law, and specifically to zoning law. . . .

Unfortunately, this common disregard of zoning law's worth reveals misperceptions of what is important to know about law and how law is known. More particularly, the legal discipline often implies, or even assumes, that knowing what judges or statutes say is more important than knowing how legal rules impact upon situations and lives, what occurs when the legal rules are at variance from cultural conceptions of justice, and how legal rules are continually constituted and reconstructed from prevailing social norms. This essay seeks to respond to these problems by arguing for the value of local knowledge[4] and by pointing out some of the illuminating features of the particularly local knowledge that zoning law entails. . . .

I. LOCAL KNOWLEDGE AS PAROCHIAL AND VENAL

Consider first, why so little attention has been paid to zoning. There are several justifications offered for the claim that zoning appeals only to a small audience. First, it may be claimed that zoning laws are less important because they are not federal laws; they are nonstandard and do not apply uniformly across the nation. Zoning cases are viewed as legally idiosyncratic, and thus, not subject to generalization. Second, some assume that zoning, particularly an ethnographic perspective on zoning, is of interest only to the members of that particular local community. The claim is: Why should you care about Peoria unless you are from Peoria? . . . Third, it is claimed that actual zoning results are flawed because they depart from the terms of the statutes, the rulings of judges, or the results that legal models predict. The venality and pettiness of local interests distorts the law and the workings of otherwise good theories and predictive legal models. Thus, the local character of zoning law is seen as venality, and venality is simply noise in the system.

. . . .

Contrary to the first claim, zoning law in various cities across the nation is uniformly structured to a rather remarkable extent. Most states follow the same basic statutory structure for municipal zoning which was promulgated in the 1920s by the United States Department of Commerce. Two standard laws, the Standard Zoning

---

[4] The term "local knowledge" was coined and developed by C. Geertz, Local Knowledge: Further Essays in Interpretive Anthropology (1983).

Enabling Act and the Standard City Planning Enabling Act, were adopted by virtually every state legislature, and continue in effect in the majority of states. This statutory uniformity provides a convenient framework against which local variation can be measured.

Addressing the second claim, the "Peoria Syndrome," it is, in fact, parochial to view Peoria as uninteresting. It is exactly Peoria's parochial character that makes it interesting. . . . The parochial character provides both the texture and necessary context for understanding legal events.

Moreover, local law is of particular relevance because many Americans are affected more directly by local zoning law than by more remote federal laws. The fact that zoning is of special importance to the inhabitants of the particular community makes it all the more intriguing, since it is in this crucible of intense feelings that the participants must conjure up arguments, must struggle with rules of justice and law, and must attempt to resolve disputes. . . .

. . . .

From observing multiple localities, one can attain an understanding of the possible, as well as the pluralist perspective that is necessary to free oneself from the mental trap of legal determinism. For example, because Iowa City, Iowa is in some regards the same as everywhere else, one can see that nothing is ever truly unique. No place is ever truly a sui generis neighborhood because all neighborhoods are gradations on a line of relative differentiation. Conversely, because Iowa City is not exactly the same as anywhere else, its uniqueness must be evaluated rather than dismissed or ignored. . . .

. . . .

As law is often expected to bring rationality to matters of public interest, so too, zoning was supposed to bring rationality to land use decisions. But it has been some time since planners naively believed that cities could be governed or laid out according to a prearranged plan and since legal theorists believed that plan jurisprudence would work as originally intended. When zoning law fails as an exercise of positive law, its failure teaches important lessons both as a failure of positive law and as a failure of rationality.

All too often the failure of zoning law is ascribed not to law's own limits, but to the venality of the local interests involved. The workings of a small community are generally viewed with suspicion for the pettiness of their concerns and the arbitrariness of their cronyism. But the local interests that are at play in zoning are neither more nor less venal than the interests at play on any other level of legal engagement. All interests and all communities are local at some level. All laws are designed by, applied to, or enforced by a community of interest that is in some sense local and about which there is a local knowledge. The contradictions that occur in local government zoning between the text and the result are simply more evident than they are in other areas of law. That such contradictions are less visible elsewhere, in statewide or national forums, does not mean they are not present.

. . . .

Notwithstanding its potential for pettiness, cronyism, and venality, a small community still offers parallel possibilities of self-sacrifice and civic-mindedness in the very best sense. Its members are bonded by shared cultural values and common experiences to a greater degree than state or national communities. An advantage of testing law in a local setting is that there is a greater possibility of cultural homogeneity in a neighborhood where, presumably, most inhabitants have chosen to live. If law cannot operate in these more culturally homogeneous settings, what are its possibilities for effectiveness across cultural gulfs? When law fails, perhaps the failure is intrinsic in the enterprise or in the expectation that law, as something distinct from culture, could matter.

. . . .

II. LOCAL KNOWLEDGE AS LEGAL REALISM

One of the noteworthy characteristics about zoning law is that the social construction of local governance is coupled with the physical construction of brick and mortar. A city's physical structure provides graphic evidence of the effect, or lack of effect, of legal constraints. What a city or neighborhood is, or what it will become, depends to a significant degree on its physical structure.

. . . .

Zoning is the primary legal mechanism through which the community attempts to influence the evolution of its physical structure. The community as a whole attempts to preserve that which it values, plan for that which it desires, and discourage or eradicate that which it dislikes. Members battle themselves and outsiders over conflicting visions of the community's future.

A. Observation of the End Result

Zoning law provides the necessary three elements for a study of law: a set of texts, a process, and a product. Most areas of law provide texts and processes, but few provide as definite and indisputable a result as zoning law. . . .

Because the result of local government zoning is verifiable, and because when there is a contradiction between text and result it is often glaring, it is possible to work backwards from these concrete facts to appraise the effect of law. This concreteness is quite rare in legal processes. The final result in many legal disputes is elusive to even the careful observer; it is difficult to really know who won and what they won. . . .

With a zoning case, however, one can observe the results of the conflict. One can visit Penn Central Station to observe whether an addition in excess of fifty stories was built (it was not). One can examine the sixty-eight acre lot between Euclid Avenue and the Nickel Plate Railroad in Euclid, Ohio to see whether an automobile plant was constructed (it was). One also can ascertain how many years passed after that landmark decision before the city granted permission to build it (over twenty years). The significance of the physical fact may still require interpretation by the contested parties, the community at large, or the disinterested observer, but the physical fact of a building or the physical presence of a land use is, nonetheless, uncontrovertible and public.

With results as clear as these, a blatant departure from the letter of the law cannot easily be ignored or papered over. A building violating the standard set-back and encroaching upon the public prospect sticks out like a sore thumb. As these results are both public and uncontrovertible, there is a means to measure the effect of the text and process of law.

B. Observation of the Law-Making Process: Cultural Signification and The Process of Fashioning Text

The difficult task of capturing the spirit of law in legally binding words is all the more real when it takes place in one's own backyard. The language of city ordinances is refreshing for its amateur, groping quality. Although many city ordinances simply copy standard language from approved sources, other ordinances are composed by a consensus of the citizens and nonlawyer council members, sometimes in response to a single instance of a land-use problem. When the community attempts to fashion its own set of restrictions, the language selected often reflects the community's particular history and the community members' understanding of the specific law's goals.

The texts of zoning ordinances, more than other laws, are fashioned and debated by the citizenry. Few small cities have the legislative drafting resources of state or national legislatures. A city ordinance, particularly in a small city, is unlikely to bring out a battery of private lawyers with a prolix array of language proposals that tends to iron the character out of the drafted word. Instead, the individual members of the city council, together with the volunteer planning and zoning commission and an often overworked city staff, try their own hands-on approach to proposing legal language. The task of making rules—considering objectives, evaluating alternative means of regulating, and considering the city's own constraints—is nearer the surface in this direct, often nonrepresentative attempt at self-governance. In smaller communities, city zoning regulations lead to face-to-face exchanges between the regulators and the regulated. The process is destined to raise the adrenaline level of those involved by the sheer participation in self-governance. Since a law's effectiveness often depends on the willing adherence of the citizenry without significant enforcement efforts, what better place to observe discussions of law, governance, and fairness that comes from the heart than through the rawness of the proceedings of a small town city council?

Local zoning ordinances contain wonderful instances of the vernacular. For example, Iowa City zoning ordinances require that "[f]lickering sources of light . . . be shielded so as not to cause a nuisance across lot lines."[37] Was the phrase "[f]lickering sources of light" intended to refer to outdoor movie theaters, blinking neon signs, Christmas displays, or electric bug lights noisily zapping wayward bugs on a hot summer night?

---

[37] Iowa City, Iowa, Zoning Code, § 8.10.18 (1977).

The Iowa City Code also provides maximum height regulations, but it exempts an odd array of structures: "Chimneys, church steeples, . . . elevator block heads, . . . monuments, . . . stage towers or scenery lofts, tanks, water towers, ornamental towers, spires, radio and television towers, grain elevators, or necessary mechanical appurtenances . . . ."[38] What accounts for the cultural acceptability of this array of tall structures, structures that cannot be accommodated within existing height limits? The list provides the basis for an inquiry into cultural signification. Clearly, the concern is not just for mass and its absence, or for light and shadow. An elevator blockhead will block light and air as completely as a small room at the top of a building, and it will do so without the aesthetic relief a cupola would provide.

. . . .

As a whole, the list contains a mixture of what the town deems tasteful and in keeping with the visual message, and what the town deems necessary and easy for the community viewer to ignore. Tall structures are prohibited unless they can be characterized either aesthetically as "ornamental towers" or "spires," or practically as "necessary mechanical appurtenances." . . .

The ordering of structures in the text of the Iowa City height ordinance is happenstance, as if each successive amendment was the result of an afterthought. Someone must have proposed a monument as high as a church steeple. In the days when live stage competed with screen in small towns, some theater must have requested the exemption for a scenery loft. Specific historical incidents and now anachronistic needs leave their mark on the accumulated body of local knowledge. One can predict that new city ordinances will respond to post-modernist architecture, roof-top satellite dishes, and solar cells, and that these issues will be resolved by whether the community believes they are sufficiently "tasteful" or unobtrusive in their visual impact.

C. Observation of the Enforcement Process: The Zoning Board of Adjustment

Observing the local zoning board of adjustment allows one to see how the law is actually applied. Under the Standard Zoning Enabling Act, each community that engages in zoning must set up a zoning board of adjustment. These local zoning boards are intended to serve the function of granting variances from the regulation when a strict application of the community's zoning ordinances poses too great of a hardship for the individual property owner. The conventional wisdom is that zoning boards of adjustment misfunction by granting many more variances than are legally permissible.[47] More recently, however, the function of zoning boards of

---

[38] Iowa City, Iowa, Zoning Code, § 8.10.22.B. 2 (1977).

[47] Dukeminier & Stapleton, The Zoning Board of Adjustment: A Case Study in Misrule, 50 Ky. L.J. 273 (1962); Shapiro, The Zoning Variance Power—Constructive in Theory, Destructive in Practice, 29 Md. L. Rev. 3 (1969); Contemporary Studies Project, Rural Land Use Regulation in Iowa: An Empirical Analysis of County Board of Adjustment Practices, 68 Iowa L. Rev. 1083, 1209 (1983).

adjustment has been reassessed as an increasingly important forum for public debate. Unlike earlier decades, most cities are no longer content to have zoning ordinances cast in those general terms that simply prescribe uses and spacing of buildings. As a result, zoning ordinances have come to function as trip wires to trigger petitions for variances, an early-warning system to notify the neighborhood of any change that might threaten the status quo.

. . . .

In its simplest form, the prevailing state law doctrine[49] provides that the zoning board is authorized to grant variances from zoning regulations only when 1) the impact of the regulation constitutes an unnecessary hardship on the petitioner, 2) granting the variance will not harm the public welfare, and 3) the situation is unique. In further judicial interpretation of the elements necessary for a variance, state supreme courts have required that the hardship to the owner be an economic hardship of sufficient severity that renders it impossible for the owner to earn a reasonable return from the property.

On first reflection, there is nothing inherently wrong with this legal doctrine. It speaks authoritatively. It attempts to limit the number of variances that can be issued because of the concern that if too many exceptions are granted to the rule, the rule will be overrun with exceptions. However, in the experience of the Iowa City Zoning Board, this doctrine led to examples of systemic failure.

The results of the Iowa City Zoning Board decisions were sometimes legally irreconcilable. In keeping with the conventional wisdom, variances were granted by the dozens, despite the directive that variances only be granted in rare cases. More surprisingly, it was often impossible to predict which variances would be granted, and in one pair of cases, . . . petitioners asking for virtually identical privileges were treated differently.

What went wrong when the Iowa City Zoning Board attempted to take doctrine seriously? Striving to be true to state court interpretations of the hardship criteria, the Zoning Board methodically focused its inquiry on each one of the three elements necessary for a variance. However, the element that was intended to be most limiting, whether the zoning restriction posed an unnecessary economic hardship in the particular case under consideration, did not lend itself to a determinate resolution in any specific case. There were no set standards to determine how much of an economic loss was too much of an economic loss for the property owner to bear. Too much compared to what? The Board had no shared understanding of what constituted a reasonable return on a property owner's property.

In fact, the criteria of "economic hardship" became something of a ruse for deciding particular matters on other, unarticulated grounds. The customary practice of the Iowa City Zoning Board was for each member, in turn, to state his or her opinion on the matter at the close of the hearing and before the official vote. On the

---

[49] Otto v. Steinhilber, 282 N.Y. 71, 24 N.E.2d 851 (1939) (discussing the three requirements necessary for the Board of Appeals to grant a variance). Otto v. Steinhilber, which has been cited in numerous jurisdictions, is considered the classic case interpreting the legal elements essential for a variance to issue.

hardship issue, opinions would be stated simply as "yes, the ordinance causes a hardship" or "no, there is no hardship," but the discussion never went much further. Board members did not, and perhaps could not, explain why they saw the ordinance as causal of some specific level of economic loss selected from the multiple figures available in the economic environment. Without a more probing discussion of reasons, individual Board members could not be certain they were using the criteria consistently. Thus, discussions of hardship tended to end abruptly in conclusory findings.

By contrast, the criterion of whether the proposed variance would harm the "public welfare" produced endless discussion by members of the Board. The Board would discuss at length whether something as seemingly innocuous as a doghouse or a swimming pool would harm the character of the existing neighborhood. The Board often discussed the characteristics of a particular project in all its facets until the time designated for conclusion of the meeting precipitated the need to vote.

Why did one element yield an extended discussion, in which members joined issue and attempted to persuade each other to share their views of the matter, when the other element produced a truncated, conclusory exchange? Was the community missing language by which it could articulate what it meant by economic hardship?

The doctrine itself seemed to create misleading expectations. Despite the fact that there were no shared views on what constituted economic hardship, there continued to be an unfounded belief that economics was an objective criteria which, when rigorously applied, would yield a single determinative answer. Focusing on "public welfare," on the other hand, opened the discussion to possibilities. "Public welfare" was not expected to have a definite, delimiting character. The criterion was expected to produce differences of opinion and, as they were produced, they were accepted and occasionally resolved in a common accord. "Public welfare" did not portend to be a determinate and reliable standard. What constituted the "public welfare" in any particular case was incapable of being determined once and for all by a fixed reference point. This indeterminateness did not render the phrase useless or harmful. Instead, the indeterminateness of this criterion may have become an important and valuable basis for opening public debate and discourse among decisionmakers over matters of community policy.

"Public welfare," though susceptible to multiple interpretations, tended to produce a more constructive discussion of the zoning rule's purpose and the community interest. In urging one definition of public welfare over another, Board members felt compelled to explain why their chosen definition was best. The Board discussed what they saw in the ordinance and whether the objective was served in the petitioner's case. This discussion made Board decisionmaking more accountable to both the public and the petitioner and had two additional beneficial results. First, such a discussion was likely to produce somewhat greater consistency between decisions. Discussion based on reasons allowed a consensus to emerge, and once Board members had formed a consensus on an issue, they were more likely to decide the issue in the same manner the next time it arose. Second, such a discussion occasionally had the potential of generating a deeper understanding of the community purposes and welfare by evoking reflection, reconsideration, and public participation.

Understandably, this method of decisionmaking produced a certain randomness of results. Only when a proposed variance request was perceived as clearly harmful to the public welfare could one predict with any certainty that it would be denied. In other cases, there was as great a chance that it would be granted as there was that it would be denied.

The problem of unequal treatment came about not only when there was sharp disagreement between Board members on what was desirable, but also when individual Board members were ambivalent as to the result. . . .

. . . .

. . . Certainly equal treatment of like cases is such a deeply embedded ethic it should have arisen from understandings of fairness in the midwestern culture itself. Instead, in this tribunal, the decisionmakers had internalized an ethic that prevented them from recreating the notion of equal treatment; they acted in accordance with the uniqueness ethic, which requires that each case be decided on its own facts. They viewed it as a mark of fairness to give each petitioner individualized justice. That "each case should be decided on its own facts" was stated frequently by Board members with the conviction that "otherwise each person would be denied his own day in court." Thus, Board members made few arguments based on earlier cases. The Zoning Board did not build a consensus on shared norms; it did not learn from earlier decisions.

. . . .

D. Organization of Placement as a Means of Social Organization

Zoning is also a study of social organization by majoritarian processes. Practically every activity takes place at a certain locus, so that by regulating the locus of space, one can indirectly regulate the activities themselves. . . .

As a result, zoning is susceptible to utilization as a means of discouraging certain types of activities that cannot be banned directly. If it is difficult to regulate pornography directly, zoning can regulate the shops that sell porn.[63] If the right to a first trimester abortion cannot be directly regulated, it can be indirectly regulated by adding requirements to the issuance of a permit for an abortion clinic to make it sufficiently difficult to acquire. Because these activities are regulated indirectly through their locus, zoning mixes issues of constitutional liberty interests and the city's police power to regulate land use—issues involving liberty and property distinctions that courts and scholars have struggled to separate for the sake of con-

---

[63] City of Renton v. Playtime Theaters, 475 U.S. 41, 47 (1986) (relegating Playtime Theaters to a relatively remote area of the city was not an unconstitutional infringement on free speech since it was a content neutral time, place, and manner regulation); *see also* Young v. American Mini Theatres, Inc., 427 U.S. 50, 72-73 (1976) (zoning ordinance prohibiting adult theaters within 1000 feet of any other "regulated uses" or within 500 feet of residential zone does not violate first and fourteenth amendments).

ceptual clarity. As a consequence, cases such as *Metromedia v. City of San Diego*,[65] that deal with the constitutionality of banning billboards, ask difficult questions which pit the government's relatively limited power to regulate speech liberties against its broad power to regulate commercial property. . . .

The same principle is true with regard to the social organization of habitation. All of those questions of class distinction that cannot be addressed directly through regulation can be enforced and reinforced through zoning. . . . [Z]oning barriers that require housing to be strictly separated by square footage, detached, semi-detached, or high-rise structures ensure that others who you know by virtue of residential proximity are those who can at least afford and gain entry to your level of housing. From location flows the social organization of where your children attend school, where you walk your dog, and where you buy your groceries. Zoning assures that others who you are most likely to bump into are on your same social level. In what other field of law can arguments that significantly limit the upward mobility of lower classes be so conveniently couched in the language of protection of property values?

E. Collective Interpretation of a Changing Canvas

As illustrated in the height maximum example, the act of zoning is also a collective attempt to signify and interpret meaning through physical structures. When undesirable buildings are built or undesirable uses commenced, the results will remain as persistent thorns in the sides of the defeated—that is, until the defeated disband, move away, die, or numb themselves to the effect of the undesired building. In a sense, the result is often "winner takes all." The canvas has changed, and the new canvas acts, in turn, as a constraint on the next set of land-use choices to be made. The next generation may very well accept the new landscape as the familiar, coming into consciousness with that new canvas as the normative background.

. . . .

What then does the observation of zoning offer to the study of law? Local government holds out the promise of allowing citizens to exercise some control over their immediate environment and, in turn, over their lives. It also holds out the possibility of obstacles for the unlucky and further traps for the powerless. As communities are allowed to evolve differently, they offer some Americans choices of environments in which to live. Other Americans will have little real choice. The incremental changes that take place in a neighborhood's evolution are channeled by the legal mechanisms which control changes in zoning. When zoning works, it works on that level of community consensus that gives us confidence in community self-governance. When zoning fails, it may be because we cannot trust ourselves or our neighbors. When that is true, then who can you trust?

---

[65] 453 U.S. 490 (1981).

PLANNING AND THE LAW
Daniel R. Mandelker
20 Vt. L. Rev. 657 (1996)[*]

. . . [T]he role of the comprehensive plan in land use administration is still a most critical and vexing problem in land planning law.

Until recently, the cases gave very little weight to the plan in zoning disputes . . . . They interpreted the Standard Zoning Act to mean the plan was only advisory, although the Act said zoning was to be "in accordance with" the plan. The Oregon Supreme Court finally got it right about twenty years ago and required zoning to be consistent with a comprehensive plan.[3] Since then, several states have adopted mandatory planning requirements and requirements that zoning be consistent with the plan.

PROBLEMS WITH THE PLANNING REQUIREMENT

Most land use professionals support statutes and court decisions that mandate planning and require zoning to be consistent with a plan. Yet these requirements create a tension in land use regulation that is difficult to resolve. An article some years ago by Robert Rider, a Hawaiian planner, put the problem very well. Although the article has not received enough attention, it is as good a statement of the land use decision-making problem as I have seen.[5] What Rider said was that the key issue in land use decision-making is the tension between the need for flexibility to make decisions and the need to limit discretion.

. . . .

Rider also argued that the adoption of a plan, far from signaling a consensus, more likely signals a new round of negotiation on land use controversies. . . .

THE NEED TO LIMIT DISCRETION THROUGH PLANNING

Consider first the need to limit discretion. . . .

. . . [T]he purpose of the plan is to control and limit arbitrary decision-making.

Some examples of arbitrary decision-making may seem surprising. Cases arising under the takings clause are one example. Many of us have believed for some time that the comprehensive plan can help protect land use regulations when landowners attack them under the takings clause. The basis for this belief is the Supreme Court's statement of what it sees as its most important takings clause principle. This principle reads a guarantee of fairness into the takings clause requirement that government may not take property without just compensation. As the Court has made clear, the takings clause is in the Constitution to ensure that government fairly distributes the burdens and benefits of land use regulation to owners of land.

---

[*]   © Copyright 1996. Reprinted by permission.

[3]   Fasano v. Board of County Comm'rs, 507 P.2d 23 (Or. 1973).

[5]   Robert M. Rider, *Local Government Planning: Prerequisites of an Effective System*, 18 URB. AFF. Q. 271 (1982).

In several recent takings cases lost by the government in the Supreme Court, the Court struck down land use regulations because they had distributed benefits and burdens unfairly. *Lucas v. South Carolina Coastal Council* is one of these cases.[9] A taking occurred when the Council denied a permit to build homes on two beachfront lots on the coast when homes existed on adjacent properties. The permit denial did not occur because of a plan or zoning ordinance, but because a beach-front law required a building setback on coastal beaches. The Lucas dwelling would have been within the coastal setback. Why the Council denied a permit to Lucas when adjacent lots were already built on is not clear. . . . The *Lucas* decision illustrates the principle that the purpose of the takings clause is to prevent unfair regulation. A plan that adopts a land use policy for coastal areas could provide a policy basis for coastal land use decisions that can prevent takings problems from arising.

The leading court decision recognizing the importance of a plan in takings cases is *Golden v. Planning Board*,[10] a New York case decided more than twenty years ago. A growth management plan postponed development in some areas for as much as twenty years. The court believed the comprehensive growth management plan the town adopted, and its commitment to necessary public facilities, justified the delay in development the plan created.

Another group of cases where courts are concerned with fairness is state cases that apply the arbitrary and capricious decision rule to strike down zoning restrictions. . . . Although the constitutional basis for the arbitrary and capricious rule is not always obvious, it clearly has a constitutional basis in the Equal Protection Clause. The rule also has a basis in the takings clause if a zoning restriction is arbitrary because it imposes a severe loss on a property owner.

. . . .

So the Supreme Court takings cases, and the state court cases holding zoning restrictions arbitrary and capricious, are examples of cases that invalidate unfair land use regulations. A comprehensive plan that determines in advance what landowners can do with their land can avoid decisions of this kind because it will prevent the unfairness problem from arising.

THE NEED FOR FLEXIBILITY IN DECISION-MAKING

The need to avoid arbitrary decisions makes the case for planning, but Rider's article also made a case for flexibility, for negotiation, and for tolerance of unpredictable results. There is a planning justification for this acceptance of political realities, and it lies in the truism that time is not cast in stone. An early criticism of planning claimed it was inflexible and rigid, that it did cast time in stone, and that it was impossible to make necessary changes. Changes in the planning process since then have tried to remedy these problems, but the need for flexibility in planning is still something we need to be concerned about.

Despite these changes in the planning process, the political concerns Rider identified demand attention. A healthy political process contemplates and encour-

---

[9] *See, e.g.,* Lucas v. South Carolina Coastal Council, 505 U.S. 1003 (1992).

[10] Golden v. Planning Bd., 285 N.E.2d 291 (N.Y. 1972), *appeal dismissed*, 409 U.S. 1003 (1972).

ages negotiation in decision-making that makes outcomes uncertain. This is why the plan often is an invitation to negotiation and not a consensus. It encourages negotiation and decision-making that leads to unpredictable results. Why is this so? This role of the comprehensive plan is best explained by a theory of democratic behavior known as process theory. Law professors and others developed this theory to explain the basis for decision-making at different governmental levels.[12]

. . . [P]rocess theory accurately describes how local government politics should work. What process theory argues is that a healthy democratic political process is pluralistic. It is one in which a variety of interest groups operate in a political arena where coalitions shift over time. It is this constant shifting in political bargains that creates uncertainty in the planning process. At one point in time, for example, the dominant coalition may favor growth. At another point in time the dominant coalition may not favor growth and adopt land use programs that limit new development.

Political bargains change over time, but the essential prerequisite to healthy bargaining is the presence of interest groups that have comparable weight in the process that produces these bargains. . . . So the call for discretion in political decision-making is really a call for the normal political bargaining that is healthy in the political process. However, this type of bargaining does not guarantee decisions that are consistent with a comprehensive plan.

BALANCING PLANNING WITH POLITICS

So how do we resolve the tension between the need to limit arbitrary decision-making, and the need for bargaining in a political process that can lead to unpredictable outcomes? Let us start from the political side and see what we can do to resolve this problem.

First, what if pluralism fails? An interest group that does not fairly represent all of the interests in a community may capture a town council and refuse to follow a plan that was produced by a balanced political coalition. . . .

One answer is to enforce the plan through litigation. If a developer comes in for approval and the council turns her down because it is dominated by an antigrowth coalition, she can go to court. There she can argue the plan controls, and that the council should approve her development because it is consistent with the plan. The difficulty with this approach is that either a court must require consistency between zoning decisions and the plan, or the state legislature must impose this requirement in order to make the policies of the plan binding. Even if consistency with the plan is required, a court may not be willing to compel a rezoning at a developer's request when the plan shows her development is consistent with the plan. The reason is that legislative decision-making is discretionary, and a court may believe it violates separation of powers to compel a legislative rezoning even if the plan shows it should be done.

---

[12] The seminal work is JOHN HART ELY, DEMOCRACY AND DISTRUST: A THEORY OF JUDICIAL REVIEW (1980).

Another difficulty with this solution is that the interest group that captured the zoning process will most likely capture the planning process over a period of time. It will go back to the plan and amend it to reflect its point of view on what development should occur. We simply have the captured and now unhealthy political process taking over the planning process and revising the plan to carry out its program. If political capture by a minority interest group is our concern, merely calling for a mandatory comprehensive plan does not necessarily solve this problem.

A remedy for dealing with capture problems does not come easy, but either a legislative or judicial solution is possible. If there is a concern that planning at the local level should reflect a politically healthy decision-making process, the legislature can amend the planning statute to prevent capture from occurring. For example, an amendment to require an affordable housing element can help remedy problems that arise when a coalition that captures a community adopts a restrictive and exclusionary plan. Many states, notably California, have required affordable housing elements for comprehensive plans for this reason.

Legislation may not be enough. Municipalities can ignore legislative planning mandates, and it is essential to provide judicial and perhaps administrative remedies to enforce legislative requirements. Effective administrative or judicial review requires legislation to confer standing to enforce legislative mandates. It also requires legislation authorizing an effective scope of judicial review once a case challenging a plan gets to court. A court must be able to invalidate a plan that does not comply with mandatory legislative requirements. Shifting review of plans to the courts, of course, does displace the legislative process that developed the plan. Some may not agree with this shift in responsibility or may not believe that courts can effectively supervise the planning process.

Courts may have to discipline the planning process even if the legislature does not impose mandatory planning requirements. In a recent article, Professor Dan Tarlock and I outlined those cases in which courts should discipline planning and zoning decisions by shifting the presumption of constitutionality against municipalities.[14] Ordinarily, any land use decision at the local government level enjoys a presumption of constitutionality, which means the burden is on the person attacking the ordinance to show it is unconstitutional. If the presumption shifts against government, the burden shifts to the municipality to justify its decision.

A presumption shift is a major change in the way in which courts review planning and zoning decisions, and I do not have the space here to make all of the arguments for it. A presumption shift should occur, however, when a captured political process produces a plan that does not represent all of the interest groups in a community. The burden should shift to the municipality to justify its planning policies in this situation.

The discussion so far has considered cases in which pluralism does not succeed in local politics. But what if pluralism succeeds and produces a consensus on land use policy, but a zoning outcome occurs that is contrary to the plan? This situation

---

[14] Daniel R. Mandelker & A. Dan Tarlock, *Shifting the Presumption of Constitutionality in Land Use Law*, 24 URB. LAW. 1 (1992).

occurs because a community may adopt a plan at one point in time when one type of coalition dominates the political process. The coalition may then shift and no longer support the plan or follow it in their land use decisions. . . .

. . . Which should take precedence, the plan or the zoning decision? Both arguably are correct if both are the products of a pluralistic political process that reaches a consensus. If the zoning process that produced the zoning denial is politically healthy but the decision is inconsistent with the plan, what should the outcome be?

The solution may again be judicial. The Florida Supreme Court solved this problem with a presumption shift, and the presumption shifts against a zoning decision if it is contrary to a plan.[15] This solution favors the plan over the zoning decision. It makes sense if controls on arbitrary decision-making are considered more important than a political process in which flexibility in decision-making can produce decisions that do not carry out planning goals.

CONCLUSION

We have completed a full circle in our discussion of the comprehensive plan as it affects the zoning process, an issue that is still critically important in land use law. The purpose of the comprehensive plan is to prevent arbitrary decision-making, but closer inspection shows that what appears arbitrary may simply be the product of a normal and healthy democratic process. The problem is to strike a proper balance between reliance on a plan to prevent arbitrary decisions, and flexibility in decision-making that can lead to outcomes inconsistent with the plan.

Note

Professor Robert Hopperton disfavors the presumption that zoning and other land use control actions are constitutional/valid, but he does not support presumption shifting. Instead, he advocates eliminating presumptions altogether in order to promote thoughtful development of fitting standards of judicial review. Robert J. Hopperton, *The Presumption of Validity in American Land-Use Law: A Substitute for Analysis, A Source of Significant Confusion*, 23 B.C. Envtl. Aff. L. Rev. 301 (1996). *See also* Daniel R. Mandelker & A. Dan Tarlock, *Two Cheers for Shifting the Presumption of Validity: A Reply to Professor Hopperton*, 24 B.C. Envtl. Aff. L. Rev. 103 (1996); Robert J. Hopperton, *Majoritarian and Counter-Majoritarian Difficulties: Democracy, Distrust, and* Disclosure *in American Land-Use Jurisprudence—A Response to Professors Mandelker and Tarlock's Reply*, 24 B.C. Envtl. Aff. L. Rev. 541 (1997).

---

[15]   Snyder v. Board of County Comm'rs, 627 So. 2d 469 (Fla. 1993).

B. Critical Assessment

A CONCEPTUAL APPROACH TO ZONING:
WHAT'S WRONG WITH *EUCLID*

Richard A. Epstein
5 N.Y.U. Envtl. L.J. 277 (1996)[*]

I
THE CONCEPTUAL FRAMEWORK

. . . [M]y topic is the relationship between the government and the market with respect to property in general and land-use regulation in particular. One central worry of our time is which activities should be undertaken by government coercion, control, or influence of one form or another, and which activities ought to be left to decentralized private decisions of individuals, who, for the most part, act rationally and steadily in their own self-interest. . . .

A. *The Owner of All You Survey*

. . . The hypothetical that I like to use for land-use planning is a very simple one. Let us suppose, somewhat weirdly, that you own all of the land on the face of the earth. . . .

Now that you are ruler of all you survey, what do you want to do with all the resources that are at your beck and call? The obvious answer is to do anything you want. . . .

When embarking on your course of conduct, you will discover that there are many things that you can do that will benefit you in some particular way. But you will also learn that you are not as free to act as you might suppose. You will quickly discover that the moment you start to alter the material universe in one respect, the consequences that flow from your actions are not necessarily limited to those you intended to bring about. You must take into account other types of consequences, some of which are known but unwelcome, and some of which are positively unanticipated. . . .

Faced with that insistent reality, your maximization process becomes rather more complicated than simply doing what you want. It also includes gathering and interpreting information as to all of the remote and indirect consequences, both positive and negative, of your actions, and then setting a course of action to maximize your anticipated advantage over all time and over all states. . . .

B. *A Shared World*

How can we start to enrich this bare bones model in order to come closer to the core issues of land-use planning? One way to complicate this model is to assume that instead of an actual person who owns the entire physical universe, it would be a legal entity or association with two or more partners that owns the universe. These partners have to decide what it is they want to do with what *they* own in a world into which some measure of personal conflict will necessarily intrude. But again, it is a world in which there are no boundary questions because our partners own everything in common.

To make matters worse, the problems that we just discussed do not disappear just because new challenges have been introduced. It is still necessary to try to value various states of the world, and to figure out the indirect, unattended, unforeseen, or unwanted consequences of various forms of human action. But in addition, there is the obvious question of conflict and disagreement: what happens when it turns out that the two individuals have rather different evaluations of what they regard to be good or bad in their world? . . .

Technically speaking, as numbers increase, what is likely to happen under these circumstances is a rising impulse toward partition. . . .

In our thought experiment, the moment two or more people own land, the single world owner model becomes untenable because the collective decision processes needed to satisfy shareholders, partners or whatever are all subject to a fundamental constraint in all social organizations: sometimes it is easier to have boundaries that have to be policed rather than to govern by collective rule. Stated another way, policing boundaries for separate assets and setting up government organizations for common assets both have their costs. One has to figure out ways to minimize the sum of these costs.

So let us examine the costs of policing boundaries. When the people focus on their partition arrangement, what sort of agreement are they going to make with respect to these noisy spillovers that are likely to take place at the boundary? . . . The moment there are boundaries, the more important it is to have some rule of trespass to regulate entry onto the other person's land (the common-law term of *close* is suggestive here). So right from the start, there is a wall between the two pieces of land.

The trespass question may be the easiest question to solve, and perhaps even the most important. But even with that said, a good deal more work remains to be done—for not all spillovers, as the term suggests, rise to the level of an actual entry. There are many things that each person can do on his or her property that will have negative effects beyond the property line. . . . Something similar to the law of nuisance will be born to police interactions at the boundary.

Next, suppose that we increase the number of people in the world by a fairly substantial factor. As the numbers increase, the obstacles to coordinated decision-making under common ownership become yet more intractable. To correct for obstacles, the people have to resort to more frequent divisions of property into smaller pieces. What typically happens, therefore—this is of course evident in or near major cities—is that the ratio of boundary lines to enclosed areas will increase. The more people that live in a given region, the more these areas will shrink in some way, shape, or form. The boundary questions that started out as essentially minor adjustments in a two-person universe turn out to raise an absolutely dominant problem in a universe with large numbers of people.

C. *Action at the Boundary*

What then do you do at the boundary? I think the first order of business is to figure out what kinds of negative spillovers the people want to stop; and these turn out to be the kinds addressed by the much-maligned law of nuisance in its traditional common-law form. This body of law does not work on a moral or deductive principle. Rather, it works on a rough empirical generalization that will be false in some cases but true in most: we should permit only those activities in which the benefits to the land owner exceed the costs from dirt and filth to the neighbor.

. . . .

The full system of land-use planning starts with a nuisance law—which operates as a general, all purpose, off-the-rack term—and couples it with a series of contract or covenant rules to allow corrections and deviations from the basic norm. This allows a whole body of voluntary transactions to take place. For example, if somebody's land is already a sewer, it may well be that it is easier to let a neighbor pollute it further at a price that leaves both sides the better. The contract thus allows the two parties to operate as one, and to divide the gains from the operation in a fashion that leaves neither unhappy and that results in no additional burdens being cast on third parties.

The process, moreover, has no externally imposed stopping point. If the value of land continues to rise, its segregation into smaller and smaller parcels will continue apace. The need for covenants to handle these distinctive, asymmetrical situations will probably increase. As a rough generalization, the more intensive the use of land, the more complicated the covenant law to adjust the position of neighbors along the boundary lines.

So far, this more robust model involves nuisance and covenant law. Yet there is a third part of the model that may sometimes arise. By breaking up large problems, it is possible to get rid of the obstacles of collective action and governance. But by the same token, it is possible that you will be hoisted by your own petard; almost inevitably, having little parcels of land helps in making daily management decisions on each parcel of land, such as who sits at the dining room table, or who plays in the fields. But this separation undermines coordination and management in that land owners have to respond to global problems that affect not only one or two parcels, but ten, fifty, a hundred, or perhaps an entire range of a city. The result is the standard market failure problem: large numbers of independent actors, all of whom would be better off if they coordinated their behavior toward a given solution, have an incentive to deviate unless the others can be brought into line. As the numbers increase, bargaining breakdowns become more frequent, costly, and difficult to overcome.

The classic argument in favor of land-use planning is based at root on some perception of market failure. The question is how these failures are best addressed. Dealing with that problem requires some guidance and constraint. Here the objective should be to replicate the win/win outcomes of voluntary exchanges. In responding to a coordination problem, a state-coerced solution should leave each party better off, and in the same proportion than before state coercion was imposed. Stated differently, the set of outcomes that result from coerced exchanges should imitate as much as possible those that derive from voluntary exchanges: namely, coerced exchanges should leave all participants, including involuntary participants, better off than they were before—after taking into account the full range of burdens and benefits created by that legal intervention.

II
THE CONSTITUTIONAL PAYOFF

By stating the point this way, you suddenly can see how a basic approach to social interactions—starting with one person owning everything and advancing to cases where many people own many little things—ties in with the just compensation model of the Constitution.[1] One has to recognize that when autonomous individuals surrender rights to the use of their land, something has been taken from them, for which compensation ought to be provided. One also has to recognize that the compensation requirement does not necessarily demand that each person receive cash for the deprivation. All that is necessary is to generate an outcome that provides benefits that all individuals can enjoy to some extent. It is best to approach the problem of market failure by conceiving of everybody as having something to sacrifice and receiving something in exchange. The social objective is to induce those kinds of social exchanges from which everybody will benefit.

I like to put the point in this particular fashion because it illustrates the intimate connection between the standard definitions of social welfare and the particular rules of land-use planning. The Epstein Constitution—which I think is basically the one that is already there, so there is no claim of originality, but only of devotion— holds that the law should allow the regulation or redefinition of the standard common-law property right only to the extent that, in the long run, it works to the average net advantage of all persons subject to regulation.

Given this view, what happens in those parts of the universe where some state initiative produces in aggregate a gain for the society at large, but leaves some individuals worse off than before? The answer is to equalize the benefits of the changed situation, not by stopping the transformation from going forward, but by making cash transfers from those who receive a disproportionate share of the gain to those individuals who are left worse off, thereby restoring the balance. The model—which, under some circumstances, allows you to find benefits from the implicit in-kind benefits of government action—also has this correlative proposi-

---

[1]   U.S. CONST. amend. V.

tion: when that condition of implicit in-kind compensation is not satisfied—and it may fail for many reasons, technical or political—then compensation from winners to losers could improve the overall situation by equalizing the gains across all persons. Such a world would have some coercive government action, but with a systematic application of the compensation requirement to approximate the preferred distributional consequences of voluntary exchanges.

The basic model of property rights articulated above tries to take into account, systematically and comprehensively, all benefits and costs to all individuals from government-initiated exchanges. How does this model compare with current law? What is it about the present land-use situation that deviates from the model?

A. Euclid's Mistake

The Just Compensation Clause allows private property to be taken for public purposes of the sort that I have just discussed, but demands the payment of just compensation to various individuals. To the extent that the basic model I have developed seems to have all the elements that are found in the Just Compensation Clause, one would expect that the legal response would be the same as my theoretical model. Ironically, the result has been exactly the opposite. Let me explain how this departure occurred and then explore whether anything can be done to change the misguided results in the future.

In *Euclid v. Ambler Realty Co.*,[3] the seminal land-use planning decision, the Supreme Court adopted a posture of deference toward a comprehensive land-use ordinance enacted by well-meaning local officials who were grappling with the difficult matters of projected interdependence in future land uses. . . . The Court said that almost anything the government wants to do in order to handle the externality questions is acceptable because the idea of nuisance is sufficiently pliable to allow virtually any form of government regulation to fall within its ambit. . . . As a result, the Court gave birth to a very powerful system of public planning without asking what risks, if any, might be prevented by the application of stricter scrutiny.

Euclid itself is suggestive of some lurking difficulties with the Court's approach. The land in *Euclid* was a sixty-eight acre parallelogram between Euclid Avenue on the south and the Nickel Plate Railroad on the north. The land owner had assembled vacant land and wanted to sell it for use as an industrial plant. The Supreme Court upheld the Euclid zoning ordinance, so that the land could not be used for the purpose for which it had been assembled because even though Euclid had designated the northern portion of the property for industrial use, Euclid had zoned the southern portion of the property for residential use. As a result of this particular action, the land's market value diminished from approximately $700,000 as an integrated industrial park to approximately $200,000 as fractured by the heavy-handed regulation.

Was this particular action justified in light of the problems that we were worried about in our hypothetical universe—coordination of multiple owners of a sin-

---

[3]   272 U.S. 365 (1926).

gle plot of land and the externality problems in trying to maintain the boundary lines between neighbors? *Euclid* fails to address these two concerns. First, there should be no social concern with the ostensible externalities that might arise among subsequent owners of the sixty-eight acre plot when and if subdivided. On the particular facts, no subdivision was going to be created at all; the owner wanted to use it for an integrated purpose. Any gain from one portion of the land that is offset by a loss on some other portion of the land will be felt by the single land owner. The owner will pay the price if its assembly lines are going to suffer from an inefficient configuration. With such powerful private monitoring over these activities, government intervention is not needed to make sure that the land is rightly configured for its own industrial purposes. Ironically, by breaking up a large parcel of land into inconsistent zones slated for different uses, the regulation has created an externality problem along the boundary between the different zones, which is most acute when one zone is industrial and the other is residential. Zoning can thus create the very externalities that it is supposed to avoid.

Once you have these boundary conditions, you not only have to police the interactions between neighbors of the old plot, but you also have to worry about boundary problems between the residents of the original sixty-eight acre plot and their neighbors who live outside it. However, these two sets of people live in different jurisdictions subject to different local planning boards. A truly comprehensive overview would take into consideration whether the plan for the original sixty-eight acre plot in town A is inconsistent with the plan for the land adjacent to it in town B. In short, local governments, like private actors, do not eliminate externalities. Rather, local governments create externalities as a consequence of operating in a hermetically sealed environment; a decision made in one township translates only with difficulty to what happens in the neighboring town. Transaction costs can bedevil governments just as they bedevil individuals, since the people who decide on land use in Euclid do not have to look beyond its borders to take their political cues. The upshot is that the problems of boundaries and externalities are not solved by zoning commissions. Indeed, zoning commissions create more friction because instead of only one land owner adjusting his or her arrangements with another, there are two layers of confusion: one between the two land owners and the other between the governing bodies of the two separate jurisdictions. Not only must neighbors come to their separate peace, but their governing bodies must come to peace as well.

The problems of coordination and externalities do not require a zoning solution. The relevant question in each case is whether government zoning aggravates or mitigates threatened harms. The first zoning case thwarted the single ownership solution to coordination problems and further aggravated externality problems that are a worry in any legal regime. Unfortunately, there is good reason to suspect that zoning, as it is currently practiced, more often than not aggravates rather than mitigates coordination and externality problems.

B. Euclid *Today*

The issue in *Euclid* carries over into the modern context. Most of the really pitched battles before zoning boards involve the future direction of undeveloped land. The endless veto powers given to immediate neighbors who suffer only minor financial loss could have powerfully negative consequences for the larger region of which that development is only a part. But political separations can prevent those costs from being registered. Developers have learned that buying land in small communities is a risky business, precisely because extensive negotiations are necessary to bring projects to fruition—projects that were stalled not because of external risks, but because neighbors thought they could extract a pound of flesh from the developer. Just as zoning boards can aggravate externality problems, so too can they aggravate coordination problems as well.

 . . . .

There is a second odd feature of zoning that is worthy of mention. In many ways the entire zoning process fundamentally misunderstands the way in which individuals wish to integrate and coordinate their activities. The clue to the difficulty lies in the fact that the original meaning of the word "zone" implied that every use inside a single zone was uniform in content. That is why we have industrial zones, commercial zones, single family zones, and multiple-family zones. This vision of the world presupposes that identical uses within single zones are wonderful, that mixed uses are to be discouraged, and, as noted, that the problems with the zoned boundaries are to be ignored.

C. *Mixed Uses*

This is a monumentally rigid vision of how the world ought to be organized. Although there is perhaps some local disadvantage to having just one deviation from that particular pattern of uses, there is a huge overall advantage. Do you allow one convenience store, for example, to exist within walking distance of a large residential area? Yes. Do you want to have an uneven concentration of homes in a neighborhood so that some space can be reserved for park land, and so forth? Yes. The same people who support zoning as a way to achieve convergent development have to worry about the question of mixed uses. Given the strong presumptions in favor of zones, the variance looks like an exceptional grant, sought by someone who wants to deviate from the normatively acceptable pattern of uses.

For all the superficial differences, the issue of mixed uses raises the same problem faced in *Euclid*. In *Euclid*, the land had to be sold to separate users. It was not kept for use as an industrial plant. Nevertheless, the single owner can sell off the land subject to covenants that can now be imposed at the front end as part and parcel of the condition of the sale. For example, if a seller wants to make a house far more attractive by laying out a golf course next door, he or she promises to dedicate the land to that use by covenant, and ensures that all buyers, present or future, can benefit from that decision. Since in cases of mixed uses, a seller can internalize gains and losses by covenant, why do we need zoning boards to review the architectural design plans whose impact, both visual and otherwise, is largely on the potential purchasers?

III
CONCLUSION: A RETURN TO LAISSEZ-FAIRE?

We must understand how the alternatives to zoning work before we can decide on its utility as a land-planning device. . . . [T]he full system of nuisance and covenants has enormous power. But it is also necessary to recognize that many forms of land-use regulation could be justified on the ground that they improve overall welfare without leaving any individual or group worse off. This just compensation element cannot be ignored. The entire interplay of principles, therefore, leads to a sophisticated set of rules whose overall strength is easy to underestimate. The full legal system, as it is fully understood, takes into account initial property rights, multiple uses, externalities, internalities, coordination difficulties, covenants by way of correction, single owners, and forced exchanges. Can zoning provide an improvement to the common-law system in proportion to its increase in costs and delay? I suspect that the answer to this question is negative, and that we should here, as in other areas, seek to find ways to clip the wings of zoning authorities. *Euclid* set the inquiry off on the wrong track. It will now take a good deal of hard work—intellectual, political, and legal—to correct the errant course of the past 70 years.

ALTERNATIVES TO ZONING: COVENANTS, NUISANCE RULES, AND FINES AS LAND USE CONTROLS
Robert C. Ellickson
40 U. Chi. L. Rev. 681 (1973)*

With increasing frequency commentators have been urging greater reliance on the market mechanism to allocate resources in a variety of fields. There has been relatively little examination, however, of the extent to which decentralized mechanisms can be used to handle the controversial social problem of conflicts among neighboring landowners. Land development in urban areas is one of the most regulated human activities in the United States. In recent decades, public regulation of urban land has increased sharply in incidence and severity, but dissatisfaction with the physical appearance and living arrangements in American cities continues to grow. Despite the evident shortcomings of present public regulatory schemes, even those commentators who propose reliance on the market mechanism in other areas tend to concur with the prevailing view that increased public planning is the most promising guide for the growth of cities. This article advances a different the-

---

sis: that conflicts among neighboring landowners are generally better resolved by systems less centralized than master planning and zoning.

. . . .

II. CRITERIA FOR EVALUATING LAND USE CONTROL SYSTEMS

. . . Problems of resource allocation have been attacked with the greatest conceptual rigor by economists. They generally judge the impact of social policies by two basic standards: efficiency and equity. A measure is inefficient if it is likely to waste resources, that is, allocate scarce goods and services in a suboptimal manner. Equity, however, is a function of the distribution of resources, or who ends up with what share of the wealth. For example, uninternalized harmful spillovers from land use activities may not only result in inefficiencies, but may also cause redistributions of wealth that are perceived as unjust. Following other legal scholars who have applied welfare economics to problems of external cost, this article employs efficiency and equity as the two basic criteria for evaluating land use control systems.

The notion of efficiency requires some dissection. When a conflict among neighboring land uses arises, three reasonably distinct types of resource diminutions may occur, singly or in combination. First, harmful externalities decrease the utility and thus the value of neighboring property. To keep the terminology as simple as possible, this factor will be called *nuisance costs*. Under a laissez faire distribution of property rights, these costs would probably be very high. A second possible source of resource diminutions will be termed *prevention costs*. This category includes nonadministrative expenditures made, or opportunity costs incurred, by either a nuisance maker or his injured neighbor to reduce the level of nuisance costs. Prevention costs will tend to be higher when either or both of the parties are compelled to undertake specific steps than when they are permitted to select voluntarily among available preventive measures. Finally, *administrative costs* may also diminish resources. This term will be used to encompass both public and private costs of getting information, negotiating, writing agreements and laws, policing agreements and rules, and arranging for the execution of preventive measures.

. . . .

. . . The overall goal from an efficiency standpoint is the minimization of the sum of nuisance costs, prevention costs, and administrative costs.

The goal of equity, however, complicates matters considerably; an efficient policy may be an unfair one, particularly when the gains of the policy are not distributed to those injured by its imposition. . . . The degree of unfairness of a system obviously cannot be quantified and persuasive arguments about fairness issues are hard to construct; nevertheless legal scholars must confront an issue so central to the law.

III. AN EVALUATION OF ZONING

The analytical framework constructed above will first be applied to zoning. . . .

. . . .

A. Zoning and Efficiency

Despite the difficulty of discussing the uncoordinated practices of over 9,000 local governments, the basic structure of zoning and present knowledge about its effectiveness will support some general observations about its likely efficiency as a land use control system.

1. *Reduction in Nuisance Costs.* Since zoning inevitably results in considerable prevention and administrative costs, large reductions in nuisance costs would have to be forthcoming for zoning to be deemed efficient. At present, zoning administrators either ban or greatly restrict the location of highly undesirable uses. Where a noxious use is permitted, planning officials generally try to place it adjacent to activities not particularly vulnerable to the type of harm caused by that use. For example, most zoning ordinances cluster industrial uses, often placing the cluster adjacent to railroad tracks. Similarly, apartment zones are commonly placed next to highways, perhaps on the assumption that if apartment dwellers must tolerate the noise coming through the party walls of their building, they should not be especially sensitive to the hum of nearby automobiles. Most ordinances also set aside large areas exclusively for single-family homes, a land use perceived as particularly vulnerable to external harm.

These locational decisions unquestionably reduce the nuisance costs that would occur if land uses were randomly distributed. Nonzoning allocations, however, may also be better than random. Urban land markets automatically reduce nuisance costs far below the level that would be found with random land use distribution. Industrial plants are not attracted to prime residential areas; instead they naturally congregate along railroad tracks, just where zoning is likely to put them. By such clustering, they are likely to achieve the benefits of convenient access to major shipping lines and supporting service industries, less vandalism, and lower risk of injury to neighborhood children. . . . Thus, even if a zoning system is more efficient than random land use, it does not necessarily follow that it reduces nuisance costs more than the market mechanism.

    . . . .

2. *Prevention Costs.* The great danger, however, is not that the drafters of zoning ordinances will fail to eliminate nuisance costs, but that they will try to eliminate them all. The pertinent goal is minimization of the sum of nuisance, prevention, and administrative costs. If zoning is directed solely toward eliminating nuisance costs, planners will impose land use controls so restrictive as to create inefficiently high prevention costs. For example, the zoning authorities in Los Angeles have focused on the slight damage that might be inflicted on a few homeowners if a small grocery store were built in the Santa Monica Mountains and banned such land uses. As a result, many mountain residents incur the prevention cost of a twenty-minute round trip to buy groceries, a total burden to them far more costly than the nuisance cost of a neighboring grocery to a few homeowners. . . . Another example is found in the common prohibition against the use of single-fam-

ily homes as business offices; this policy prevents professionals and small businessmen from economizing on rental expenditures and travel costs, and deprives residential areas of conveniently located professional and business services. . . .

Structural restrictions may also be a major source of prevention costs. For example, fixing minimum lot sizes larger than consumers demand increases the amount of urban land that must be consumed in order to accommodate a given population increase; thus metropolitan areas tend to spread farther than they would under a free market, increasing transportation and utility costs throughout the urban network. . . .

. . . .

3. *Administrative Costs*. The most conspicuous administrative cost of zoning is the direct cost of operating a public planning agency. Local governments, however, are tightfisted in budgeting for their planning staffs, and direct public costs are actually quite low. . . .

Planning and zoning operations also impose more indirect expenses on local governments. . . . Since land use regulation is one of the major activities of local government, a significant fraction of general governmental costs should be attributed to it. Conflicts over land use regulation that are judicially resolved may impose another sort of public cost. Local governments seek to shift many of these public costs to private parties by imposing fees for efforts to change existing regulations, or for securing permits to proceed under them.

The private administrative costs necessitated by zoning systems far exceed the public costs. Developers of urban land, and traders of urban property, must investigate any public land use restrictions governing development. The existence of zoning means that builders, land speculators, civil engineers, architects, financial institutions, lawyers, and others involved in land development must maintain libraries of local land use regulations and spend time studying them. These information costs are greatly increased by the rapid changes in the regulations.

. . . .

The total public and private administrative costs of zoning are far from insubstantial. These costs, when added to the high prevention costs zoning is likely to involve, may be so great that an entire zoning ordinance is inefficient; that is, the reduction in nuisance costs is less than the concomitant prevention and administrative costs. . . .

B. Zoning and Equity

Zoning can promote equity by prohibiting unneighborly acts, thereby protecting some landowners from privately inflicted losses. As it is usually operated, however, zoning is an inequitable system; the Achilles' heel of zoning is that it does not correct the changes in wealth distribution it causes. When a zoning decision increases the value of a parcel, the owner is generally not obligated to disgorge the increased value. Conversely, when a zoning action reduces property values, an owner is not compensated for any losses unless he can obtain a judicial decision that the ordinance constitutes an unconstitutional "taking."

. . . .

The situation is aggravated, from a fairness standpoint, by the aggrieved landowner's knowledge that zoning decisions are not random. Zoning is not a perfectly balanced roulette wheel, randomly bestowing its wins and losses. In most communities the wheel is warped; friends of the house come out winners while others are losers. Given the huge amounts at stake, it is not surprising that special influence problems have plagued zoning from its inception. . . .

The pervasiveness of special influence is inherent in the zoning system. Judicial insistence on uniform standards for decision, a basic way of preventing favoritism in government, is not possible in the case of zoning; the name itself suggests a system of nonuniform regulation. Since the courts cannot easily distinguish good planning from bad, judicial checks on unfair variations in land use restrictions have been minimal. Studies have documented the lawlessness of zoning variance decisions in most communities. Many courts have stopped trying to police local zoning and consistently sustain the local government's action under the "presumption of validity" given to zoning provisions.

. . . .

The inequities of zoning are not limited to its effect on landowners. Recent legal commentary about zoning has emphasized its potential as a vehicle for segregation of racial minorities and low income groups. . . .

The separation of families by income . . . is . . . abetted by many zoning ordinances, primarily through minimum lot size, lot frontage, and floor area requirements for residences, and the total exclusion of apartments and mobile homes. Needless to say, income discriminations often have racial ramifications. . . .

In the United States zoning generally works to the detriment of the poor and near-poor, racial minorities, and renters; it operates for the benefit of the well-to-do, particularly homeowners, by artificially increasing the supply of sites on the market usable only for expensive homes and thus reducing their cost. . . .

C. Reforming Zoning

. . . .

Most of the zoning reforms that have been proposed do not address the three fundamental weaknesses of the institution: (1) exclusive reliance on mandatory public standards, (2) concentration on prospective development with little attention to existing land use problems, and (3) sharp and frequent variability of regulations among zones.

1. *The Inefficiency of Mandatory Public Standards.* Compliance with zoning laws is mandatory. Potential violators are denied permits; existing violators, unless specially protected, may be forced to comply with zoning standards through mandatory injunctions. Zoning is thus an example of what Calabresi terms a system of specific deterrence.[101] Specific deterrence systems impair the efficiency of

---

[101] G. CALABRESI, [THE] COST OF ACCIDENTS [(Student ed., 1970)] . . . , at 95-106. Another example of specific deterrence is injunctive relief in a nuisance action.

resource allocation to the extent that they require compliance with a standard even when the prevention costs involved in compliance exceed the resulting reduction in nuisance costs. . . .

. . . .

2. *The Problem of Scant Retrospective Application.* Since the application of zoning regulations to preenactment land uses is politically unpopular, the first zoning map drawn in a jurisdiction will closely mirror existing land uses. The main thrust of the regulations thus focuses on the prospective development of vacant land. Zoning is forced into a "hands off" attitude toward most existing nuisances because it is mandatory and extinction is usually both politically undesirable and an inefficient remedy. Zoning's incapacity to deal with existing land use problems severely limits its effectiveness.

3. *The Inequity of Multiple Zones.* The variability of restrictions on topographically identical parcels of land is the third fundamental weakness of zoning systems. The growing number of zones in most cities reflects an attempt to refine an increasingly precise hierarchy of land uses ranked according to their levels of nuisance costs. The efficiency of this additional complexity is a close question, but largely irrelevant. The main point is that nonuniform regulation by local government is almost inevitably unfair regulation. The amounts of money at stake in switching parcels of land from one zone to another assure that zoning will continue to be an arbitrary and largely corrupt system. In addition, as long as multiple residential zones are tolerated, zoning will tend to be used to segregate the residences of different income classes and thus restrict equality of opportunity.

With the inherent shortcomings of zoning as a backdrop, this analysis now turns to the fundamental issues that underlie land use conflicts—the proper distribution of rights among landowners and optimal systems for their enforcement. That investigation will lead to the construction of an alternative model to zoning that alleviates the impact of the three problems just discussed without causing greater ones.

IV. COVENANTS, MERGER, AND OTHER CONSENSUAL SYSTEMS OF LAND USE REGULATION

. . . .

Covenants negotiated between landowners will tend to optimize resource allocation among them. In other words, the reduction in future nuisance costs to each party will exceed the sum of the prevention and administrative costs each agrees to bear, with all costs discounted to present value. For example, when a developer drafts covenants that will bind people who move into his subdivision, market forces prompt him to draft efficient ones. Covenants will enhance the developer's profit only if they increase his land values by more than the cost of imposing them. His land values will rise only if his home buyers perceive that the covenants will reduce the future nuisance costs they might suffer by an amount greater than the sum of their loss of flexibility in use and future administrative costs. The developer will suggest, therefore, only those covenants that provide each purchaser with a reduction of nuisance costs greater than the purchaser's loss in flexibility plus his enforcement cost plus a pro rata share of the developer's administrative costs. Not all conflicts between neighbors can be solved by covenants, but covenants generated by market forces will tend to promote efficiency.

In addition to promoting efficiency, covenants will not usually cause unfair wealth transfers among landowners. Absent fraud, duress, and the like, a party will not agree to a contract that he perceives as unfair. Thus, assuming equal bargaining power and information, consensual covenants will not involve inequitable gains or losses to any party.

. . . .

V. Assigning Rights Among Landowners: A Reformulation of Nuisance Law

More efficient and more equitable resource allocation will sometimes be achieved by altering the laissez faire distribution of property rights so as to place the risk of loss from external harms on the landowner carrying out the damaging activity. . . . [N]uisance law provides the most important source of common law rules for shifting the risk of loss for external harms.

A. Existing Nuisance Law as a Land Use Control System

Nuisance law is today suffering from neglect. Its doctrines receive little attention in modern casebooks on torts and property. Scholarly analysis of nuisance problems has been minimal, perhaps because nuisance law is widely viewed as an archaic means of handling land use problems. As a result, the confusions and inefficiencies in the law of nuisance are considerably more serious than in most other areas of the law.

Many of the doctrinal difficulties in nuisance law have arisen when courts have tried to avoid granting injunctive relief, the traditional remedy in nuisance cases. An injunction often imposes prevention costs that exceed the reduction in nuisance costs it achieves; the closing of a factory may be more costly to the economy than the losses caused to neighbors by its operation. As courts became sensitive to this danger they responded by limiting the circumstances in which they were willing to find a nuisance, rather than denying injunctive relief while still allowing damages. Nuisance law thus came to provide no relief in many cases where the risk of loss could appropriately have been shifted to the landowner carrying out the damaging activity.

In many instances courts avoided finding actionable nuisances by applying a type of balancing test; the social utility of the actor's conduct was compared to the total amount of harm caused. This test is proper for deciding whether to grant injunctive relief. Unfortunately most courts applied the test to the initial question of whether a nuisance existed at all, incorrectly limiting the availability of damage awards that would internalize the harmful externalities. . . . Illogical doctrines of this type have greatly reduced the value of nuisance law as a land use control system.

. . . .

B. Nuisance Law: The Prima Facie Case

. . . .

. . . Any unexpected alteration of the distribution of rights among landowners is almost certain to affect their relative shares of wealth. Decisions on the distribution of rights in cases of external costs thus must accommodate the complex considerations of administrative costs and fairness.

The following reformulation of nuisance law is an estimate of how rights should be distributed among neighboring landowners when these considerations are taken into account. The analysis follows a rather traditional legal mold: the development of a prima facie case, to be pleaded and proved by the injured neighbor, and the articulation of various defenses. . . .

1. *Assigning Rights To Promote Efficiency: A Preliminary General Rule.* Efficient resource allocation is accomplished through the minimization of the sum of the nuisance costs, prevention costs, and administrative costs arising from land use conflicts. A party compelled to bear a nuisance cost can be expected to adopt all preventive measures he perceives as efficient. A measure will appear efficient to a party if its prevention cost and the administrative cost of carrying it out are less than the reduction in nuisance costs achieved. Prevention costs cannot be diminished by shifting the assignment of rights; those costs are only affected by technological innovation. Legal rules may, however, affect the administrative costs involved in the execution of a specific preventive measure. Rights should therefore be assigned to reduce administrative costs in order to increase the number of preventive measures that parties perceive to be in their self-interest. . . .

. . . .

Since this article focuses primarily on land use problems in urban areas, the general liability of a host landowner is proposed both for intentional changes and for damaging events on his property that arise through the workings of nature. In both situations the urban landowner is likely to be the most efficient bearer of liability.

2. *Toward a Tripartite System of Internalization: The Unneighborliness Requirement.* . . .

. . . .

Normalcy has become a central concept in law as well as language, but the reasons for this importance have not yet been adequately explored. This article contends that normalcy is often used as a legal standard because the concept promises substantial efficiencies. In order to promote economically productive behavior that cannot be easily achieved by bargaining and to satisfy community desires to reward virtuous activities, legal rules should seek to transfer wealth from those whose actions have unusually harmful external impacts and to those whose actions are unusually beneficial to others. That pattern of transfers is now accomplished through a tripartite set of rules incorporating the normalcy standard: meritorious behavior is sometimes rewarded through quasi-contract doctrines and other devices, normal behavior is treated neutrally, and substandard behavior is penalized through liability rules and other sanctions.

. . . .

The following modification in the general rule of host landowner liability is proposed to establish the tripartite system: a change in land use should result in liability of the host landowner only if the change is perceived as unneighborly according to contemporary community standards. In cases where only part of a complex land use is unneighborly, only the damage done by its unneighborly aspects should be compensable. For example, if a gas station blocks a scenic view, but a typical residence would also have blocked the view, damages from view blockage should not be included in the gas station's liability.

An unneighborliness test is a democratic and dynamic method of assuring that neighbors of an enterprising landowner do not receive excessive endowments of property rights. The unneighborliness concept is analogous to the emphasis on unreasonableness in current nuisance law, but the latter test is avoided here since it has been used in far too many situations to protect host landowners from liability, often by courts trying to avoid the harshness of injunctive relief.

. . . .

Under the system described above an aggrieved landowner establishes a prima facie case for nuisance when he shows that his neighbor has damaged him by carrying on activities, or harboring natural conditions, perceived as unneighborly under contemporary community standards. . . .

3. *Compensable Damage: The Problem of Aesthetics.* The formulation of the prima facie case discussed above allows recovery without a physical invasion of the damaged property, for example where the sole injury is to a landowner's psychological comfort or sense of aesthetics. This possibility represents a departure from prevailing legal doctrines . . . .

. . . .

4. *Measuring Damage: Bonuses for Consumer Surplus.* Where compensation is to be allowed, a system must be designed to measure its proper amount. The golden mean of normalcy would seem to be achieved by requiring the defendant to pay to the plaintiff an amount equal to the drop in the market value of the plaintiff's property that would be caused by the defendant's unneighborly use if there were no right to recovery. If periodic rather than permanent damages were awarded, they would equal the lost rents over the relevant period discounted to present value. . . .

Use of market values for measuring damages in nuisance cases, however, may be inappropriate. There is a minimum price at which any person would voluntarily exchange any item of his property. The excess of this subjective value over market is termed "consumer surplus." . . .

. . . .

. . . [T]here are types of nonfungible property to which most owners attach considerable consumer surplus. Possessions such as long-occupied single-family homes in stable residential areas tend to attract increasing subjective valuations as the tenure of ownership increases. The property owner with a *common* nonfungible surplus is normally sensitive, not hypersensitive, and consequently not likely to be the best avoider of losses of that surplus. A desirable system for dealing with this problem is to award damages for the drop in market value plus a bonus award to compensate for loss of the commonly held irreplaceable consumer surplus. To limit administrative costs such bonuses could be defined through legislated schedules, perhaps as specific percentages of the market value award. . . .

5. *The Requirement of Substantial Harm.* Prevailing nuisance law requires that the plaintiff suffer "substantial harm" to be entitled to relief. This condition is essential to an efficient prima facie case. If plaintiffs are allowed to bring suits for trivial damages, the administrative costs involved are likely to exceed the efficiency gains of permitting such suits. . . .

. . . .

6. *Remedies: The Plaintiff's Choice between Damages and Purchasing an Injunction.* In a recent and stimulating article Calabresi and Melamed observed that there are four possible rules on remedies in nuisance cases.[201] Under the first rule the plaintiff is entitled to enjoin the defendant's nuisance. Second, the plaintiff is entitled to damages from the defendant but not to injunctive relief. The third rule is that the plaintiff may neither enjoin the defendant's conduct nor collect damages. The fourth rule, generally ignored by legal commentators, permits the plaintiff to enjoin the defendant's conduct, but only if he compensates the defendant for the defendant's losses caused by the injunction. When a nuisance exists, present principles always allow the plaintiff to invoke rule two (damages) and in a great many situations to invoke rule one (injunction).

Nuisance law would function better if, in general, a plaintiff in a nuisance case were limited to choosing between the remedies of rule two (damages) and rule four (compensated injunction). Adoption of this recommendation would obviously constitute a major reformation of prevailing nuisance doctrine. . . . Rules one and three are recognized as appropriate, however, in certain unusual nuisance situations where they are essential to protect the fundamental rights of one of the parties.

. . . .

C. Nuisance Law: Defenses

. . . Affirmative defenses involve additional administrative costs. Nonetheless, four defenses to the prima facie case are now proposed: the first two to protect the defendant's liberty and the last two to promote efficiency. These defenses will often be incomplete, and in such cases the parties in conflict will ultimately be required to split the contested cost between them.

---

[201] Calabresi & Melamed, [*Property Rules, Liability Rules, and Inalienability: One View of the Cathedral*, 85 HARV. L. REV. 1089 (1972)] . . ., at 1115-23.

1. *The Defense of Freedom of Expression.* . . . [E]very landowner should possess rule three entitlements that protect him from liability for exercising certain freedoms and immunize him from the risk that a neighbor will stop these activities by purchasing the right to their termination through rule four. A landowner's basic rule three entitlement should be that his activities may not be disturbed unless a neighbor can make out a prima facie case in nuisance against him. In addition, rule three protection is warranted even when activities are unneighborly, to the extent that those activities constitute exercises of fundamental rights of free expression. Bizarre architecture or landscaping may be as significant a mode of self-expression as unusual clothing or hairstyles, activities lately protected by rule three. . . .

. . . .

2. *The Defense of Equality of Opportunity.* Unavoidable physical characteristics of a landowner may be perceived as unneighborly and thus cause an unusual decline in his neighbors' property values. In a society valuing equality of opportunity, however, rule three should be used to protect people with unpopular racial, ethnic, or morphological characteristics from liability and coerced disruptions. . . .

. . . .

3. *The Defense of Hypersensitivity.* . . . The general rule placing liability on the landowner must now be modified to deal with those types of cases where the affected neighbor, not the landowner, typically has better knowledge, organization, and/or control over at least part of the potential loss. This relationship occurs primarily where the neighbor is hypersensitive to harm or where he fails to mitigate damages after a change on the landowner's property. In hypersensitivity cases the neighbor generally has better knowledge of the risk; in mitigation cases he is at least equally aware of the risk of further damage and controls the property on which the most efficient preventive steps can be taken. Efficiency defenses based on these two situations, unlike the liberty defenses discussed above, should not entitle the defendant to rule three protection, but should rather benefit him by shifting more in his favor the assessment of payments due under rules two and four.

. . . .

4. *The Defense of Failure to Mitigate Damages.* A major flaw in existing nuisance law is its disregard for the sequence of actions of the parties to a conflict and its consequent failure to induce a plaintiff to minimize damages by adopting measures uniquely within his control. Although the duty to mitigate damages is imposed in many areas of the law to provide such incentives, it is rarely recognized in nuisance cases. The efficiency considerations that lead courts to impose a duty to mitigate in tort and contract cases, however, also hold in nuisance cases. The lack of such a doctrine for land use conflicts is particularly unfortunate since the cases generally involve continuing harms to plaintiffs and thus present many opportunities for mitigation. . . .

. . . .

VI. A Tentative Sketch of a More Privatized System of Land Use Regulation

... This article proposes that private nuisance remedies become the exclusive remedy for "localized" spillovers—that is, those that concern no more than several dozen parties. Private nuisance remedies, however, are not the optimal internalization system for all types of harmful spillovers from land use activity; in particular private remedies are likely to be an inefficient means of handling insubstantial injuries from "pervasive" nuisances that affect many outsiders. More centralized systems for internalizing pervasive harms may be capable of achieving savings in administrative costs that outweigh the inevitable allocative inefficiencies of collective regulation. ...

A. The Superiority of Nuisance Law for Localized Harms

Many land use activities now constrained by zoning ordinances raise only localized threats that would be better handled through private nuisance remedies supplemented by covenants and good manners. The system of private nuisance law outlined above avoids the allocative inefficiencies threatened by mandatory regulations or injunctions. It relies upon a decentralized policing system that is triggered more efficiently than a centralized system, and it can easily be used to internalize existing nuisances, not merely future ones. It also assures the availability of compensation to parties substantially injured by nuisances.

The major drawback of the nuisance approach is potentially excessive administrative costs. Even in localized conflicts, the costs of assessing and distributing payments ... might be so high as to make the nuisance approach inferior to one of its alternatives. Some economies should be possible, however, through proper structuring of the public administrative apparatus used for handling nuisance disputes. Land use conflicts arise frequently in urban areas and present specialized and repetitive issues. A single adjudicative authority with exclusive jurisdiction over these cases could resolve them with greater facility and consistency than courts of general jurisdiction.

1. *Nuisance Boards*. The following administrative structure would be a good start. First, the state would enact the nuisance rules suggested above. The state would then establish metropolitan Nuisance Boards and grant them primary jurisdiction over nuisance cases and exclusive rule making power over land use problems in their metropolitan area. Each Nuisance Board would then use this power principally (a) to publish regulations stating with considerable specificity which land use activities are considered unneighborly by that metropolitan population at that time, (b) to identify hypersensitive uses with similar specificity, (c) to establish threshold levels of "substantial harm," and (d) to promulgate schedules of bonus payments for losses of common nonfungible consumer surplus. By thus clarifying entitlements, the Board would assist the private settlement of disputes and thus lower administrative costs.

In adjudicating cases the Board would be authorized to award compensated injunctions and either periodic or permanent damages. To reduce administrative costs, the Board could assign hearing officers to find facts and determine appropriate awards. These decisions would be reviewable first by the Board and then by courts of general jurisdiction, a pattern of appeals characteristic of many administrative agencies. Where they would simplify Board decisions and encourage private settlements, the Board could promulgate schedules of damages for typical harms. User fees imposed on litigating parties could also be structured to encourage private settlements.

. . . .

Nuisance remedies, whatever their structure, will undoubtedly involve substantial administrative costs, but so do the alternative land use control systems. The nuisance approach will be desirable in situations where its allocative and administrative inefficiencies are less serious than those of alternative systems.

. . . .

2. *Nuisance Boards in Action.* Some examples will illustrate how the nuisance system might apply to localized problems now regulated by zoning.

a. *Side and rear yards.* Construction of a building by a landowner close to his side or rear lot line will generally affect the property values of only one of his neighbors, and never more than three or four, assuming the usual configuration of urban lots. Nearly all localities regulate such construction through mandatory minimum side and rear yard requirements. When enforced, these restrictions impose massive prevention costs by making a large fraction of urban land unimprovable. Private civil remedies would permit the bargaining out of more individualized solutions, an eminently feasible process in such localized disputes. Moreover, in a new subdivision the nuisance approach would allow the developer, initially the landowner on both sides of the lot line, great flexibility in determining the side and rear setbacks best suited to consumer demands.

A Nuisance Board would handle conflicts over side yard uses in the following manner. First, to assist parties in understanding their entitlements, the Nuisance Board would promulgate general rules establishing threshold distances for unneighborly side yard construction in its metropolitan area. If a landowner were violating the threshold, the adjacent neighbor would be entitled to choose between collecting damages under the reformulated nuisance rules and purchasing injunctive relief against the side yard incursion. . . .

. . . .

B. The Necessity of More Collective Internalization Systems for Pervasive Harm

A pervasive nuisance may inflict substantial harm on nearby neighbors and also cause legally insubstantial injuries to a large number of more distant parties. Entitlement to nuisance remedies assures those suffering large injuries compensation for their losses. Use of nuisance remedies to internalize the insubstantial pervasive harms, however, would pose an intolerable administrative burden. One of the more collective internalization systems—fines, regulatory taxes, mandatory standards, mandatory prohibitions—may prove to be a more efficient intervention by eliminating the task of assessing and distributing many small awards. . . .

. . . .

1. *Uniform Standards Enforced Solely through Fines.* Welfare economists have historically favored fines as solutions to problems of external cost. Unlike mandatory standards and prohibitions, fines can be applied retrospectively to existing nuisances without imposing the drastic prevention costs that deter many zoning administrators from eliminating nonconforming uses. Fines are also more flexible than mandatory regulations since a landowner is free to buy, in effect, the right to violate an inefficient standard. A system of fines requires establishment of standards for imposition of the fines, rules for calculating their amounts, and an administrative structure for assessment and collection.

Standards can take either of two forms: performance standards, setting performance levels to be achieved, or specification standards, detailing exact technologies that are, and are not, acceptable. For example, performance standards on light stanchions in gas stations might consist of limits on the lumens detectable at a specified distance; specification standards would list approved or disapproved types of poles, hoods, and bulbs. These approaches can also be used in combination. . . .

. . . .

The metropolitan Nuisance Boards would be the logical authority to administer the fine system since those boards would already be involved with the nuisance rules. For flexibility, the Boards could be authorized to levy either periodic fines or permanent fines. The fines should be lienable and given priority over most other creditors. Actual collection of fines might be handled through the property tax assessor's office.

Although fines are an attractive land use control, they are not necessarily the best system for all types of pervasive nuisances. Fines work best as an internalization device when the harmful activity presents a simple and objective index of noxiousness; the amount of the fine is then easily keyed to that index. If no such index exists, the administrative costs of calculation will be higher, and the amount of individual fines are likely to be so arbitrary that courts will have a difficult time preventing graft and discrimination. Even where a simple, objective index can be applied, rapid changes in index variables may make fines unworkable by requiring maintenance of expensive monitoring devices.

There are, however, several pervasively harmful land use activities now regulated by mandatory governmental controls that are well suited to being controlled with fines. These activities all present a reasonably objective index of noxiousness that is negligibly volatile over time.

. . . .

c. *Front yard setbacks.* Front yards affect more people than side or rear yards because they determine the light, air, and views available to passing pedestrians and motorists and the ability of those travellers to avoid cross-traffic at intersections. Mandatory front yard setbacks are now imposed prospectively and enforced through preconstruction design reviews. This problem might be more flexibly handled through a system of fines triggered by violations of specification standards issued by Nuisance Boards. The index for calculating fines might include such variables as distance from the street, street width, and proximity to intersections.

d. *Building heights.* Mandatory height restrictions are becoming popular in many coastal cities where skyscrapers are perceived as threatening pervasive harm. Fines are again a possible alternative; they are easily indexed to height and area of silhouettes. . . .

2. *Mandatory Enforcement of Uniform Standards and Prohibitions.* When an activity that causes pervasive harm presents no reasonably objective indexes of noxiousness a system of fines is likely to be both administratively costly and arbitrary. In these instances mandatory enforcement of minimum standards may be the best method for limiting damage caused by pervasive nuisances. . . .

Mandatory standards may be the best land use control system for regulating activities like subdivision design. Subdivision activity may pervasively disrupt the community road, utility, and drainage networks. There is no apparent simple index for assessing fines against violations of normal standards on subdivision design, and regulatory taxes that equal the actual damage inflicted would be both expensive to calculate and difficult for courts to scrutinize. . . .

. . . .

VII. Conclusion

The most prevalent systems of land use control in the United States are neither as efficient nor as equitable as available alternatives. Detailed mandatory zoning standards inevitably impair efficient urban growth and discriminate against migrants, lower classes, and landowners with little political influence. The elimination of all mandatory zoning controls on population densities, land use locations, and building bulks is therefore probably desirable. The alternative proposed in this article relies primarily on a variety of less centralized devices to internalize the external costs of unneighborly land use activities . . . .

. . . .

Note

Other scholars also have proposed substitutes for the existing land use control regime. *See* Jerry Frug, *The Geography of Community*, 48 Stan. L. Rev. 1047 (1996); Douglas W. Kmiec, *Deregulating Land Use: An Alternative Free Enterprise Development System*, 130 U. Pa. L. Rev. 28 (1981).

C. Reappraisal and Outlook

ZONING: A REPLY TO THE CRITICS
Bradley C. Karkkainen
10 J. Land Use & Envtl. L. 45 (1994)[*]

I. INTRODUCTION

In November 1993 voters in Houston narrowly rejected a referendum to establish zoning in that city. This was the third time in a half-century that Houston voters had rejected zoning. Thus Houston remains the only major city in the United States without zoning. To zoning's supporters, Houston represents an unenlightened backwater that has stubbornly resisted the tide of twentieth century land use regulation. To zoning's critics, Houston stands as a lonely beacon of economic rationality, or at least a living laboratory in which alternatives to zoning can be fairly tested.

Extensive academic literature critical of zoning has accumulated in the last twenty years, beginning with Bernard Siegan's landmark 1970 study lauding Houston's non-zoning approach,[3] and followed shortly thereafter by Robert Ellickson's broader theoretical critique of zoning.[4] Subsequent academic literature has been almost as uniformly critical of zoning[5] as public policy has been uniformly in favor of it. Although few academic defenders of zoning have stepped forward, governmental decision-makers have proceeded with zoning apace, apparently untroubled by the academic onslaught. By some estimates, 9,000 municipalities, large and small, in every region of the country and representing at least 90% of the nation's population, have zoning schemes in place. The closeness of last November's vote, and Houston's status as the only major holdout against zoning, can give little

---

[*] Copyright © 1994 by the Florida State University Journal of Land Use and Environmental Law. Reprinted by permission.

[3] Bernard H. Siegan, *Non-Zoning in Houston*, 13 J.L. & ECON. 71 (1970) (arguing that land use patterns in Houston are similar to those in other cities, but the patterns are achieved more efficiently because of the absence of zoning).

[4] Robert C. Ellickson, *Alternatives to Zoning: Covenants, Nuisance Rules, and Fines as Land Use Controls,* 40 U. CHI. L. REV. 681, 779-80 (1973) [hereinafter Ellickson, *Alternatives*] (recognizing the need for land use regulation to control negative externalities, but arguing that restrictive covenants, modified nuisance law, and administrative fines would operate more efficiently and fairly than zoning).

[5] *See, e.g.,* WILLIAM A. FISCHEL, THE ECONOMICS OF ZONING LAWS: A PROPERTY RIGHTS APPROACH TO AMERICAN LAND USE CONTROLS (1985); ROBERT H. NELSON, ZONING AND PROPERTY RIGHTS: AN ANALYSIS OF THE AMERICAN SYSTEM OF LAND USE REGULATION (1977); Douglas W. Kmiec, *Deregulating Land Use: An Alternative Free Enterprise Development System,* 130 U. Pa. L. Rev. 28 (1981); Jan Z. Krasnowiecki, *Abolish Zoning,* 31 Syracuse L. Rev. 719 (1980); Andrew J. Cappel, Note, *A Walk Along Willow: Patterns of Land Use Coordination in Pre-Zoning New Haven (1870-1926),* 101 Yale L.J. 617 (1991).

cheer to zoning's critics. No trend toward abolishing zoning appears on the horizon, and indeed, non-zoning in Houston hangs by a thread.

. . . .

. . . [T]he purpose of this article is not to offer a general defense of zoning. Its task is the more modest one of showing that many of the critiques, despite the broad claims of their authors, should not be taken as general indictments of zoning, but rather as indicators of particular dysfunctions that must be addressed if zoning is to work effectively.

II. TRADITIONAL JUSTIFICATIONS FOR ZONING

Initially, the question of why we even have zoning must be addressed. Zoning's proponents traditionally have offered two rationales, neither of which stands up to close scrutiny. First, zoning advocates suggest that zoning is necessary to protect or enhance property values, particularly the values of residential properties (and especially single-family homes). On this analysis, zoning serves principally to protect property owners from the negative externalities of new developments. Without zoning (or some comparable system of land use regulation), residential property owners would face plummeting property values if a development with significant negative externalities—a junkyard or brick factory, for example—moved in next door. . . .

A significant problem with the property values rationale for zoning, however, is that such a rationale is difficult to support with empirical evidence. It has not been clearly established that zoning results in higher market values for residential property. Another problem with this rationale is that zoning's advocates have not clearly established that zoning is the only means, or even the most effective or efficient means, of controlling externalities.

Second, zoning is defended as a tool of a broader scheme of comprehensive urban planning. However, in many smaller communities that cannot afford their own planning agencies, zoning is often not accompanied by comprehensive planning. Furthermore, critics suggest that in bigger cities that do have planning departments, planners often find zoning a bothersome, time-consuming, and highly technical distraction from what they regard as their more important planning functions, i.e., charting the future of that area. Therefore, it is not clear that zoning has ever been well-integrated with the other tools at a planner's disposal. . . .

More recently, some zoning advocates have suggested the prevention of "fiscal freeloading" as a third rationale.[19] According to this view, some new developments place a greater burden on public services than they contribute in new taxes. Zoning is a means by which such developments can be screened out in favor of

---

[19] This view is most prominently associated in academic literature with Bruce Hamilton. *See, e.g.,* Bruce W. Hamilton, *Zoning and Property Taxation in a System of Local Governments,* URB. STUD., June 1975 (arguing that, in a metropolitan area with a large number of competing municipal jurisdictions, the use of zoning as a neutral fiscal device can make residential property taxes function as an efficient price for public services).

developments that pay their fair share. This may indeed be one of the ways zoning is used in some exclusive, and exclusionary, suburban communities, but it does not appear to be a major factor in big-city zoning schemes. Moreover, where the fiscal freeloading rationale is employed, it has troublesome normative implications. Typically, it is lower-income, multi-family rental housing developments that are thought not to "pay their own way."[23] . . . Thus, the fiscal freeloading argument may become a rationale for excluding lower-income (and often minority) persons from suburban residency and opportunities for economic advancement.

III. The Critiques

Most of the critiques of zoning fall into four broad categories. Two concern fairness or equity and the other two are based on considerations of economic efficiency. . . .

A. Zoning Is Unfair To Some Property Owners

Some critics contend that zoning is fundamentally unfair because it grants special privileges to some property owners (typically, current owner/occupants of single-family homes) at the expense of others, including principally those (usually non-resident) owners who wish to develop their property for non-residential purposes.[27] . . .

At one time, this argument was of constitutional dimensions, but *Village of Euclid v. Ambler Realty Co.*[31] settled the dispute by holding that zoning is constitutionally permissible, at least on due process grounds. Absent a constitutional or positive law norm prohibiting unequal treatment of different classes of property owners, advocates of this position must rely on some deeper moral principle. Yet

---

[23] [Michael H.] Schill, [*Deconcentrating the Inner City Poor*, 67 Chi.-Kent L. Rev. 795 (1991)] . . . , at 812-14; Siegan, *supra* note 3, at 120. *But cf.* Robert C. Ellickson, *Suburban Growth Controls: An Economic and Legal Analysis,* 86 Yale L.J. 385, 406 n.55 (1977) [hereinafter Ellickson, *Growth Controls*] (stating that because tenant families usually have fewer school-age children and apartment buildings are often subject to higher effective property tax rates, apartments are *more* likely to "pay their own way" in property taxes than are modest single-family homes).

[27] *See* Richard A. Epstein, Takings: Private Property and the Power of Eminent Domain 263-66 (1985) (zoning frequently results in uncompensated taking of private property in violation of constitutional principles and fundamental norms of fairness). Epstein recognizes, however, that zoning sometimes has beneficial outcomes such as controlling nuisances or benefiting the regulated party along with her neighbors, "so it is out of the question to invalidate all zoning per se." *Id.* at 265; Ellickson, *Alternatives, supra* note 4, at 699 (arguing that zoning reduces some property values while raising others; the losers are typically not compensated, and the winners reap a windfall); Ellickson, *Growth Controls, supra* note 23, at 438-40 (arguing that some forms of land use controls effectively allow current homeowners to skim off developers' profits, violating principles of horizontal equity); Robert C. Ellickson, *Three Systems of Land-Use Control*, 13 Harv. J.L. & Pub. Pol'y 67, 72-73 (1990) . . . (stating that political processes of zoning are biased in favor of local residents).

[31] 272 U.S. 365, 389-90 (1926) (upholding local zoning ordinance against claims that it unconstitutionally deprived landowners of property without due process of law).

our legal system recognizes many other kinds of unequal burdens by type of property, such as differential tax treatment. This suggests that under contemporary notions of property, the moral and legal norms implicated here are at best very weak. Ultimately, this type of critique must rest on a highly controversial (and ultimately insupportable) natural rights notion of property in which property rights are seen as having some nearly-inviolable, pre-political status.[33]

B. Zoning Is Exclusionary

This argument, in its attenuated form, has already been alluded to in the prior discussion on fiscal freeloading. In its more general form, the argument is that zoning, because it is prohibitory in nature, is fundamentally a device of exclusion. It is further argued that, in fact, zoning is widely used to exclude racial groups, economic classes, and economic activities that are deemed to be undesirable.[35] These arguments are more commonly directed at suburban zoning[36] because big cities, by their very nature, tend to be less exclusionary, taking all comers. It does appear, however, that while big cities do not use zoning to exclude groups entirely, some neighborhoods within the cities do use zoning as an exclusionary device. At first glance these arguments have some appeal, but they often are stated vaguely. Once we unpack them, it becomes clear that they should not stand as a general indictment of zoning.

The idea that some racially discriminatory applications of zoning should somehow taint all zoning is a peculiar one. If zoning is consciously used to achieve racial segregation, then a serious problem exists. But this problem should be addressed by constitutional and statutory equal protection claims, not by scrapping zoning. . . . Since it is not zoning on its face, but rather its application that results in discrimination, those particular applications, and not all zoning, should be eradicated.

More difficult is the claim that zoning is used to exclude persons by economic class, resulting in the side effect of racial exclusion, because racial minorities generally are not as affluent as the white majority. Again, this charge is typically made against suburbs rather than big cities because big cities embrace a greater diversity of income classes. The problem with this claim is that our legal and political culture is at best ambivalent about the principle of equal treatment on the basis of economic status. Even if society were committed to that principle, the appropriate

---

[33] *See, e.g.*, EPSTEIN, *supra* note 27, at 36 (describing property rights as pre-political "natural rights" with which government may interfere only if it provides dollar-for-dollar compensation). As Epstein recognizes, however, claims based on this theory are ultimately takings claims, resting on the notion that the government's action diminishing the value of A's property is wrong, regardless of how the government treats B. *Id.*

[35] *See* Joel Kosman, *Toward an Inclusionary Jurisprudence: A Reconceptualization of Zoning*, 43 CATH. U. L. REV. 59, 71-77 (1993) (arguing that zoning is inextricably tied to invidious forms of racial and class exclusion).

[36] *See, e.g.,* Leonard Rubinowitz, *Exclusionary Zoning: A Wrong in Search of a Remedy*, 6 J.L. REFORM 625 (1972); Lawrence G. Sager, *Tight Little Islands: Exclusionary Zoning, Equal Protection, and the Indigent*, 21 STAN. L. REV. 767, 791 (1969). . . .

remedy would not be to reject zoning as an institution, but to challenge particular applications of the zoning power based on impermissible categories of economic status. Alternatively, the states or perhaps Congress could enact statutes prohibiting the use of zoning to exclude on the basis of economic status.

More fundamentally, exclusion on the basis of economic status appears to be the entire *raison d'être* for the most exclusive suburbs. Although zoning is one tool used to achieve that goal, it is not the only tool, and abolishing zoning would not necessarily effect a cure. Finally, even if all public regulation of land use were abolished, private devices like restrictive covenants might still be used to achieve the goal of exclusion.

Another variant on the exclusion argument is not concerned with exclusion by economic status, but with exclusion of certain legal but locally undesirable (yet socially necessary) land uses. This is the NIMBY (Not-In-My-Back-Yard) syndrome. It is said that zoning benefits the best-organized and politically most powerful residents who are able to block the siting of locally undesirable economic activities in their own communities. Yet those same residents get some portion of the social benefits of those activities when they take place in other, less politically powerful communities. . . .

. . . .

The critics' recurring mistake is confusing the zoning power itself with the application of that power to achieve a goal they find objectionable. If suburban zoning is too restrictive and produces NIMBY-like results, then perhaps the problem is not with zoning generally, but with the particular goals and practices of suburban zoning, or even with the existence of suburbs themselves as exclusive enclaves within the larger metropolitan community. Some suburbs are intended to be communities that keep out certain kinds of economic activities; zoning is but one tool used to achieve that result. If NIMBY is a problem, then perhaps the solution is a return to the requirement that zoning allow all otherwise-legal economic activities to take place somewhere within its bounds.

A final variant on the exclusion argument is that politically well-connected developers are often able to win the zoning changes they need, while political neophytes and outsiders are disadvantaged. An even harsher version is that self-seeking, entrepreneurial local officials are able to use the zoning power to "shake down" developers for campaign contributions, bribes, patronage jobs, and other private benefits. Only those who "ante up" are awarded the zoning approvals they need. There is substantial evidence that these practices do take place. This has led some to conclude that land use regulation should be more rule oriented. Others argue that the solution is to make zoning more scientific and professional, and less political. Still others argue that these practices are so widespread, and such an unavoidable part of the zoning power, that no solution short of abolition of zoning will suffice. This article addresses these concerns in Part IV, arguing that zoning decisions must be policed both from the top-down and from the bottom-up, using processes that encourage neighborhood residents to participate actively in decision-making.

C. Zoning Adds Unnecessary Transaction Costs

Most proponents of this argument concede that some form of local land use regulation is necessary to control the negative effects of certain types of land uses. Typically, they argue that some alternative form of regulation would be more efficient than zoning because of lower transaction costs. The direct governmental administrative costs of zoning are generally conceded to be relatively low. The higher costs are shifted to developers, especially when the development requires approval for a variance, special use permit, amendment, or planned unit development. Yet these transaction costs are only part of the total cost equation.

Though critics of zoning contend that zoning advocates focus only on the costs of the externalities they seek to prevent (ignoring the transaction costs added by the zoning system itself), the critics themselves may focus only on the transaction costs. In particular, some critics would rely, in whole or in part, on private covenants to perform some of the nuisance-avoidance functions of zoning.[60] As has been frequently noted, however, the transaction costs of getting all residents of an existing neighborhood to agree to restrictive covenants are prohibitively high. Thus, private covenants are likely to be effective only in previously undeveloped areas where a private developer can impose them as part of the subdivision of a large parcel.

Moreover, that alternative schemes of land-use regulation would result in lower transaction costs is both a controversial and unproven assertion. . . .

D. Zoning Produces Inefficient Land Use Allocation Decisions

In its purest form, an economic critique of zoning might argue that zoning (or any scheme of land use regulation) is inherently inefficient because it forces landowners to make land use allocation decisions other than those they would make in a free market. According to classical economic theory, free markets efficiently allocate economic resources, and neither legislative-type categorical regulations nor case-by-case decisions by bureaucratic regulators can make such decisions as efficiently as the market. Thus, land use decisions made under a regulatory scheme inevitably result in inefficient distortions of the market.

The classic objection to such a pure laissez-faire approach is that it does not take into account externalities or spillovers from land uses. Internalizing the externalities requires some kind of regulatory scheme. The laissez-faire response argues that land-use conflicts involve highly localized and concentrated externalities. Therefore, only a few neighboring properties are significantly affected. No major obstacles exist to Coasean bargaining[68] to resolve that conflict efficiently. In addi-

---

[60] *See* Siegan, *supra* note 3, at 142; Ellickson, *Alternatives, supra* note 4, at 711-19 (urging expanded use of covenants as substitute for zoning).

[68] *See* Ronald H. Coase, *The Problem of Social Cost*, 3 J.L. & ECON. 1 (1960) (positing that in a world free of transaction costs parties will bargain to efficient outcomes regardless of initial assignments of entitlements). Here, it is suggested that with few parties affected, transaction costs are low, and parties will be more likely to bargain to efficient outcomes.

tion, the existing common law of nuisance offers landowners remedies for negative "spillovers" from noxious uses of neighboring properties. This common law should produce efficient results where neighbors recover damages for such negative spillovers.

. . . .

Most of zoning's critics recognize the need to control negative externalities through some regulatory scheme, but do not make the pure laissez-faire "market distortions" argument. Since any regulatory scheme is arguably subject to the laissez-faire market distortions objection, their objections to zoning principally turn on equity and transactional efficiency arguments. Many critics suggest that zoning produces some distortions in land use decisions. . . .

Jane Jacobs' classic critique of zoning[77] might be considered a sociological variant on the distortions argument. Jacobs argues that healthy, lively, innovative, and economically dynamic cities are founded upon diversity within their neighborhoods. Zoning renders cities sterile and uncreative, by stifling the diversity of land uses within neighborhoods and generally segregating land uses by type. Thus, to Jacobs, zoning distorts the natural allocation of land use within cities in a way that is detrimental not only to economic innovation and growth but also to the flowering of culture and the natural pleasures of city life.

IV. ZONING: ANOTHER LOOK

A. Zoning To Protect The Neighborhood Commons

This article contends that both supporters and critics of zoning have misconceived the nature of zoning. Zoning is only partially about protecting individual property owners against the effects of "spillovers" or negative externalities that adversely affect the market values of their property. Specifically, zoning protects a homeowner's consumer surplus in a home and in the surrounding neighborhood, that lies above the market value of that home. This consumer surplus has essentially been overlooked and is fundamental to an understanding of zoning.

. . . .

Although typically not addressed in the literature, which generally discusses only objectively measurable market values, the notion of consumer surplus in an individual parcel of property is quite straightforward. The concepts of "home" in general, and "home ownership" in particular, are areas where consumer surplus are particularly important. What distinguishes a mere "house" from a "home" is the consumer surplus we have in the latter. "Home" provides continuity, security, familiarity, and comfort for our most intimate and satisfying life experiences. The intimately bound ideas of home and family strike deep emotional chords in our culture. Since most people feel that these values cannot be reduced to dollars, people tend to be especially sensitive when the use and enjoyment of the home is threat-

---

[77] JANE JACOBS, THE DEATH AND LIFE OF GREAT AMERICAN CITIES (1961).

ened. In part, this reflects the importance of a homeowner's financial stake, which typically represents a substantial part of that homeowner's net worth. If the only concern were to protect financial investments, however, monetary compensation for any loss of market value would be acceptable. Part of zoning's appeal lies in the fact that it allows homeowners to protect *all* the value we place in a home, including the consumer surplus that lies above and beyond the market price of the home.

The failure of zoning's critics to account for the importance of "home" to the homeowner suggests that their critiques are based on an incomplete cost-accounting. But the notion of individuals' consumer surplus in their homes, by itself, is not sufficient to explain or justify zoning. An adequate account of zoning must also deal with the *collective* values zoning seeks to protect. Zoning is a device that protects a neighborhood from encroachments by land uses inconsistent with its character, regardless of the positive or negative effects of a proposed development on the market values of individual properties.

Neighborhoods are not just made up of individual parcels, but include collective resources comprising a neighborhood commons, and the property rights of an urban neighborhood dweller typically consist both in specified rights in an individual dwelling and inchoate rights in a neighborhood commons. This commons consists of open-access (but use-restricted) communally-owned property, such as streets, sidewalks, parks, playgrounds, and libraries. It also includes restricted-access but communally-owned property, such as public schools, public recreational facilities, and public transportation facilities.

It further includes privately-owned "quasi-commons" to which the public generally is granted access, but with privately-imposed restrictions as to use, cost, and duration. These generally include restaurants, nightspots, theaters, groceries, and retail establishments. It will include (risking the appearance of an oxymoron) "private commons," like churches, temples, private schools, political organizations, clubs, and fraternal and civic organizations. These are essentially private associations, but are characterized by some substantial degree of open access to members of the community. Finally, the neighborhood commons will include other intangible qualities such as neighborhood ambiance, aesthetics, the physical environment (including air quality and noise), and relative degrees of anonymity or neighborliness.

These features together make up the "character" of a neighborhood. They are what give the neighborhood its distinctive flavor. A purchaser of residential property in an urban neighborhood buys not only a particular parcel of real estate, but also a share in the neighborhood commons. Typically, differences in the neighborhood commons may be as crucial to a decision to purchase as differences in individual parcels.

To some extent, differences in the neighborhood commons will be reflected in the market values of individual parcels. If, for example, other things being equal, neighborhood A has better public schools and more desirable parks than neighborhood B, property in neighborhood A will have a higher market value than similar property in neighborhood B. But because different people value different features in a neighborhood, not all such neighborhood differences will be reflected in property values.

. . . .

Apart from consumer surplus, even those neighborhood features that are capitalized in market value come in different mixes from neighborhood to neighborhood. I may be more concerned about parks and less concerned about public transportation, and you vice-versa. While better parks and better public transportation may both make positive contributions to market values, I may prefer a neighborhood with good parks and mediocre public transportation, while you prefer a neighborhood with good public transportation and mediocre parks. Properties in the two neighborhoods may be similarly priced, but you and I will place entirely different values on the characteristics unique to each neighborhood.

Some neighborhood differences are simply inconsistent. For example, I might prefer a quiet, neighborly, low-density neighborhood of single-family homes, with access to parks and good neighborhood schools; you might prefer the faster pace, excitement and anonymity of a high-rise condominium in a high-density neighborhood featuring interesting restaurants, bistros, music venues, and trendy boutiques. Yet my house and your condo may have identical market values because some people are willing to pay the same price for my house as others are willing to pay for your condominium. In this example, the individual properties are themselves not interchangeable, but additional subjective value attaches to the features of the neighborhood that we each find desirable.

However, some of the same neighborhood features that add value to your property in your neighborhood might detract value from my property in my neighborhood. A hot new jazz club, for example, might be a welcome addition in your lively, trendy neighborhood, but would be a nuisance in my quiet neighborhood. To some extent, the spillover effects on your individual property are different; noise, traffic congestion, and heavy pedestrian traffic are presumably of less concern to you.

This example illustrates that *some* land uses are incompatible with the neighborhood commons that current property owners have come to rely on. It further illustrates that negative externalities are contextual. A land use that would have severe negative externalities in my neighborhood may be an amenity in your neighborhood.

It is not always the case, however, that inconsistent uses will lower *market* values. Suppose my quiet single-family neighborhood is located within a few blocks of some successful high-rise developments. Absent some system of land-use control, a developer might acquire the previously single-family parcels adjacent to mine, and proceed to put up more high-rises. The value of my *house* may go down because of spillover effects from the new high-rise, but the value of my *land* may increase, as my property becomes attractive as a potential site for additional high-rise developments. Under a market value based system, I would be entitled to no relief since my property is worth exactly what it was before. Yet under these circumstances many homeowners would feel aggrieved by this development. In part this is because the direct spillovers (e.g., noise and aesthetics) would interfere with the use and enjoyment of my home. To recoup that loss by selling my home would subject me to the additional cost and inconvenience of moving. More importantly, however, my loss of consumer surplus in this particular home would go uncompensated.

Additionally, my neighbors and I may be equally concerned about the effect of the new high-rise development on the neighborhood. The coming of the first high-rise means, at least initially, more intensive uses of the neighborhood commons (e.g., streets, sidewalks, on-street parking, public transportation facilities, etc.) which means that more people are competing for diminishing shares of fixed resources (e.g., on-street parking). Again, since land prices may rise, the result may be that I suffer no net financial loss. But what I suffer now (in addition to my uncompensated loss of consumer surplus in my own home) is a loss of consumer surplus in my interest in the neighborhood commons. In short, the neighborhood is taking the first step toward becoming something other than the neighborhood where I chose to live. Although difficult to place in quantitative terms, the loss is great.

What's wrong with this? Well, nothing, I suppose, unless you were that home-owner who had been quite happy with your home and neighborhood but now find them to be no longer what they were. Of course you can move, but it may not be easy (and in some crucial respects is impossible) to replicate those features of your old home and neighborhood that made your life what it was.

Zoning is aimed at preventing, or at least limiting, precisely these kinds of changes in the use of property that are disruptive of a neighborhood's character because they are inconsistent with current uses of the neighborhood commons. These include changes in density, as well as shifts from residential to commercial or industrial uses.

. . . .

This article has argued that, although ultimately we can never be certain, zoning may be welfare-maximizing. Since we must decide amidst uncertainty, we should choose the course that appears most likely to simultaneously protect the welfare of current neighborhood residents and reinforce community values, resources and institutions (which themselves contribute to the welfare of current and future neighborhood residents). We should also recognize that the limits of our knowledge mean that our initial choice of zoning regulations may sometimes be wrong. Sometimes a neighborhood may be willing to accept a proposed development not permitted by the regulations in exchange for other benefits. By limiting the terms of that bargain to community benefits, however, we retain community-reinforcing norms. Zoning thus can be seen as a peculiar kind of property rule—one in which developers can in limited ways "buy" the rights to develop contrary to the zoning entitlement, but only by compensating the community for its loss.

In this idealized model zoning gives current neighborhood residents a kind of "right of prior appropriation" over the neighborhood commons. This right trumps the right of other property owners to use their land in ways that interfere with, or are inconsistent with, current uses of the neighborhood commons. Developments may proceed as long as they are either consistent with current uses of the neighborhood commons, or in ways the neighborhood has agreed in advance (through the political process) to allow. This protects the expectations of neighborhood residents. Moreover, neighborhood residents have the right to change course and to agree to modify the rules to permit developments facially inconsistent with the presumptive prohibitions. But the only compensation that may be offered or accepted for such exceptions is compensation that benefits the community as a whole, i.e., that preserves a healthy and vibrant commons.

B. Normative Implications

This analysis has several further normative implications. First, zoning should not be understood solely as a means of protecting property market values. Instead, it protects values that may be only partially captured in market values. Second, it suggests that zoning should not be understood principally as a tool of rational/scientific urban planning. Indeed, the visions of planning bureaucrats may sometimes stand in sharp contrast to the values of neighborhood residents, who seek to protect the neighborhood in which they have chosen to live. This analysis further suggests that rather than seeking to impose a rigid uniformity over all residential neighborhoods, zoning should seek to accommodate diversity among neighborhoods.

Not all neighborhoods are alike, nor should they be. The whole point of urban land use zoning is to allow people to live in the kind of neighborhood they want. Imposed uniformity defeats that goal. Some residential neighborhoods, for example, may be more tolerant of certain kinds of, or higher concentrations of, commercial activities than others. Thus a zoning scheme should be designed with a sensitivity toward the neighborhood context, taking into account the particular needs, interests, and desires of the residents of particular neighborhoods.

A zoning scheme also should not attempt to freeze a neighborhood in time. Despite the apparent conservatism inherent in the notion of "protecting" a neighborhood against inconsistent changes in land uses, this does not imply that all changes are unwelcome. For instance, a new restaurant may be entirely consistent with neighborhood residents' vision of the kind of neighborhood in which they have chosen to live, while a new liquor store may be inconsistent with that vision. A properly designed zoning scheme should attempt to predict, from consultation with current neighborhood residents, what kinds of changes would be welcome in a particular neighborhood and accommodate those changes while presumptively (though not conclusively) ruling out other changes.

. . . .

This underscores the need for flexibility in zoning. Zoning should accommodate changes over time, through mechanisms that encourage individual variances and amendments when supported by neighborhood residents, as well as periodic comprehensive updates of the zoning scheme to reflect larger-scale shifts in neighborhood values.

C. Zoning And Bargaining

A zoning scheme, because it is inherently rule-like, may appear fundamentally incompatible with this kind of fine-grained contextual sensitivity to neighborhood preferences and flexible accommodation of changes over time. Rather than conceiving of zoning as consisting of legislative-type rules, we should under-stand zoning as establishing mere presumptions or baseline rules that precipitate and provide a convenient substantive starting point for negotiations between developers and representatives of neighborhood interests.[134]

. . . Zoning . . . can actually facilitate such bargaining and reduce information costs (an important part of transaction costs) in several ways.

Foremost, zoning establishes brightline rules under which some categories of land uses are automatically permitted. As a practical matter, bargaining is therefore unlikely to be necessary in these cases. . . .

Secondly, zoning establishes categories of proposed land uses which are presumptively prohibited, signaling to the developer that the proposed development must win approval of the municipality, acting as the neighborhood's representative, in order to proceed. The developer will then bargain for such approval (so long as the developer expects the costs of such bargaining, including both transaction costs and the costs of any additional concessions likely to be required to win approval, will be less than the benefits to the developer of the proposed development).

Third, by empowering an identifiable party to grant variances, amendments, and/or wholesale revisions of the zoning scheme, the zoning ordinance identifies a single party with whom the developer can initiate bargaining without the need to identify and bargain individually with all potentially affected homeowners. This promotes efficiency of both time and money.

Fourth, by placing bargaining power directly in the hands of elected officials (or, alternatively, in the hands of persons accountable to elected officials) zoning creates political incentives for the neighborhood's representative to bargain on the neighborhood's behalf.

Finally, by initiating such bargaining, zoning opens channels for the transfer of information between the developer and the neighborhood. The neighborhood acquires the necessary information about the proposed development needed to gauge whether the proposed development is consistent with neighborhood interests, while the developer learns more about the needs and interests of the neighborhood and can gauge whether, given the costs and benefits, it is sensible to proceed. Thus, zoning can actually reduce transaction costs, by supplying and channeling information useful to both community residents and potential developers.

D. Zoning As A Participatory Democracy

The core functions of zoning can best be served if zoning is decentralized and participatory. A decentralized and participatory neighborhood zoning process, which gives neighborhood residents a direct voice in zoning decisions affecting their neighborhood, is critical for several reasons. First, neighborhood residents, not

---

[134] *See* Carol Rose, *Planning and Dealing: Piecemeal Land Controls as a Problem of Local Legitimacy*, 71 CALIF. L. REV. 837 (1983) . . . .

planners or elected officials, are in the best position to evaluate their own consumer surplus in their homes and in their neighborhoods. To the extent zoning is designed to protect these values, the most effective way to elicit that information is through residents' participation in neighborhood zoning decisions. Second, decentralized and participatory zoning is essential to shift zoning decision-making out of the "interest group" paradigm—in which neighborhood residents are just one of a number of competing interest groups, and a weak and disorganized one at that—into something more akin to the "median voter" model in which decision-making more clearly reflects neighborhood preferences. Third, . . . citizen participation is essential to combat bribery and the corrupting influence of political contributions by developer interests.

. . . .

E. Corruption And Favoritism In Zoning

The problems of corruption and favoritism . . . must be addressed in any normative account of zoning. To some extent, these are problems associated with government generally, and especially local government. . . .

I submit that zoning, while a particularly important power of local government, is not so different from other powers and institutions of local government. We should be concerned about corruption and work to eradicate it. Our response to corruption in other areas, in the form of swift and tough prosecution of offenders, more effective policing, institutional safeguards, and requirements of openness in transactions, should apply here as well. Zoning may also require special policing, for example, through a special state agency with broad investigatory powers, established solely to monitor and investigate zoning corruption cases.

Ultimately, as with other avenues of municipal corruption, what matters most is effective policing from the bottom up through effective participatory democracy. . . . [O]n the whole, graft becomes impossible (or at least ineffective, and therefore not worthwhile for the developer) under the watchful eyes of the citizenry and its active involvement in the zoning process.

. . . .

V. CONCLUSION

This article has argued that, by limiting their analyses of zoning costs and benefits to monetizable values, both defenders and critics of zoning have substantially missed the mark. While zoning does have significant effects on the market values of individual parcels, and larger-scale economic consequences as well, a complete cost accounting must also consider zoning's role in protecting crucial, non-monetizable values. These include each homeowner's surplus in his or her home, as well as neighborhood residents' interest in preserving the unique set of common neighborhood resources—the neighborhood commons—upon which they rely. Far from being trivial, or mere ancillary values, "home" and "neighborhood" are central components of our identities. Precisely because these values are notoriously insusceptible to objective valuation, we afford them property rule protection in the form of zoning laws.

Thus conceived as a means of protecting the legitimate interests of current neighborhood residents, zoning regulations should be flexible to change over time, sensitive to unique neighborhood concerns and contexts, and based upon a participatory process. Citizen participation both gives voice to the interests of current neighborhood residents and provides the most effective safeguard against corruption of the zoning process.

THE TWILIGHT OF LAND-USE CONTROLS: A PARADIGM SHIFT?
Charles M. Haar
30 U. Rich. L. Rev. 1011 (1996)*

. . . .

An Evolutionary Process

Change in land-use practices occurs at an uneven pace. The distance of nearly a century makes it difficult to comprehend today how radical and innovative was the first comprehensive zoning ordinance adopted by New York City in 1916. A culmination of the efforts of diverse, often contending, interest groups over many years, and shaped by the lively interchanges at the annual National Conferences on City Planning, the first zoning ordinances marked a revolutionary leap in the treatment of individual property rights. Even more startling is an ensuing reflection that all planning of land-uses must pass the test of constitutional scrutiny and that the validation of the extensive cutting into private property rights in *Euclid*[3] came during the heart of the *Lochner*[4] era of jurisprudence. . . .

Nevertheless, a relative quiescence has prevailed since that stormy period. What has persisted over the long history of land-use controls since the 1920s is a continuation of the equilibrium that the *Euclid* decision evoked. . . .

. . . .

In short, over an extended period of practice and of criticism, land-use law in the different states and municipalities proceeds on even course, between contending, but certainly not overwhelming, waves of "too far" or "not far enough."

---

*   Copyright © 1997. Reprinted by permission.

[3]   *See* . . . [Village of Euclid v. Ambler Realty Co.], 272 U.S. 365 [(1926)] (reducing the value of plaintiff's land from $10,000 to $2500 per acre).

[4]   *See* Lochner v. New York, 198 U.S. 45 (1905) (ruling that a New York law regulating the hours of bakery workers violated a fundamental right to contract).

Sometimes emotions run high over amendments and variances or the foray of a NIMBY (not in my back yard). Essentially, though, the stability of land-use controls is the striking factor—the system's ability to adapt to startlingly new transportation technologies, changes in financing and the flow of capital, even transformations of family values. Land-use controls continue to provide the setting in which cities and suburbs exist today.

. . . .

The Current Challenge: The Reiterated Need for Periodic Examination and Revision

. . . .

The reality of the assault upon land-use laws . . . from so many sides is hard to evaluate, often catching truths but pushing them to ideological distortions. Partisans are replete with slogans and cliches, pitting, on the one hand, the essentiality of private property in a democratic community against the despoliation of the landscape by ruthless exploiters. Nevertheless, do recent arguments against the current system have merit? Is there something essential being recognized here? Is the long period of stasis about to be punctuated by a sharp break?

As a prelude, it should be noted that the existing land-use legal system, sadly, does display soft underbellies that pose appropriate targets for invasion: questions aroused by sloppy draftsmanship; ordinances that are unclear in definition and ambiguous in defining responsibilities; and troubles deciphering the general intent of the enactor. Without much difficulty, one can point out vague declarations of principles in the city planning documents. Confusion is often encountered in the allocation of powers among zoning commissions, planning boards, landscape and design commissions, and the local legislatures. Even on the federalist level, the proper division among the national, state, regional, and local levels is continuously shifting and unclear.

More than sprucing up language or clarifying ambiguities spurs the current challenges. Strangely, and ironically, the local land-use control instrumentalities are under fire as a result of at least two pressures emanating from the national level.

One pressure is the emerging property entitlement emphasis. A recent series of Supreme Court opinions, *Lucas,*[10] *Nollan,*[11] and *Dolan,*[12] have propelled the Fifth Amendment of the Constitution to center stage. The opinions of Justice Antonin Scalia especially seek to employ the compensation knife to cut through government efforts to set a non-market framework for public and private development or, on the expansive side, to upset a community determination of the appropriate physical setting for urban and suburban existence. Issues involving property "takings" are prominent in the conservative agenda. Congress and various state legislatures seem to be following through with property rights bills, with varying diminutions

---

[10] Lucas v. South Carolina Coastal Council, 505 U.S. 1003 (1992).

[11] Nollan v. California Coastal Comm'n, 483 U.S. 825 (1987).

[12] Dolan v. City of Tigard, 512 U.S. 374 (1994).

in value requiring the balm of full compensation for property restrictions caused by environmental and land-use controls. The ultimate effect of reification of the bundle of property rights, but for the nuisance exception, is a chilling of planning innovations.

A second pressure arousing unease among adherents of the current system is a looming retreat by courts from the scope of lenient judicial review that has been the accepted standard since *Euclid*. The benevolent standard of reasonableness—a minimum threshold that is easily passed over by most land-use regulations—may be ending. Indeed, footnote three of *Nollan*[14] may someday be noted as the first shot of the counter-revolution.

   . . . .

The American Political Culture

Digging below the surface in order to understand the remarkable persistence of zoning, subdivision, and other land-use controls, one conclusion emerges surprisingly and starkly: land-use controls in the United States are truly representative of American culture, and fit tightly into the classical liberal tradition so prevalent in our political thinking at large.

   . . . .

. . . The typical zoning ordinance is a quintessential product of a series of pragmatic compromises; it finds working arrangements in situations where people disagree over particular choices; it emerges with a minimal *modus vivendi* for a pluralist undertaking. In sum, there is no overall framework of priorities. Like American society, zoning is profoundly middle-class and liberal in basic orientation toward rights and deeply Lockean in character. On the other hand, it seeks to absorb contending viewpoints of the existence of a public interest without shaking the core belief system. Consequently, land-use controls embody on a local scale, and in a physical sense, the national ambivalence and ambiguity. In addition, by not bringing conflicts out in the open, but seemingly adopting all views at one and the same time, the ordinances are again typically American in the desire not to highlight conflict or probe the darker side.

Hence, the appeal of zoning (as well as the reason for recent attacks upon it from those who resent the lack of dominance of their credo) lies in surface reconciling rather than repressing competing conceptions of the good life and rival notions of society's claims upon the individual property owner. The popularity of zoning lies in its melting pot quality: while it embodies the strand of local *democracy* and political and legal, if not economic, *equality*, its most powerful attachment is to a free market operated on by individual *liberties*. But, at the same time, the public interest of a larger society asserts itself. The constraints that judicial inter-

---

[14] 483 U.S. 825, 836 n.3 (1987) (stating, in part, "[w]e have required that the regulation 'substantially advance' the 'legitimate state interest' sought to be achieved.").

pretations of equality place on the democratic expression of local wills put the management of the resulting tensions at the heart of post-modern controls. Occasionally, the uneasy and imperfect coexistence of the three goals is out in the open; from time to time, the honeymoon of the three strands turns into a tense cohabitation.

. . . .

Some Specific Examples

. . . The following are a few prevalent examples of unifying compromise, carrying with them the underlying axiom of a continued dominance of the private sector, but slowed or modified by social restraints.

1. *Height and bulk restrictions* set by the zoning envelope obviously do cut into the private decision-maker's freedom. In the 1990s, one cannot build another Equitable Building in the Wall Street area of New York, concentrating 13,000 people in one block (plus casting a shadow on Trinity Church, a too symbolic dominance, perhaps, of the new money religion over the old). Under the zoning ordinance, skyscrapers will not be allowed to blot out the sky completely, yet corporations can build towering IBM and AT&T headquarters cheek-by-jowl on Madison Avenue. Profitable high rises are not extinct—although they cannot loom too high on the skyline.

2. *Zoning shapes the size and character of the community*, but not too extensively. Property values are to be respected and stabilized as far as possible. Ramapo[15] in the East, and Petaluma[16] on the opposite coast, with their growth plans, can limit the number of building permits they will issue, and force private development along lines of existing public infrastructure. Yet the timing-based restraint must be reasonable, the period limited in years, and self building of infrastructure allowed. Overall, any growth-system control must be slow-paced.

. . . .

3. *Dramatic changes in traditional Euclidean districting* that incorporate the design flexibility advocated by professional city planners occurred in the 1960s and 1970s. Ensconced within them are continued compromises. The arrival of planned unit developments, floating zones, development rights transfer, and cluster zoning can be cited as counterexamples of my thesis of slow-paced and evolutionary change in land-use controls. And they do present important modification of the traditional system. . . .

---

[15] *See* Golden v. Planning Bd., 285 N.E.2d 291 (N.Y. 1972), *appeal dismissed,* 409 U.S. 1003 (1972); John D. Landis, *Do Growth Controls Work? A New Assessment,* 58 J. AM. PLAN. ASS'N 489 (1992).

[16] *See* Construction Indus. Ass'n v. City of Petaluma, 522 F.2d 897 (9th Cir. 1975), *cert. denied,* 424 U.S. 934 (1976).

The new techniques widen the range of the operation of individual liberty, with the size of the physical tract making feasible new land development arrangements. . . .

4. *Localism is rampant*, attachment to grass roots and closeness to neighborhoods is the chosen course in the United States for exercise of the restrictive land-use power. Local preeminence flows from the classical notion of limited and decentralized power. Increasingly, however, evolutionary change may increase its hold, as this tenet becomes subject to review by state courts and by state legislative mandates to take local spillovers and externalities into account.

This raises a sharp conflict in the system. Implementation of housing and land policies is clustered at the local level. Over the long-run, however, metropolitan solutions (whether by regional agencies or by state governments) seem to be the only ways to solve pressing environmental, social, and economic problems. . . .

More precisely, as several state courts are gingerly advocating, suburbs need to shoulder low-income housing responsibilities; and, as part of regional land policies and regional economic development, pay for the fair share of the costs derived from the benefits of their siting within the metropolitan area. Most dramatically, the general welfare attack on exclusionary zoning by the *Mount Laurel*[21] cases may foster a new attitude toward class and race relations. Land needs to be made available at prices that are affordable for moderate and low-income housing. Calls for equality will intrude on democracy and individualism.

5. *The countervailing force of neighborhood groups and participatory democracy*—forces uniquely at play in the land-use control area—can subvert the purported supremacy of local legislative sovereignty. From the outset, the Standard Zoning Enabling Act provided that no regulation would become effective until after a public hearing, at which parties in interest and citizens should have an opportunity to be heard. Especially with NIMBYs and affordable housing, can subgroups apply pressures for excluding unwanted uses or for expansion of desirable facilities. Citizen associations are quite powerful. The introduction of mandated citizen review boards is a way of controlling bureaucratic power, but it legitimizes conflicting pulls that will shatter temporary equilibria, often to replace them with assertions of private property rights.

6. *Segregation of uses*—the essence of zoning—has dark overtones in certain contexts, such as the segregation of users, rather than uses. As early as 1917, overly blatant divisions were outlawed by the courts. But more sophisticated and indirect controls, such as minimum acreages or overzoning industrial land, have escaped the

---

[21] *See, e.g.,* Southern Burlington County NAACP v. Township of Mount Laurel (*Mount Laurel II*), 456 A.2d 390 (N.J. 1983); Southern Burlington County NAACP v. Township of Mount Laurel (*Mount Laurel I*), 336 A.2d 713 (N.J.), *appeal dismissed and cert. denied,* 423 U.S. 808 (1975).

judicial lens. Too often the public power has been deployed to divide communities in ways antithetical to the American Dream. Gated suburbs, surrounded by legal walls of exclusionary zoning, are a blot on the domestic scene. . . .

. . . .

This difficult and troubling aspect of land-use controls needs a resolution that may prove wrenching to the traditional delegation of land-use powers to the small units of government; avoiding the serious social strains by an agreement to tiptoe around race and class issues is a fantasy—and the movement for environmental justice is but the latest push toward greater openness over submerged misuses of land-use powers. . . .

7. The overriding of individual property owners through *the exercise of the compulsory acquisition power* may seem a contradiction of the theme of Lockean prevalence. Yet the justification for the modern extensive broadening of the public use doctrine, and the most difficult arena for repealing contrary precedent, is recycling by another private developer of property taken from a private owner. Facing the quandary of upholding a taking of land by an authority that would then turn it over not to another public agency, but to a private owner, Justice Douglas, in *Berman v. Parker*,[27] had to content us with a legal fiction, one that refused to look beyond the iron curtain of the taking and so could disregard the ultimate disposition and resting place of the land. Again, the various federal and state urban redevelopment legislations, and the ensuing variants of judicial justifications for broad exercises of the eminent domain power, even with the payment of just compensation, can be argued to be indirect ways of extending the individual sovereign powers of selected private sector developers. . . .

8. The nature of the *local comprehensive plan* that enunciates future land policies and sets out the vision that is to guide the implementing regulations in practice too often turns into an American compromise. From the outset, the draftsmen of the Standard Planning Enabling Act have been divided on the extent and type of private development that should fall within the ambit of the plan. The debate concerns whether public planning should go beyond the spatial. The diametrically opposite versions of Bettman (planning entails social and economic factors) and of Basset (land-use planning relates to physical aspects alone) appear with equal force in the same standard planning statute, coexisting in an incredible contradiction. This ambiguity persists throughout the enactment of state enabling statutes.

Huge investments are required to produce the dwelling units and the infrastructures—another name for the economists' "public goods"—that turn a series of individual homes into a neighborhood. This concentrates attention on the physical aspects of development. Since externalities are more obvious, government intervention also seems safer with respect to accepted tenets than does broad-scale planning. Perhaps, also, competence on the part of administrative agencies is more

---

[27] 348 U.S. 26 (1954).

prevalent in design components. When the need for a powerful emotional impetus to budge any rigidities of a social system is added to these considerations, it becomes clear why emphasizing the physical setting of land-use controls becomes so appealing. Clearance of physical blight, with its call for the eradication of dilapidated housing and slums, arouses a middle-class constituency. This is also more likely to receive the approval of reviewing courts as being indeed a constitutional public use. Furthermore, it means that the subtleties, contradictions, and intractabilities of human nature do not have to be taken into account by blunt government action. How else can one explain the apparent naivete of the belief, held by many of the originators of urban renewal, that by tearing down deteriorating structures, they would transform people's lives; and that somehow, by blotting out the visible physical evil and substituting new forms of concrete structures, urban life would be enhanced? Fortunately, awareness of the economic, social, and even racial consequences of physical siting and location is emerging in public opinion polls; however, ambivalence still persists as to how wide the community may cast its net.

. . . .

9. The efficiency of the Adam Smith market has yielded on other occasions in consideration of land-use problems. Urban land's monopolistic nature makes *the need for a safety net* more obvious. The admission is widespread that the ruthless market needs to be tempered by the needs of disadvantaged groups. This can be achieved through techniques such as inclusionary zoning, development exaction fees, linkages, and low-income housing density bonuses. The general belief in economic growth is modified in these cases to protect those who otherwise suffer from change. Contempt for the economically disadvantaged and politically disenfranchised characteristic of a social Darwinism in other areas of economic activity is tempered in the land-use area. Consequently, the controls are often shaped, and even initiated, by this realization, and they further justify extending actions by governments.

Part and Parcel of the System

All of these examples illustrate that zoning, as an outcrop and interpretation of American political thought and culture, is nowhere near a substitution of a collectivist ethos for individual decision-making over land. . . .

. . . Zoning is an effort to mediate opposing conceptions of the good. Within this typical American approach, zoning neither clearly establishes liberal values, nor espouses communitarian values.

Nor have land-use controls come to a final resting point concerning the deference to be paid to popular democracy. Zoning is the Mozart of adjustment. No institution does it better. It establishes a shifting balance that is temporary in nature, but at the same time a fixed balance. The theory of the untrammelled market seems dominant, but having let the genie of public interest out of the bottle, it cannot be shoved back in no matter how impassioned the later efforts. . . .

. . . .

The Positive Side: Enter the Joint Venture

One evolutionary trend may ultimately bring about sharp changes. This trend is widening the scope of controls by emphasizing the "welfare" term of the police power quartet. In the marketplace of ideas, zoning can be justified as expunging imperfections in the market, rather than replacing it wholesale or interfering with its operations. The real estate market is traditionally an inefficient one—primarily local, characterized by imperfect knowledge of supply and pricing, and dominated by lack of data or awareness of national trends. Hence there is a need for legislative enactment to rectify these shortcomings, but one that still owes allegiance to the untrammelled theory of the market. My guess is that, though far short of a revolutionary break such as repeal, society is ready to move the equilibrium further than in the past, most particularly against the prevailing legal constraint of a separation between the public and private worlds.

Recognition of affirmative potentials may provide the more likely impetus for rewriting the current agenda. It is the positive side, the potential of land-use planning and ordinances operating in conjunction with the Lockean owner, by way of enhancement and of synergies, that may differentiate newly emerging land-use controls from the compromises of the past. . . .

. . . .

It is too early to say whether the joint-venture approach is for better or worse. The marriage of market and regulatory strategies rests on different but complementary conceptions: business as the motor force in our capitalist economy and the developer of metropolitan land; and government as public conscience, minor market manipulator, and, in areas where the profit motive cannot work, the purveyor of funds or the initiator of programs. The traditional attachment to private enterprise—and the force of its constituent lobbies—leads not to complete substitution of public goals for those of the private decision-maker, but rather to the stimulation of joint participations.

. . . .

At its most complex, the joint-venture format has come to mean cooperation among three significant groups: private developers and lenders, local municipal and state governments, and relevant federal agencies. Ideally, bargains struck among them can result in coexistence of private profits and public benefits. It should be noted that gains would be made in each sector that could not be obtainable through individual efforts alone. As experience has introduced the reality principle, the approach explicitly encourages participants to pursue their own ends as they best envision them—a reinterpretation of self-interested maximization that is the settled norm in the society—redeemed by the belief that a framework of properly designed programs, through a coordination process, will produce benefits for everyone.

. . . .

Cultural change would have to accompany, indeed precede, legal change. A prerequisite for success of a joint venture program is overcoming business disdain of government and government distrust of business. Moreover, the time has come for modifying the corrosive pessimism over local government will and capacities.

A principal task for government is to win over the average developer by eliminating genuine fear of administrative bureaucracy, red tape, delays, and perceived inefficiency—especially when actions of several levels of government are required. The public sector can take two major steps to encourage the joint-venture approach: (1) streamlining local land-use controls and federal regulatory procedures, and (2) developing a cohesive institutional strategy in its comprehensive plan formulation. Realignment and coordination among city and federal departments that influence land development, coupled with a simplified application and approval procedure, could increase private support, understanding, and participation.

At the same time, the private sector must work to gain the trust of a government wary of its continuous pushing of the zoning envelope, overexploitation of infrastructure, red-lining practices, poor management, and undertones of ethnic or racial discrimination. Developers need to understand, and work to achieve, the social goals of a project while keeping their eye on the bottom line. This may require prodding. Voluntary, cooperative solutions are difficult to maintain. While some corporations may be considering environmental values in making pollution decisions, they do so, at least in part, because of laws and sanctions regulating pollution.

. . . .

Finally, the need at strategic moments for direct government intervention and decision-making for human settlements grows more clearly recognized, even by a Lockean private-property oriented society. The imperfections of the private land market, set forth glaringly by the absence of affordable housing, are all too obvious in the metropolitan area. Thus, one should keep in mind the use of urban development corporations, or metropolitan land-bank associations equipped with eminent domain powers to compulsorily acquire land, and authority to either (1) package large-scale, mixed-use land developments for private investments, or (2) actually carry entire projects themselves. They may be the next evolutionary phase of controls. Ultimately, the joint-venture organization of metropolitan land development challenges the capacity and willingness of a society to engage in deliberate social change.

Where public tax funds or exercises of sovereign powers enhance land value, recapture by society of some proportion of values generated by its efforts should be acknowledged. This will also be the test of the new forms of joint-venture controls. If planning and land-use controls cannot prove that they pay for themselves either by compensating those property owners who have to undergo the costs of use restrictions, or by making an economic return on infrastructure investments or joint ventures, then there is little reason for them to put forth claims in a world of limited resources. Hence, public efficiency has to be added to distributive goals if communitarian values are to play a stronger role in the post-Lockean society of the joint venture.

Conclusion

. . . .

Public action, in the form of land-use controls, is unavoidable in the provision of infrastructure generated by existing and proposed transportation and utilities systems, the availability and affordability of housing, the revitalization of central cities, and the coping with emerging regional environmental needs. Again, large-scale undertakings are too intimidating to the private sector without subsidies, incentives, or guarantees. This also means prevention of potential conflicts in land-uses (when the nuisance equitable anticipatory injunction is not available). Only through the action of the community can the demands for a better life, and the need for a vision in the physical setting of the metropolitan area, be met. The police power enables society to uniformly regulate a wide variety of land-use activities in order to protect the health, safety and general welfare of the citizenry. The empirical experience denies drastic revision or repeal of the land-use regulatory system as a realistic option. *Gotterdämmerung* on the operatic stage, yes; in real life developments, no.

. . . .

. . . [T]he long period of stasis in land-use controls is not about to be interrupted by abrupt change. The call for expanded private property rights is especially simplistic. The task of the next decades is not that of total recasting of the land-use and environmental systems with an earlier halcyon form of market ordering, but to improve and enhance the present structure so that it continues the evolutionary pattern of meeting the needs of continually evolving economic and social arrangements.

MOVING TOWARD THE BARGAINING TABLE: CONTRACT ZONING, DEVELOPMENT AGREEMENTS, AND THE THEORETICAL FOUNDATIONS OF GOVERNMENT LAND USE DEALS
Judith Welch Wegner
65 N.C. L. Rev. 957 (1987)[*]

I. INTRODUCTION

Market-oriented approaches to land use management have generated considerable interest among legal scholars in recent years. Proponents of deregulation urge local governments to limit sharply their intervention in the workings of real estate markets. . . .

Others reason that local governments must continue to assume responsibility for land use control, but argue that traditional regulatory approaches should be reformed to mirror more closely the functioning of the market. A number of scholars and practitioners have probed the practical benefits attainable through use of bargaining as a means of resolving land use disputes;[4] they view the public role in establishing site-specific development controls and obligations as an exercise in mediating private disputes.[5] Recent legal scholarship has contributed significantly to this discussion by developing a jurisprudential basis for government land use "dealing," that is, mediation activity that allocates rights among competing private claimants.[6] The theoretical foundations for government land use deals, however, remain far from complete.

To describe the dynamic of government-citizen-developer decisionmaking as "dealing" raises a fundamental question concerning the character of such government activity: Does the activity remain wholly the exercise of police power authority, or does it somehow implicate the government's contracting power? . . .

---

[*]   Copyright 1987, North Carolina Law Review Association, reprinted with permission.

[4]   *See, e.g.*, J. KIRLIN & A. KIRLIN, PUBLIC CHOICES—PRIVATE RESOURCES 59-74 (California Tax Found. 1985) (discussing consequences of increased bargaining that reallocates responsibility for financing capital infrastructure); MANAGING DEVELOPMENT THROUGH PUBLIC/PRIVATE NEGOTIATIONS (R. Levitt & J. Kirlin ed., Urb. Land Inst. and American Bar Ass'n 1985) (discussing negotiation techniques and strategies, and related issues); T. SULLIVAN, RESOLVING DEVELOPMENT DISPUTES THROUGH NEGOTIATIONS 25 (1984) (explaining hypothesis that "the results of ad hoc efforts to resolve development disputes encourage a wider use of negotiations either as a complement to the existing structures for resolving conflicts, or as an alternative path that citizens and government officials may find attractive for certain classes of disputes"); Butler & Myers, *Boomtime in Austin, Texas*, AM. PLAN. A., Autumn 1984, at 477-78; Kmiec, *The Role of the Planner in a Deregulated World*, LAND USE L. & ZONING DIG., June 1982, at 4.

[5]   *See, e.g.*, Rose, *Planning and Dealing: Piecemeal Land Controls as a Problem of Local Legitimacy*, 71 CALIF. L. REV. 837, 891 (1983) (advocating adoption of "mediation" jurisprudence in which "dealing" is a natural part of dispute resolution process). . . .

[6]   *See* Rose, *supra* note 5 (distinguishing between traditional plan jurisprudence and mediation jurisprudence that explains legitimacy of piecemeal changes in land use controls).

Adoption of a "dealing" methodology also raises questions concerning the continued need for standards that ensure fairness and efficiency of outcomes. "Dealing" has a number of potential benefits. It allows for individualized decisions that take into account the unique features of a particular parcel or project and the availability of measures capable of mitigating adverse land use effects. A carefully tailored set of land use requirements based on a bargaining process may be fairer than traditional regulation: rather than simply treating roughly similar land equally, it takes into account specific characteristics and problems that justify variations from a potentially overbroad norm. Furthermore, the bargaining process may be more efficient because it facilitates cost-efficient outcomes and substitutes a potentially cheaper decisionmaking process that fosters prompt and amicable compromises while avoiding the costs attendant to protracted administrative and judicial appeals.

Yet dealing is not without its perils. Unfair or inefficient outcomes may result from imbalances in power or skill that either distort the dealings of participating parties, or result in failures to consider the interests of affected nonparticipants. In extreme cases involving government parties, power imbalance may result in the creation of "naked preferences," that is, the treatment of one group or person different from another solely because of a raw exercise of political power in the absence of a broader and more general justification or public value. Such preferences may take various forms including preferences favorable to the government itself or the public as a whole (public abuse), or those favorable to individuals or a small segment of the community (private abuse). Decisionmakers and courts accordingly need standards as they seek either to avoid such perils at the outset, or to resolve legitimate challenges after the fact. At the same time, such standards may have to be shaped to ensure that the potential benefits associated with the dealing methodology can in fact be gained.

Finally, to ensure that dealing provides a truly fair and efficient system of dispute resolution, attention must focus not only on threshold issues of deal creation, but also on issues of noncompliance. . . .

. . . .

II. Lessons From the Contract Clause

Analysis of the theoretical framework governing public-private land use deals should begin with a consideration of the Contract Clause of the United States Constitution, a provision which specifies that "No State shall . . . pass any . . . Law impairing the Obligation of Contracts."[12] . . .

. . . .

---

[12] U.S. Const. art. I, § 10, cl. 1.

A. *Characterization of Public-Private Relationships*

. . . .

The Contract Clause . . . offers a first basic lesson: The characterization of public-private relationships may involve a subtle analysis of factors such as legislative language, circumstances surrounding government action including its purpose and effect, the parties' expectations including the consideration afforded, and causation-reliance links. This lesson provides a framework for further analysis in the context of land use dealing.

B. *Development and Application of Standards*

Contract Clause cases also establish certain criteria that determine whether the blend of contract and police powers that infuses many public-private relationships is basically legitimate or fundamentally flawed. This facet of Contract Clause theory is often described as the "reserved powers" doctrine.[31] . . .

. . . .

At least two lessons may be drawn from the reserved powers doctrine. First, the coalescence of certain factors suggests an incompatible blending of contract and police powers that may give a court grounds for invalidating a resulting relationship: the absence of reasonably clear government authority, marginal or unwarranted private expectations, and a strong, circumstance- and time-dependent public interest that has been affected adversely. At the same time, however, the criteria are notably ambiguous. In any given case it may be extremely difficult to judge and balance the clarity of authority, reasonableness of expectations and inherent adverseness of effects on important public interests. Taken together, however, these lessons indicate that the question of fundamental incompatibility must be addressed thoughtfully and flexibly in the course of developing an appropriate theoretical framework to govern land use deals.

C. *Noncompliance Issues*

Contract Clause precedent suggests that special rules may be needed to address noncompliance issues that arise in connection with public-private deals. . . .

---

[31] This Article uses the phrase "reserved powers doctrine" to refer to the rule that state and local governments lack the capacity, at the outset, to enter into contracts that convey away certain of their sovereign powers, including the police power. . . .

. . . .

1. Threshold Level of Noncompliance: Rules About Impairment

The United States Constitution does not prohibit noncompliance with contracts; it only bars "impairment" of contractual obligations. This language has accordingly provided a vehicle for decisions requiring some threshold level of noncompliance before a constitutional violation occurs. . . .

. . . .

A review of the impairment doctrine . . . offers the following critical lesson: It may be appropriate or necessary in the interest of public policy to distinguish between types or levels of interference with private expectations that result in the event of government noncompliance with contractual obligations. Considerable difficulty, however, may accompany such distinctions, particularly when they concern public-private agreements.

2. Justification of Noncompliance: The Role of the Police Power

A major issue in Contract Clause litigation has been whether any justifications immunize government action in derogation of contract rights from constitutional challenge. . . .

. . . .

In effect . . . the [Supreme] Court has recognized that at times government action in derogation of public contract rights may be justified, but only under circumstances that reflect an appropriate balance between the need to respond to police power concerns and the obligation to avoid public and private abuse of that power. Inquiry regarding the purpose of government action assures that a public purpose exists, not the private purpose of a narrow faction that seeks to employ the police power for selfish ends to the disadvantage of another small segment of the community. By scrutinizing closely the impact on private expectations, courts can conduct a reasoned analysis of the extent to which private property rights are implicated, and they can make an informed judgment concerning the fairness of any proposed accommodations between private property rights and the police power. Perhaps most significantly, the "reasonable and necessary" facet of the Court's analysis forces a government, which has entered into a contract, to demonstrate that a proposed modification represents an independent exercise of the police power dictated by changed circumstances and unforeseen events; furthermore, the Court's analysis requires that public necessity dictated the government's decision, not the mere convenience of shifting an additional burden to a bargaining partner who may be an easy target for the imposition of public costs.

The role of police power justifications for noncompliance likewise offers useful lessons in developing a theoretical framework to govern public-private dealing. Public policy requires that government parties retain police power prerogatives for use notwithstanding binding contractual obligations. Careful assessment of the proposed exercise of that power is clearly needed, however, to ensure that governmental action results in an appropriate and nonabusive accommodation of public and private interests.

3. Remedies for Noncompliance

. . . .

Two major factors determine what remedies a court will award in the event of governmental noncompliance. First, the court must consider the nature of governmental noncompliance to determine whether the government party intended a simple breach of contract or whether, instead, it intended an outright repudiation of contractual obligations. If only a breach is involved, traditional compensatory relief in the form of a damages award remains available, while more extreme remedies may be provided in the event of a repudiation and resulting impairment, as discussed below. . . . .

If governmental noncompliance amounts to repudiation and impairment, rather than a simple contract breach, a second factor—whether the impairment is justified—must be considered. If an adequate justification for the government's action does exist—for example, if governmental noncompliance is based on a well-founded concern for public safety—the aggrieved private party can rely on neither damages nor declaratory or injunctive relief. On the other hand, if no justification exists to satisfy the "reasonable and necessary" test described above, the court will invalidate the government's noncomplying action and in effect require the government party to specifically perform its contractual agreement. . . . .

. . . .

III. CONTINGENT ZONING

. . . Rezoning decisions are a chronic source of litigation, because deeply held expectations of neighborhood stability are often at war with deep-seated desires for handsome profits, against a backdrop of uncertain jurisprudence and unpredictable judicial dispositions. Carefully constructed compromises that focus on the legitimate concerns of residents, developers, and local governments offer an appealing alternative.

Such compromises may take several forms and may be implemented in several different ways. Often it may be desirable to limit the types of use that may be made of particular property, notwithstanding the wider range of uses otherwise permissible in a given district: for example, residential neighbors may find a rezoning to commercial use more palatable if only certain types of uses are allowed. Other requirements might mitigate adverse environmental effects by, for example, restricting building placement or specifying that a property owner utilize buffering and landscaping. Alternatively, adverse effects on community infrastructure might be addressed by specifying that a property owner dedicate land, undertake construction, or contribute funds for road improvements or for other purposes. These and other compromises might be incorporated in express or implied agreements between a developer and a local government, in covenants between a developer and a neighborhood association, or in rezoning ordinances passed by local legislative bodies.

. . . .

A. *Characterization*

Courts and commentators to date have employed several different terms and phrases to characterize the type of land use deal just described. A number of courts have referred to rezoning decisions tied to explicit or implied government-private agreements as "contract zoning." Others have used the phrase "conditional zoning" as a means of characterizing decisions of this sort, commonly, but not universally, when no express agreement is present. Some courts and commentators have avoided these two basic catch phrases; in an effort to recast a troublesome doctrinal mold, they have adopted modified descriptors by, for example, focusing on the use of "unilateral contracts" or "concomitant" agreements.

Care must be taken in evaluating this body of precedent to determine whether the terminology adopted was intended to characterize the land use control mechanisms in question for purposes of defining the applicable theoretical framework, or whether instead, it was adopted for purposes of describing the ultimate disposition of the case. An examination of the cases supports the latter view. Early cases adopting the "contract zoning" terminology seemed intent to condemn the proposed arrangements on reserved powers as well as other grounds. . . . Courts deliberately chose the "conditional zoning" terminology, on the other hand, in contravention of the earlier designation as a means of describing rezoning arrangements perceived as legitimate. . . .

More full-blown consideration of the characterization question, however, may assist in the development of an overall theoretical framework. The Contract Clause doctrine previously discussed provides a useful benchmark for this purpose; it suggests that additional attention should focus on the legislative language, circumstances, and expectations associated with novel rezoning devices.

. . . .

This reasoning then leads to three key conclusions. First, all rezoning arrangements, with or without agreements, arise against a single backdrop provided by governing legislation, relevant circumstances, and the parties' expectations. Second, careful consideration suggests that all such arrangements are primarily regulatory in character, and the theoretical framework for their development and use should reflect that fact. Thus, this Article adopts the neutral term "contingent zoning" to describe all types of individualized rezoning arrangements, instead of the more traditional dichotomy "contract" and "conditional zoning" or the more recent references to "unilateral contracts" or "concomitant agreement zoning." A final conclusion follows from the first two: To the extent that contingent zoning arrangements run the gamut between involuntarily imposed conditions and bilateral agreements, all are potentially affected by the presence of a bargaining process. Thus, although governmental police power primarily shapes the theoretical framework governing such arrangements, it may also be appropriate to draw on contract principles or doctrine, or otherwise to modify the theoretical framework, to take this special feature into account.

B. *Standards*

. . . .

1. Per Se Invalidity

. . . .

Several prominent early cases, which involved both express and unstated agreements, condemned the contingent zoning device as per se invalid. Specifically, these courts concluded that zoning legislation failed to provide clear authority for adoption of a contingent zoning strategy, or that this strategy failed in various respects to conform to the literal terms of traditional zoning legislation. . . .

Other courts, including many of the more recent cases, have upheld contingent zoning in the face of charges of per se invalidity. These courts have concluded that traditional zoning legislation provided ample authority, and that textual restrictions designed to guide the implementation of other types of zoning simply did not apply. . . .

Courts that reject the per se invalidity argument clearly have the better view. Ample statutory authority exists in the form of traditional zoning legislation that may be construed to support this novel regulatory device. The key question instead is whether such authority should be narrowly or broadly construed. Many states have traditionally opted for narrow construction of enabling legislation to ensure against unwarranted action by local governments, but the present trend is toward a more expansive view of local government powers and a more generous interpretive view. A growing number of state legislatures have confirmed the wisdom of the latter position by adopting legislation specifically authorizing contingent zoning in at least some circumstances.

. . . .

2. Specific Standards

Courts rejecting the per se invalidity argument have developed procedural and substantive standards as a means of distinguishing between appropriate and inappropriate contingent zoning arrangements. . . .

a. Procedural Standards

Contingent zoning is employed within a well-defined procedural context. Statutes and ordinances establish detailed procedures, which rezoning decisions generally must follow. They require notice and an opportunity for a hearing, and special super-majority voting requirements may apply. . . .

. . . .

Along with these traditional requirements, the courts gradually have adopted what seem to be common-law criteria designed to guarantee the integrity of the contingent zoning process. Outcomes in many cases have been influenced significantly by factors that bear on the independence of the legislative body's judgment in reaching a contingent zoning decision. Thus, the character of express or implicit promises between the local government and the property owner often proves significant. It is much more likely that a unilateral promise, which the landowner makes contingent, of course, on the rezoning's becoming effective, would pass legal muster, than a bilateral promise in which the local government also agrees to take action, most probably to rezone. At times courts have invalidated bilateral agreements outright; they may also preserve the agreement but reinterpret the local government's pledge more narrowly, for example, by requiring only that rezoning be considered or that, once granted, it be subject to later change.

. . . .

b. Substantive Standards

Courts have also required that contingent zoning arrangements satisfy both traditional and more novel substantive standards. . . . To date, courts have inquired whether contingent rezoning is consistent with a jurisdiction's comprehensive plan, whether it is warranted in light of changed circumstances, and whether other substantive factors relevant to legitimate land use decisions weigh in favor of the proposed rezoning. . . . It appears, in any event, that the more numerous and qualifying the conditions required to insure the achievement of sound public policy, the more skeptical a court is likely to be in evaluating the resulting arrangement.

Courts have developed additional standards that focus on the particular conditions or obligations incorporated into a contingent zoning arrangement. In decisions to date, the courts have indicated that such conditions or obligations may be imposed only as a means of addressing public needs that result from development proposed in conjunction with the requested rezoning. Need may be measured in terms of adverse land use effects that require mitigation, or it may be based on demands for public services that must be addressed. Benefit to the affected landowner will not suffice as an alternative justification.

Perhaps not surprisingly, the cases appear to reflect subtly different approaches to the evaluation of need and the requisite relationship between need and conditions or obligations imposed. . . .

. . . .

C. *Noncompliance*

Contingent zoning arrangements impose many requirements that either necessitate immediate, one-time compliance, or create ongoing obligations deemed problematic from the outset. Accordingly, their validity has commonly been challenged under the theories just described as part of an appeal from the original disposition of a rezoning petition, rather than as part of litigation addressing subsequent noncompliance. In those few cases that have considered questions relating to noncompliance, however, the courts have generally varied very little from traditional police power doctrine.

. . . .

The courts' tendency to hew more closely to traditional doctrine when the landowner or local government does not comply contrasts sharply with their willingness to adopt more novel standards designed to govern dealing that results in the initial formulation and terms of contingent zoning arrangements. This approach might be explained in terms of relevant expectations: landowners should not and cannot reasonably expect that local governments will refrain from future rezoning under appropriate circumstances; similarly, governments should not and cannot expect that they can accomplish future rezonings without full-scale review. An equally plausible hypothesis, however, is that accommodations to facilitate a bargaining dynamic will be made only to the extent warranted in the public interest. In the context of contingent zoning, the formulation of individualized requirements and obligations may be significantly advanced by a process of individualized dealing, but no comparable need exists to vary rules concerning noncompliance and remedial norms. . . .

IV. DEVELOPMENT AGREEMENTS

Although contingent zoning primarily provides individualized answers to problems of incompatible uses and overstrained public facilities that arise in conjunction with rezoning decisions, deals and dealing methodology can be used to resolve a variety of other land use issues. For example, development agreements have been used to facilitate agricultural land preservation, to compensate for lost tax revenues, to foster community redevelopment, and to bolster available low and moderate income housing supplies. This part of the Article focuses on one particular type of development agreement—that which includes not only land use conditions and exaction obligations, but which also provides for municipal services and a regulatory freeze.[203] . . .

A. *Characterization*

The very phrase "development agreements" suggests that contract principles heavily influence the theoretical framework governing this device, including its initial characterization. This premise can best be evaluated with an eye to relevant statutes and analogous precedent, because little case law has directly assessed the legality of development agreements. The states of California, Hawaii, Nevada, and Florida have led the way in developing detailed legislation that authorizes the use of development agreements. . . .

. . . .

---

[203] Such agreements typically go further than contingent zoning arrangements and embody deals that fall outside the bounds of traditional police power requirements, both insofar as landowners agree to contribute more extensive exactions, and insofar as local governments make various concessions in return. . . .

. . . .

A strong case can be made for the proposition that development agreements undertaken pursuant to these statutory provisions give rise to rights properly characterized as contractual in nature. To date, writers have simply assumed this proposition. An examination of relevant language, circumstances, and expectations, as suggested by the earlier Contract Clause discussion, arguably confirms their view. . . .

. . . .

Before adopting this view, however, an alternative perspective should be considered. A respectable case can be made for the proposition that development agreements quite simply constitute a novel packaging of regulatory requirements, one that implicates very little contract doctrine. From this viewpoint the use of the language "development agreement" in statutes and ordinances creates a convenient term of art, without necessarily giving rise to doctrinal implications. Just as occurred in the contingent zoning context, in which agreements form but one facet of an all-encompassing regulatory context, development agreements embody detailed requirements that a local government might otherwise impose through an ordinary permit scheme . . . .

. . . .

Careful analysis thus indicates that development agreements may legitimately be seen as both contractual and regulatory in character. If this is indeed true, two parallel lines of precedent and related theoretical constructs may eventually emerge in litigation involving this land use device, much as has occurred in the contingent zoning context. A better, alternative approach would assume, at the outset, that development agreements possess a dual or hybrid character, and that standards and rules concerning noncompliance should be formulated with that character in mind.

B. *Standards*

1. Per Se Invalidity

. . . .

As was true with contingent zoning, a significant body of authority involving public-private agreements finds certain such agreements invalid per se. Many courts adopting this view have focused on the arguably problematic blend of contract and police powers that characterizes particular agreements. In contrast to the contingent zoning cases, and cases under the Contract Clause, these courts have stopped short of a full-blown consideration of statutory authority, the parties' expectations, and governmental interests; instead they have relied on traditional, but flawed, distinctions between governmental and proprietary functions as a means of resolving this initial question.

. . . .

. . . As happens in other areas in which the proprietary/governmental dichotomy has been used, such decisions may be criticized as arbitrary and inconsistent, and insufficiently sensitive to the full range of policy considerations that should shape the analysis.

Perhaps not surprisingly, in view of these serious flaws, other courts have adopted a case-by-case rather than a categorical approach that treats certain types of government contracts as invalid per se. These courts have tended to focus on one or more of the factors evident in Contract Clause analysis: the existence of adequate authority, the parties' expectations, and the governmental interest involved.

. . . .

. . . In sum, a significant body of case law recognizes that sensitive analysis on a case-by-case basis best serves critical policy concerns, rather than the categorical application of a rule of per se invalidity.

With this precedent in mind, it is possible to return to the difficult question whether regulatory freeze provisions included in many development agreements can be upheld in at least some instances. . . . The parties' expectations . . . support the recognition of the legitimacy of certain regulatory freezes. Development agreement legislation has authorized such freezes precisely because the common law vested rights and equitable estoppel doctrines had arguably failed to consider private development expectations adequately, particularly those that arose in connection with complex multistage projects. When the legislature has authorized a new strategy for establishing expectations, and the public and private parties have solidified such expectations in an individual case through appropriate public hearings, these expectations appear to be well and firmly fixed, at least absent materially changed circumstances that implicate significant health and safety concerns or other statutory exceptions. Government interests may also be well served by regulatory freezes in appropriate cases. Adoption of appropriate specific substantive standards can ensure that beneficial rather than adverse effects will result. The need to preserve essential police power prerogatives is better served by insistence on preservation of suitable discretion, rather than by the outmoded and insensitive dichotomy between governmental and proprietary activities. Similarly, the need to exercise the police power at a later time can be protected adequately by developing standards that limit the duration of regulatory freezes, or by permitting government noncompliance with agreements under special circumstances as described below. In short, ample reason exists to reject a rule of per se invalidity for regulatory freezes, and to adopt sound substantive standards as proposed in the following section.

2. Specific Standards

. . . .

a. Procedural Standards

Two major procedural issues have emerged in recent discussions of development agreements: (1) what procedural standards govern adoption of such agreements; and (2) to what extent may citizens use initiative and referendum procedures to prevent their implementation? Although procedural standards applicable to

development agreements are fairly clear, more uncertainty surrounds the availability of referendum and initiative procedures.

. . . .

b. Substantive Standards

. . . [S]tate legislation provides the relevant starting point for determining the
substantive standards that govern use of development agreements. Zoning enabling
legislation or local ordinances may include standards that control related decisions
to rezone or issue permits authorizing the use of land subject to a development
agreement. Development agreement legislation specifies that development agreements likewise must conform to underlying land use plans and policies, much as
common-law doctrine concerning contingent zoning required consistency with
the local government's comprehensive plan. Just as was true for contingent zoning,
additional careful thought must be given to the substantive standards needed to
ensure that individual facets of an agreement avoid the pitfalls of possible public
or private abuse. . . .

i. *Analytical Framework*

Development agreements tend to be even more multifaceted than contingent zoning arrangements. They may include not only promises by a developer to abide by
certain land use conditions or to make specified infrastructure contributions, but also
commitments by a government agency to provide public services and to freeze regulatory requirements. Moreover, each of these multiple promises may itself involve
a combination of obligatory and optional aspects—that is, aspects that embody
obligations of government agencies and private parties that would exist even in the
absence of a development agreement, as well as aspects that reflect a commitment to
undertake additional actions that would not be required under such circumstances.

Not surprisingly, therefore, a multifaceted, multidimensional approach to
developing and applying substantive standards appears necessary. As a first step,
individual promises or facets of the agreement must be considered in isolation to
determine to what extent obligatory and optional aspects have been included. In
making this determination, standards that traditionally govern the obligatory provision of public services, imposition of conditions and exaction requirements,
and protection of vested rights outside the development agreement context may be
employed. It is then possible to turn to a second stage of analysis, which focuses
on the optional aspects of the agreement individually and in combination. At this
stage, once it is evident to what extent the agreement varies from the traditional
obligatory norm, subtly different standards drawn from contract and regulatory
incentive doctrine may be employed to determine whether public or private abuse
has affected this distinctive dimension of the development agreement.

. . . .

ii. *Standards Defining Obligatory Aspects*

With this basic framework in mind, it is next possible to consider in more detail the substantive standards traditionally used to define obligations of local governments and private parties with respect to the major development agreement provisions of interest in this Article—those relating to the provision of public services, to land use conditions, to exactions, and to regulatory freezes.

Development agreements may address the availability and content of terms under which a municipality will provide public services such as water and sewer. Specific statutes typically regulate this area in the individual states, but a few generalizations may be made. At least within municipal limits, municipalities must extend services on a nondiscriminatory basis, as must private providers of utility services. Municipalities traditionally have considerable discretion in determining how new service areas will be defined. In some states adequate service must be provided within a certain period following annexation. Rules and user charges must likewise have a rational basis.

Conditions concerning use of land, availability of mitigating measures, and other similar matters are also frequently included in development agreements. As the discussion on contingent zoning previously noted, only "reasonable" conditions may be imposed without a permit or rezoning applicant's consent. Judgments regarding reasonableness may vary from jurisdiction to jurisdiction.

Exactions of property, infrastructure, or fees play a particularly important role in development agreements. Statutes and case law in virtually all jurisdictions have developed specialized tests of the "reasonableness" of exactions. . . .

  . . . .

Recently, doctrine governing exactions has been expanded to address the use of "impact fees." To protect against government overreaching in this context, jurisdictions universally require that any fee be reasonably related both to the burden created by and the benefit to be afforded to a development project. . . .

It is also likely that development agreements will include regulatory freezes. Two pockets of established precedent are most relevant in assessing the obligatory character of such provisions. Courts traditionally have used the vested rights and equitable estoppel doctrines to distinguish between circumstances in which a development can proceed under preexisting regulations—in effect freezing those regulations in place—and circumstances in which changed regulations may apply. In effect, therefore, the closely entwined vested rights and equitable estoppel doctrines define the point at which a regulatory freeze must begin. Courts commonly recognize vested rights when a developer demonstrates substantial reliance, in good faith, on affirmative acts attributable to the regulating government. Some jurisdictions have applied this rule in more stringent, and others in more lenient, ways. . . .

A related question, of course, is how long regulatory freezes must remain in effect. Two analogies are possible. Traditional nonconforming use doctrine recognizes that the protection afforded such uses need not continue if forces of nature destroy the relevant structures, or if the owner's action removes them from use. Perhaps more to the point, case law concerning amortization of nonconforming uses in many states allows their termination, without compensation, after a "reasonable" period. Reasonableness is judged, for these purposes, in terms of the adverse effect of termination on the property owner's expectations—including the level of and return on investment, and the life expectancy and condition of improvements—and the social harm that results from continued use—taking into account the type of use and effect on the surrounding neighborhood. . . .

It is therefore evident that while a reasonableness standard runs throughout these several distinct contexts, it means subtly different things in each. . . .

Certain guidelines, however, may prove helpful. Case law concerning the reserved powers doctrine and contingent zoning suggests that individual obligatory provisions should, at a minimum, result in no adverse impact on the public interest. What that means in practice depends heavily on the facts when issues such as height, density, or infrastructure exactions arise. Rules of thumb may more readily be applied to determine whether public service commitments or regulatory freeze provisions are of unreasonably long duration, so as to violate the government's obligation to set appropriate limits on their length.

In these contexts a key issue is whether the government in question has considered the appropriate range of possible durations, taking into account relevant factors. Factors likely to affect the appropriate length of service commitments include the typical length of commitments in the community, the remaining capacity of existing public facilities, and the anticipated time needed for the proposed development to come on line. Factors likely to affect the appropriate length of regulatory freezes include the range of durations recognized in the area or the country, and the frequency of administrative review, the anticipated start-up time, the level of investment, recognized market characteristics, and past experience regarding type and frequency of regulatory change.

iii. *Standards Governing Optional Aspects*

Once a determination has been made regarding the extent to which obligatory aspects may be incorporated into a development agreement, it will be apparent that any additional obligations or opportunities included must be optional in nature. Although a reasonableness test likewise provides the key substantive standard governing provisions of this type, it is important to recognize that a somewhat different application of that standard is required in this context.

The inclusion of optional provisions can be regarded either as the exercise of a local government's contract powers, or as the provision of regulatory incentives through expanded use of the police powers. Contract doctrine provides government with rudimentary protection against private abuse. . . . [C]ourts will uphold a government contract if it . . . had a proper purpose, and was reasonably calculated to achieve that end. A similar standard would govern government contracts entered into in a proprietary capacity. Courts have used the common-law unconscionability doctrine to overturn contracts that are unfair and unreasonable, at least in extreme cases also involving questionable negotiation processes. . . .

Police power analysis leads to a similar conclusion. A government decision to afford a bonus or incentive as part of its regulatory scheme must satisfy due process requirements. Thus, the incentive scheme must have a legitimate purpose. It cannot result in unjustified confiscation—public abuse—or in unwarranted give aways—private abuse—but must seek to gain an appropriate public advantage or remedy a public necessity. The incentive arrangement also must reasonably relate to the purpose at hand. . . .

In effect, therefore, optional development agreement provisions must satisfy a comparable reasonableness standard, whether contract or police power doctrine controls. Attention may, therefore, turn to the application of the test to . . . typical fact patterns, assuming that the inclusion of contested provisions as part of a development agreement does not waive the right subsequently to pursue a judicial challenge.

A local government might . . . consider requesting a developer to include a child care center as part of a mixed use residential/commercial development, and a commitment to build such a center and dedicate it to the town might be incorporated in the development agreement. The first question, for purposes of this Article's proposed analysis, would focus on whether construction and dedication of a center is obligatory or optional in nature. Arguably, the center responds to a development-related need for child care facilities to service residents and assist employees, and easy access to day care provides a measurable benefit to those associated with the new development. Whether a particular jurisdiction's courts would accept this argument is likely to depend on the language of applicable statutes and the courts' tendency to apply the rational nexus test in a strict or lenient fashion.

Assuming, however, that construction and dedication of a day care center could not be required by the local government, this facet of the development agreement would be viewed as optional in character. A legitimate public purpose underlies the local government's desire to provide for the training and care of young children and the peace of mind of their employed parents. Because an additional burden or obligation is imposed, the development agreement would need to provide for at least some special benefit or opportunity; for example, the agreement could authorize increased height or density of residential or commercial structures, or an extended regulatory freeze. It is possible to show a relationship between burden and benefit, or between obligation and opportunity, by demonstrating that the added cost of including the day care facility constituted a factor in determining what offsetting height or density or length of freeze to provide.

. . . .

C. *Noncompliance*

. . . .

1. Landowner Noncompliance with Conditions and Exaction Requirements

. . . .

Development agreement statutes clearly address the problem of developer noncompliance. Periodic administrative review of project progress is generally required, so that developer noncompliance becomes immediately evident. So long as it complies with applicable procedures, the government may terminate a development agreement if it demonstrates developer noncompliance.

Development agreements often include additional language specifying when nonperformance is excused, and what remedies may be available. . . .

. . . .

2. Government Failure to Provide Promised Services

Although case law has addressed the consequences of government failure to provide promised services in the context of annexation agreements, precedent concerning this issue has yet to address development agreements themselves. . . .

. . . Annexation agreement case law has indicated that both actual and consequential damages may be levied against a noncomplying municipality. Development agreement statutes which specify only that injunctive relief may be available perhaps limit such monetary awards in some states. The parties may also have specified that certain unusual remedies should be available in the event of municipal noncompliance, and at least in some circumstances courts will enforce the availability of such novel relief.

3. Government Noncompliance with Regulatory Freeze Provisions

Considerable scholarly attention has focused on the obligation of governing bodies to observe regulatory freeze provisions included in development agreements. The issue has recently arisen in litigation concerning development agreements designed to encourage agricultural land preservation. . . . [G]overnmental noncompliance with such provisions raises questions involving the constitutional taking and impairment of contract doctrines, as well as common-law contract law. Under each of these lines of analysis, courts will excuse governmental noncompliance only when it serves essential public interests, such as the interest in public safety.

. . . .

V. Conclusion

Public-private dealmaking as a means of fashioning land use controls continues to have its critics who rightly fear that untrammeled use of such an approach may lead to public or private abuse of government power. This Article has argued that the development of appropriate theoretical constructs can protect against these perils while resulting in a more flexible, equitable, and efficient approach to this critical social problem. It has urged that a thorough understanding of the interplay of contract and police power principles must inform such theoretical constructs. It has suggested that doctrine developed in connection with the United States Constitution's Contract Clause provides a useful model that teaches important lessons concerning the characterization of deals, the design of standards, and the responses to noncompliance in the land use context. The Article has drawn from two subtly different but somewhat similar examples of public-private land use deals—contingent zoning and development agreements—to illustrate how an appropriate balance can be established between private expectations and the public interest. Whether the substantial potential implicit in the dealmaking model can be brought to fruition with the aid of this or other theoretical models remains to be seen.

Note

Do the Supreme Court decisions in *Nollan v. California Coastal Commission,* 483 U.S. 825 (1987), and *Dolan v. City of Tigard*, 512 U.S. 374 (1994), have an impact on contractual arrangements between a municipality and a developer?

PART III

Takings

Takings analysis rightfully dominates land use discourse. The appropriate relationship between government and property owners may be defined and interpreted in innumerable ways. The articles in this part reflect this diversity of views. For a book on takings that has justifiably garnered widespread attention, see Richard A. Epstein, Takings: Private Property and the Power of Eminent Domain (1985).

A. Regular Proceedings

The Economics of Public Use
Thomas W. Merrill
72 Cornell L. Rev. 61 (1986)[*]

The fifth amendment to the United States Constitution, as well as most state constitutions, provides that private property shall not be taken "for public use" unless just compensation is paid. American courts have long construed this to mean that some showing of "publicness" is a condition precedent to a legitimate exercise of the power of eminent domain. Thus, when a proposed condemnation of property lacks the appropriate public quality, the taking is deemed to be unconstitutional and can be enjoined. In practice, however, most observers today think the public use limitation is a dead letter. Three recent decisions, upholding takings that courts would very likely have found impermissible in the past, support this view.

In the first case, *Poletown Neighborhood Council v. City of Detroit*,[3] the Michigan Supreme Court approved the city of Detroit's plan to condemn a 465-acre tract of land and reconvey it on favorable terms to the General Motors Corporation (GM) for construction of an automobile assembly plant.[4] GM had previously

---

[*] © Copyright 1986 by Cornell University. All Rights Reserved. Reprinted by permission from the Cornell Law Review, Vol. 72, No. 1, Nov. 1986.

[3] 410 Mich. 616, 304 N.W.2d 455 (1981).

[4] Although the projected cost of the condemnation to Detroit exceeded $200 million, GM subsequently purchased the property from the city for slightly more than $8 million. *Id.* at 656, 304 N.W.2d at 469 (Ryan, J., dissenting).

announced its intention to relocate certain Detroit-based manufacturing operations if the city did not provide a new plant site. The purported public benefits of the condemnation (the "public use") included retaining over 6,000 jobs, preserving tax revenues, and avoiding the social deterioration caused by a declining industrial and population base. The Poletown Neighborhood Council, representing approximately 3,400 area residents whose homes, shops, and churches were to be bulldozed to make way for the plant, opposed the project, claiming it did not satisfy the public use requirement. Over two vigorous dissents, the Michigan Supreme Court held the proposed taking a legitimate public use.

The second case, *City of Oakland v. Oakland Raiders*,[7] sustained an even more unconventional exercise of eminent domain. The Oakland Raiders professional football team, after failing to renew its stadium lease with the city of Oakland, announced that it intended to move to Los Angeles. The city responded by seeking to condemn the intangible contractual rights associated with the Raiders' franchise, including player contracts. The city apparently contemplated operating the team for a brief period while seeking a private owner willing to keep the team in Oakland. Although not deciding conclusively that the proposed taking served a public use, the California Supreme Court held that neither the plan's exotic object—the intangible contractual rights of a professional sports team—nor the possibility of a resale to a private party precluded an exercise of eminent domain.

Finally, *Hawaii Housing Authority v. Midkiff*[9] is probably the most important of the three cases, because it is the United States Supreme Court's first pronouncement on the meaning of "public use" since *Berman v. Parker*[10] was decided in 1954. At issue in *Midkiff* was the constitutionality of the Hawaii Land Reform Act of 1967, which allows persons renting homes in development tracts of five or more acres to condemn their landlord's interest and thereby acquire an estate in fee simple. A unanimous Court, citing figures suggesting that land ownership in Hawaii is highly concentrated, sustained the Act as a constitutional means of "[r]egulating oligopoly and the evils associated with it,"[12] in particular the inability of renters to purchase homes at a "fair" price.[13] Although declaring that courts play a role in enforcing the public use clause, and that a "purely private taking" would be unconstitutional,[14] the Court nonetheless characterized the historical judicial posture as one of extreme deference: "where the exercise of the eminent domain power is rationally related to a conceivable public purpose, the Court has never held a compensated taking to be proscribed by the Public Use Clause."[15]

These three decisions suggest several common themes. First, and most clearly, they suggest that modern courts will tolerate very wide-ranging uses of eminent

---

[7]   32 Cal. 3d 60, 646 P.2d 835, 183 Cal. Rptr. 673 (1982).

[9]   467 U.S. 229 (1984).

[10] 348 U.S. 26 (1954).

[12] *Midkiff*, 467 U.S. at 242. . . .

[13] *Id.* . . .

[14] *Midkiff*, 467 U.S. at 245.

[15] *Id.* at 241.

domain. Legislatures may use eminent domain to promote the construction of a privately owned factory (*Poletown*), to force a favored tenant to remain in a government-owned facility (*Oakland Raiders*), or to engage in "land reform" (*Midkiff*). Second, the cases suggest that modern courts are exceedingly deferential to legislative definitions of a permissible public use. Indeed, *Midkiff* hints that the public use analysis parallels the "minimum rationality" standard applied to equal protection and substantive due process challenges to economic legislation. Third, and perhaps most important, the cases suggest that courts have no theory or conceptual foundation from which meaningful standards for judicial review of public use issues might originate. Instead, the cases are filled with cliches regarding the "breadth" and "elasticity" of the "evolving" concept of public use, language indicating a dearth of theory—or perhaps a lack of any desire to develop one.

From an economic perspective, the extreme deference to legislative eminent domain decisions reflected in these cases is puzzling. After all, eminent domain entails coerced appropriation of private property by the state, and there is an important difference between coerced and consensual exchange. Consensual exchange is almost always beneficial to both parties in a transaction, while coerced exchange may or may not be, depending on whether the compensation is sufficient to make the coerced party indifferent to the loss. The distinction is equivalent to that drawn by Guido Calabresi and Douglas Melamed[19] between property rules, which allow an owner to protect a right or entitlement from an unconsented taking by securing injunctive relief, and liability rules, which afford protection only through an ex post award of damages. It seems peculiar that in the eminent domain area, which so often parallels private law doctrine, courts have effectively declared that liability rules alone shall protect all private property rights.

In Part I of this article, I propose an explanation for the extreme judicial deference we see in public use cases. The underlying source of this deference, I suggest, is a historical focus on ends rather than means. Public use analysis has traditionally examined the ends of a government taking—the purpose or use to which property will be put once acquired. With the transition from the minimalist state to the activist state, however, courts have become increasingly uncomfortable in defining the correct or "natural" ends of government. Not surprisingly, therefore, courts have adopted a hands-off posture regarding questions of public use. In contrast, the property rule/liability rule distinction familiar to economists regards eminent domain as a *means* of achieving governmental ends. From this perspective, eminent domain offers just one of several possible means of acquiring resources, ranging from voluntary exchange at negotiated prices at one extreme to confiscation without compensation at the other. In this view, even if courts refuse to challenge legislative decisions about the ends to which property is put, they still might, and perhaps should, play some role in choosing the appropriate means to reach those ends.

. . . I attempt in Part II to construct a theory that would guide judicial review of a legislature's choice of eminent domain as a means. Drawing on economic analysis, I argue that eminent domain's purpose is to overcome barriers to voluntary exchange created when a seller of resources is in position to extract economic

---

[19] *See generally* Calabresi & Melamed, *Property Rules, Liability Rules, and Inalienability: One View of the Cathedral*, 85 HARV. L. REV. 1089 (1972).

rents from a buyer. This "thin market" setting, as I will call it, can lead to monopoly pricing by the seller, to unacceptably high transaction costs, or to both. This conception of eminent domain's purpose is not new, but I attempt to explore the basic idea, and certain important qualifications to it, more thoroughly than have others. This exploration produces two models of eminent domain: what I call the "basic model" and the "refined model." Each model carries different implications for judicial review of the exercise of eminent domain. The basic model sanctions virtually unlimited judicial deference to the legislature whereas the refined model supports heightened judicial scrutiny in certain limited circumstances.

Judicial theory is one thing; judicial decisions are another. Notwithstanding the tradition of judicial deference associated with the public use limitation, I seek in Part III to determine whether judicial decisions actually reflect a sensitivity to the choice-of-means issue. . . .

Finally, in the concluding section, I return to *Poletown, Oakland Raiders,* and *Midkiff,* and consider how courts might resolve those cases under the economic models developed in Part II.

. . . .

II

EMINENT DOMAIN AS A MEANS: AN ECONOMIC APPROACH

. . . .

A. The Basic Model

The purpose of eminent domain is analogous to that of other liability rules, in that eminent domain applies where market exchange, if not impossible to achieve, is nevertheless subject to imperfections. To illustrate the point, consider the most common situation in which we see the exercise of eminent domain: a public or private project requiring the assembly of numerous parcels of land. Suppose, for example, that an oil refining company wants to construct an underground pipeline to transport crude oil from a producing field to a refinery several hundred miles away. Suppose further that only one feasible pipeline route exists. Without an exercise of eminent domain, the company must obtain an easement from each of hundreds of contiguous property owners. Each owner would have the power to hold out, should he choose to exercise it. If even a few owners held out, others might do the same. In this way, assembly of the needed parcels could become prohibitively expensive; in the end, the costs might well exceed the project's potential gains.

. . . .

In the final analysis, whether one describes the assembly problem in terms of antitrust economics or transaction cost economics does not matter. In either case, the underlying predicament is the same: market conditions allow the seller to seek economic rents, that is, to charge a price higher than the property's opportunity cost. The oil pipeline hypothetical illustrates the potential for rent seeking. The opportunity cost of any one landowner's interest is near zero. But when this interest combines with other similar interests to form a right of way for a pipeline, its potential value becomes considerable. The difference between these two sums—the property's negligible opportunity cost and its value as part of the pipeline project represents a potential economic rent to the seller.

Assembly projects, however, do not exhaust a seller's rent-seeking opportunities. For example, rent seeking can occur when a buyer wants access to land that he already owns, but which is surrounded by the seller's land. It can also arise when a buyer needs to expand an existing site by acquiring adjacent land; when the buyer will lose undepreciated improvements if he does not acquire certain property from the seller; or when the seller owns property uniquely suited for some undertaking by the buyer, such as promontory for a lighthouse or a narrows for a bridge. I will hereinafter refer to any situation where a seller can extract economic rents from a buyer as a "thin market." Conversely, I will call any situation where market conditions do not allow a seller to extract economic rents from a buyer a "thick market."

Whatever a thin market's source, its potential for engendering rent seeking may make it economically efficient to confer the power of eminent domain on a buyer. . . .

Before completing discussion of the basic model, however, we must consider another important factor. So far we have focused exclusively on what might broadly be termed the transaction costs of market exchange. But we must also consider the administrative costs of eminent domain, and compare these costs with the costs of market exchange in either thick or thin market settings.

There is reason to believe, at least in thick market settings, that eminent domain is more expensive than market exchange. First, and most important, legislatures must authorize the exercise of eminent domain. It is thus necessary to persuade a legislature to grant the power of eminent domain, or, if a general grant of the power already exists, to persuade officials to exercise it. Second, the due process clauses of the fifth and fourteenth amendments, as well as local statutes and rules, impose various procedural requirements upon the exercise of eminent domain. At a minimum, these include drafting and filing a formal judicial complaint and service of process on the owner. Third, nearly all jurisdictions require at least one professional appraisal of the condemned property, something generally not done (or not done as formally) in a private sale. Finally, both court-made and statutory law guarantee a person whose property is subject to condemnation some sort of hearing on the condemnation's legality and the amount of compensation due. Of course, the parties to condemnation proceedings, like the parties to most civil litigation, typically settle before a trial. But the possibility of trial clearly increases the expected administrative costs of condemnation.

Given what might collectively be called the "due process" costs of eminent domain—obtaining legislative authority, drafting and filing the complaint, serving process, securing a formal appraisal, the possibility of a trial and appeal, and so forth—it is safe to conclude that, in a thick market setting, eminent domain is a more expensive way of acquiring resources than market exchange. This conclusion has important implications for the basic model. In effect, it means that the decision whether to use eminent domain should be, from an economic perspective, self-regulating. In thick markets, where the model initially suggests that eminent domain is inappropriate, the acquiring party should in fact utilize market exchange because eminent domain would consume more resources. Conversely, in thin market settings, where the model suggests that it is appropriate to use eminent domain, the acquiring party should in fact use eminent domain, so long as the administrative costs are less than the costs of market exchange.

. . . .

If, as the basic model suggests, the decision to use the power of eminent domain is essentially self-regulating, this holds important implications for judicial review of public use issues. Most obviously, there would seem to be little point in courts second-guessing legislative and executive determinations of public use. Judicial review would add only uncertainty and expense . . . . It is simply not clear, *a priori*, that this tighter rationing of eminent domain is desirable.

In sum, the basic model suggests that courts, in setting the limits of eminent domain, should ensure that just compensation is paid and enforce the due process "tax"—the legislative and constitutional requirements that push the administrative costs of eminent domain above the costs of market exchange in thick market settings. Otherwise, the basic model suggests that courts need do nothing to limit the use of eminent domain. Thus, the basic economic model reinforces the principle, enunciated in *Berman* and *Midkiff*, that courts should give virtually complete deference to legislative determinations of public use.

B. The Refined Model

Despite the basic model's appealing simplicity, with its thick market/thin market distinction and its modest conception of the judicial role, the model raises a number of troubling economic and noneconomic questions. To avoid unduly complicating the argument, I will discuss only the economic objections.

The broadest and best-known economic objection to eminent domain is that it is unnecessary. The critics who raise this objection first note that acquiring parties generally use eminent domain to assemble large tracts of land. They then point out that real estate developers and others are frequently able to assemble such parcels by using buying agents, option agreements, straw transactions, and the like. If private developers and the like can get by without eminent domain, the critics ask, then why cannot the government?

This broadscale objection meets with two answers. First, simply because the market can overcome the assembly problem (and presumably other thin market problems) some of the time, this does not mean that market mechanisms, by themselves, always produce optimal land assembly. The market may work well enough for shopping centers and commercial office buildings, but these projects entail relatively small amounts of land, are not strictly site-dependent, and often generate very high gains from trade. It does not necessarily follow that market mechanisms would work for such things as interstate highways, wilderness areas, or urban renewal projects. . . .

Second, although buying agents, option agreements, and straw transactions may work well for private developers, it is unclear whether government can use these devices effectively. The necessary ingredient of these techniques is secrecy, and governments, at least in an open society like the United States, are not very good at keeping secrets. . . .

The broadscale denial of the need for eminent domain therefore fails. Nevertheless, I believe that there are three narrower economic objections that have greater merit. Each objection requires a partial modification of the basic model, and a corresponding refinement of the model's conception of the judicial role.

1. *Uncompensated Subjective Losses*

The basic model posits that eminent domain is designed to increase social wealth by facilitating certain transactions that otherwise would not take place, or that would take place only at an inefficiently high cost. Eminent domain, to use a familiar metaphor, is an instrument for increasing the size of the pie. But eminent domain also contains an implicit decisional rule for allocating the gains and losses associated with these forced transactions. This rule, manifested in eminent domain's compensation requirement, dictates that a condemnee is entitled to the fair market value of his property in its highest and best use *other than* the use proposed by the condemnor. In other words, the condemnee is entitled to an award equal to the opportunity cost of his contribution to the condemnor's project, no more and no less.

This opportunity cost compensation formula, however, fails to compensate the condemnee for all of his losses. The formula awards the condemnee what he would obtain in an arm's length transaction with a third party, but does not compensate him for the subjective "premium" he might attach to his property above its opportunity cost. In some cases, such as those involving undeveloped land, there may be no subjective premium. But in other cases, the premium may be quite large and may reflect several potential concerns: a condemnee may have a sentimental attachment to the property, or may have made improvements or modifications to accommodate his unique needs, or may simply wish to avoid the costs and inconvenience of relocation. In addition, other personal losses which do not "run" with the property, such as lost goodwill, consequential damages to other property, relocation costs, and attorney fees, are also not compensable.

. . . .

The foregoing concerns counsel a qualification of the basic model's core conception of the judicial role. Specifically, they suggest that courts should closely scrutinize the decision to condemn whenever an owner's subjective losses are high. . . . In effect, courts would provide a condemnee faced with large subjective losses an additional "trump card," in the form of a higher probability that the project would be enjoined as failing the public use requirement. This additional leverage should induce the government to increase its settlement offer, thus offsetting, at least in part, the subjective losses.

2. *Secondary Rent Seeking*

A second objection to the opportunity cost compensation formula is that it encourages rent seeking by condemnors. Eminent domain almost always generates a surplus—a resource's value after condemnation is almost always higher than before. The present compensation formula allocates 100% of this surplus to the condemnor, and none to the condemnee. Commentators have questioned such a division on fairness grounds.

. . . .

The danger of secondary rent seeking suggests that it may be appropriate to add a second qualification to the basic model. In cases where eminent domain is most likely to foster secondary rent-seeking behavior—where one or a small number of persons will capture a taking's surplus—courts should closely scrutinize a decision to confer the power of eminent domain. Cases involving delegation of eminent domain to one or a few private parties, or involving condemnation followed by retransfer of the property to one or a few private parties, present the primary situations where such secondary rent seeking is likely to occur.

3. *Market Bypass*

In addition to the foregoing limitations derived from eminent domain's compensation formula, there is a third objection that would apply even if questions of compensation never produced distorted incentives. Suppose a buyer facing a relatively thick market for a resource declines to engage in market exchange, but later changes his position such that, ex post, he faces a thin market. Should eminent domain be available to buyers who have either deliberately or negligently bypassed a thick market exchange?

. . . .

. . . Clearly, a buyer who takes all reasonable and prudent steps while engaging in thick market exchange, only to later face the need for further exchange in a thin market, should be allowed to use eminent domain. On the other hand, a buyer who intentionally bypasses a thick market by taking action . . . that leaves him in a thin market should not be allowed to use eminent domain. Disallowing eminent domain under such circumstances is necessary to prevent the transformation of all property rules into liability rules. Intermediate cases are more troublesome. Suppose a buyer's mistake derives from mere negligence . . . . [C]ourts should at the very least closely scrutinize cases in which condemnors face thin markets as a result of their own intentional acts or negligence, leaving the meaning of "negligence" to be fixed on a case-by-case basis.

. . . .

III
CASE SURVEY

Although courts almost invariably discuss the public use issue in terms of government ends, *Poletown*, *Oakland Raiders*, and *Midkiff* suggest that courts have no theory as to what those ends might be. Indeed, courts seem to have abandoned the idea that they should articulate and enforce a conception of permissible government ends. Nevertheless, one still finds state courts declaring that a proposed taking does not serve a public use. This state of affairs—no agreement on general principles, frequent statements of broad deference, and intermittent holdings of no public use—has led several courts and commentators to a kind of legal realist despair. . . .

Nonetheless, the judiciary's failure to articulate either a coherent theory of public use or a theory of the judicial role in enforcing the public use limitation does not imply that public use cases are wrongly decided from an economic perspective. The very absence of coherent legal doctrine effectively allows courts to justify any result that strikes them as intuitively correct. With this thought in mind, I undertook a fairly large survey of appellate opinions concerning contested public use issues to determine whether the outcomes of these cases are consistent with the economic models developed in Part II. My operating hypothesis was that courts operating in a common law fashion, although interpreting an open-ended constitutional provision rather than fashioning rules of common law per se, would tend to embrace efficient results.

A. Description of the Survey

To test both the basic and refined versions of the economic model, I surveyed all reported appellate cases decided between *Berman v. Parker*[107] and January 1, 1986, that involved a contested public use question. . . . The net result: a sample of 291 state and 17 federal appellate decisions, or a total sample of 308 cases.

Berman served as the survey's starting point for two reasons. . . . [O]ne was manageability. Second, such an approach enabled me to review the state and lower federal courts' acceptance of *Berman*'s deferential approach to legislative public use determinations. *Berman* dealt with the taking clause of the fifth amendment, and thus is not binding on state courts interpreting their own constitutions. Nevertheless, the decision is widely regarded as an important watershed . . . .

Before discussing specifics, a few general observations about the survey are in order. First, virtually all the cases involved acquisitions of interests in land—either fees simple or easements. Other than *Oakland Raiders,* only four cases challenged the use of eminent domain to acquire interests in personal property . . . .

Second, of the 308 opinions in the sample, 261, or 84.7%, held that the proposed taking served a public use; conversely, 47, or 15.3%, held that it did not. Given *Berman*'s and *Midkiff*'s assertion that a legislative public use determination is virtually dispositive of the issue, the relatively high number of cases finding no public use is somewhat surprising. The apparent anomaly disappears, however, once we separate federal decisions from state decisions. Although the survey contained only 17 federal cases, each upheld a legislative public use determination, suggesting that lower federal courts have been faithful to *Berman*'s deferential standard of review. State courts, on the other hand, seem more willing to depart from *Berman*'s virtual abandonment of judicial review. Looking at the state appellate decisions alone, we find that 16.2%, roughly one in six, held that a proposed taking did not serve a public use.

Third, the survey failed to reveal any clear regional patterns. . . .

Finally, the survey did disclose a clear—and surprising—temporal pattern. When we divide the survey cases into five-year periods, we find that the total number of public use cases is fairly constant, ranging from 42 to 61 cases in each

---

[107] 348 U.S. 26 (1954).

period from 1954-1985. But the percentage of cases holding that a taking does not serve a public use generally increases throughout the 31-year period. The percentages are as follows: 1954-1960, 11.8%; 1961-1965, 12.5%; 1966-1970, 13.1%; 1971-1975, 13.7%; 1976-1980, 21.4%; and 1981-1985, 20.4%. These figures suggest that, most commentary notwithstanding, judicial enforcement of the public use requirement is not a thing of the past. On the contrary, it is generally on the rise.

B. Testing the Basic Model

The survey revealed that contested public use cases tend to fall into certain recurrent categories. Significantly, each category reflects what I have termed a thin market situation: the condemnor would be susceptible to a seller's rent-seeking behavior if an open market transaction were attempted. . . .

1. *Assembly*

By far the largest category of cases involved projects . . . requiring the assembly of a large tract of land or of numerous contiguous easements in land. For reasons previously discussed, the assembly presents the condemnor with a thin . . . market. . . . [O]f the total sample, 185, or 60.1%, at least "arguably" involved assembly. . . .

Eminent domain is used to overcome a broad range of assembly problems. Most common among the contested cases were utility easements, urban renewal projects, and dam sites. Some of the more unusual examples of assembly included a site for a Sears, Roebuck department store, acquisition of a scenic easement along a highway, and an effort to straighten out jigsaw-like lot lines in Guam.

2. *Expanding Existing Facilities*

A second category of contested cases involved efforts to expand existing facilities. In a typical expansion case the condemnor or the beneficiary of the condemnation has invested capital to improve a particular piece of property, only to find later that the resulting facility is too small for his needs. The only way to expand is to acquire additional land. If the only land feasible for expansion is owned by one seller, then the condemnor faces a thin market. . . . [O]f the total sample of cases, 41, or 13.3%, arguably involved expansion.

During the 1954-1985 period, one of the most frequently litigated expansion issues involved parking lots. As automobile travel became more popular in the postwar era, government buildings, department stores, and sports facilities found their parking areas inadequate. Frequently, the only way to acquire needed parking space was to condemn an adjacent lot or structure. Other expansion cases involved airports and airport runways, public utilities, wildlife refuges, and public recreation areas.

3. *Landlocked Property*

A third category of cases, encountered with virtually the same frequency as the expansion cases, involved rights of access to landlocked property. When someone owns land completely surrounded by another owner's property, or by variously owned parcels where there is only one feasible route of access, the landlocked owner faces a thin market for an access easement to his land. The landlocked property cases thus fit comfortably within the basic model. . . . [O]f the total sample of cases, 41, or 13.3%, arguably involved landlocked property.

Access roads presented the most frequently litigated problem in this area, followed by condemnations of utility easements to landlocked property. One unusual case involved construction of a road to a landlocked bog used for duck hunting.

4. *Unique Property*

The fourth most frequently litigated issue involved property uniquely suited to the condemnor's enterprise. A good example is *Williams v. Hyrum Gibbons & Sons Co.*[133] In that case, the company needed to acquire an elevated parcel of city land unobstructed by surrounding buildings to operate a radio station for mobile telephone and radio paging services. Because such property was in short supply, the owner of a parcel having these characteristics could extract economic rents from the buyer. . . . [O]f the total sample of cases, 14, or 4.5%, arguably fell into this category.

5. *Specific Capital*

The fifth category, appearing with about the same frequency as the fourth, involved the condemnor who has committed specific capital which would be lost or reduced in value if he did not acquire an additional interest in land. The specific capital problem can arise in a variety of ways: perhaps a condemnor improved land belonging to someone else, made improvements before discovering a defect in his chain of title, or made improvements under a lease which the landlord refuses to renew. Because of the condemnor's commitment of specific capital, the holder of the rights to the additional land can extract economic rents (perhaps, more accurately, "quasi rents") as a condition of sale. Consequently, the condemnor faces a thin market. . . . [O]f the total sample of cases, 14, or 4.5%, arguably involved specific capital.

---

[133] 602 P.2d 684 (Utah 1979).

6. *Condemnations in Thick Markets*

Not all contested cases involved thin markets; several opinions reflected the exercise of eminent domain where a market transaction should have been possible at or near the property's opportunity cost. . . . [O]f the total sample of cases, 13, or 4.2%, arguably involved a thick market. . . .

. . . .

7. *Summary*

Recapitulating the foregoing six categories, we find that . . . of the total sample of cases, 295, or 95.8%, arguably involved a thin market. These figures forcefully confirm the basic economic model. Regardless of courts' conclusions about whether a taking is for a public use, condemnors rarely use the power of eminent domain unless it is necessary to overcome barriers to voluntary market exchange— monopoly pricing or strategic bargaining. Thus, if we adhere to the basic model and ignore the refined model's three qualifications, eminent domain is in effect self-regulating.

The distinction between thin and thick markets is also useful in predicting appellate definitions of public use. In the five thin market categories, courts held that a taking serves a public use at a fairly consistent rate, ranging from 75.6% (landlocked property) to 100% (unique property), with the largest single category (assembly) coming in at 90.3%. In the few thick market cases (13 in total), courts found a public use only 15.3% of the time. These numbers suggest that the basic model at least partially explains the pattern of decisions reached by courts in deciding what constitutes a public use.

C. Testing the Refined Model

Can the refined model do even better? To find out, I adopted a two-part strategy. First, I tried to identify those cases involving one of the three conditions that the refined model suggests justify heightened scrutiny: high subjective value, potential for secondary rent seeking, and intentional or negligent market bypass. I then compared the relative frequency of nonpublic use holdings in these cases with the average frequency of 15.3%, and sought to discover any relationship between the size of the surplus and the public use determination. Second, I focused on the 47 decisions holding that a taking was not a public use to determine how often the three limiting conditions appeared in these cases.

Unfortunately, the data in the appellate opinions did not allow me to make these estimations in a very precise manner. First, of the three limiting conditions, only the second, potential for secondary rent seeking, clearly emerged from the statements of facts contained in most of the opinions. Appellate judges nearly always recite facts indicating whether a taking transfers property to a few previously identified parties. However, the other two factors, high subjective value and market bypass, could not be established from the statements of facts in most cases. Consequently, I did not obtain a satisfactory case sample presenting the first and third factors.

Second, even in those cases that did clearly suggest the presence of one of the three limiting conditions, the courts only occasionally supplied enough information to estimate the size of the taking's surplus. In order to make even a rough guess about the surplus's size it is necessary to have some information regarding the property's use before and after the taking. Surprisingly, the opinions often failed to report even this seemingly elementary data. . . .

Given these two shortcomings, I could not rigorously assess the accuracy of the refined model. Nevertheless, the survey did yield some suggestive results.

. . . .

In the end, the survey provides a degree of support for the refined model, although it does not support the refined model as much as the basic model. The data generally suggest that state courts are fairly sensitive to an ex post consideration of a taking's surplus and will more readily sustain a taking when the added wealth to society appears large. Thus, when we factor in the size of a taking's surplus, the refined model is reasonably predictive. However, it is less clear that courts are concerned with uncompensated subjective loss, or with the ex ante incentive effects of secondary rent seeking or market bypass. Some evidence suggests that these factors influence courts, but the impact of these factors, by themselves, seems minimal and inconsistent.

Perhaps more striking is that the opinions contain so little factual information relevant to the refined model. This must count against the model. One would think that if concerns like uncompensated subjective value or market bypass influenced courts, they would at least mention facts that would tend to support or refute the presence of these elements in any given case. Thus, if the refined model is at work, it operates at a fairly subconscious level.

CONCLUSION

Explaining public use in terms of choice of means seems moderately successful, at least as a positive model for predicting the outcome of contested public use cases. In concluding, I consider how courts might apply this perspective as a normative standard. To do so, I return to the three cases that introduced this study: *Poletown*, *Oakland Raiders*, and *Midkiff*.

The basic model posits that eminent domain seeks to overcome thin market barriers to negotiated exchange. The basic model also posits that beyond assuring proper procedures and just compensation, courts need not intervene to limit the exercise of eminent domain, because the higher administrative costs associated with eminent domain render it essentially self-regulating. Nevertheless, it is instructive to ask how the three cases might have come out if the deciding courts had explicitly employed the thin market/thick market distinction in determining the limits of eminent domain.

Poletown presents a straightforward assembly problem. Hence, it easily conforms to the basic model. Because of holdouts, General Motors would have encountered tremendous difficulties had it tried to acquire a 465-acre tract in the middle of a major urban area by voluntary negotiation. Without eminent domain, GM would almost certainly have built the plant elsewhere, or at least not built it on the same scale.

Oakland Raiders presents a unique property case, and is thus also consistent with the basic model. The number of National Football League franchises is artificially restricted: the league, which controls the formation of new franchises, has created only 28 to date, and seems reluctant to add new ones. Realistically, Oakland had only one source for an NFL lessee for its stadium—the Raiders—making the case a classic example of bilateral monopoly. Moreover, the Raiders had been based in Oakland for approximately 20 years, and the residents of the area had developed a strong identification with the team—thus entailing a kind of reverse subjective loss when the Raiders sought to leave.

Midkiff appears at first blush to be another unique property case; after all, the Supreme Court's opinion emphasized that Hawaii's supply of residential property had been "artificially" restricted, and suggested that the price of single family homes had soared beyond the reach of most would-be purchasers. However, the Court's figures suggest that the residential home market in Hawaii is neither a monopoly nor a cartel, and is thus not subject to noncompetitive pricing. In all probability, the litigants and the Court mistakenly equated a "housing shortage" caused by high demand with oligopolistic pricing by sellers. . . .

. . . Perhaps a better explanation for the Land Reform Act is that it addressed a specific capital problem. From this perspective, the refusal of Hawaii's land magnates to sell their land in fee simple did not motivate the statute; rather, it was motivated by their transfer of the land through long-term ground leases that were either coming due or up for renegotiation. The expiration or renegotiation of the ground leases rendered tenants with substantial capital investments in the property vulnerable to rent-seeking behavior by landlords. A landlord could charge a lease-renewal price that included not only the unimproved land's opportunity cost, but also the value of improvements previously paid for by the tenant. The Land Reform Act would have represented a rational response to this problem. In fact, there is evidence that tension between landlords and tenants over lease renewals was a contributing factor in the statute's enactment.

Thus, under the basic model's thin market/thick market distinction, all three cases present proper occasions to exercise eminent domain. True, an opinion sustaining these takings under the basic model would be drafted quite differently from those the courts actually produced. But an opinion written from the basic model's vantage point would at least embody a coherent vision of eminent domain as a means, and would thus possess a degree of intellectual credibility. This is more than can be said for the decisions in *Poletown*, *Oakland Raiders*, and *Midkiff*.

As one might expect, the analysis under the refined model is a good deal more complex. *Poletown* involves both high subjective value and secondary rent seeking. The taking displaced thousands from their homes and businesses and destroyed a community irreplaceable at any cost. The uncompensated subjective loss was undoubtedly large. Furthermore, the condemnation transferred the property to a single entity, General Motors, and accordingly presented a high potential for secondary rent seeking. Under the refined model, both factors suggest that heightened judicial scrutiny was appropriate.

. . . .

. . . Thus, under the refined model, we can perhaps conclude that *Poletown* was wrongly decided. It must be stressed, however, that all of the evidence demanded by the model is unavailable, and a confident assertion on this score is simply impossible.

Oakland Raiders also seems to involve uncompensated subjective losses and a high potential for secondary rent seeking. Most NFL owners probably view their team as not only a business venture, but as a personal hobby as well. Thus, one can reasonably conclude that Al Davis, owner of the Raiders, would incur uncompensated subjective losses if stripped of his ownership rights in the team. Given that the condemnation also involved players' and coaches' contracts, we should also consider the possibility that the players and coaches attached subjective value to playing for Davis. In addition, *Oakland Raiders* presents an open invitation to secondary rent seeking. A general practice of allowing municipalities to condemn corporate franchises to prevent businesses from relocating elsewhere could easily foster abuses, as municipalities sought to use eminent domain to keep businesses offering high-paying jobs and tax dollars from relocating. . . .

. . . .

. . . So, when we add together both the subjective losses and the potential for secondary rent seeking, *Oakland Raiders*, like *Poletown*, was probably wrongly decided under the refined model.

At first blush, *Midkiff* involves none of the refined model's qualifying factors. The gentry of Hawaii may derive a certain psychological benefit from the size of its holdings, but it probably views any particular parcel as fungible wealth. Thus, the condemnees probably cannot claim great uncompensated subjective losses. Moreover, because triggering the takings mechanism required petition by one-half of the renters in a tract, or 25 renters, whichever is less, the Land Reform Act does not satisfy the conditions that suggest a high probability of secondary rent seeking. The benefits of "land reform" will necessarily be spread among a sizeable group of people.

If the earlier speculation about the true purpose of the Act is correct, however, *Midkiff* may involve a market bypass problem. . . . [W]hen the renter makes his initial commitment of capital, he faces a relatively thick market. Only later, when lease termination is imminent and the renter has invested a great deal in improvements, does he face a thin market. This suggests that the renters in *Midkiff* who sought to condemn their landlord's reversionary interest negligently bypassed opportunities for thick market exchange.

However, two other considerations, both quite speculative, suggest that even if *Midkiff* presents a market bypass situation, that fact perhaps should not invalidate the taking. First, although commercial tenants seem to cope successfully with the problems of long-term lease renewal, the experience may be relatively novel for residential tenants, especially if they have emigrated from parts of the continental United States where such leases are uncommon. Thus, the "negligence" in the *Midkiff* market bypass may not be very great. Second, as in any case involving specific capital in the form of structures, the renter's subjective premium guarantees at least some surplus from condemnation. Taking these factors into consideration, perhaps a more complete account of the facts in *Midkiff* could justify the taking under even the refined model. Here again, however, the reported decision simply does not provide enough information to apply the model with confidence. If the legal system were to adopt the refined model as a normative standard, clearly courts and lawyers would have to develop a different kind of record as a basis for appellate review.

In sum, under the basic model, *Poletown, Oakland Raiders*, and *Midkiff* were rightly decided; under the refined model the result is less clear, but possibly two and arguably all three were wrongly decided. The choice of the model thus bears directly upon the degree of deference that courts will give legislative decisions, and accordingly upon the outcome of contested public use cases. How then should courts decide which model to adopt as an interpretation of the meanings of public use?

I will offer only a few tentative thoughts on this question. The case survey summarized in Part III suggests that federal courts have adopted a highly deferential approach to public use, an approach consistent with the basic model. State courts applying state constitutional provisions, however, present a more mixed picture, with some state courts adopting an interventionist stance consistent with the refined model. Perhaps this dichotomy reflects an appropriate division of authority under our system of constitutional government.

. . . .

. . . [T]he Supreme Court has declared that the Constitution does not create property rights; instead, "they are created and their dimensions are defined by existing rules or understandings that stem from an independent source such as state law."[183] This suggests that perhaps state law should determine and elaborate upon the contours of the prohibition against takings for private use, an incident of private property rights. De-federalizing public use would allow us to take advantage of the twin virtues of federalism: experimentation and competition among states. If the interventionist judicial stance implied by the refined model works well, we can expect other states to emulate the refined model. If, on the other hand, the refined model's additional litigation and uncertainty seem not to justify the effort, we can expect states to follow the federal courts toward greater judicial deference.

Note

Ascertaining the measure of compensation due the owner of property taken by the government is treated in Glynn S. Lunney, Jr., *Compensation for Takings: How Much Is Just?*, 42 Cath. U. L. Rev. 721 (1993).

---

[183] Board of Regents v. Roth, 408 U.S. 564, 577 (1972).

B. Substantive Due Process Compared

PUBLIC USE, SUBSTANTIVE DUE PROCESS AND TAKINGS—AN INTEGRATION

Lawrence Berger

74 Neb. L. Rev. 843 (1995)[*]

I. INTRODUCTION

In differing ways the three related doctrines of public use, substantive due process, and takings all provide landowners a measure of protection from various unlawful impingements by government upon their rights to own, possess, use, or transfer realty. The three sets of rules all stem from one sentence in the Fifth Amendment to the Constitution: "No person shall be deprived of life, liberty or property without due process of law; nor shall private property be taken for public use without just compensation." That sentence, *inter alia*, raises the following questions that are respectively discussed here under the above three rubrics: (1) As interpreted the Constitution permits the government to condemn private property only when it is for a "public use." Under what circumstances may it be said that a taking is for that purpose? (2) The Supreme Court has held that the Due Process Clause provides more than a mere guaranty that when the government seeks to deprive a person of his life, liberty, or property, it must do so with fair procedures; rather the protection of the clause extends to substantive matters as well. Under what circumstances may it be said that a government regulation is so substantively illegitimate that its implementation would deprive a person of his property without due process? (3) In what kinds of situations, other than the obvious one of a complete governmental seizure of the title to and possession of property, may it be said that the government has "taken" a person's property thus requiring that he be compensated for its activity?

Though it is clear that the three doctrines deal with quite different issues and should not be conflated, we shall see that unfortunately the Court has failed to maintain clear lines of demarcation between the substantive due process and takings rules and has introduced some unnecessary overlap and confusion in their application. As a result it has failed to recognize that since the two have entirely different purposes and underlying policies, appropriately the remedies for their breach should necessarily be quite different from each other. On the other hand, though the

---

[*]   Copyright 1995. Reprinted by permission.

substance of the Court's rules about what is a public use is subject to criticism, it has applied an appropriate remedy for its breach, and there has certainly been no confusion of the doctrine with the other two.

This Article first recapitulates the often uncertain content of the three doctrines and in the process discusses the purposes and policies of each. It then argues the courts should keep in mind those different purposes and policies in devising the appropriate remedies for enforcing each of the rules in order to avoid handling functionally equivalent land use problems in ways that are irrationally inconsistent with each other. Finally, . . . the Article attempts to outline an approach that integrates the purposes and policies of the rules with the appropriate means of enforcing them.

II. THE PUBLIC USE DOCTRINE

This doctrine prevents government from condemning property unless it is for a "public use." Its obvious purpose is to prevent government from seizing, even with compensation, the property of one person merely to benefit another private person. Historically there was a fierce debate over whether the rule required that the property seized by the government be taken for actual use by the public or merely that the taking resulted in some benefit to the public. However, that issue has seemingly been finally settled at least as a federal matter by the Supreme Court's latest opinion on the subject, *Hawaii Housing Authority v. Midkiff*.[4] In that case, a Hawaii statute authorized a state agency to condemn realty so that it could be resold to the tenants occupying the properties. The purpose of the statute was to break up the land holdings of the few families that owned almost half of the state's land in fee simple so that their properties could be turned over to those other private parties. Clearly no use of these lands by the public or any segment thereof was contemplated.

In upholding the law's constitutionality, the Court said: (1) a law authorizing realty condemnation is valid as for a public use if it is "rationally related to a conceivable public purpose";[5] (2) "[t]he 'public use' requirement is . . . coterminous with the scope of a sovereign's police powers";[6] and (3) "[r]egulating oligopoly and the evils associated with it"[7] was a valid "classic exercise of a States's police powers."[8]

The Court also dealt with the standard for reviewing whether the means of condemnation was rationally directed toward achieving the articulated public purpose. It said that it will uphold the condemnation if the state "rationally could have believed that the [Act] would promote its objective" and that "[w]hen the legisla-

---

4   467 U.S. 229 (1984).

5   *Id.* at 241.

6   *Id.* at 240.

7   *Id.* at 242.

8   *Id.*

ture's purpose is legitimate and its means are not irrational, [the] cases make clear that empirical debates over the wisdom of takings—no less than debates over the wisdom of other kinds of socioeconomic legislation—are not to be carried out in the federal courts."[9]

Broad as the Court saw the eminent domain power to be, still it recognized that there remain some limits to the purpose that government can lawfully have as its reason for a taking. In the same opinion the Court noted that, "[t]o be sure, the Court's cases have repeatedly stated that 'one person's property may not be taken for the benefit of another private person without a justifying public purpose even though compensation be paid,'"[10] and that a statute authorizing condemnation would be invalid if it were passed "for no reason other than to confer a private benefit on a particular private party."[11]

In other cases, courts have upheld, *inter alia*, the condemnation of an entire neighborhood consisting of private homes, churches, and places of business, for the purpose of turning the properties over to a private manufacturer who would employ many persons in the area[12] and even rights of way to a public road for owners of landlocked realty.

In summary, it can be said that as the law has developed, the public use doctrine looks to the purposes or ends of direct condemnations and upholds those that have a conceivable public purpose while it generally forbids only those which are done for strictly private purposes. The standard is a loose one and if a particular condemnation benefits both a private party and an important segment of the general public, the tendency of the courts is to uphold the right of the government to condemn the property (with, of course the concomitant duty to pay compensation). The remedy where there is a breach, however, is crucial. When a condemnation is held to violate the public use doctrine, it is not enough for the government to pay the owner compensation; rather the court completely forbids the taking. And properly so, for it is perfectly appropriate for the courts to wholly prevent the government from engaging in a particular activity when its purposes are wholly illegitimate and outside the scope of its delegated powers.

III. SUBSTANTIVE DUE PROCESS—MEANS/ENDS REVIEW

Unlike public use inquiries, substantive due process reviews do not scrutinize direct condemnations but deal only with the validity of government regulations and regulatory activities. But like public use, substantive due process scrutinizes the

---

[9]   *Id.* at 242-243.

[10]   *Id.* at 241.

[11]   *Id.* at 245.

[12]   Poletown Neighborhood Council v. City of Detroit, 304 N.W.2d 455 (1981).

legitimacy of the government's ends and the rationality of the means chosen to achieve them.

. . . .

It was not until after the Civil War . . . that the Supreme Court began to take a serious interest in using the Due Process Clauses of the Fifth Amendment and the recently ratified Fourteenth Amendment for the purpose of reviewing the substance of various federal and state regulations. Starting with the cases examining the reasonableness of utility rate regulation, the Court over time expanded the reach of its substantive reviews to all manner of government regulations. . . .

. . . [T]here were a number of cases that struck down purported exercises of the police power as violations of substantive due process, but what became the archetypal case was *Lochner v. New York*.[25] In *Lochner*, the U.S. Supreme Court was reviewing the affirmance by the New York Court of Appeals of an employer's conviction for violating a state statute which had made it a misdemeanor for bakery employees to be required or permitted to work more than sixty hours per week or ten hours per day. In what proved to be one of the most controversial decisions in its history, the Court, in a far-ranging opinion by Mr. Justice Peckham, reversed the conviction on substantive due process grounds. . . .

. . . .

In his famous dissent to *Lochner*, Mr. Justice Holmes argued that the Court was attempting to import its economic theories into the Constitution. . . .

Despite the protestations of Holmes and Harlan (who also dissented), the Court in *Lochner* effectively reserved unto itself the power to decide whether: (1) the proclaimed end of the statute under review was legitimate; (2) the proclaimed end was "really" the end of the legislature at all or there was perhaps another illegitimate purpose animating the law-making body; and (3) even if the end was a legitimate one, the means selected were truly directed toward reaching it.

Over the next thirty years, the Court reached inconsistent results in the application of substantive due process to various economic regulations, while the theory itself was under violent attack by the commentators. By the 1930s the Court, manned with different personnel and facing the economic disaster of the Great Depression, was ready to give government much broader latitude in attacking the problems of the day. In a series of cases beginning with *Nebbia v. New York*[36] and *Home Building and Loan Association v. Blaisdell*[37] and ending with *Ferguson v. Skrupa*,[38] the Court turned completely away from substantive reviews of economic regulation. . . .

Ferguson represented the definitive end (at least for this period in our history) of the Court's substantive reviews of the legitimacy of ends and effectiveness of means with respect to what it called "economic legislation." However, the Court

---

[25] 198 U.S. 45 (1904).

[36] 291 U.S. 502 (1934).

[37] 290 U.S. 398 (1934).

[38] 372 U.S. 726 (1963).

has continued to this day to make such reviews with respect to land use regulation[40] and has felt forced to resurrect substantive due process to protect certain "fundamental rights"[41] such as the right to privacy and freedom of association.

One can reasonably argue that the Court is justified in giving special substantive due process protection to certain defined fundamental rights. But its decisions, wherein it continues to act as a "superlegislature" in land use cases but not in other kinds of economic regulation cases, have never been satisfactorily explained. The truth of the matter, of course, is that the Court has never given up its power to make this kind of a review when it wishes to. At the moment it chooses not to do so as to most economic regulation, while it does so in various other kinds of cases. But is there any doubt that it would resurrect substantive due process—either by that name or another—in an economic regulation case, if the facts were egregious enough? . . .

In addition to those cases of the Supreme Court already mentioned,[44] there has been a voluminous number of modern U.S. Court of Appeals cases involving substantive due process reviews of land use regulations. These have typically involved suits under § 1983 of the Civil Rights Act[46] seeking damages and injunction for arbitrary and capricious denials of such things as building permits, subdivision approvals, or certificates of occupancy or for unreasonably impeding the development of property.

It should be emphasized, however, that the remedy available in all of these substantive due process cases, like the remedy in the case of the public use doctrine, has been to grant specific relief—in this case to void the regulation or regulatory activity at the option of the person harmed by it. In addition damages under § 1983 have been available for the harm done while the government imposition has been in effect.

. . . .

IV. EARLY TAKINGS LAW

Unlike the doctrines of public use, which deals with direct government condemnations, and substantive due process, which deals with the validity of government regulations, takings doctrine, as it has evolved, deals with the validity of

---

[40] Nollan v. California Coastal Comm'n, 423 U.S. 825 (1987); Agins v. City of Tiburon, 447 U.S. 255 (1980); Penn Central Transportation Co. v. City of New York, 438 U.S. 104 (1978); Goldblatt v. Hempstead, 369 U.S. 590 (1962); Nectow v. City of Cambridge, 277 U.S. 183 (1928) (striking down as a violation of substantive due process a zoning ordinance that did not bear a substantial relation to the public health, safety, morals, or general welfare); Village of Euclid v. Ambler Reality Co., 272 U.S. 356 (1926) (upholding the power of municipalities to zone).

[41] In United States v. Carolene Products Co., 304 U.S. 144 (1938), Justice Stone in his famous footnote 4 foreshadowed the fact that the Court would exercise strict scrutiny in reviewing laws that infringe on fundamental rights specifically guaranteed by the first ten amendments while giving much greater deference to laws that merely involved economic legislation.

[44] *See supra* note 40.

[46] 42 U.S.C. § 1983 (1988).

governmental ongoing activities *and* regulations. Though, as we shall see, the Court has recently said that takings rules, like those of substantive due process, are aimed at making sure that the means used by government in its regulatory activities are directed toward a legitimate public purpose, that was not their function as originally conceived. The rules were historically designed to make sure that compensation was given for what were regarded as implicit takeovers of property by the government. Thus, early on, the Court took the position that a taking would occur when the government authorized the physical invasion of a person's property. . . .

When it came to losses caused by government *regulation*, however, the matter was less clear. Some of the Court's early cases could be read to hold that when the challenge was to a state regulation that completely destroyed the value of the owner's property, this could not be a taking because there was no physical invasion of the owner's property. In *Mugler v. Kansas*,[56] for example, the Court took the position that the Takings Clause did not apply at all to a statute, which outlawed the manufacture or sale of intoxicating beverages, thus destroying the value of the defendant's brewery. . . .

. . . *Mugler* stood for the proposition that though a value-destroying regulation could not be a taking requiring compensation, it could be a deprivation of property without due process of law if it did not have a legitimate police power objective, such as the suppression of a nuisance. However, with respect to the takings point, some commentators have read *Mugler* to stand for a somewhat different principle known as the "noxious use doctrine."[58] Under that view the Court did not take the position that no land use regulation could be a taking, but rather the more limited view that a regulation aimed at prohibiting harmful activities could not be deemed a taking. According to that notion, if the nature of the use adversely affected by the government regulation was found to be noxious, wrongful, harmful, or prejudicial to the health, safety, or morals of the public, then government might validly regulate it and thereby decrease its value without the necessity of paying compensation to the owner.[59]

. . . .

In *Lawton v. Steele*,[62] the Court indicated for the first time that a confiscatory land use regulation, that is, one "unduly oppressive upon individuals"[63] might be

---

[56]   123 U.S. 623 (1887).

[58]   *See, e.g.,* Joseph L. Sax, *Takings and the Police Power*, 74 Yale L.J. 36 (1964).

[59]   Though the early cases stood for no such proposition, Professor Ernst Freund stated the principle in the alternative: "[I]t may be said that the state takes property by eminent domain because it is useful to the public and under the police power because it is harmful." Ernst Freund, The Police Power 546-47 (1904).

   In other words, Freund held that if the result of governmental regulation was to achieve a benefit for the community, compensation must be paid; but if it was to terminate a harmful activity, no compensation was necessary. The original noxious use cases stood only for the second of the two propositions, but as we shall see, the courts later accepted Freund's formulation.

[62]   152 U.S. 133 (1894).

[63]   *Id.* at 137.

unconstitutional. However, it did not make clear whether it considered this to be a taking or a deprivation of due process. . . .

Finally in *Pennsylvania Coal Co. v. Mahon*,[67] the Court, . . . in an opinion by Justice Holmes, . . . made it absolutely clear that it rejected any notion that an onerous land use regulation could not be a taking. In that case, the Court struck down a state statute upheld by the state courts, that, with certain exceptions not relevant, prohibited the mining of anthracite coal in such a way as to cause the subsidence of structures used for human habitation. The suit was an action brought by a superadjacent individual private homeowner to enjoin the defendant Coal Company from violating the statute by mining in a way that would cause the collapse of his house. Defendant Coal Company's defense was that the plaintiff's title stemmed from a deed made by it, which granted to the plaintiff surface rights, while reserving to the defendant the right to mine the subsurface coal, with the plaintiff also agreeing to waive all right to damages which might occur from such mining. Under the law of Pennsylvania, this gave the plaintiff a surface estate, while the Coal Company had the subsurface estate and a separate support estate. The Court viewed the matter as an unconstitutional taking of the entire separate support estate. . . .

In *Pennsylvania Coal* the Court laid down the doctrine, known as the diminution in value test, that a land use regulation that was too onerous could in certain circumstances be a taking. This obviously left open the question of when the regulation might be said to go "too far." Certainly it does not happen too often, for it is interesting to note that in the seventy year period from 1922, the date of *Pennsylvania Coal*, until 1992, when it finally issued the opinion finding a taking in *Lucas v. South Carolina Coastal Council*,[69] the Court never found a regulation that went "too far." And though the cases are relatively infrequent, state courts have on occasion used the doctrine to strike down various individual land use control regulations that they deemed too onerous, such as industrial zoning and various development prohibitions.

The policy of the Takings Clause was made clear by *Pennsylvania Coal*, however. It was later best, if cryptically, expressed in an opinion by Mr. Justice Black in *Armstrong v. United States*.[71] . . .

The case is not notable for what it held, but is often cited for Justice Black's delineation of the basic policy underlying the takings rules, hereinafter designated as the Armstrong Policy: "The Fifth Amendment's guarantee that private property shall not be taken for a public use without just compensation was designed to bar Government from forcing some people alone to bear public burdens which, in all fairness and justice, should be borne by the public as a whole."[72] Solving the riddle of when "fairness and justice" require that society rather than the individual

---

[67] 260 U.S. 393 (1922).

[69] 112 S. Ct. 2886 (1992).

[71] 364 U.S. 40 (1960).

[72] *Id.* at 49.

should bear the cost of government impositions has proved to be one of the most difficult questions the Court has ever had to face. . . .

V. THE REMEDY FOR REGULATORY TAKINGS

It is important to note the remedy that the Court used in *Pennsylvania Coal* when it held the statute was an unconstitutional taking of the Coal Company's support estate, viz., to refuse to enforce the statute, thus effectively voiding it and enjoining its enforcement. The unfortunate result of that was to allow the Company to continue its mining operations unhampered and consequently to destroy the homes of the superadjacent landowners.

If it had been available, a different remedy would have reached a result much sounder and fairer to both sides, while still leaving intact the basic taking decision. The remedy follows logically from the Armstrong Policy which underlies all takings rules—that of preventing the state from imposing upon an individual those burdens which in fairness ought to be borne by the general public. That better approach would be to give the regulator the option of compensating the Company and allowing the regulation to go into effect, thereby protecting the homes from collapse, or, in the alternative, acquiescing in the Court's voiding of the regulation, thereby, of course, imperiling them. If the regulator chose the former option, both sides would be protected by a procedure that allowed the homeowners to keep their homes and the Coal Company to be compensated for the taking of its property. The remedy was not available in *Pennsylvania Coal* because the regulator (in this case the state) was not a party to the suit. But in most cases challenges to regulations do involve the regulator as a party (or it can be made one), and it should be available.

The history of the compensation remedy for governmental acts deemed a taking is rather a complicated one and will only be briefly described here. First of all, compensation has always been available when the government act involved a physical takeover of the owner's property. The appropriate action was (and is) a suit in "inverse condemnation" where the plaintiff injured landowner sued the government wrongdoer for damages.

The real controversy has always been whether an owner who was the victim of a "regulatory taking" had a similar remedy in inverse condemnation, or the courts were limited to a declaration that the regulation was void and therefore unenforceable. . . .

. . . .

Finally in *First English Evangelical Lutheran Church v. County of Los Angeles*,[82] the Court faced the issue head-on and ruled in favor of the remedy. . . .

. . . .

The importance of the *First English* case lies in its establishment, conclusively for the first time, of a right to compensation for temporary regulatory takings. But

---

[82]   482 U.S. 304 (1987).

there is perhaps greater significance in what the Court had to say about damages for permanent takings. In two places in the opinion, it indicated that where a regulation is held to be a taking, the government has the option of continuing to enforce it permanently upon payment of damages or to acquiesce in its being voided. This is a perfectly appropriate result. If the regulation has a legitimate public purpose, the government should be allowed to continue it in effect, as long as it is willing to pay those people who, in the words of *Armstrong*, should not be forced "alone to bear public burdens which, in all fairness and justice, should be borne by the public as a whole."[94]

The rule has some other virtues as well. Importantly, it will force regulators to take into account the costs and benefits of the regulations they put into effect. Finally it will help put to an end the pernicious practice of some municipal regulators of what might be called serial regulation. For example, a developer wants to put in a shopping center on his property, and the city to forestall that passes an ordinance zoning the property as single family residential. When the state supreme court after four years of litigation voids the regulation, the city passes another ordinance zoning the property for multi-family residential. Other ordinances can be passed as needed to prevent the desired development. In the end no landowner is able to win a battle in which the city passes one law after another to frustrate his purposes. The inverse condemnation rule will help to end that kind of abuse.

VI. EARLY MUDDLING OF TAKINGS AND SUBSTANTIVE DUE PROCESS

. . . In pure form, due process now questions the legitimacy of the government impositions—does the regulation have a lawful objective and are the means utilized directed to reaching it? In contrast, takings rules deal with the *weight* of government impositions—even though in a particular case the government has a lawful objective and its means are directed to reaching it, is it fair under the circumstances for one person to bear all the costs of the imposition or would it be more just to require society to bear them?

It is perfectly obvious that it makes little difference what labels one puts on these very different concepts as long as sound rules are applied to each. The problem has been that historically the Court often neither carefully distinguished between the basic concepts nor consistently applied the same labels to them. Often it has tended to put the two doctrines together in an unintelligible muddle. . . .

In the land use area, the Court also failed to distinguish between the two concepts. In the two cases that purported to deal with the constitutional limits upon zoning, *Village of Euclid v. Ambler Realty Co.*[102] and *Nectow v. City of Cambridge*,[103] the Court dealt with the issue as a matter of substantive due process. In the first it upheld generally the power of government to zone, holding that sepa-

---

[94] Armstrong v. United States, 364 U.S. 40, 49 (1960).

[102] 272 U.S. 365 (1926).

[103] 277 U.S. 183 (1928).

ration of land uses was a legitimate end and that zoning was a rational means of getting there. In the second, it struck down as a violation of substantive due process a particular regulation that the master below felt was irrational under the circumstances. Neither case discussed takings jurisprudence though they both involved substantial decreases in value as a result of the zoning regulation, and they both came after Justice Holmes' decision in *Pennsylvania Coal.*

VII. THE MODERN MERGER OF TAKINGS AND DUE PROCESS

After *Pennsylvania Coal, Euclid* and *Nectow*, the Court, with very few exceptions, pretty much ignored local land use control problems for the next fifty years. In 1978, however, with the case of *Penn Central Transportation Co. v. City of New York*,[105] it initiated a new period of intensive work in the area and also began what now seems to be an irreversible and unfortunate merger of the due process and takings concepts. . . .

. . . .

The *Penn Central* case was an opening wedge in what became the final rejection of the noxious use doctrine by the Court and its replacement in takings analysis by what is very difficult to distinguish from a substantive due process standard in *Agins v. City of Tiburon*,[118] *Nollan v. California Coastal Commission*,[119] and *Lucas v. South Carolina Coastal Council*.[120] The noxious use doctrine had allowed the destruction of property values by regulation as long as its purpose was to prevent some "public harm." But the shift to a rule permitting the justification of a regulation by a showing that it serves the public health, safety, welfare, or morals allowed a much broader compass for regulation.

. . . .

In *Penn Central* Mr. Justice Brennan had stated that a regulation that advanced the public welfare was not a taking. A few years later in *Agins v. City of Tiburon*[124] the Court, in upholding the validity of a zoning ordinance limiting plaintiff's land to residential use against a taking challenge, stated in dictum the converse proposition that a regulation that did *not* advance the public welfare *was* a taking. "The application of a general zoning law to particular property effects a taking if the ordinance does not substantially advance legitimate state interests . . ., or denies an owner economically viable use of his land."[125] The Court agreed with the state supreme court's view that the ordinance advanced a legitimate public interest by discouraging the "premature and unnecessary conversion of open-space land to urban uses."[126]

---

[105] 438 U.S. 104 (1978).
[118] 447 U.S. 255 (1980).
[119] 483 U.S. 825 (1987).
[120] 112 S. Ct. 2886 (1992).
[124] 447 U.S. 255 (1980).
[125] *Id.* at 260.
[126] *Id.* at 261.

In *Nollan v. California Coastal Commission*,[127] the Court, in the first modern case to do so, actually struck down as a taking, rather than as a denial of substantive due process, a regulation that flunked a means/ends nexus review. Stated more precisely, the Court held to be a taking a regulation, wherein, though the ends sought by the regulators were legitimate, the means selected were not fairly directed toward those ends. . . .

. . . .

. . . In other words, the *Nollan* opinion stands for the propositions that, for such a regulatory exaction to be valid: 1) the owner's proposed activity must create or contribute to the creation of a public need; and 2) the exaction must tend toward the satisfaction of that same need.

In the recent case of *Dolan v. City of Tigard*,[134] the Court made more clear exactly what a regulatory body has to show under the first point to justify the exactions that it requires in exchange for permission to develop. It borrowed from state cases in the subdivision exaction area that required a "reasonable relationship" between the exaction and the need created by the proposed development, but the Court modified that rule by substituting for it the standard that there must be a "rough proportionality" between the two factors.

The *Nollan* opinion was notable in at least two respects. First, it established with finality, if the question was still in doubt, the dubious notion that judicial review of the nexus between means and ends, which was traditionally viewed as an issue of substantive due process, was a takings question as well. The Court was apparently enshrining as a permanent fixture in constitutional law a heedless merger of the very different concepts and policies involved in substantive due process and takings rules. Second, although the Court held that basically the same issue was involved in both the takings and due process inquiries, it carefully distinguished the burden of proof required under each, requiring heightened judicial scrutiny (similar to that given sex discrimination under the Equal Protection Clause) in reviews under the Takings Clause but mere rational basis scrutiny in reviews under substantive due process. Thus, under *Nollan*, the same regulation might fail a means-ends test as a takings matter but pass it as a due process one. As a practical matter, then, the takings review, being the stricter one, would henceforth control the determination of whether a land use regulation would be held to be constitutional or unconstitutional in a means-ends review.

Though Justice Scalia did not purport to limit the application of his doctrine that it is a taking if the means are not reasonably directed toward reaching the regulator's articulated end, that doctrine must clearly be confined to cases involving regulatory *exactions*. For *Nollan* does not really answer the question of what the result should be when a regulatory *prohibition* is argued to be unconstitutional as a taking or deprivation of due process, on the ground that the means are not rationally directed toward the regulator's admittedly lawful purpose. To illustrate the

---

[127] 483 U.S. 825 (1987).

[134] 114 S. Ct. 2309 (1994).

problem, take the *Nollan* facts and suppose the regulation of the Commission was not an attempted easement exaction but a broad-gauged prohibition against any new construction on the property. Again suppose the purpose advanced for the regulation was that the Commission was seeking to preserve the view of those persons already on the beach—an obvious subterfuge. If the Commission had no other lawful purpose in mind, or if it had an unlawful purpose, (e.g. to succumb to the whimsical obsession of an influential next-door neighbor that he have the largest house in the neighborhood), then it is submitted that the regulation should be voided as a violation of substantive due process, and that the government should not have the option of enforcing the regulation even upon payment of full compensation. The reason is that the government's exercise of power to pass legislation having only a private purpose is illegitimate, and just as in the case of a condemnation having a private purpose in violation of the public use doctrine, the government should be completely prevented from so acting.

. . . .

VIII. THE *LUCAS* CASE AND THE NUISANCE DOCTRINE

When the Court decided to review the case of *Lucas v. South Carolina Coastal Council*,[139] it was expected that, with the changes in the composition of the Court, some radical remodeling of the law might occur. Change there has been, but it is not yet clear that it could be properly called "radical.". . .

. . . .

An important part of the opinion deals with the Court's rejection of the noxious use doctrine and its replacement with the background principles of nuisance rule. One might ask what difference the change will make in the actual decision of cases and indeed, when the matter is carefully analyzed, whether the Court has really made a substantive change at all. First of all there is an obvious similarity between the two rules: the conventional (though as we shall see, historically inaccurate) statement of the noxious use doctrine is that the challenged regulation is not a taking when its purpose is to forbid a use which is "harmful" to society, but is a taking when its purpose is to secure a benefit for the community. The rule applies to all regulations adversely affecting value, even those completely reducing it to zero. On the other hand, the nuisance rule holds that when a regulation wreaks a total decrease in value, it is categorically a taking, except where common law principles of private and public nuisance indicate "that the proscribed use interests were not part of [the landowner's] title to begin with."[148] An ostensible difference between the two rules is that the noxious use doctrine exempts from takings challenges *any* regulatorily-caused diminution in value, while the nuisance rule applies only as an exception to the rule that *total* diminutions in value are categorical takings. But that difference is illusory, for if the nuisance rule insulates cases of total

---

[139] 112 S. Ct. 2886 (1992).

[148] Lucas v. South Carolina Coastal Council, 112 S. Ct. 2886, 2899 (1992).

diminution from takings challenges, then *a fortiori* it would serve to exempt cases of lesser decreases in value.

There are some other important points to be made about Justice Scalia's rejection of the noxious use rule as well. A problem lies with his statement that the doctrine hinged on the distinction between harm prevention and benefit extraction. If one examines the classic cases in this area, involving prohibition of brickyards,[149] fertilizer manufacturing plants,[150] breweries[151] and cedar trees[152] one can look long and hard to find any statement contrasting those two factors. The complete emphasis of these landmark cases was upon the nuisance or at least the harmful nature of the proscribed uses. The benefit extraction part of the rule seems to have arisen from the statement made by Professor Ernst Freund in his book on the police power.[153]

If one grants that the noxious use doctrine as originally formulated looked only at the nuisance or harmful aspect of the activity, that doctrine and Justice Scalia's nuisance rule become strikingly similar. Both rules, it appears, are seeking to allow the government great latitude in dealing with the problems of harmful or damaging land use activity without having to pay compensation. But Justice Scalia's criticism of the noxious use doctrine as useless because of the impossibility of distinguishing between harm-preventing and benefit-conferring regulations, does seem disingenuous when one considers what the original noxious use doctrine really said. And while his critique would seem fair enough if one were to accept his assertion of what that doctrine held, still his argument rings a little hollow when one considers that the common law of nuisance itself has always been considered notably amorphous and uncertain.

Still the question remains: what can one authoritatively say about the effect of this new rule upon the decision of actual cases? To answer that, it would be well to examine the famous above-described U.S. Supreme Court noxious use cases of the past involving prohibitions upon pre-existing breweries, brickyards, fertilizer manufacturing plants, and cedar trees. In each the Supreme Court upheld the constitutionality of the proscribing regulations based upon the notion that the government had the right under the police power to regulate those noxious activities to promote the public welfare. And in each the Court mentioned the *nuisance* nature of the regulated party's activities but without purporting to refer to the state's common law as such. Thus, it would appear that under the old noxious use doctrine, the courts were left completely free to use "general principles" in deciding questions of harm and nuisance, while they would apparently be tied to the state's common law of nuisance, with all of its variables and uncertainties, in deciding similar issues under the new rule. Each one of the above activities involved might or might not

---

[149] Hadacheck v. Sebastian, 239 U.S. 394 (1915).

[150] Fertilizing Co. v. Hyde Park, 97 U.S. 659 (1878).

[151] Mugler v. Kansas, 123 U.S. 623 (1887).

[152] Miller v. Schoene, 276 U.S. 272 (1928).

[153] . . . FREUND, *supra* note 59, at 546-47.

be a nuisance at the common law depending upon a number of circumstances, including, of course, the suitability of the plaintiff's use and of the defendant's allegedly wrongful use to the locality involved, the priority in time issue considered below, as well as other factors. Justice Blackmun asserted in his dissent in *Lucas*, that the brewery in *Mugler* (as well as the brickyard in *Hadacheck*, the cedar trees in *Miller*, and the gravel pit in *Goldblatt*) were not common law nuisances;[160] that undoubtedly was true at least at the time that the parties started using their property in what later became an offending way.

It should also be emphasized that the full strength of the nuisance rule applies only where there is a complete destruction of value. Under *Lucas*, where there is such and there is no nuisance, that would categorically be a taking, but where the diminution is less than total—overwhelmingly the most common situation—the Court would be relegated once again to deciding the taking question by the admittedly uncertain method of balancing various factors and "engaging in . . . essentially ad hoc factual inquiries."[161]. . .

. . . .

Only time will tell whether this change to a takings law more protective of the landowner will occur. It may be that, sooner or later, the Court will feel impelled to pull back from a full-blown application of its nuisance doctrine. Whether it should or not is another question. . . .

In summary, it appears that the net result of the change to the common law nuisance standard will be a tendency for the courts, in the very few cases where there has been a complete destruction of value, to strike down more regulations than they would have under the old noxious use doctrine, as they feel somewhat constrained by the admittedly uncertain contours of traditional nuisance law. That certainly was the effect in the *Lucas* case itself, where the South Carolina courts upheld the regulation under the noxious use doctrine but were forced to strike it down when they were held to be bound by the state's common law of nuisance. But because the rule in *Lucas* only applies to those rare cases where the decrease in value is total, the overall effect of the case will undoubtedly be much less than conservative takings reformers hoped for before the opinion was handed down.

IX. A SOUND TAKINGS RULE

The Armstrong Policy should be the touchstone used in devising a sound takings jurisprudence. Takings rules deal with the fairness of imposing upon one person or a small group of persons burdens that benefit a large segment of society. In a sense, then, they have an equal protection component; they attempt to decide whether when government bears down harder on one person than the rest of society, there is some valid justification for its doing so. Such justification might be the

---

[160] Lucas v. South Carolina Coastal Council, 112 S. Ct. 2886, 2913 (1992) (Blackmun, J., dissenting).

[161] Penn Central Transportation Co. v. City of New York, 438 U.S. 104, 124 (1978).

wrongful or tortious conduct of the person, which the nuisance rule addresses, or that any detriments visited upon the person are *de minimis* or offset by a corresponding benefit to him. The latter point is what Justice Holmes meant in his discussion in *Pennsylvania Coal* of the "average reciprocity of advantage." It would not be a justification, however, that imposing a substantial burden results in great public benefit, if the person is without fault and fortuitously in the position where it becomes cheaper and easier to have him rather than society to bear the cost.

This, of course, raises the question of what is meant by "without fault." By that I mean, not fault in the sense of moral culpability, but in the sense that the person exercised the care normally employed by a reasonable person to prevent economic loss to himself. Thus if the burden was reasonably expectable at the time of the owner's purchase of the property, no compensation should be due him, because presumably the price he paid would reflect that expectation. And if at such time, he made a property improvement which later suffered in value as a result of those reasonably predictable governmental acts, no recompense should be payable for such diminution in value.

The real weakness of takings rules in general and the *Lucas* case in particular lies in the requirement that the challenged regulation cause a total decrease in value before an owner is afforded full takings law protection against a governmental imposition. *Lucas* holds that if the decrease is 100 percent, a categorical takings rule applies, but if it is only 98 percent, a different set of rules—involving the balancing of a number of factors—applies. The case can be fairly criticized for making so much rest on so little. Would it really be fair in a case like Mr. Lucas' to say that he would be entitled to a $975,000 recovery if his property was rendered worthless by the regulation but he would be entitled to nothing if its value was reduced a mere $965,000 to $10,000? . . .

. . . .

XI. CLEARING UP THE MUDDLE—SUMMARY AND CONCLUSION

. . . [T]he recent merger of substantive due process and takings rules has resulted in an unfortunate muddle. Properly, due process analysis—looking to whether there is a valid public purpose for a challenged regulation or regulatory activity, and/or whether the means are fairly directed to reaching it—should decide the question of whether the government's imposition is legitimate and therefore whether it has the *power* to so act. This is the same kind of an issue as is addressed by the public use doctrine which outlaws outright government condemnations that are illegitimate because they are strictly for the benefit of a private party. That doctrine grants specific relief against the governmental seizure; the payment of compensation does not cure the defect. Similarly when a regulation fails a substantive due process means/ends nexus test, the exercise of governmental law-making power is illegitimate and the law should, at the option of the party harmed, be completely voided; even payment of full compensation should not be sufficient to sustain it. And of course, compensation should be paid under § 1983 of the Civil

Rights Act for the temporary injustice visited upon the owner for the period until the regulation is invalidated.

On the other hand, takings analysis—properly analyzed, looking to whether it is fair to impose the burden of a regulation, having a valid public purpose, upon one person rather than upon society in general—should decide the question of whether upon the exercise of the regulatory power, government must pay compensation to sustain it. It follows that when a law is fairly directed to a public purpose but unjustly bears upon an owner in such a way as to constitute a taking, the law should be upheld as long as the government is willing to pay compensation to validate it, but if it is not so willing, it should be voided. And when the government decides not to pay compensation but rather to acquiesce in the voiding of a regulation, damages for the temporary taking should be available under the *First English* case.

Using the above analysis, not only does the means/public ends test bear upon the legitimacy of the exercise of law-making power, but takings tests that purport to examine the purpose of regulations should be viewed as involving similar questions. Thus the former noxious use test and the *Lucas* nuisance test logically go not only to the takings issue but also to the question of whether there is a valid public purpose for a regulation. And the consequence of there not being such a nuisance or noxious use—assuming there is no other valid purpose for the regulation— should be unconditionally to strike the law down as an illegitimate exercise of governmental power. This, of course, is just another illustration of the notion that, if a regulation has a private rather than a public purpose, even paying full compensation should be insufficient to sustain it; the regulation should be stricken down as an improper usurpation by government.

It is unfortunate that in the recent jurisprudence of the Supreme Court in cases such as *Nollan* and *Lucas* the Justices have failed to make the basic distinction between illegitimate governmental impositions and unfairly onerous ones. The result of this will be a failure to achieve sound results in a fair number of cases where government regulations lack a legitimate public purpose.

C. Regulatory Takings

The subject of regulatory takings is addressed by Professor Berger in the immediately preceding article. This section focuses on that perplexing concept. For a book analyzing regulatory takings from an economist's perspective, see William A. Fischel, REGULATORY TAKINGS: LAW, ECONOMICS, AND POLITICS (1995).

1. Procedural Matters

RIPENESS AND FORUM SELECTION IN FIFTH AMENDMENT TAKINGS LITIGATION
Thomas E. Roberts
11 J. Land Use & Envtl. L. 37 (1995)[*]

I. A MESSAGE UNHEARD, MISUNDERSTOOD, OR RESISTED

The 1985 decision in *Williamson County Regional Planning Commission v. Hamilton Bank*[1] imposed significant ripeness and forum selection requirements on Fifth Amendment takings claims. The recent takings decisions of *Lucas v. South Carolina Coastal Council*[3] and *Dolan v. City of Tigard*[4] expand the rights of property owners. However, they have only a modest effect on the rules of ripeness and forum selection, which remain formidable hurdles in land use litigation. Although a spate of takings legislation offered around the country has emerged with the aim of further limiting public control over land use, these bills generally do not address ripeness and forum limitation issues.

Hamilton Bank sets out a two prong test. The first prong—called the final decision requirement—requires a property owner to obtain a final decision from local land use authorities for an "as applied" challenge. If dissatisfied with the devel-

---

[*] Copyright © 1995 by the Florida State University Journal of Land Use and Environmental Law. Reprinted by permission. (The article's initial footnote, which has been omitted, indicates that "[t]his article is a revised version of" a chapter in an American Bar Association book. *See* Thomas E. Roberts, Chapter 3—*Ripeness and Forum Selection in Land-Use Litigation, in* TAKINGS: LAND-DEVELOPMENT CONDITIONS AND REGULATORY TAKINGS AFTER *DOLAN* AND *LUCAS* 46-79 (David L. Callies ed., 1996) (© 1996 American Bar Association).)

[1]   473 U.S. 172 (1985).

[3]   112 S. Ct. 2886 (1992). . . .

[4]   114 S. Ct. 2309 (1994).

opment rights denied or limitations imposed in seeking a final decision, or if making a facial challenge, the second prong—called the compensation requirement—requires the property owner to seek compensation in the state courts. The rationale of prong one is that a regulation is only a taking if it goes "too far," and a court cannot answer this question without knowing how far the regulation goes.[8] The second prong is based on the nature of the Fifth Amendment claim; the Constitution does not proscribe takings, only takings without compensation. To receive compensation, the property owner must initiate an inverse condemnation action.[9]

Despite these requirements, case reporters over the past decade are filled with suits that have been filed prematurely in both state and federal courts without a final decision from the local authorities. The reporters also carry numerous instances of property owners seeking compensation directly from the federal courts. This suggests that the requirements of *Hamilton Bank* have either not penetrated the consciousness of property owners and their lawyers, or that the property owners' affinity for federal court is so great that they are willing, against great odds, to spend their time and money attempting to fall within narrow exceptions to the rules.

. . . .

Some of these premature litigation efforts are understandable in light of the uncertainty regarding the finality of a decision for the purposes of prong one and the difficulty in distinguishing finality from exhaustion. Property owners may encounter difficulty ascertaining the number of applications for development, to whom the applications must be submitted, and the need to apply for development permission when to do so seems futile. Clarity is needed in the prong one final decision rule.

Confusion also exists regarding prong two, the compensation requirement. Despite the fact that the Constitution mandates a compensation remedy, some litigants and courts question the availability of such claims in state courts. The lack of recognition of the res judicata implications of prong two complicates the claim. In this respect, the ripeness label applied to prong two is misleading for it suggests that a claim may be heard in federal court after a state court denies compensation. This is generally not true. Once tried in state court, the claim cannot be relitigated in federal court. Characterizing prong two as a forum restricting rule, rather than a ripeness rule, provides more accuracy and safety.

II. The Leading Cases

. . . .

To summarize, *Hamilton Bank* and *MacDonald* require that, prior to filing suit in federal court, developers obtain from state courts a final decision on a mean-

---

[8]   MacDonald, Sommer & Frates v. County of Yolo, 477 U.S. 340, 348-49 (1986). . . .

[9]   *MacDonald, Sommer & Frates*, 477 U.S. at 350.

ingful application for development. If a variance procedure exists that might permit a project to proceed, it must be used unless application would be futile. If development permission is denied, compensation must be sought by way of an inverse condemnation action in state court. For a property owner's lawyer, this approach is "easier said than done."

. . . .

VI. CONCLUSION: ARE THE RIPENESS RULES UNDUE BURDENS OR A HOAX?

Critics disagree over whether compliance with the final decision rule is more analogous to fording a raging river or stepping over a trickle of a stream. . . .

My view is that some clarification is needed and that an accurate reading of *Hamilton Bank* and *MacDonald* would do the job. Much of the stringency of the final decision rule has come from the lower federal courts' expansion of those cases beyond their bounds. This, presumably, is traceable in large part to the desire of these courts, for good and bad reasons, to keep land use cases off their dockets.

Statutory solutions should also be explored. Florida's property rights legislation adopted in 1995, for example, creates final decision ripeness by compelling a municipality to issue a ripeness determination after the property owner files notice of intent to sue.[257] The ripeness determination must list the allowable uses for the property. This commendable solution comes after a statutorily mandated settlement process. The government will have had ample opportunity to review the desired reach of its laws and can hardly complain of being prematurely hauled into court. Furthermore, the property owner has an assurance that enough requests have been filed.

More troubling is prong two and the paradoxical consequences that result from the mixture of ripeness law and the law of full faith and credit. One understandable reaction to the prong two requirement of *Hamilton Bank* is that it perpetrates a fraud or hoax on landowners. The courts say: "Your suit is not ripe until you seek compensation from the state courts." When the property owner complies, a federal court suit is barred by collateral estoppel and res judicata. While it is unfortunate that courts continue to use misleading ripeness language, the result is justifiable if one thinks that one lawsuit is enough.

Beyond the misleading ripeness language, the litigant incurs no harm simply by being barred from federal court. If the property owner's lawyer knows the law, the property owner can avoid a wasted effort in federal court. In the alternative, if

---

[257] *See* 1995, Fla. Laws ch. 95-181. The statute authorizes a property owner to file a notice of claim after having an application for development permission turned down. The governmental entity must then "put up or shut up." It can develop a number of settlement offers. If no settlement is reached, section 1 (5)(a) compels a written ripeness determination. A federal court would still need to determine that an Article III controversy existed.

. . . .

the property owners come to federal court, they come with the knowledge that they are likely to fail if the government defendant or the court *sua sponte* raises the jurisdictional defense of ripeness.

There is a denial of a federal forum but our dual system presumes state court competency. No injury inures to property owners as a class unless one thinks that state courts are likely to be hostile to property owners' rights. Undoubtedly, state courts vary in the deference they accord local land use decisions. Even if hostility exists in some courts, the same would likely be true in federal courts. Numerous federal judges have decried being turned into super zoning boards of appeal. Judge Posner has complained of federal courts hearing "garden variety zoning dispute[s] dressed up in the trappings of constitutional law."[259] The denigrating tone of these pronouncements suggests that the outcome for property owners in many instances would be no better, and might be worse, in federal court.

Two solutions emerge if the matter is thought to be in need of change: rewrite the law of res judicata and full faith and credit or rewrite the law of the Fifth Amendment. In rewriting the law of res judicata, the Court or Congress might address the paradox and conceivably say that the second suit in federal court is not barred by the full faith and credit statute. Such a ruling or statute, however, would require a decision as to whether the principles and policies behind full faith and credit and the law of finality of judgments should give way to replication of matters once litigated. Ironically, an unripe suit is barred at the moment it comes into existence. Like a tomato that suffers vine rot, it goes from being green to mushy red overnight. It is never able to be eaten. This anomaly, however, is not necessarily bad. The additional lawsuits might not cause the federal judiciary to collapse, but they would use the limited resources of courts already busy.

If one insists on opening the lower federal courts to these suits, judicial economy would be better served by having just one lawsuit. This could be achieved by reexamining the rule that the Fifth Amendment does not require pre-taking compensation. This rule lies behind prong two's view of the Fifth Amendment that no cause of action exists until demand is made on the state, and the state refuses to pay. The language of the Fifth Amendment does not dictate this rule.

In the context of inverse condemnation, the Fifth Amendment could be read as providing that a taking occurs upon the adoption or application of an excessive or illegal regulation. Regarding as applied claims, a property owner would have to obtain a final decision. After obtaining a final decision, the property owner would then sue either in state or federal court. As to facial claims, prong one not being applicable, the choice of forums would exist upon enactment. With this reinterpretation, at least only one lawsuit would be viable. The state, the wrongdoer in the sense that it took property without paying, could hardly complain that it must defend itself in federal court for violating federal rights. The increased workload on the lower federal courts might affect the inclination to overturn this longstanding rule of inverse condemnation. That, in part, may depend on whether those

---

[259] *Coniston v. Village of Hoffman Estates*, 844 F.2d 461 (7th Cir. 1988). . . .

courts are already obligated to hear land use claims under the Due Process and Equal Protection Clauses of the Fourteenth Amendment. If so, perhaps the takings claim related to the same facts might be seen as an insignificant addition.

I do not advocate these changes. Federal courts are busy enough. State judges are more familiar with land use disputes and can do a better job of evaluating local and state interests. Further, the bar is not total. Where state courts have definitively ruled out takings claims, a federal action will lie. Finally, I am not convinced that state judges in general harbor hostilities to property owners that would, if true, support the availability of the more independent federal judiciary.

REGULATORY TAKINGS AND RIPENESS IN THE FEDERAL COURTS
Gregory M. Stein
48 Vand. L. Rev. 1 (1995)[*]

I. INTRODUCTION

. . . .

. . . [R]egulatory takings law and the ripeness doctrine frequently operate at cross purposes. Plaintiffs whose rights must be protected quickly if they are to be protected at all may be fatally delayed by a doctrine that is designed—with good reason—to limit their access to federal court. Defendants who blunder into effecting a taking will pay unnecessarily large awards, augmented by the years of regulatory bickering during which the just compensation meter was silently ticking. And federal courts have shown little inclination to address this doctrinal clash, with few courts even acknowledging that they appreciate the problem.

. . . .

II. REGULATORY TAKINGS AND RIPENESS

At first glance, the jurisdictional ripeness standard might seem unlikely to thwart the just compensation requirement—in fact, the two appear to have little relationship to each other. . . .

In spite of their apparent disjunction, these two doctrines tend to become entangled, because regulatory takings cases by their nature are likely to raise ripeness issues as well. A regulatory taking, as the Supreme Court has defined that term, is not an event. Rather, it is a post hoc conclusion about an earlier, often prolonged series of events. Landowners commonly initiate litigation as this sequence

---

of events is unfolding, when a court is not yet in a position to determine whether a taking has occurred. As a result, the Supreme Court has applied a particularly tough ripeness standard in land use cases, thereby ensuring that regulatory takings law and ripeness doctrine remain intertwined. . . .

A. Regulatory Takings Law

. . . .

While the Court has resolved many of the major issues that arise in direct condemnation cases, inverse condemnation law remains unsettled. . . .

As far back as 1922, the Supreme Court recognized that governments can "take" property by regulatory action without explicitly condemning it. In Justice Holmes's language for the Court, "[W]hile property may be regulated to a certain extent, if regulation goes too far it will be recognized as a taking."[21] Although the Court continues to wrestle with the question of how far is "too far," it resolved in *First English*[23] the related question of what remedies are available to the plaintiff who suffers an inverse condemnation.

In *First English*, appellant owned twenty-one acres in a canyon that flooded after a forest fire. The flood destroyed several church-owned buildings, including facilities used for a summer camp. Fearing more floods in the future, Los Angeles County passed a temporary emergency ordinance prohibiting any construction in the canyon. Appellant brought suit in state court alleging that the ordinance constituted a compensable taking. The California Superior Court ruled against the church on a pre-trial motion, the Court of Appeal affirmed, and the California Supreme Court denied review.

On appeal, the United States Supreme Court could not determine whether a regulatory taking had actually occurred, given the absence of a trial. But the Court nonetheless held that "where the government's activities have already worked a taking of all use of property, no subsequent action by the government can relieve it of the duty to provide compensation for the period during which the taking was effective."[25] In other words, if a municipality takes some action that a court determines years later to have worked a regulatory taking, then the municipality must provide compensation accruing from the point when the interference first effected the taking.

Although *First English* resolved the uncertainty surrounding the appropriate remedy for an inverse regulatory taking, it left to the lower courts the challenging details of how to calculate compensation. Significantly, the Court offered no suggestion as to how to determine when a temporary regulatory taking begins and ends.

---

[21] *Pennsylvania Coal v. Mahon*, 260 U.S. 393, 415 (1922) (Holmes, J.). . . .

[23] [*First English Evangelical Lutheran Church v. County of Los Angeles*,] 482 U.S. 304 [(1987)].

[25] *First English*, 482 U.S. at 321. . . .

B. *The Ripeness Doctrine*

1. Ripeness, in General

The ripeness doctrine is a tool designed to determine when judicial review is appropriate. . . . [R]ipeness seeks to protect courts from deciding cases whose times have not yet come.

The ripeness doctrine is generally viewed as being both constitutionally required and judicially prudent. The constitutional mandate results from Article III's requirement that federal courts hear only cases or controversies.[31] The prudential restrictions result from the fact that most courts would rather avoid speculative cases, defer to finders of fact with greater subject matter expertise, decide cases with fully-developed records, and avoid overly broad opinions, even if these courts might constitutionally hear a dispute. . . .

. . . .

2. Modifying the Ripeness Doctrine for Land Use Cases

The ripeness doctrine applies to federal courts that have been asked to rule on federal challenges to the application of state or local land use laws. As in any federal case, Article III requires a case or controversy, and federal courts would be prudent to avoid rendering speculative opinions based upon incomplete records. Nonetheless, federal courts afford somewhat different procedural treatment to regulatory takings plaintiffs. These differences are byproducts of the unique nature of the Takings Clause.

The Supreme Court has stated clearly that exhaustion of administrative remedies is not required in federal cases alleging state takings. . . . [A] requirement similar to that of exhaustion is already built into the ripeness test that the Court applies in takings cases. For while exhaustion is excused, a plaintiff is required to seek just compensation in state court before she can present a ripe case or controversy in federal court. . . .

. . . .

The prudential portion of the ripeness test also turns out to be extremely difficult to meet in takings cases. Both the highly fact-specific nature of takings claims and the unusually ad hoc nature of takings case law make federal courts particularly reluctant to hear these cases until a record has been fully developed. . . .

. . . .

3. The Land Use Ripeness Cases

The Supreme Court has developed a well-defined ripeness doctrine for land use matters in its recent cases. . . .

. . . .

---

[31] U.S. Const., Art. III, § 2. . . .

. . . [B]y 1980, the Court had suggested the beginnings of a ripeness test. At the outset, a landowner may challenge the offending ordinance on its face. She need not take this step, and she will have a difficult time prevailing on the merits if she does elect this alternative. If the owner foregoes a facial challenge or undertakes such a challenge unsuccessfully, her next option is to submit a development plan to local officials. This may not be sufficient to ripen her claim, but . . . it is a necessary first step for a litigant who is challenging an ordinance as applied.

. . . .

The Court outlined additional steps required to obtain federal judicial review of a land use decision in *Williamson County Regional Planning Commission v. Hamilton Bank of Johnson City*.[79] Respondent bank's suit, arising from the denial of approval for a subdivision, included a claim that the commission had taken its property without just compensation, in violation of Section 1983 and state law. The Court acknowledged that respondent had submitted the development plan required by *Agins* [*v. City of Tiburon*, 447 U.S. 255 (1980),] and *San Diego Gas* [*& Electric Company v. City of San Diego*, 450 U.S. 621 (1981)], but nonetheless found that respondent had not taken either of two additional necessary steps: (1) the landowner never received a final decision regarding the application of the local land use laws to its property; and (2) the landowner never used the procedures available under state law for obtaining just compensation.

To begin with, respondent never received a final decision on its application because it never sought the variance that would have allowed it to proceed, even though the local zoning appeals board had the power to grant such a variance and might have done so. A court could not determine whether petitioner had unreasonably interfered with respondent's investment-backed expectations because the extent of the interference was not yet known. . . .

Moreover, respondent did not avail itself of the state procedures available for obtaining just compensation. The Fifth Amendment prohibits only the uncompensated taking of property, so there is no way to know if a violation has occurred until the landowner seeks payment and is rejected. A municipality's alleged constitutional violation is not complete unless it fails to provide adequate compensation for the taking. Until that happens, the case continues to ripen.

. . . .

The Court added yet another layer to the ripeness test in *MacDonald, Sommer & Frates v. Yolo County*.[86] In *MacDonald*, appellant challenged the rejection of its subdivision proposal, seeking declaratory and monetary relief. . . . After reaffirming the ripeness doctrine it had developed . . . , the Court carried its analysis a step further, noting that "[r]ejection of exceedingly grandiose development plans does not logically imply that less ambitious plans will receive similarly unfavorable reviews."[88] Thus, two or more variance applications may sometimes be required before a landowner's case ripens.

---

[79]   473 U.S. 172 (1985).

[86]   477 U.S. 340 (1986).

[88]   Id. at 353 n.9.

The Court finally resolved the remedial question the following year in *First English*, holding that regulatory takings are always compensable.[90] . . .

. . . .

. . . [S]een in retrospect and as a group, these cases are clear and coherent. A case will not be heard until it is ripe, and there are several steps that a plaintiff must take to ripen her case. Before bringing an as-applied challenge to a regulation in federal court, a landowner will ordinarily be required to apply to the local board for a development permit, seek a variance if her application is denied, and seek just compensation in state court. Once she takes these steps and ripens her federal claim, she has the opportunity to prove a regulatory taking and the right to compensation if she succeeds.

These cases also leave some important questions unresolved. First, while the Court has established several explicit ripeness thresholds, its decisions do not make it possible to ascertain in advance exactly when a federal court will find a given case to be ripe. . . .

In addition, assuming that a case is ripe and a court finds a regulatory taking, *First English* does not reach the knotty problem of calculating the just compensation that is automatically due. . . .

III. Pinpointing the Four Critical Moments in a Successful Regulatory Takings Claim

Four moments are critical in any federal regulatory takings claim in which the landowner prevails. First, a taking must become effective. Second, a takings claim must ripen, allowing a federal court to exercise jurisdiction. Assuming that a ripe claim exists, the third critical moment is the point when the court makes its decision that a taking has occurred. Finally, there may be a fourth moment when the temporary taking ceases. . . .

A. *The Effective Moment*

. . . .

Initially, establishing the Effective Moment may appear to be a simple task: If a government regulation is intrusive enough that it amounts to a taking of property, then the taking would appear to have commenced when the regulation became effective. But while these two events can occur simultaneously, there is no reason why they must. Not every landowner suffers equally from the enactment of a municipal ordinance that might in some instances amount to a taking. Regulations often become effective long before individual owners form development plans and long before they suffer any actual injury, and compensation should accrue only from that later point when subsequent events combine with the regulation to effect

---

[90] 482 U.S. at 318. . . .

a taking as applied to a given landowner. It would be unfair to municipalities and a windfall to some landowners if courts were always to treat the effective date of a regulation as the Effective Moment and were always to calculate awards from that point forward.

Courts instead should presumptively define the Effective Moment as the point when the landowner's last required variance application is finally denied by the highest administrative body with the power to consent. This is ordinarily the first time that the municipality states with administrative finality exactly what its position is. . . .

. . . .

B. The Ripeness Moment

. . . .

The definition of the Ripeness Moment is fairly clear, given the intense Supreme Court interest in this issue since 1978. But pinpointing the Ripeness Moment in a specific case sometimes proves to be a challenge because of the fact-specific nature of each of these thresholds. . . .

C. The Decision Moment

The "Decision Moment" occurs at the instant when a federal court decision in favor of the landowner becomes irrevocable. At its earliest, this moment occurs when a federal district court enters judgment in favor of the property owner, assuming that the municipality decides not to appeal. At its latest, this moment occurs when the Supreme Court decides in favor of the landowner or declines to hear the case. Whatever the procedural setting of the case, the Decision Moment is the moment when the landowner prevails irreversibly.

. . . .

D. The Cessation Moment

What alternatives does a local governing body have after a federal court finds that a municipality's actions amount to a regulatory taking? *First English* addresses this question directly: "Once a court determines that a taking has occurred, the government retains the whole range of options already available—amendment of the regulation, withdrawal of the invalidated regulation, or exercise of eminent domain."[127] But no matter which of these options it chooses, the municipality is required under *First English* to compensate the owner for the period beginning with the Effective Moment and continuing through the point when it amends or withdraws the regulation or explicitly exercises its eminent domain power. This Arti-

---

[127] *First English*, 482 U.S. at 321. . . .

cle will refer to this latter moment, which marks the end of the period for which there is an ongoing obligation to compensate, as the "Cessation Moment."

. . . .

IV. The Problematic Sequence of Events in a Successful Regulatory Takings Case

. . . .

Ascertaining when these four Moments occur is a daunting task, but accomplishing it is only a necessary first step. For it is the *sequence* of these four Moments that demonstrates most vividly the discord between regulatory takings law and ripeness doctrine. . . .

. . . .

A. The Sequence of Critical Moments in a Successful Case

. . . .

. . . The Effective Moment must precede the Ripeness Moment, which must precede the Decision Moment; and . . . [t]he Cessation Moment can occur at any time after the Effective Moment and need never occur at all.

. . . .

B. Typical Regulatory Takings Cases Are Highly Sensitive to Delays

. . . .

1. The Typical Regulatory Takings Plaintiff

. . . .

. . . [T]he ripeness requirement serves to weed the field of potential plaintiffs, removing those owners whose takings claims are seen as tenuous or distant. That, after all, is the point of both the constitutional and prudential elements of the ripeness requirement. The ripeness doctrine narrows the universe of potential claimants to those owners of truly substantial interests in real property—primarily fee simple holders and long-term ground lessees—who wish to develop their land or modify its use in the immediate future.

A substantial number of these landowning entities will be partnerships, corporations, and limited liability companies, as these are the ownership forms most likely to be used by real estate developers. . . .

But the business entities involved in many major real estate development projects frequently lack the staying power to survive protracted litigation. In spite of the fact that these entities, in contrast with their human counterparts, may endure perpetually, for all practical purposes they must either produce or perish within a period of just a few years. Partners or shareholders invest in these entities with the expectation of seeing returns, or at least construction, within months or years, not decades. The carrying costs of the development parcel, which may include principal and interest on an acquisition loan, real estate taxes and assessments, maintenance of existing structures, insurance, and security, coupled with the costs of ripening and then litigating a regulatory takings claim, can bankrupt a real estate development entity before it ever breaks ground. . . . Practically speaking, the universe of plaintiffs with the financial ability to survive the lengthy ripening process is small.

2. The Typical Regulatory Takings Transaction

The nature of development transactions and the business practices that development entities often employ magnify the problems these typical landowners may face. Rather than purchasing the land at the outset, the developer would rather secure the rights to the development parcel in an option agreement or a contract of sale conditional upon receipt of all necessary permits and approvals. Option agreements and conditional contracts nearly always contain outside closing dates that may arrive and pass while the option holder or contract vendee is seeking permits or pursuing a takings claim. . . .

Developers typically obtain construction and permanent loan commitments early in the development process; such commitments will expire during a prolonged permitting process, leaving developers with the risk of interest rate increases and uncertainty as to the availability of any funds at all. Contractual commitments from architects, contractors, subcontractors, and consultants may expire during the permitting process, and potential tenants may seek other locations. And the business cycle flows forward relentlessly—a project that seemed feasible in 1987 may be out of the question in 1995. Thus, the nature of the typical plaintiff and the nature of the typical transaction combine to dictate that these "perpetual" entities either build or exit within a very short period of time. The ripeness requirements, which delay a landowner's access to court, can be fatal to these sorts of plaintiffs engaged in these sorts of transactions.

3. The Typical Regulatory Takings Defendant

The effects of the ripeness doctrine are intensified further by the nature of the typical defendant. Regulatory entities are municipal bodies, often at the local level, that are inherently slow moving and that possess numerous incentives to delay their final decisions. As elected officials or appointees of elected officials, regulators may be under intense community pressure to deny or delay building permits and variances, in the hope that the applicant will give up or wither away. Their knowledge that developers cannot survive forever and that business cycles fluctuate may lead them to stretch the process out as much as possible, in the hope that the need to decide will evaporate. . . .

In short, certain types of plaintiffs tend to enter into certain types of transactions, for which they need the approval of certain types of defendants. This pattern results in an environment in which the landowner occasionally suffers harsh treatment at the hands of an otherwise fitting ripeness doctrine. The Supreme Court's response to this problem has not been to streamline the process but to raise the cost of the occasional loss for the municipality. By holding that the Takings Clause is self-executing, the Court has told local regulatory bodies that a miscalculation is not just a mistake, but a very expensive mistake. Local boards now face a small risk of huge liability, but only if the plaintiff survives long enough to ripen its claim.

. . . .

V. SOME POSSIBLE SOLUTIONS

. . . .

This Part offers a number of solutions to the problems caused by the synergy of regulatory takings law and ripeness doctrine. Each of these proposed solutions relies upon two premises. The first premise is that solutions to procedural problems should address procedure and not the substantive takings law governing these claims. The second premise is that each party in a regulatory takings case possesses at least one legitimate substantive argument.

. . . .

A. Reexamining the Effective Moment and the Ripeness Moment

1. Reaching the Earliest Possible Ripeness Moment under Existing Law

The most obvious way in which to expedite a landowner's access to federal court is to interpret existing ripeness requirements in such a way that the Ripeness Moment arrives at the earliest possible time. This result can be accomplished even within the confines of current ripeness doctrine, for while the Supreme Court has laid down explicit ripeness thresholds, there is some elasticity built into each one. By applying the various requirements more flexibly, federal courts could comply with the Supreme Court's ripeness demands while allowing more cases to ripen earlier.

Two examples will illustrate this point. First, recall that the Supreme Court held, in *MacDonald, Sommer & Frates v. Yolo County*,[184] that a single building permit application is not sufficient to ripen every regulatory takings case; in some cases, "exceedingly grandiose development plans" that are rejected must be followed up with "less ambitious plans."[185] By interpreting the phrase "exceedingly grandiose" narrowly, a court would be following the Supreme Court's mandate while rejecting the smallest possible number of cases on these grounds. If courts

---

[184] 477 U.S. 340. . . .

[185] 477 U.S. at 353 n.9.

find only the occasional proposal to be exceedingly grandiose, then only one permit application will be required most of the time, and some cases will ripen more
quickly. The result will be that more plaintiffs will be heard in federal court, and
heard earlier.

Second, a court could interpret broadly the futility exception, which excuses a
plaintiff's failure to clear one of the ripeness hurdles when such an attempt would
plainly be futile. . . . A broader reading of the futility exception would violate neither the letter nor the spirit of Supreme Court precedent and would allow courts to
decide some cases earlier in their lives.

. . . .

2. Reaching an Earlier Ripeness Moment by Modifying Existing Law

Federal courts could expedite the ripening process in a far more sweeping manner if the Supreme Court were to relax its ripeness rules expressly. . . .

. . . Relaxing these requirements would frequently place lower federal courts
in the position of having to reach substantive judgments based on guesswork. The
Court should not add overruled cases and increased uncertainty to an area of law
that is already plagued both by the doctrinal clash described in this Article and by
substantive questions that inherently demand ad hoc resolution.

3. Creating Exceptions to the Ripeness Test: The Analogy to Mootness

. . . .

. . . In a takings case, the plaintiff may disappear before the issue ripens, and
the litigation process . . . may provide no better alternative than an exception to a
general timing rule. If issues that inherently evade review form an exception to the
mootness doctrine, perhaps plaintiffs that are incapable of surviving the judicial
process merit an exception to the ripeness doctrine.

. . . .

4. Redefining the Effective Moment

Part III recommended that courts define the Effective Moment presumptively
as the point when the landowner's last required variance application is finally
denied by the highest administrative body with the power to consent. . . . Because
the placement of the Effective Moment has a significant impact on the ripening
process and on the magnitude of regulatory takings awards, it is appropriate here
to reevaluate the proposed definition.

Moving the Effective Moment earlier would affect regulatory takings case law
in two related but distinct ways. First, it would increase the size of the awards that
occasionally will result. This point should be obvious, given that compensation is
measured from the time the government's activities effect a taking. If the municipality effects a taking earlier in the process, awards will increase correspond-

ingly. Second, it would freeze the consequences of municipal activities earlier in the permitting process. . . .

. . . .

This approach must be rejected for two reasons. First, it would force the municipality to pay compensation for an extended portion of the permitting process even though it ordinarily could not have divined that early in the process what the legal effects of its actions would be. . . . It is unfair to the municipality to find a compensable violation to have become effective early in the decision process, while municipal officials were still evaluating incomplete facts and struggling to reach an initial decision. . . .

. . . .

This redefinition of the Effective Moment must be rejected for a second reason. . . . By redefining the Effective Moment, a court would be . . . awarding compensation for a significant portion of the normal permitting process. . . .

. . . .

B. Streamlining the Ripening Process

An entirely different approach to resolving the conflict between regulatory takings law and ripeness doctrine is to minimize its effect by shortening the lengthy permitting process. If legislators and judges can reduce the time between the initial permit application and the final decision, then the significance of the problem is reduced. . . .

1. Creating a State Land Use Court

One method of shortening the permitting process would be for a state legislature to create a special land use court. This new court would, ideally, have jurisdiction over compensation claims arising after variance denials by local regulators. By limiting this court's docket to land use cases, the legislature could minimize the delay between the final variance denial and the state court decision, and the land use judges would develop expertise in state land use matters.

The creation of a land use court would neither change the constitutional definition of a regulatory taking nor modify the constitutional and prudential aspects of the ripeness doctrine. Landowners would still have to obtain a final decision at the local level and regulators would still face the specter of regulatory takings awards. But a state land use court could minimize the negative effects that often ensue when these two doctrines are combined. Once a landowner receives a final administrative decision, his state-level claim would be ripe and would be heard in the land use court in an expeditious manner.

This speedy judicial review would minimize the delay between the asserted Effective Moment and the Ripeness Moment. As a result, it would also reduce the time during which the landowner must remain immobilized and would reduce the size of the award that an offending municipality would have to pay. Moreover, the expertise that land use judges would develop should lead to greater consistency and predictability within each state, reducing the number of borderline cases that need to be litigated and increasing the likelihood of settlements. . . .

The suggestion that states create specialized land use courts has its drawbacks. During times of shrinking resources, state legislatures may not believe they can afford the luxury of new special purpose courts, particularly in states with small numbers of land use cases. Moreover, there are strong arguments to be made that various subject matter areas should not be carved out of the state civil court system and placed in single purpose courtrooms. . . .

Most importantly, this proposal addresses only one aspect of the problem of delay. It provides for the speediest and most consistent possible resolution of claims in which the municipality has already reached a final decision, without inducing the municipality to reach that decision more quickly. . . .

. . . .

2. Enacting a Model State Inverse Condemnation Act

A related but more extensive proposal would be the promulgation of a Model State Inverse Condemnation Act. The wide variety of existing land use regulations and procedures means that a prior land use case may be of little precedential value even within a single state because the local ordinance that was the subject of an earlier case differs materially from the ordinance at issue in a subsequent dispute. This results in inconsistency and unpredictability even within a single jurisdiction, leaving parties uncertain as to the legal significance of their actions.

. . . .

Various aspects of inverse condemnation procedure would be covered in a broad Model Act. The Act would list the steps that a landowner must take before an as-applied inverse condemnation claim is ripe, in both the constitutional and prudential senses. It would establish standard procedures for local regulators, thereby providing assurance that the state legislature views these procedures as reasonable. By placing time limits on the various actions that landowners and regulators may take, a Model Act would shorten the permitting process and increase the likelihood that a landowner could survive for its duration, while decreasing the potential liability facing a municipality that reaches a wrong result. . . .

. . . .

Recall that both the ripeness doctrine and the just compensation requirement are mandated by the United States Constitution. The widespread adoption of a model state law is no guarantee that the problem of harmonizing these two doctrines will be addressed. However, one of the concerns facing state and local lawmakers is the fear that each new attempt at a land use law or procedure might run afoul of the United States Constitution, thereby visiting untold liability upon government bodies. A possible response to this concern is the development of a consistent and streamlined set of procedures which, upon withstanding federal court challenges in some jurisdictions, would be widely seen as relatively secure. While not solving the problem of harmonizing the two doctrines, a Model Act could sharply reduce its consequences by limiting the uncertainty that has become so damaging to municipalities and landowners.

C. Rethinking the Relevance of the Due Process Clause

Parts V.A and V.B proposed several ways of reducing the conflict between regulatory takings law and the ripeness doctrine that either redefine the takings Moments or streamline the permitting process. These recommendations focus on the elements of the ripeness doctrine and seek to minimize its more harmful effects on regulatory takings law. But if the extended permitting processes that certain municipalities employ cause some portion of this problem, then courts can find a partial solution beyond the ripeness doctrine, in the Due Process Clause.

. . . .

1. Takings Law Contrasted with Procedural Due Process Law

In his *First English* dissent, Justice Stevens questioned the bright line that the majority had drawn between "normal delays" and "going too far."[225] "[N]ormal delays in obtaining building permits, changes in zoning ordinances, variances, and the like" are not compensable, said the Court.[226] However, "[w]here the government's activities have already worked a taking of all use of property, no subsequent action by the government can relieve it of the duty to provide compensation for the period during which the taking was effective."[227]

The Court's analysis suggests that "normal delays" and "takings" represent the two alternative findings that a court can reach, but this is not the case. . . .

. . . .

If a landowner claims that a municipality has delayed her application unfairly, her claim should not depend upon whether the municipality ultimately granted her a building permit. Nor should it turn upon whether any permit denial was proper or improper. Rather, the procedural inquiry should focus on procedural questions, such as whether the municipality took a reasonable amount of time to decide. Challenges to procedures should focus on those procedures, irrespective of the final decision and the substantive propriety of that decision.

And if the procedural analysis should center on procedures, the substantive analysis should center on substantive regulatory takings law. The substantive takings decision should not turn upon whether a delay was normal or not, and the procedures employed ought to be just one of the many factors that a court examines in assessing a takings claim. . . .

. . . .

---

[225] *First English*, 482 U.S. at 334 (Stevens, J., dissenting).

[226] *First English*, 482 U.S. at 321.

[227] Id. . . .

2. The Ripeness Standard Applicable to Procedural Due Process Cases

The plaintiff with a ripe regulatory takings claim, then, also may possess a viable procedural due process claim. The primary concern of this Article, however, is the plaintiff with an *unripe* takings claim, who seeks due process relief long before a federal court can hear her takings claim. If procedural due process claims are subject to the same ripeness standards as regulatory takings claims—if the second claim must wait as long as the first—then this plaintiff is little better off than she was before. She still must survive long enough to enter federal court; she now has two claims that may never ripen instead of one. The Due Process Clause offers land use plaintiffs an alternative that is useful earlier only if the ripeness test federal courts apply in procedural due process cases is easier to meet than the ripeness test they apply in regulatory takings cases. . . .

. . . .

. . . [I]f a state actor randomly and without authorization deprives a landowner of a protected property interest, and if due process is not provided after this deprivation, then the landowner should be viewed as having a ripe and valid procedural due process claim even though any regulatory takings claim may still be years from ripening.

3. Procedural Due Process Claims in the Lower Federal Courts

Several circuits have heard procedural due process claims before any regulatory takings claim could have ripened. . . .

. . . .

Federal courts should continue to recognize that the elements of a procedural due process violation differ from the elements of a regulatory taking. The question in these cases is not whether a long series of actions amounts to a taking; rather, it is whether a shorter series of activities denies a landowner the process she is due. As a result, it is possible for this type of due process violation to occur in its entirety during the time when a regulatory takings claim is just beginning to ripen. . . . Although a federal court is properly precluded from hearing a regulatory takings claim while the elements of that claim are still developing, there is no reason why it should not hear and decide a procedural due process claim that has developed completely.

. . . .

D. Putting These Suggestions Together

1. Recognizing Interim Due Process and Takings Violations

. . . .

The permitting process operates in fits and starts. Sudden bursts of activity punctuate prolonged periods of delay, and most of these delays are ordinary and reasonable. In a small number of cases, however, these delays will violate the applicant's procedural due process rights and in an even smaller number of cases they will constitute regulatory takings. The federal courts must recognize that violations of both types can occur during the permitting process and not just as a result of the process. Moreover, interim takings arising out of procedural errors are sufficiently different from the substantive final-decision takings that might result months or years later to warrant their own, more precisely tailored ripeness test. Once federal courts recognize that interim due process and takings violations can occur and ripen during the permitting process, landowners will be better able to nudge the process forward judicially when municipalities improperly impede their administrative alternatives.

2. Combining These Proposals

Part V has suggested a number of ways in which ripeness doctrine and regulatory takings law can be harmonized. . . .

. . . [E]ach of these suggestions addresses at least one of the problems caused by the conflict between regulatory takings law and ripeness doctrine, and various permutations of these proposals may blend well. In addition, these suggestions are directed to a variety of different audiences. Federal and state courts and state and local legislative and administrative entities all may have different ideas as to how best to resolve these legal tensions. Different bodies may take different approaches in different jurisdictions, and the many participants in the land use process can observe and learn from each others' successes and failures.

. . . .

E. Consigning Regulatory Takings Cases to the State Courts or to Non-Judicial Forums

Several of the proposals described above would require action at the state or local level. This dispersal of responses is necessary because the effect of federal ripeness doctrine, and perhaps its primary purpose, has been the removal of many regulatory takings cases from the federal courts. The ripeness doctrine, after all, assumes that there is no federally justiciable case or controversy until a certain sequence of events occurs at the local and state levels, and the ripeness cases since 1978 have progressively added steps to this sequence. So while federal regulatory takings law arises directly under the Fifth Amendment of the United States Constitution, the federal courts have been making it more and more difficult for regulatory takings plaintiffs to enter federal court. The Supreme Court may be recognizing a federal claim that is cognizable only in state court for most or all of its life. . . .

But a plaintiff who litigates in state court may find a subsequent federal claim barred for one of several reasons. Once a state court has determined that compensation is not owing, the doctrines of res judicata and full faith and credit, may preclude relitigation in federal court. . . .

. . . .

There is evidence in the case law . . . to suggest that some federal courts are using the ripeness doctrine as one of several ways of relegating inverse condemnation cases to the states. . . .

A more extreme view of the ripeness doctrine is that the federal judiciary may be attempting to remove regulatory takings cases from the courts altogether. Under this view, the federal courts are attempting to route these cases to non-judicial forums. Landowners and municipalities who observe the many other cases that drag on for years may opt out of the court system entirely. Perhaps the ultimate result of the ripeness cases, whether intended or not, will be to encourage settlements and other forms of non-judicial resolution.

VI. Conclusion

Ripeness doctrine and regulatory takings law are inherently contradictory, and to some degree these inconsistencies cannot be avoided. This Article has proposed a variety of ways in which to address this doctrinal clash. . . . Each of these proposals attempts to synthesize the two doctrines in a manner that is both fair and predictable, something that existing law fails to accomplish. . . .

. . . .

Note

In Suitum v. Tahoe Regional Planning Agency, 117 S. Ct. 1659 (1997), the Supreme Court determined that landowner-Suitum's action alleging a regulatory taking passed the "final decision" portion of the ripeness test. The Court concluded that Suitum had received a "final decision" that her land could not be developed. This was true notwithstanding her failure to endeavor to obtain agency approval to convey the transferable development rights she received under the regulatory scheme in question.

2. Origin Examined

"THE FOUNDATION OF OUR 'REGULATORY TAKINGS' JURISPRUDENCE": THE MYTH AND MEANING OF JUSTICE HOLMES'S OPINION IN PENNSYLVANIA COAL CO. V. MAHON

Robert Brauneis
106 Yale L.J. 613 (1996)[*]

. . . .

Genealogists of . . . regulatory takings jurisprudence have found their Adam in *Pennsylvania Coal Co. v. Mahon*,[7] a 1922 Supreme Court decision with a majority opinion by Justice Oliver Wendell Holmes. The *Mahon* Court concluded that a Pennsylvania statute prohibiting mining of coal so as to cause surface subsidence was unconstitutional. "The general rule at least," Holmes wrote, "is, that while property may be regulated to a certain extent, if regulation goes too far it will be recognized as a taking."[9] The Holmes opinion, Chief Justice Rehnquist concludes, was "the foundation of our 'regulatory takings' jurisprudence."[10] . . . A bevy of scholars has come to the same conclusion.[12]

The Holmes opinion in *Mahon* is lauded, not just as the common ancestor of all regulatory takings decisions, but also as the progenitor of particular features of current regulatory takings doctrine. The Supreme Court and Congress have both embraced a tradition of looking to *Mahon* for a diminution in value test; scholarly

---

[*] Reprinted by permission of The Yale Law Journal Company and Fred B. Rothman & Company from The Yale Law Journal, Vol. 106, pages 613-702.

[7] 260 U.S. 393 (1922).

[9] *Id.* at 415.

[10] . . . [Keystone Bituminous Coal Ass'n v. DeBenedictis], 480 U.S. [470 (1987)] at 508 (Rehnquist, C.J., dissenting).

[12] *See, e.g.*, DAVID L. CALLIES ET AL., CASES AND MATERIALS ON LAND USE 245 (2d ed. 1994) ("In [*Pennsylvania Coal Co. v. Mahon*], the regulatory taking doctrine was born."); STEVEN J. EAGLE, REGULATORY TAKINGS § 1-1, at 2 (1996) ("[T]he Supreme Court . . . never had found governmental activities short of a physical invasion to constitute a taking. This changed abruptly with Justice Holmes's famous declaration in *Pennsylvania Coal Co. v. Mahon*."); DANIEL R. MANDELKER, LAND USE LAW § 2.11, at 29 (3d ed. 1993) ("Pennsylvania Coal Co. v. Mahon, a landmark decision, was the first Supreme Court case to hold a land use regulation unconstitutional under the taking clause."); Jed Rubenfeld, *Usings*, 102 YALE L.J. 1077, 1086 (1993) ("[I]n *Pennsylvania Coal v. Mahon* . . . the Court for the first time struck down a regulation as an uncompensated taking."); William Michael Treanor, *The Original Understanding of the Takings Clause and the Political Process*, 95 COLUM. L. REV. 782, 782 (1995) ("In 1922 . . . the Supreme Court's decision in *Pennsylvania Coal v. Mahon* established a new takings regime.").

recognition has preceded and accompanied that embrace.[15] At other times, the Court has cited *Mahon* for a balancing test . . . . Academic acknowledgment of a balancing test in *Mahon* runs a close second to acknowledgment of a diminution in value test.

But if *Mahon* is celebrated for its originality and fecundity, it is also blamed for the muddled state of regulatory takings doctrine. . . . Bruce Ackerman's conclusion best sums up the conventional praise and criticism of Justice Holmes's opinion in *Mahon*: It is "both the most important and most mysterious writing in takings law."[22]

My goal in this Article is to unveil the mystery. The *Mahon* opinion, I will argue, is best understood as a terse expression of Justice Holmes's theory of the constitutional protection of property, and of his views about the textual basis for that protection, both of which he had developed over decades. Much of that theory and those views was unique to Holmes; other Supreme Court Justices agreed with him at most in part. There was, however, broader agreement on the Court about several features of the *Mahon* opinion. In the modern campaign to force *Mahon* into the role of a seminal regulatory takings case, most of its original meaning—to Holmes and to the other members of the *Mahon* Court—has been obscured. The opinion has come simultaneously to mean more, and less, than it did as written and handed down.

. . . .

I. The Jurisprudence of the Holmes Opinion in *Mahon*

All that can be expected from modern improvements is that legislation should easily and quickly, *yet not too quickly*, modify itself in accordance with the will of the *de facto* supreme power in the community . . . .[24]

The jurisprudence of *Mahon* requires extended discussion, but a succinct summary of its facts will suffice. The law at issue in *Mahon* was the Kohler Act, a 1921 Pennsylvania statute that prohibited underground mining of anthracite coal that caused the surface above to collapse. The prohibition applied only to surfaces that were not owned by the miner and that supported specified uses including streets, hospitals, schools, factories, and houses. When the Pennsylvania Coal Company notified Mr. and Mrs. Mahon of its intention to mine underneath their house, the Mahons sued under the Kohler Act to enjoin the company from mining in such a way as to cause their house to sink. The company's defense was that the Act was

---

[15] *See, e.g.,* Carol M. Rose, Mahon *Reconstructed: Why the Takings Issue Is Still a Muddle,* 57 S. Cal. L. Rev. 561, 562 n.9, 565-66 (1984); Rubenfeld, *supra* note 12, at 1086-87; Joseph L. Sax, *Takings and the Police Power,* 74 Yale L.J. 36, 41 & nn.33-35 (1964); Treanor, *supra* note 12, at 799.

[22] [Bruce A.] Ackerman, [Private Property and the Constitution (1977)] . . . , at 156.

[24] 1 Oliver Wendell Holmes, Jr., *Summary of Events: Great Britain, in* The Collected Works of Justice Holmes 323, 325 (Sheldon M. Novick ed., 1995) (emphasis added) [hereinafter Collected Works]. . . .

unconstitutional. The company noted that when it had originally sold the surface rights to the Mahons' lot, it had not only retained the mineral rights, but had also specifically obtained a waiver of all claims against the company due to subsidence to the surface. By effectively nullifying the waiver, argued the company, the Kohler Act deprived it of property without due process of law, took its property without just compensation, and impaired the obligation of a contract. The company won in the Pennsylvania trial court, but lost on the Mahons' appeal to the Pennsylvania Supreme Court, and persuaded the United States Supreme Court to hear the case on writ of error. Of the eight Supreme Court Justices who heard the case, seven agreed with the company that the Act was unconstitutional; Justice Louis D. Brandeis was the sole dissenter. Chief Justice William Howard Taft assigned the opinion of the Court to Justice Holmes. . . .

Holmes produced a short opinion of about 1500 words, covering less than five pages in the United States Reports. Yet within those limits, Holmes outlines and demonstrates a distinctive, coherent approach to the constitutional protection of property. That approach is best discussed in three stages. First, Holmes defines the "property" protected by the Constitution and suggests criteria for a successful theory of constitutional property protection. In doing so, Holmes establishes his position in relation to both of the main American traditions of constitutional property jurisprudence: the vested rights tradition and the substantive rights/police power tradition. Second, Holmes attempts to develop and apply a theory for deciding constitutional property cases that remains true to his definition of constitutionally protected property. Under that theory, judges must determine how drastically a challenged law has departed from basic principles, or as Holmes once referred to them, "structural habits," embedded in preexisting positive law. The body of Holmes's opinion is best read as an application of that theory to the issue of whether the Kohler Act is constitutional as applied both to private homes and to publicly owned property. Third, Holmes suggests the limits of his own theory—limits at which he only hints in *Mahon*, but more fully develops in other opinions and writings. Legal theories and doctrines, Holmes contends, are irreducibly historical and collective: They are developed over time and by more than one judge. Holmes demonstrably did not view *Mahon* as the application of a settled, comprehensive calculus of constitutional property, but as one more step in developing a series of guiding precedents. . . .

. . . .

II. THE MYTHS OF MODERN *MAHON*

[T]he holding in *Pennsylvania Coal* . . . has for 65 years been the foundation of our "regulatory takings" jurisprudence. . . . [O]ur repeated reliance on that opinion establishes it as a cornerstone of the jurisprudence of the Fifth Amendment's Just Compensation Clause.[237]

---

[237] Keystone Bituminous Coal Ass'n v. DeBenedictis, 480 U.S. 470, 508 (1987) (Rehnquist, C.J., dissenting).

There is no reason to think that any other member of the *Mahon* Court, let alone a majority, embraced or even appreciated the whole of Justice Holmes's constitutional property jurisprudence. Thus, it would be a mistake to suggest that the true Holmesian meaning of *Mahon* was once known to all, and has since become obscured. But Chief Justice Rehnquist's comment, suggesting that the Supreme Court's understanding of and reliance on *Mahon* remained consistent over the sixty-five years between 1922 and 1987, is equally inaccurate. The frequency of citation of the Holmes opinion in *Mahon*—a telling indicator of its influence—has varied widely over that period. Most dramatically, after being cited in a moderate number of Supreme Court opinions between 1922 and 1935, *Mahon* all but disappeared from the United States Reports for over two decades. In the twenty-two years from 1936 through 1957, *Mahon* appeared in a single obscure dissent by Justice Frankfurter. After 1957, the Court's understanding of *Mahon* differed drastically from its understanding before 1936. In their haste to appropriate Holmes's reputation and utilize his striking turns of phrase in a new constitutional era, Supreme Court Justices of every stripe began to ignore key points of understanding between Justice Holmes and the 1922 Court. By the mid-1980s, the Court had embraced a new understanding, or new understandings, of Justice Holmes's *Mahon* opinion. . . .

A. *The Court's Original Understanding*

Justice Holmes and the 1922 Supreme Court shared three key points of understanding about *Mahon*, all of which have since been lost. First, Holmes and the 1922 Court understood *Mahon* to be a Due Process and Contract Clause case, not a Takings Clause case. Second, rather than viewing *Mahon* as a seminal case, they understood the decision as one among many that incrementally established the limits of the police power. Although *Mahon* was part of a trend toward accepting that the constitutionality of nontrespassory regulations could turn on the provision of compensation, it was not the first case to so hold. Third, both Holmes and the Court recognized and accepted *Mahon*'s use of a historical method that looked to traditional legal principles and categories, and that considered both the purpose and effect of legislation important to the constitutional inquiry.

1. *The Textual Basis*

Holmes and the 1922 Court agreed that *Mahon* should be decided under the Contract and Due Process Clauses, not the Takings Clause. At the same time, the Due Process Clause was thought to protect a right of just compensation upon expropriation of property. Holmes's references to the textual basis for the *Mahon* decision, although brief, are quite straightforward. Holmes refers explicitly to the textual basis of the decision once: The police power must be limited, he contends, "or the contract and due process clauses are gone."[240] Three coupled references to

---

[240] Pennsylvania Coal Co. v. Mahon, 260 U.S. 393, 413 (1922).

contract and property rights elsewhere in the opinion underscore this dual textual basis.[241] Later in the opinion, Holmes notes that the Fifth Amendment provides that private property "shall not be taken for [public] use without compensation."[242] He recognizes, however, that *Mahon* is not being decided under the Fifth Amendment, which applies only to the federal government. Holmes notes carefully that "[a] similar assumption is made in the decisions upon the Fourteenth Amendment."[243] The case he cites makes clear—although in 1922 this hardly needed to be made clear—that the pertinent provision of the Fourteenth Amendment was the Due Process Clause.

. . . .

2. *Regulation and Just Compensation*

A second point of common understanding between Holmes and the 1922 Court was that *Mahon* did not announce a radically novel doctrine; rather, it was one of a series of cases articulating the boundaries between governmental power and constitutional property rights. *Mahon* is now widely understood, by Supreme Court Justices and academic commentators alike, to be a landmark: the first "regulatory takings" case. This honor is ambiguous; but under any of the principal resolutions of the ambiguities, *Mahon* does not deserve it. I have already argued that the claim is invalid under one interpretation: *Mahon* was not the first case to hold that "regulatory" legislation could violate the Fifth Amendment Takings Clause, because *Mahon* was not a Fifth Amendment case.

Assume, next, that "regulatory" legislation is that which does not affect the physical possession of property but only its use and enjoyment. Perhaps the claim is that *Mahon* was the first case to hold that use and enjoyment rights were constitutionally protected property, whether under the Due Process Clause or the Takings Clause. But under classical substantive due process, already well established when *Mahon* was decided, constitutionally protected property rights included the right to acquire wealth through bargaining for the sale of one's labor, and the right to set the price at which one's property would be sold. Thus *Mahon* is too late to claim the honor of expanding constitutional property protection beyond physical possession.

Another possibility is that "regulatory taking" refers to legislation that would be constitutional if and only if accompanied by just compensation. Under this interpretation, the textual basis for the just compensation obligation is unimportant; it

---

[241] *See id.* at 412 (noting that Pennsylvania Supreme Court concluded that "the defendant had contract and property rights protected by the Constitution of the United States"); *id.* at 413 ("As applied to this case, the statute is admitted to destroy previously existing rights of property and contract."); *id.* at 414 ("[The Kohler Act] purports to abolish what is recognized in Pennsylvania as an estate in land . . . and what is declared by the Court below to be a contract hitherto binding the plaintiffs.").

[242] *Id.* at 415.

[243] *Id.*

could be either the Fifth Amendment Takings Clause or the Fourteenth Amendment Due Process Clause. The claim would be that *Mahon* was the first case to hold that the constitutionality of a regulation could turn on the provision of just compensation. This claim fails as well, but it is a more interesting and substantial one. . . .

. . . .

Numerous cases of that sort had already been decided before *Mahon* reached the Court. . . .

These opinions suggest the Court's willingness, both before *Mahon* and through Justices other than Holmes, to use an eminent domain model to analyze government alterations of property rules falling short of physical dispossession and to strike them down for lack of compensation. That willingness deprives *Mahon* of the title of first "regulatory eminent domain" case.

3. Traditional Legal Categories

Holmes's contemporaries on the Supreme Court also shared a familiarity with and acceptance of the historical and purpose-based analyses Holmes used in *Mahon*. . . . *Mugler v. Kansas*, for example, appeals to the common law category of public nuisance.[285] *Munn v. Illinois*[286] looks to the common law for the category of businesses "'affected with a public interest.'"[287] Finally, *Lochner v. New York*[288] looks to, among other things, the common law contract doctrine of incapacity.[289]

. . . .

B. Mahon *Lost and Found*

After 1935, *Mahon* appeared to be destined for oblivion, along with many other minor substantive due process cases. For over two decades, it failed to surface in a single Supreme Court majority opinion. Between 1935 and 1958, its only appearance in the United States Reports was in a dissent by Holmes admirer Justice Frankfurter in *United States v. Commodities Trading Corp.*,[313] an obscure 1950 case about the amount that the United States should pay for the black pepper it requisitioned during World War II. . . .

By 1958, *Mahon* had a future only if each of the points of understanding about the case between Holmes and the 1920s Court could be forgotten or ignored. The constitutional revolution of the late 1930s rejected the Due Process Clause as a textual home for substantive economic rights. Rejected, too, was *Lochner*'s

---

[285] . . . 123 U.S. 623, 669 (1887).

[286] 94 U.S. 113 (1876).

[287] . . . *Id.* at 125-26 (quoting Matthew Hale, *De Portibus Maris, in* A COLLECTION OF TRACTS RELATIVE TO THE LAW OF ENGLAND (London, T. Wright 1787)). . . .

[288] 198 U.S. 45 (1905).

[289] . . . *Id.* at 57.

[313] 339 U.S. 121 (1950) (Frankfurter, J., dissenting in part).

ahistorical approach to protection. In the process, the new regime also abandoned the inquiries into traditional legal categories and legislative purposes that Holmes's approach shared with the *Lochner* ahistoricists. Viewed as a run-of-the-mill due process case, *Mahon*—along with the three key points of its original understanding—was hopelessly obsolete.

In the post-1937 world, however, a judge who wanted to reestablish some sort of constitutional discourse about the governmental regulation of property rights could find alternative uses for *Mahon*. It might be the best precedent available in support of a discourse that was not vulnerable to charges of either textual or methodological Lochnerism. First, the matter of text. The keys here are Justice Holmes's posthumous reputation as a determined opponent of economic substantive due process and *Mahon*'s mention of the Fifth Amendment Takings Clause, which, if not examined too closely, could be taken to indicate reliance on that text.

. . .

. . . .

If a new constitutional property discourse could not be based on the Due Process Clause, neither could it invoke the methods of *Lochner* ahistoricism. It was no longer acceptable to look to common law rulings and categories to give content to a phrase like "health, safety, and general welfare," which was supposed to define the proper sphere of the police power. . . . Nor was it acceptable for courts to conduct anything but the most cursory examination of the purposes of ordinary economic legislation or of the relationship of the legislature's means to its purported ends. . . .

Although Justice Holmes's inquiries into tradition and purpose had a different ultimate theoretical basis, no one considered whether that basis provided a justification for those inquiries that could survive the rejection of *Lochner* ahistoricism. Rather, courts sought to construct a takings inquiry that placed little reliance on tradition and purpose. As Justice Stewart declared in *Hughes v. Washington,*[345] "the Constitution measures a taking of property not by what a State says, or by what it intends, but by what it *does*."[346] *Mahon* survived because it contained language suggesting a test that seemed to fulfill Justice Stewart's hopes for an objective takings jurisprudence: the diminution in value test. To measure the effect of a regulation on a property's value, one need not know anything about the regulation's purpose or its relationship to a legal tradition. Thus, when *Mahon* reappears after its twenty-three-year hiatus, it is cited for the propositions that "action in the form of regulation can so diminish the value of property as to constitute a taking"[347] and that "governmental action in the form of regulation ca[n] be so onerous as to constitute a taking which constitutionally requires just compensation."[348]

---

[345] 389 U.S. 290 (1967).

[346] *Id.* at 298 (Stewart, J., concurring).

[347] United States v. Central Eureka Mining Co., 357 U.S. 155, 168 (1958).

[348] Goldblatt v. Town of Hempstead, 369 U.S. 590, 594 (1962).

C. Mahon *in the Last Two Decades*

Although *Mahon* had shown its new textual and methodological face by the early 1960s, the Supreme Court did not devote serious, sustained attention to its "regulatory takings" doctrine until the late 1970s. When it did, however, *Mahon* became a critical, contested authority in a number of major doctrinal battles that continued to reshape perceptions about the case's textual basis and methods of analysis.

1. Mahon *and the Constitutional Text*

Mahon's reconstruction as a Takings Clause case, rather than a substantive due process case, was fortified in the battle over whether the Constitution mandated a retrospective damages remedy for those temporarily subject to excessively burdensome regulation. By 1980, it was established that the Takings Clause itself entitled an owner whose property had been taken to bring an "inverse condemnation" action, seeking just compensation.[349] Moreover, owners whose property had been taken temporarily—for example, owners whose land or buildings had been taken over by the federal government to be used in the war effort during World War II—could recover just compensation for the period when they had been dispossessed, even after the government returned possession to them.[350] It appeared that if regulations were subject to review under the Takings Clause, the Constitution guaranteed damages for the time during which an excessive regulation was in effect, even if the government agreed to lift the regulation once a court found it to effect a taking. Those opposed to awarding damages for temporary regulatory takings did not question this logic. Rather, they developed the argument that regulations were subject to review only under the Due Process Clause, which did not provide an inverse condemnation action or require interim damages.

Into this debate came *Mahon* and Justice Holmes's comment that "if regulation goes too far it will be recognized as a taking."[352] Did this mean that the Court had decided in 1922 that regulations were reviewable under the Takings Clause? The state courts that had decided against a temporary damages remedy maintained that Justice Holmes had used the word "taking" only in a "metaphorical" sense and that the real issue in *Mahon* was whether the Kohler Act was "an invalid exercise of the police power under the due process clause."[353]

---

[349] *See* United States v. Clarke, 445 U.S. 253, 257 (1980).

[350] *See, e.g.,* Kimball Laundry Co. v. United States, 338 U.S. 1 (1949); United States v. General Motors Corp., 323 U.S. 373 (1945).

[352] Pennsylvania Coal Co. v. Mahon, 260 U.S. 393, 415 (1922).

[353] Fred F. French Investing Co. v. City of New York, 350 N.E.2d 381, 385 (N.Y. 1976); *see* Agins v. City of Tiburon, 598 P.2d 25, 29 (Cal. 1979), *aff'd*, 447 U.S. 255 (1980) (stating that Holmes used word "taking" to "indicate the limit by which the acknowledged social goal of land control could be achieved by regulation rather than by eminent domain").

In 1981, however, Justice Brennan rejected this interpretation in his dissent in *San Diego Gas & Electric Co. v. City of San Diego.*[354] While the majority in *San Diego Gas & Electric* held that the Court lacked jurisdiction to decide the temporary damages issue, Justice Brennan, joined by three others, enlisted *Mahon* in support of his conclusion that the Constitution did mandate damages for temporary takings. . . .

After *San Diego Gas & Electric*, the Court failed in two other cases to reach the temporary damages issue. In the 1987 case of *First English Evangelical Lutheran Church v. County of Los Angeles,*[358] however, the Court adopted Justice Brennan's position that the Constitution mandated a damages remedy for temporary regulatory takings, and with it, Brennan's interpretation of *Mahon*. In the view of the *First English* Court, when Holmes stated that "'if a regulation goes too far it will be recognized as a taking,'" he meant a Fifth Amendment taking, and he meant to acknowledge that the Fifth Amendment provided a damages remedy regardless of whether the government had formally instituted condemnation proceedings. Together, *San Diego Gas & Electric* and *First English* contributed mightily to *Mahon*'s reputation as a seminal Takings Clause case.

. . . .

2. Mahon *and Methods of Takings Analysis*

If *First English* and its precursors have influenced recent perceptions of *Mahon*'s textual basis, two other developments in takings law have influenced perceptions of Justice Holmes's analysis in *Mahon*. The first is the evolution of economic impact takings, culminating in the creation in *Lucas v. South Carolina Coastal Council*[367] of a per se takings category for regulations that "den[y] all economically beneficial or productive use of land."[368] The second is the Court's decision in *Keystone Bituminous Coal Ass'n v. DeBenedictis,*[369] narrowly upholding a coal mining subsidence statute quite similar to the statute *Mahon* struck down. The line of cases leading to *Lucas* is, along with the earlier cases of *United States v. Central Eureka Mining Co.*[370] and *Goldblatt v. Town of Hempstead,*[371] responsible for the perception of *Mahon* as a "diminution in value" case. *Keystone* is responsible for the perception that *Mahon* turned on a balancing test.

. . . .

---

[354] 450 U.S. 621 (1981).

[358] 482 U.S. 304 (1987).

[367] 505 U.S. 1003 (1992).

[368] *Id.* at 1015.

[369] 480 U.S. 470 (1987).

[370] 357 U.S. 155 (1958).

[371] 369 U.S. 590 (1962).

D. *A Role for Rediscovered* Mahon?

What impact, if any, should a rediscovered *Mahon* have on current takings jurisprudence? My goal in the last Section of this Article is to suggest a variety of issues that judges and scholars must face before they can decide whether to adopt a Holmesian approach to constitutional property. The issues divide into two groups. The first concerns the feasibility of Holmes's approach: Is implementation possible? The second concerns its desirability: Do we want such an approach?

1. *Feasibility*

The most basic issue of feasibility is whether law actually is organized the way that Holmes assumed it was for purposes of adjudicating constitutional property cases. Holmes assumed that the positive law of a jurisdiction can be described as a *body* of law, organized around multiple principles, poles, or paradigm cases. But perhaps this organization is illusory, or perhaps there is a more or less equally convincing principle to justify any result one wishes. If that is the case, then Holmes's approach may be just one more failed attempt to separate law from politics and the adjudication of constitutional property cases may be indistinguishable from legislation.

Even if we could imagine describing positive law as an organized body, there remain other crucial questions in a legal system as large and complicated as that of the United States: How many separate bodies of law are out there and on which body do we need to focus in deciding constitutional property cases? After *Erie Railroad Co. v. Tompkins*,[407] the correct answer to the first question seems to be that each state has its own body of law and legal tradition, as does the federal government. It would seem that in assessing the change wrought by a piece of legislation we would have to identify the sovereign from which the legislation issues and analyze its relationship to the body of law connected with that sovereign. In practice, however, Holmes was not particularly concerned about distinguishing the legal traditions of each sovereign. In *Mahon*, he does allude to one tradition peculiar to Pennsylvania: the treatment of support rights as a separate estate in land. But he considers other principles—public nuisance, personal safety, and so on—without regard to Pennsylvania precedent.

. . . .

The confusion caused by the failure to reconcile the theory and practice of identifying law with a particular sovereign is even greater in federal constitutional property law than in private law. For it would seem that some of the principles developed over time in elaborating federal constitutional property law would be federal principles, applicable regardless of the particular jurisdiction at issue, whereas principles developed in elaborating primary private law might be specific to particular jurisdictions. But where is the dividing line between those two sets of

---

[407] 304 U.S. 64 (1938).

principles? Holmes seems to suggest that the result in *Mahon* might have been different if Pennsylvania did not treat support rights as a separate estate in land . . . . The implication seems to be that the constitutional constraints on the Pennsylvania legislature may be different from those on another state's legislature. Does this mean that a state that traditionally had a strict law of trespass might be subject to a per se takings rule for permanent physical occupations, whereas a state that traditionally treated trespass more flexibly might not be? Holmes never addresses this issue directly. He seems to assume that, although the legal traditions of the states are independent in theory and occasionally different in small details, they are largely parallel in fact, all drawing from one Anglo-American legal tradition. A greater sensitivity to differences in legal traditions among particular jurisdictions, however, may raise both theoretical and practical problems with developing a federal constitutional property jurisprudence.

A third issue is the practical and psychological feasibility of the Holmesian inquiry within the constraints of actual litigation: Do judges have the time and inclination to consider all of the relevant "structural habits" in a body of law and sufficient detachment not to be swayed by their own views of the desirability of the particular policy in question? Many have criticized the Supreme Court, along with other courts, for practicing "law office" history, whether due to bias or time constraints that necessitate reliance on parties' briefs and cursory independent inquiries. Of particular relevance to this Article, a number of scholars have argued that the Court has relied on the mistaken historical assumption that land-use regulation was uncommon in colonial and early American times and began to expand only at the end of the nineteenth century.[415] In addition, Jeremy Paul has argued that psychological pressures on judges might make it difficult to implement a model of takings depending on an assessment of change from preexisting law. Paul contends that a judge will find it difficult to determine the preexisting law uninfluenced by the fiscal consequences of her decision about whether compensation is necessary for a challenged statute.[416]

The fourth issue of feasibility relates directly to the Holmesian project of specification. In constitutional property law as in the law of negligence, Holmes imagined, broad, imprecise standards would eventually be replaced by more specific, predictable rules. Holmes recognized that this project would be threatened by rapid legal and societal change, but he believed that change, though inevitable, occurred slowly. One of the most astonishing statements in *The Common Law*, to modern eyes, is that "the standards for a very large part of human conduct do not vary from century to century."[418] Can we believe this anymore? . . . Holmes's answer in areas of rapid change was to leave the question to the jury, which would

---

[415] *See* John F. Hart, *Colonial Land Use Law and its Significance for Modern Takings Doctrine*, 109 HARV. L. REV. 1252, 1287-93 (1996); William J. Novak, *Common Regulation: Legal Origins of State Power in America*, 45 HASTINGS L.J. 1061 (1994).

[416] *See* Jeremy Paul, *The Hidden Structure of Takings Law*, 64 S. CAL. L. REV. 1393, 1425 (1991).

[418] 3 HOLMES, *The Common Law*, *in* COLLECTED WORKS, *supra* note 24, at 109, 179.

express "the existing average standards of the community."[422] Perhaps those who advocate formalizing the use of community standards in constitutional property law, such as Robert Ellickson,[423] followed most recently by William Fischel,[424] are the true modern heirs of the Holmesian tradition.

2. *Desirability*

Even if the Holmesian project is feasible, is it the right project to graft onto the Fifth and Fourteenth Amendments? The issues that this question raises conveniently divide into issues of scope and issues of approach.

Two issues of scope seem to be most important. First, shouldn't we read the Takings Clause to apply only to physical dispossession and the Due Process Clause to be concerned only with matters of procedure? William Michael Treanor is only the most recent of a series of scholars to have adduced considerable evidence indicating that the Takings Clause was originally meant to apply only to physical appropriation of land and goods.[425] . . .

Judges and scholars, however, have rarely been able to resist the temptation to read broader protections of property into the Constitution, whether the chosen textual hook is the Contract Clause, the Due Process Clause, or the Takings Clause. Even Treanor, after establishing that the Takings Clause originally applied only to physical appropriations, ends up arguing that the Takings Clause should be applied to protect discrete and insular minorities from harms caused by political process failures, such as the harms caused to racial minorities by placing hazardous waste dumps in or near their neighborhoods—harms that hardly fit within the category of "physical appropriation."[431] It appears that courts will continue to read the Constitution to authorize broader protections of property.

The second issue of scope concerns limiting the reach of "property" if physical appropriation is not to be the exclusive focus. The Holmesian project focuses on changes in positive law and does not appear to be clearly limited to one subset of those changes. But very few people would agree that all changes in positive law implicate property rights. Consider, for example, a law that bans previously allowed musical performances in public parks, or one that raises the minimum age for drinking from eighteen to twenty-one. Do these changes affect property rights? If not, how do we define that portion of positive law that is concerned with property, once we agree that takings are not limited to physical appropriation? The rel-

---

[422] 3 HOLMES, *The Common Law*, *in* COLLECTED WORKS, *supra* note 24, at 109, 179.

[423] *See* Robert C. Ellickson, *Alternatives to Zoning: Covenants, Nuisance Rules, and Fines as Land Use Controls,* 40 U. CHI. L. REV. 681 (1973); Robert C. Ellickson, *Suburban Growth Controls: An Economic and Legal Analysis,* 86 YALE L.J. 385 (1977).

[424] *See* [WILLIAM A.] FISCHEL, [REGULATORY TAKINGS: LAW, ECONOMICS, AND POLITICS (1995)] . . . , at 351-55.

[425] *See* Treanor, *supra* note 12, at 785-97.

[431] *See* Treanor, *supra* note 12, at 872-78.

evant Holmesian comments do not suggest an easy answer to this question. . . . One possibility is to look once again to the legal tradition of the jurisdiction in question: If we are considering a challenge to a Pennsylvania statute, how does Pennsylvania law develop distinctions between property rights and other rights? That approach, however, seems to leave what is supposed to be federal law in a completely fragmented state.

The second group of issues of desirability concerns the basic approach to the protection of property. The basic value underlying Holmes's approach is continuity. In Holmes's view, because law and society are always in flux, settled expectations can never be completely protected. In most cases, a court must allow legislatures to destroy those expectations. When a court intercedes to protect property, however, it intercedes to protect against discontinuities—changes in positive law that cannot be justified or explained in evolutionary terms.

That is an important view of the role of property, but certainly not the only one. One might, for example, see property as inextricably connected to a whole range of substantive moral values, of which continuity is only one. The problem with continuity is that it equally preserves the wicked and the good. Although preservation of the wicked might be justified to avoid the greater evils produced by radical discontinuity, on a larger moral view that is not a matter that can be decided in advance once and for all. This issue, however, was not a pressing one for Holmes, the convinced amoralist.

Alternatively, one may conclude that property rights, as well as all sorts of other rights, are adequately protected by the pluralist political process so long as that process is not stacked against "discrete and insular minorities."[437] On that view, the Takings Clause should be invoked whenever a judge finds a sufficiently grave defect in the political process affecting property rights, but not otherwise. Holmes undoubtedly would have scoffed at the idea that a well-oiled democratic process would lead to a fair distribution of resources, or even that fair distribution was or could be the goal underlying the constitutional protection of property, but we might think otherwise.

The choice of a Holmesian framework is partly or wholly independent of other choices about the constitutional protection of property. . . . The choice of a Holmesian approach is undoubtedly also, to some degree, independent of a commitment to the reasons Holmes himself formulated. One does not need to be a moral skeptic, for example, to find merit in Holmes's method of recognizing and protecting expectations. Yet, in spite of the fact that Holmes's approach neither determines particular results in particular cases nor flows from one particular set of beliefs about the nature of property and law, it is worthy of consideration as an attempt to provide a coherent theory of constitutional property protection.

---

[437] United States v. Carolene Prods. Co., 304 U.S. 144, 152-53 n.4 (1938). . . . For applications of process theory to the Takings Clause, see [WILLIAM A.] FISCHEL, [REGULATORY TAKINGS: LAW, ECONOMICS, AND POLITICS (1995)] . . . , at 100-40; Treanor, *supra* note 12, at 855-87.

III. CONCLUSION

Justice Holmes's opinion in *Pennsylvania Coal Co. v. Mahon* has been simultaneously acclaimed as the seminal case in the law of "regulatory takings" and blamed for the doctrinal confusion in that area. Both the commendations and the accusations, however, have been largely misplaced. *Mahon* was not the "first regulatory takings case." It was not decided under the Takings Clause. It was not the first case to hold that the Constitution protected nonphysical property or property as value. And it was not the first case to hold that a use restriction might be constitutional if and only if accompanied by just compensation. Its supposed status as the progenitor of all regulatory takings cases is the result of erroneous genealogy.

On the other hand, Justice Holmes's opinion in *Mahon* does not deserve all of the blame it has attracted. Holmes had worked out a theory of constitutional property that was far more sophisticated than a mere "diminution in value" or "balancing" test. He decided that the "property" the Constitution protected was the set of advantages that an owner could count on the state to enforce as existing positive law. The Constitution did not protect the owner against every change in law. Change was a fact of life, and no one assumed that all change would be accompanied by compensation. The Constitution did, however, protect the owner against radical, discontinuous alterations. These degrees of change were not measured solely, or even primarily, by the yardstick of economic value. Rather, change was measured as deviation from fundamental principles, or structural habits, embedded in the organized body of standing positive law.

The story of *Mahon*'s reputation and interpretation is a case study in legal evolution, selective borrowing, and amnesia. After the 1937 constitutional revolution, *Mahon* was the best case upon which to rebuild a constitutional property discourse. It was rediscovered—and to some extent reinvented—as the "foundation of regulatory jurisprudence." But in order to serve that role, a number of its features had to be ignored or misunderstood, and they were. One result is that American law does have a jurisprudence of regulatory takings, supported in part by the existence of *Mahon*, a Supreme Court case written by the great *Lochner* dissenter that affirmed the existence of constitutional protections for property. Another result is that the jurisprudence is confused, at least in part because a thin reading of *Mahon* was necessary to make it pass as a Takings Clause case with rules of decision fit for modern consumption. This left courts with very little framework within which to decide constitutional property rights cases.

Understanding Justice Holmes's theory in *Mahon* is important for at least three reasons. First, it sets the historical record straight. Second, it helps us see the range of choices to be made in constructing a theory of constitutional property, especially revealing the connections between theories of constitutional property and basic issues of jurisprudence. Finally, it makes clear the theoretical choices that one of the most important judges and legal thinkers in the United States made, thus providing a model that may be useful as courts and scholars continue to ponder the issue of the constitutional protection of property rights.

3. Overarching Constructs

Property, Utility and Fairness:
Comments on the Ethical Foundations of
"Just Compensation" Law
Frank I. Michelman
80 Harv. L. Rev. 1165 (1967)[*]

. . . .

"Taking" is, of course, constitutional law's expression for any sort of publicly inflicted private injury for which the Constitution requires payment of compensation. Whether a particular injurious result of governmental activity is to be classed as a "taking" is a question which usually arises where the nature of the activity and its causation of private loss are not themselves disputed; and so a court assigned to differentiate among impacts which are and are not "takings" is essentially engaged in deciding when government may execute public programs while leaving associated costs disproportionately concentrated upon one or a few persons.

. . . .

The compensation problem is, of course, familiar to constitutional lawyers who have faced the difficulty of distinguishing between valid exercises of the "police power," valid even though, in the course of "regulating" a person's activities, they cause him to be less well off than he was before the regulation; and governmental "takings" of "property," not permitted unless monetary "just compensation" is paid. . . .

. . . .

Such questions as those of distinguishing the "police power" from the "power of eminent domain" and of calculating "just compensation" thus seem to derive from a broader question: When a social decision to redirect economic resources entails painfully obvious opportunity costs, how shall these costs ultimately be distributed among all the members of society? Shall they be permitted to remain where they fall initially or shall the government, by paying compensation, make explicit attempts to distribute them in accordance with decisions made by whatever process fashions the tax structure, or perhaps according to some other principle? Shall the losses be left with the individuals on whom they happen first to fall, or shall they be "socialized"?

. . . .

This essay differs from what has gone before in its provisional abandonment of the assumption that case-by-case adjudication should or must be the prime method for refining society's compensation practices. This departure is in no way

---

meant to deny that compensability, insofar as the question is thrust upon courts by the duties of judicial review, is a legal as well as an ethical problem; or that one must approach the problem, in its legal aspect, determined to arrive at some sort of solution which finds expression in decisional rules. It is intended, rather, to give due recognition to the circumstance—herein documented—that the attempt to formulate rules of decision for compensability cases has, with suggestive consistency, yielded rules which are ethically unsatisfying. This observation seems to justify the hypothesis that decisional rules simply cannot be formulated which will yield other than a partial, imperfect, unsatisfactory solution and still be consonant with judicial action.

Examination of that hypothesis requires willingness to return as far as may be necessary to first principles in order to form a clear understanding of just what purposes society might be pursuing when it decrees that compensation payments shall sometimes be made. A substantial part of this essay will be devoted to such an inquiry. Through it, I shall argue that the only "test" for compensability which is "correct" in the sense of being directly responsive to society's purpose in engaging in a compensation practice is the test of fairness: is it fair to effectuate this social measure without granting this claim to compensation for private loss thereby inflicted? I hope to show that the test of fairness, while no doubt obvious, is not a truism; that departures from it in practice are common and can often be identified with confidence; that it can and to some extent always has served, and increasingly is serving, as a guide to public policy; and that its most important immediate implication for public policy pertains to the assignment of responsibility for ensuring that compensation is paid whenever it ought to be.

Full elaboration of the problem requires both some detailing of the failure of the rule-of-decision approach, and a tour over the route which leads to formation and specification of the idea of fairness as the key to compensability. . . .
. . . .

II. SOME RULES OF DECISION

Examination of judicial decisions and of legal commentary focused on them indicates that one of four factors has usually been deemed critical in classifying an occasion as compensable or not: (1) whether or not the public or its agents have physically used or occupied something belonging to the claimant; (2) the size of the harm sustained by the claimant or the degree to which his affected property has been devalued; (3) whether the claimant's loss is or is not outweighed by the public's concomitant gain; (4) whether the claimant has sustained any loss apart from restriction of his liberty to conduct some activity considered harmful to other people.

There follow some brief comments on each of these four "tests." The discussions are, at this point, tentative and incomplete. Their purpose is the limited one of showing that none of the standard criteria yields a sound and self-sufficient rule of decision—that each of them, when attempts are made to erect it into a general principle, is either seriously misguided, ruinously incomplete, or uselessly over-broad. . . .

. . . .

III. Some Theories of Property

Our survey of the general "tests" most commonly discussed in connection with judicial judgments of compensability has yielded no conclusions save that none of the tests is adequately discriminating and reliable. Even without a clear concept of the precise purposes of compensation, to which an "adequate" test ought to answer, we have been able to reject various proposed rules on account of more or less obvious flaws.

We turn now from deck clearing to theory building or, more accurately, to theory hunting. We are looking for a clear and convincing statement of the *purposes* of the compensation practice, in the form which shows us how to state with precision the variables which ought to determine compensability. . . .

. . . .

IV. Utility, Fairness, and Compensation

A. *Compensation and Utility*

A strictly utilitarian argument leading to the specific identification of "compensable" occasions would have a quasi-mathematical structure. Let us define three quantities to be known as "efficiency gains," "demoralization costs," and "settlement costs." "Efficiency gains" we define as the excess of benefits produced by a measure over losses inflicted by it, where benefits are measured by the total number of dollars which prospective gainers would be willing to pay to secure adoption, and losses are measured by the total number of dollars which prospective losers would insist on as the price of agreeing to adoption. "Demoralization costs" are defined as the total of (1) the dollar value necessary to offset disutilities which accrue to losers and their sympathizers specifically from the realization that no compensation is offered, and (2) the present capitalized dollar value of lost future production (reflecting either impaired incentives or social unrest) caused by demoralization of uncompensated losers, their sympathizers, and other observers disturbed by the thought that they themselves may be subjected to similar treatment on some other occasion. "Settlement costs" are measured by the dollar value of the time, effort, and resources which would be required in order to reach compensation settlements adequate to avoid demoralization costs. Included are the costs of settling not only the particular compensation claims presented, but also those of all persons so affected by the measure in question or similar measures as to have claims not obviously distinguishable by the available settlement apparatus.

A measure attended by positive efficiency gains is, under utilitarian ethics, prima facie desirable. But felicific calculation under the definition given for efficiency gains is imperfect because it takes no account of demoralization costs caused by a capricious redistribution, or alternatively, of the settlement costs necessary to avoid such demoralization costs. When pursuit of efficiency gains entails capricious redistribution, either demoralization costs or settlement costs must be incurred. It follows that if, for any measure, both demoralization costs and settlement costs (whichever were chosen) would exceed efficiency gains, the measure is to be rejected; but that otherwise, since either demoralization costs or settlement costs must be paid, it is the lower of these two costs which should be paid. The compensation rule which then clearly emerges is that compensation is to be paid whenever settlement costs are lower than both demoralization costs and efficiency gains. But if settlement costs, while lower than demoralization costs, exceed efficiency gains, then the measure is improper regardless of whether compensation is paid. The correct utilitarian statement, then, insofar as *the issue of compensability* is concerned, is that compensation is due whenever demoralization costs exceed settlement costs, and not otherwise.

. . . .

B. Compensation and Fairness

It is not the purpose of this essay to make a case for utilitarian ethics. Unquestionably, the provisional assumption of a utilitarian stance towards efficiency, property, and security is clarifying to a critical study of actual compensation practices. But there is no basis for concluding that the question of compensability is intelligible only when compensation is regarded as an instrument of utilitarian maximizing. Many observers, though they may admit that the question of compensability can logically be viewed as a question of efficiency, will insist that it can also be viewed as a question of justice to be decided without regard to the effect of the decision on the net social product. We must consider whether, in the name of justice, a person might not claim compensation (or society might not refuse compensation) regardless of the consequences for the net social product.

. . . .

V. The Rules of Decision Revisited

A brief recapitulation of the discussion up to this point may be helpful. We have, in effect, been searching for a useful and satisfying way to identify the "evil" supposedly combatted by the constitutional just compensation provisions, and have now suggested equating it with a capacity of some collective actions to imply that someone may be subjected to immediately disadvantageous or painful treatment for no other apparent reason, and in accordance with no other apparent principle, than that someone else's claim to satisfaction has been ranked as intrinsically superior to his own.

. . . .

To argue at length for the unamazing proposition that the true purpose of the just compensation rule is to forestall evils associated with unfair treatment, is to imply that the proposition, for all its obviousness, is insufficiently understood or recognized in practice. We should, then, consider carefully the extent to which the "fairness" or utility rationale is already reflected, even if inexplicitly, in the judicial doctrines which presently compose the main corpus of our just compensation lore. My conclusion is that these doctrines do significantly reflect the line of thought which has been elaborated in these pages, and that this approach, indeed, derives some indirect support from its power to explain much that is otherwise mysterious about the doctrines. Nevertheless, the courts fall too far short of adequate performance to be left without major assistance from other quarters.

A. Physical Invasion

. . . [T]he factor of physical invasion has a doctrinal potency often troublesome on two counts. First, private losses otherwise indistinguishable from one another may, as in the flight nuisance cases, be classified for compensability purposes according to whether they are accompanied by a physical invasion, even though that seems a purely fortuitous circumstance. Second, purely nominal harms—such as many which accompany street-widenings or subterranean utility installations—are automatically deemed compensable if accompanied by governmental occupation of private property, in apparent contradiction of the principle that the size of the private loss is a critically important variable. Both these seeming oddities may now seem easier to understand.

Actual, physical use or occupation by the public of private property may make it seem rather specially likely that the owner is sustaining a distinctly disproportionate share of the cost of some social undertaking. Moreover, there probably will be no need, in such a case, to trace remote consequences in order to arrive at a reasonable appraisal of the gravity of the owner's loss—a loss which is relatively likely to be practically determinable and expressible as a dollar amount. Furthermore, to limit compensation to those whose possessions have been physically violated, while in a sense arbitrary, may at least furnish a practical, defensible, impersonal line between compensable and noncompensable impositions—one which makes it possible to compensate on some occasions without becoming mired in the impossible task of compensating all disproportionately burdened interests.

The most obvious argument, then, for physical invasion as a discriminant of compensability would be that it combines a capacity to hold down settlement costs—both as to determining liability and as to measuring damages—with at least some tendency to draw the line so that compensable losses do, as a class, exceed in magnitude those deemed noncompensable. To the extent that the physical invasion criterion really does have these attributes, it should satisfy the test of fairness whether viewed as independent of or as subservient to a test of utility.

But this justification for a physical invasion criterion is really rather weak. The capacity for such a criterion to minimize settlement costs is beyond question, but its capacity to distinguish, even crudely, between significant and insignificant losses is too puny to be taken seriously. A rule that no loss is compensable unless accompanied by physical invasion would be patently unacceptable. A physical invasion test, then, can never be more than a convenience for identifying *clearly compensable* occasions. It cannot justify dismissal of any occasion as *clearly noncompensable*. But in that case, the significance of the settlement-cost-saving feature is sharply diminished. We find ourselves accepting the disadvantage of a test requiring compensation on many occasions where losses in truth seem relatively insignificant and bearable, in return for the convenience of having a simple way to identify some—but by no means all—compensable occasions. This seems a questionable bargain.

There may be a way of shoring up the physical invasion test—viewing it as a way of identifying some but not all compensable occasions—if we are inclined to take a utilitarian rather than an "absolute" view of fairness. This requires some reflection on psychic phenomena. Physical possession doubtless is the most cherished prerogative, and the most dramatic index, of ownership of tangible things. Sophisticated rationalizations and assurances of overall evenness which may stand up as long as one's possessions are unmolested may wilt before the stark spectacle of an alien, uninvited presence in one's territory. The psychological shock, the emotional protest, the symbolic threat to all property and security, may be expected to reach their highest pitch when government is an unabashed invader. Perhaps, then, the utilitarian might say that as long as courts must fend with compensability issues, to lay great stress on the polar circumstance of a permanent or regular physical use or occupation by the public is sound judicial practice—even though, at the same time and in a broader view, to discriminate on such a basis seems unacceptably arbitrary.

It is this evident arbitrariness which seems to require outright disapproval of the physical invasion criterion if we judge it by the standards of "absolute" fairness. For, true as may be the utilitarian controller's judgment that physical invasion raises special risks to the sense of security he wishes to inculcate, the rational actors of the fairness model must be expected to see that the relevant comparison is between large losses and small losses—not between those which are and are not accompanied by partial evictions.

B. Diminution of Value

. . . .

The method of identifying compensable harms on the basis of the degree to which "the affected piece" of property is devalued offers several parallels to that of discriminating on the basis of physical invasion. Both methods, though they seem obtuse and illogical so long as the purpose of compensation is broadly stated to be that of preventing capricious redistributions, gain in plausibility given the more refined statement that the purpose of compensation is to prevent a special kind of suffering on the part of people who have grounds for feeling themselves the victims of unprincipled exploitation. Moreover, the appeal of both methods rests ultimately in administrative expediency, in their defining classes of cases whose members will (a) usually be easy to identify and (b) usually, under certain behavioral suppositions, present a particularly strong subjective need for compensation.

As applied to the diminution of value test, these statements require explanation. We may begin by noticing a refinement, not mentioned earlier, which might initially seem only to deepen the mystery. It will be recalled that Justice Holmes, writing for the Court in the famous *Pennsylvania Coal* case,[111] held that a restriction on the extraction of coal, which effectively prevented the petitioner from exercising certain mining rights which it owned, was a taking of property and so could be enforced only upon payment of compensation. Holmes intimated strongly that the separation in ownership of the mining rights from the balance of the fee, prior to enactment of the restriction, was critically important to the petitioner's victory. But why should this be so? We can see that if one owns mining rights only, but not the residue of the fee, then a regulation forbidding mining totally devalues the owner's stake in "that" land. But is there any reason why it should matter whether one owns, in addition to mining rights, residuary rights in the same parcel (which may be added to the denominator so as probably to reduce the fraction of value destroyed below what is necessary for compensability) or residuary rights in some other parcel (which will not be added to the denominator)?

The significance of this question is confirmed by its pertinency to many comparable judicial performances. . . . [M]any courts award compensation to persons deprived by government action of the benefits of private building restrictions, without asking any questions about how much value, or what fraction of some value, has been destroyed. Thus, government activity, on land adjacent to the complainant's, which would otherwise give rise to no claim to compensation, may support such a claim if it violates a building restriction of which the complainant is a beneficiary. If a justification exists for such a difference in treatment, it would seem to be that one's psychological commitment to his explicit, formally carved out, appurtenant rights in another's land is much more sharply focused and intense, and much nearer the surface of his consciousness, than any reliance he places on his general claim to be safeguarded against nuisances. This proposition, if valid, would not affect the "fairness" of noncompensation, but it means that a utilitarian, with his eye on the actual long term psychological effects of his decisions, will be wary of denying compensation to the affronted servitude owner.

. . . .

The "fraction of value destroyed" test, to recapitulate, appears to proceed by first trying to isolate some "thing" owned by the person complaining which is affected by the imposition. Ideally, it seems, one traces the incidence of the imposition and then asks what "thing" is likely to be identified by the owner as "the thing" affected by this measure? Once having thus found the denominator of the fraction, the test proceeds to ask what proportion of the value or prerogatives formerly attributed by the claimant to that thing has been destroyed by the measure. If practically all, compensation is to be paid.

All this suggests that the common way of stating the test under discussion—in terms of a vaguely located critical point on a sliding scale—is misleading (though

---

[111] Pennsylvania Coal Co. v. Mahon, 260 U.S. 393 (1922).

certainly a true representation of the language repeatedly used by Holmes[116]). The customary labels—magnitude of the harm test, or diminution of value test— obscure the test's foundations by conveying the idea that it calls for an arbitrary pin-pointing of a critical proportion (probably lying somewhere between fifty and one hundred percent). More sympathetically perceived, however, the test poses not nearly so loose a question of degree; it does not ask "how much," but rather (like the physical-occupation test) it asks "whether or not": whether or not the measure in question can easily be seen to have practically deprived the claimant of some distinctly perceived, sharply crystallized, investment-backed expectation.

. . . .

C. Balancing

Earlier it was argued that while the process of striking a balance between a compensation claimant's losses and "society's" net gains would reveal the *efficiency* of the measure responsible for those losses and gains, it would be inconclusive as to compensability. By viewing compensation as a response to the demands of fairness we can now see that the "balancing" approach, while certainly inconclusive, is not entirely irrelevant to the compensability issue.

What fairness (or the utilitarian test) demands is assurance that society will not act deliberately so as to inflict painful burdens on some of its members unless such action is "unavoidable" in the interest of long-run, general well-being. Society violates that assurance if it pursues a doubtfully efficient course and, at the same time, refuses compensation for resulting painful losses. In this situation, even a practical impossibility of compensating will leave the sense of fairness unappeased, since it is unfair, and harmful to those expectations of the property owner that society wishes to protect, to proceed with measures which seem certain to cause painful individual losses while not clearly promising any net social improvement. In short, where compensability is the issue the "balancing" test is relevantly aimed at discovering not whether a measure is or is not efficient, but whether it is *so obviously* efficient as to quiet the potential outrage of persons "unavoidably" sacrificed in its interest. This conclusion does not, of course, detract from our earlier conclusion that even the clear and undisputed efficiency of a measure does not sufficiently establish its fairness in the absence of compensation.

D. Harm and Benefit

For clarity of analysis the most important point to be made about asking whether a restrictive measure requires a man to "benefit" his neighbors or only stops him from "harming" them is that this distinction (insofar as it is relevant and valid at all) is properly addressed to an issue different from, and antecedent to, the issue of "compensation" as we have now come to view it. We concluded earlier that

---

[116] In addition to the *Pennsylvania Coal* opinion, *see* Tyson v. Banton, 273 U.S. 418, 445-46 (1927) (dissenting opinion).

the harm-benefit distinction was illusory as long as efficiency was to be taken as the justifying purpose of a collective measure. But we have for many pages past been treating the compensation problem as one growing out of a need to reconcile efficiency with the protection of fair, or socially useful, expectations. The issue we have been trying to clarify does not exist apart from the collective pursuit of efficiency. In this scheme of things, the office of the harm-benefit distinction cannot be to help resolve that issue. But the distinction, properly understood, does have a related use. It helps us to identify certain situations which, although in most obvious respects they resemble paradigm compensability problems, can be treated as raising no compensation issues *because the collective measures involved are not grounded solely in considerations of efficiency.*

The core of truth in the harm-prevention/benefit-extraction test—and the reason for its strong intuitive appeal—emerges when we recognize that some use restrictions can claim a justification having nothing to do with the question of what use of the available resources is the most efficient. If someone, without my consent, takes away a valuable possession of mine, he is said to have stolen and is called a thief. When theft occurs, society usually will do what it can to make the thief restore to the owner the thing stolen or its equivalent, either because "commutative justice"[119] so requires or because it is felt that there will be an intolerable threat to stable, productive social existence unless society sets its face against the unilateral decisions of thieves that they should have what is in the possession of others. The case is not essentially different if I own a residence in a pleasant neighborhood and you open a brickworks nearby. In pursuit of your own welfare you have by your own fiat deprived me of some of mine. Society, by closing the brickworks, simply makes you give back the welfare you grabbed; and, since you were not authorized in the first place to make distributional judgments as between you and me, you have no claim to compensation. The whole point of society's intervention negates any claim to compensation.

The point, then, is that the appeal of the tendered distinction between antinuisance measures and public benefit measures lies in the fact that the activities curbed by the first sort of measure are much more likely to have been "theft-like" in their origin than are activities restricted by the second sort. Measures of the "public benefit" type can usually be justified *only* in terms of efficiency, a justification which leaves the compensation issue unresolved, while "antinuisance" measures may be justified by considerations of commutative justice, or of the protection of orderly decision making, which negate any possible claim to compensation.

It should be clear, however, that no sharp distinction is thus established between the two types of measures. Activity which is obviously detrimental to others at the time regulations are adopted may have been truly innocent when first instigated. Failure to act upon this plain truth is responsible for some of the most violently offensive decisions not to compensate. The brickyard case is the undying classic.[121] The yard is established out of sight, hearing, and influence of any other

---

[119] *See* THE ETHICS OF ARISTOTLE (THE NICOMACHEAN ETHICS) bk. V, ch. 4 (Thomson transl. 1955).

[121] Hadacheck v. Sebastian, 239 U.S. 394 (1915).

activity whatsoever. The city expands, and eventually engulfs the brickyard. The brickmaker is then ordered to desist. That order reduces the market value of his land from 800,000 dollars to 60,000 dollars. There is no question here of disgorging ill-gotten gains: brickmaking is a worthy occupation, and at the time of its establishment the yard generated no nuisance. No incompatibility with any use of other land was apparent. To say that the brickmaker should have foreseen the emergence of the incompatibility is fantastic when the conclusion depending from that premise is that we may now destroy his investment without compensating him. It would be no less erratic for society to explain to a homeowner, as it bulldozed his house out of the way of a new public school or pumping station, that he should have realized from the beginning that congestion would necessitate these facilities and that topographical factors have all along pointed unerringly in the direction of his lot.

. . . .

In sum, then, it would appear that losses inflicted by "nuisance prevention" may raise serious questions of compensation, while losses fixed by "public benefit" measures may not even involve any redistribution. If that is so, then surely we ought to be wary of any compensation rule which treats as determinative the distinction between the two types of measures. Such a rule has overgeneralized from relevant considerations which are somewhat characteristic of, but not logically or practically inseparable from, measures in one or the other class. If the relevant considerations can be kept in view without the oversimplified rule, then the oversimplified rule is merely a menace to just decision and should be dismissed.

Clarity of analysis is, at any rate, greatly improved by treating these considerations as logically antecedent to compensability issues. If efficiency-motivated social action has a painfully uneven distributional side-effect, the issue of compensability must be faced and resolved. But social action which merely corrects prior, unilaterally determined redistributions, or brings a deliberate gamble to its dénouement, raises no question of compensability. The true office of the harm-prevention/benefit-extraction dichotomy is, then, to help us decide whether a potential occasion of compensation exists at all. If one does, the compensability discussion must proceed from that point.

. . . .

VI. INSTITUTIONAL ARRANGEMENTS FOR SECURING JUST COMPENSATION

We tend naturally to think of fairness as a standard against which to test political action, a discipline to be administered specifically and with deliberation, an extrinsic constraint to be imposed on an intrinsically nonfair political process. Such a conception is likely to lead without further conscious thought to an assumption, which for many surely will have an a priori feel, that the task of assuring the fairness of political action lies principally and ultimately with the courts. Thus it is that, when legal specialists turn their attention to the "legal system's" part in promoting fairness in collective undertakings through such a means as establishing a duty to pay "just compensation," they immediately perceive the problem as one to be solved by the promulgation of sound rules of decision. One can nonetheless challenge the attribution of preeminent responsibility to the judiciary, identify institutional impediments to adequate control of fairness by courts, and explore the possible advantages of *self*-discipline by legislatures and public administrators. . . .

. . . .

A. *The Difficulty of "Judging" Fairness*

The question to be investigated at this point is whether there is something about the content of fairness as a standard for testing the legitimacy of political action which unfits it for judicial use, and so suggests that reliance would be better placed on political self-discipline than on judicial discipline.

However difficult the fairness standard may be to formulate and apply, there is no obvious reason for supposing that political actors should be able to understand it better or handle it more deftly than judges can. There is, indeed, some ground for supposing the contrary. One way to define fairness is to say that a political output is fair when it approximates the expected output of a fairness machine—a system yielding results similar to those which unanimity would yield, but somehow freed from the operational costs attendant upon an actual unanimity rule. In making this comparison, the judge has an obvious advantage of detachment over the legislator who is actually involved on terms inconsistent with the hypothetical terms governing the fairness machine. But the judge may labor under a serious disadvantage too. In order to make use of the fairness machine comparison, he would need access to information which the legislator may have but which the judge usually cannot have; that is, he would need to see the decision which has been challenged in litigation in its whole systematic context—to know, for example, what vote trades, explicit and implicit, concerning past and future measures have been connected with it—in order to employ the objectified conception of fairness as an approximation to the output of a fairness machine.

. . . .

Our question about fairness as an apt standard for judging thus reflects not a suspicion that judicial personnel are less able than other men to understand or apply the content of the standard, but doubt stemming from a judicial predilection—one which we normally applaud because we deem it healthily responsive to limits we wish to keep in place around the judicial province—to seek an articulate doctrinal packaging for all judgments. The problem is that fairness resists being cast into a simple, impersonal, easily stated formula.

. . . .

B. *The Usefulness of Artificial Settlements*

A serious objection to the habit of leaving fairness discipline to the courts is that we may thereby miss opportunities to make good use of settlement methods too artificial or innovative for judicial adoption. A court, it seems, must choose between denying all compensation and awarding "just" compensation; the loss is either a "taking" of "property" or it is not. If "just" compensation is essentially incalculable, or if the cost of computing it is very high, the court may be led to classify a situation as noncompensable. If choice must be relegated to this framework, we shall not be able to exploit the substitutability of settlement costs and demoralization costs. It may be that even though that settlement which would reduce demoralization costs to zero would be prohibitively costly, there exists some relatively cheap form of settlement which would reduce demoralization costs so effectively that, by using it, we can reduce the total of settlement plus demoralization costs below what they would be in the absence of any settlement. Such a settlement technique, if one exists, is very likely to require legislative adoption.

. . . .

C. The Need for Administrative Conscientiousness

Settlement schemes, whether of legislative or judicial origin, are bound to be imperfect. There will be occasions on which recognition of these imperfections should spell the difference between approving and disapproving some collective undertaking. A danger of automatically entrusting the fairness discipline to courts is that public administrators may fail to take appropriate notice of this problem.

. . . .

THE ORIGINAL UNDERSTANDING OF THE TAKINGS CLAUSE AND THE POLITICAL PROCESS
William Michael Treanor
95 Colum. L. Rev. 782 (1995)[*]

The original understanding of the Takings Clause of the Fifth Amendment[1] was clear on two points. The clause required compensation when the federal government physically took private property, but not when government regulations limited the ways in which property could be used. In 1922, however, the Supreme Court's decision in *Pennsylvania Coal v. Mahon*[2] established a new takings regime. In an opinion by Justice Holmes, the Court held that compensation must be provided when government regulation "goes too far"[3] in diminishing the value of private property. Since that decision, the Supreme Court has been unable to define clearly what kind of regulations run afoul of Holmes's vague standard. Attempts to

---

[*]   This article originally appeared at 95 Colum. L. Rev. 782 (1995). Reprinted by permission.

[1]   "[N]or shall private property be taken for public use, without just compensation." U.S. Const. amend. V.

[2]   260 U.S. 393 (1922).

[3]   Id. at 415.

do so, including the Court's recent decisions in *Lucas v. South Carolina Coastal Council*[4] and *Dolan v. City of Tigard*,[5] have created a body of law that more than one recent commentator has described as a "mess."[6]

The Court and leading commentators have not seriously considered the possibility that there was an underlying rationale, worth reviving, that explains why the Takings Clause and its state counterparts originally protected property against physical seizures, but not against regulations affecting value. This Article contends that the limited scope of the takings clauses reflected the fact that, for a variety of reasons, members of the framing generation believed that physical possession of property was particularly vulnerable to process failure. The Article then argues on both originalist and non-originalist grounds for a process-based theory of the Takings Clause that departs dramatically from current takings jurisprudence.

. . . .

I. TAKINGS LAW THROUGH *PENNSYLVANIA COAL*

. . . In colonial America, government routinely acted in ways that affected private property, and the political process determined when compensation was due. No judicially enforceable compensation requirement existed during this period. Even after the establishment of a compensation requirement, it applied only to interference with physical ownership, and government routinely acted in ways that diminished the value of private property without providing compensation.

. . . .

II. MISUNDERSTANDING (OR IGNORING) THE ORIGINAL UNDERSTANDING

The predecessor clauses to the Fifth Amendment's Takings Clause, the original understanding of the Takings Clause itself, and the weight of early judicial interpretations of the federal and state takings clauses all indicate that compensation was mandated only when the government physically took property. Despite this clear history, the Supreme Court in 1922 in *Pennsylvania Coal* held that a government regulation could give rise to a requirement of compensation. Neither that decision, nor any subsequent Supreme Court decision, nor any of the leading takings scholars, has seriously considered the possibility that there was a principle of relevance today that would explain why the requirement of compensation originally applied only to physical seizures of property.

---

[4] 112 S. Ct. 2886 (1992).

[5] 114 S. Ct. 2309 (1994).

[6] Daniel A. Farber, Public Choice and Just Compensation, 9 Const. Commentary 279, 279 (1992); Saul Levmore, Just Compensation and Just Politics, 22 Conn. L. Rev. 285, 287 (1990).

A. Pennsylvania Coal

. . . .

Pennsylvania Coal involved a challenge to Pennsylvania's Kohler Act, which barred coal companies from removing coal when such removal would cause subsidence. An exception was recognized for lots on which the coal company owned the surface rights. The Court found that this regulation violated the Takings Clause. Writing for the majority, Holmes framed the decision in terms of first principles, and simply ignored the precedents in which the Court had held that regulations did not fall within the Takings Clause. . . . The previous brightline test—regulations were never a taking—was replaced by a far more imprecise test: "The general rule at least is, that while property may be regulated to a certain extent, if regulation goes too far it will be recognized as a taking."[105] It was the role of the court to determine when a regulation "goes too far," and one factor that the court was to consider was the "extent of the diminution"[106] of value caused by the regulation. Underlying this view was a suspicion of the legislature. "When this seemingly absolute protection [for property] is found to be qualified by the police power, the natural tendency of human nature is to extend the qualification more and more until at last private property disappears."[107]

. . . .

Holmes's position has an intrinsic appeal. Why should one form of property receive strong protection under the Takings Clause and others none? There are, however, two problems with the *Pennsylvania Coal* approach. First, compared to the earlier approach, it makes the decision about when courts should direct compensation a very difficult one. The text, original understanding, and early interpretations of the Takings Clause explain clearly when a court should order compensation—when the government physically takes private property. In contrast, the *Pennsylvania Coal* inquiry into when regulation "goes too far" is open-ended and unconstrained. Second, the *Pennsylvania Coal* approach rests on the implicit premise that the question *why* the framers protected physical possession rather than other forms of property does not merit serious inquiry. In other words, Holmes assumes that, because anything of economic value is property, anything of economic value also merits protection under the Takings Clause. Despite these problems, *Pennsylvania Coal* established the pattern that has dominated modern takings law. The Supreme Court has consistently held that a regulation that "goes too far" can give rise to a compensable taking.

---

[105] [Pennsylvania Coal Co. v. Mahon, 260 U.S. 393 (1922)] . . . at 415.

[106] Id. at 413.

[107] Id. at 415.

B. *The Modern Supreme Court, Original Understanding, and Takings Law*

In fashioning a modern takings jurisprudence, the Supreme Court has essentially ignored the original understanding of the Takings Clause. . . . The Court's recent decisions in *Lucas* and *Dolan* illustrate the willingness of its members to disregard the original understanding of the Takings Clause.

After David Lucas had paid almost $1,000,000 for two beachfront lots, the South Carolina Beachfront Management Act was passed, significantly restricting the use of all beachfront property in the state. The state coastal commission, acting pursuant to the Act, subsequently barred Lucas from building any habitable structure on his lots. Lucas claimed that the commission's determination was a taking under the Fifth Amendment. In a majority opinion by Justice Scalia, which Chief Justice Rehnquist and Justices White, O'Connor, and Thomas joined, the Court announced that when a regulation deprives property of all its value, compensation is due. It accordingly found that, because Lucas's property had lost all economic value, the regulation blocking development of the property was presumptively a taking. The Court, however, framed an exception to this general rule: Regulation that concerns a common law nuisance or is in accordance with background principles of property law does not give rise to a taking. The case therefore was remanded for a determination of the relevant South Carolina law.[119]

. . . .

Justice Scalia's approach in *Lucas* is at odds with his announced commitment to a doctrine of originalism and his explanation of what originalism means. For example, in "Originalism: The Lesser Evil," Justice Scalia contended that original meaning as revealed in the contemporaneous record should control constitutional adjudication.[139] A constitutional clause should be treated as capable of evolution only "on the basis of some textual or historical evidence."[140] Nonetheless, in *Lucas*, Justice Scalia seemed to be treating the Takings Clause as capable of evolution, without making a case for why it should be so treated.

Lucas is an anomaly in that the original understanding is at least discussed. At the same time, the case neatly illustrates the irrelevance of the original understanding for modern takings jurisprudence. The Justice who invokes original understanding apparently does not actually believe that it should be used to decide the case. The Justice who is most closely associated with a jurisprudence of original intent essentially dismisses it as irrelevant.

Dolan v. City of Tigard[141] is a more typical example of the peripheral role of history in takings law. Florence Dolan wished to expand her hardware store and applied for a permit to develop the site. The Tigard City Planning Commission

---

[119] See Lucas v. South Carolina Coastal Council, 112 S. Ct. 2886, 2900-02 (1992).

[139] See Antonin Scalia, Originalism: The Lesser Evil, 57 U. Cin. L. Rev. 849, 862-64 (1989) [hereinafter Scalia, Originalism]. . . .

[140] Scalia, Originalism, supra note 139, at 862.

[141] 114 S. Ct. 2309 (1994).

approved her application, subject to the conditions previously imposed by the municipality's Community Development Code for new developments in the central business area, where the store was located. In exchange for permission to expand, Dolan was required to dedicate to the city that part of her property lying within the 100-year floodplain for use in a storm drainage system, and she was also required to dedicate a fifteen-foot strip of land adjoining the floodplain for use as a bikepath. Dolan sought a variance, and when it was denied by the Planning Commission and by the Land Use Board of Appeals, she brought suit, claiming a taking.

The Supreme Court divided sharply in response to the case. Chief Justice Rehnquist wrote for a five-member majority that found in Dolan's favor, while Justices Stevens and Souter dissented. The Court held that the Takings Clause required that, to avoid compensation, there had to be an "essential nexus" between a legitimate state interest and the permit condition and, in addition, that the government bore the burden of demonstrating the existence of "rough proportionality" between the harm associated with the expansion—additional water run-off and additional car and bike trips to the larger store—and the burdens imposed on Dolan. The Court concluded that the findings relied on by the municipality did not satisfy the rough proportionality test and that burdens imposed in the absence of such a showing were unconstitutional conditions.

None of the . . . opinions in the case contains any focused discussion of original intent. Only Justice Stevens touched on the issue, and he did so obliquely. . . .

C. Academic Commentary and Original Intent

As the above discussion indicates, the original understanding has played at most a marginal role in modern Supreme Court takings jurisprudence. Like the Court, scholars have not seriously considered the possibility that the framers' requirement of compensation for physical seizures but not for regulations might be based on a principle relevant to modern constitutional discourse. This section discusses the academic disregard of original intent and what are probably the two most prominent exceptions to this trend: Joseph Sax's "Takings and the Police Power"[151] and Richard Epstein's *Takings*.[152] Both Sax and Epstein use original intent to support their conceptions of takings law, yet dismiss the significance of the fact that the Takings Clause was originally limited in scope. In doing so, they fail to grasp the full significance of the Takings Clause.

. . . .

III. UNDERSTANDING THE ORIGINAL UNDERSTANDING

If we are to take seriously the original understanding of the Takings Clause, we cannot focus only on its animating principle, but must also focus on the clause's

---

[151] [Joseph L.] Sax, . . . [Takings and the Police Power, 74 Yale L.J. 36 (1964)].

[152] [Richard A.] Epstein, . . . [Takings: Private Property and the Power of Eminent Domain (1985)].

limiting principle. As Professor James Ely has written, "For all their devotion to property rights, the framers were content to rely primarily on institutional and political arrangements to safeguard property owners."[188] Why did the people who drafted and enacted the Takings Clause and its state counterparts decide that the interest in physical possession of property needed substantive protection, but that other property interests did not? . . .

This Part begins by considering why the framers did not require compensation for any government act that affected the value of property. To this end, it examines the prevalent views of property during the framing period. Drawing on recent historical scholarship about the ideologies of republicanism and liberalism at the time of the framing, it suggests—contrary to Epstein—that Lockean liberalism, which treats the right to property as prepolitical, was not the single dominant ideology of the time. Rather, republicanism, which values the right to property but subjects it to majoritarian delineation, was also extremely influential. The power of the republican view of property during this period shows that there was no consensus among the framers that majoritarian decisionmakers could not be trusted to determine the appropriate level of protection for property interests.

After advancing this explanation for the initially limited scope of the Takings Clause, this Part then considers why possessory property interests in particular received substantive protection. It rejects the explanation that the limited scope of the Takings Clause resulted from the framers' limited conception of property and regulation. Instead, it examines the rise of the just compensation requirement in various state constitutions and in the Bill of Rights and concludes that in each case it was produced by the fear of process failure.

Finally, this Part turns to Madison, whose sophisticated conception of the clause and its purpose accords with the general reasons for which others sought special protection for physical possession of property. . . . Physical possession received such heightened protection because of Madison's concern that the political process would not fairly consider certain possessory interests, specifically the ownership of land and slaves.

. . . .

IV. A POLITICAL PROCESS-BASED THEORY OF THE JUST COMPENSATION CLAUSE

. . . This Part . . . argues for a political process-based theory of the Takings Clause, inspired by its original meaning and purpose, yet modified to reflect the changes in economic and political circumstances since the late eighteenth century.

. . . This Part argues that translating the original understanding into a contemporary takings jurisprudence means that courts today should protect those whose property interests are, given modern political realities, particularly unlikely to receive fair consideration from majoritarian decisionmakers. Thus, the translation

---

[188] [James W.] Ely, [Jr., The Guardian of Every Other Right (1992)] . . . , at 47.

of the original understanding outlined here would interpret the Takings Clause to provide heightened protection to the property interests of those who have been singled out and the property interests of discrete and insular minorities.

. . . .

A. *Why Translate?*

An originalist model of constitutional interpretation is attractive for two related reasons. First, it constrains judicial decisionmaking to a significant degree. Rather than deciding independently what factors are relevant to a case, originalist judges defer to already established choices. As a result, originalism accords with the belief that the rule of law requires judges to follow externally imposed rules, rather than resolve cases in accordance with their own personal views. Second, originalism connects constitutional decisionmaking with majoritarian decision-making. Originalist judges are implementing the considered choices made by "We the People" under circumstances that fostered careful deliberation and that "We the People" have not subsequently altered.

Under the traditional originalist approach to constitutional interpretation, judges construe a text as it was construed at the time of its ratification. . . .

The translator is also an originalist, but she looks not to the concrete constitutional understandings of "We the People," but to the underlying values that "We the People" embraced. . . .

From an originalist standpoint, translation is a better model than traditional originalism because the available evidence suggests that it better reflects the original approach to constitutional interpretation. The framers were not traditional originalists. They created a terse, open-ended constitution whose meaning would change in response to changed circumstances. . . .

. . . .

B. *Translating the Original Understanding*

. . . .

1. *The Original Understanding.* — As we have seen, the federal Takings Clause and its predecessor clauses, as they were originally understood, divided governmental actions affecting property into two groups. When the government physically took property, it owed compensation. Any other governmental action, no matter how severely it affected the value of property, did not give rise to a compensation requirement. This requirement applied to physical takings because the framers believed that majoritarian decisionmaking processes would not give fair consideration to the individual's interest in not having her property physically seized by the government.

The clause sought to remedy failures in the political process. But the underlying idea was *not* that all majoritarian decisions should be reviewed to determine whether the process behind any particular decision was fair or unfair. Rather, heightened constitutional protection was provided only for the limited category of decisions in which unfairness was most likely. At the same time, while the clause only mandated compensation in a limited sphere, it had a broader significance: It was also designed to teach the people that governmental actions that arbitrarily affected property interests (including the value of property) were illegitimate.

. . . .

2. *The Takings Clause and Changed Circumstances.* — At the time of the framing and ratification of the Takings Clause and its predecessor clauses, different people were concerned with risks to different possessory interests, but there was nonetheless a close match between the end served by the clause—remedying process failure—and the means adopted—requiring compensation for physical takings. Today, protection of physical possession no longer advances the broader end of remedying process failure.

Slaveownership obviously no longer falls within the ambit of the clause. Madison believed that slaveowners were particularly politically vulnerable because those who did not own slaves would be unlikely to enter into political combinations with them. However, the Thirteenth and Fourteenth Amendments rendered this aspect of the clause moot by requiring uncompensated emancipation of all slaves.

The situation with respect to landownership is more complex, but the essential point—that the affected property interest no longer needs heightened protection—is also applicable here. Critical factual presuppositions that animated Madison are inconsistent with contemporary realities. Madison anticipated that in the near future most Americans would not own land. Moreover, in accordance with republican theory, he thought landowners would be particularly weak because employees, dependent on their employers for support, would follow their employers' wishes and most employers would be engaged in trade or industry, rather than farming. Neither assumption is accurate today. According to the most recent census report, sixty-four percent of Americans own their own homes. In addition, voter studies indicate that voting behavior reflects variables like class, gender, ethnicity, region, and age, not the voting orientation of one's employer.

Indeed, a group of landowners faced with seizure of their land for a public use are particularly well situated to secure compensation from majoritarian decision-makers. As Professor Daniel Farber has observed, "[I]f public choice theory has any one key finding, it is that small groups with high stakes have a disproportionately great influence on the political process. Thus, landowners have some political advantages in seeking compensation."[382] . . .

. . . .

In sum, because of changes that have occurred over time, many (although not all) of the property interests that in the late eighteenth century were considered to be inadequately protected by the political process either no longer exist or are now adequately protected by that process. Thus, special protection for possessory property interests no longer serves the principle underlying the Takings Clause. The job

---

[382] Daniel A. Farber, Economic Analysis and Just Compensation, 12 Int'l Rev. L. & Econ. 125, 130 (1992). . . .

of the translator, therefore, is to determine what property interests must now be protected if we are to be consistent with the original purposes of the clause.

3. *The Translation. . . .*

a. *Public Choice Theory.* — In recent years, Professors Farber,[392] Fischel,[393] and Levmore[394] have offered public choice theories of the Takings Clause. Like the original understanding of the Takings Clause, these theories treat the central concern of the Takings Clause as protecting those who suffer property losses because of process failure. These public choice theories, however, offer different accounts of what type of process failure needs to be averted. Because of their different focuses, the theories provide useful bases for consideration of how a translated Takings Clause would guard against process failure.

Fischel's model offers the broadest protection to property owners. He argues that courts construing the Takings Clause should direct compensation when property owners are "victims of democratic excess."[396] . . . The governmental entity making the decision is of critical significance in Fischel's theory . . . . In our system, larger units of government are characterized by pluralist politics—with logrolling and the opportunity for deal-making—and this gives property owners "a realistic opportunity to politically protect themselves."[399] In contrast, empirical studies indicate that local government decisionmaking is characterized by majoritarian politics, rather than by deal-making. Because local governments typically have one legislative chamber, rather than two, and because their legislative agenda has a relatively limited number of items, there are fewer opportunities for logrolling. As a result, special interests are likely to lose consistently. Such interests will not be able to bargain in order to protect themselves, and therefore need judicial protection. When a larger unit of government is involved, such protection is generally unnecessary. . . . Judicial action directing compensation for decisions made by higher level governmental entities is appropriate only when there has been unfairness . . . .

Although Fischel does not claim to offer an originalist vision of any type, his concern with process failure initially appears a good translation of the original understanding. However, his account is ultimately an inadequate translation because it fails to accord enough respect to the Takings Clause's limiting principle—the principle of deference to the political process, except where it is most prone to failure. Fischel's theory imposes a high level of judicial scrutiny on decisions made by most localities and states. While scrutiny is less rigorous when larger

---

[392] See Farber, supra note 6 . . . .

[393] See [William A.] Fischel, . . . [Exploring the Kozinski Paradox: Why is More Efficient Regulation a Taking of Property?, 67 Chi.-Kent L. Rev. 865 (1991)].

[394] See Levmore, supra note 6 . . . .

[396] Fischel, supra note . . . [393], at 890.

[399] Id. [at 911].

governmental entities are involved, even decisions by such entities receive only a limited degree of deference, as Fischel's suggestion that *Lucas* was correctly decided indicates.

. . . .

While Fischel's theory is too broad for the translator, it is nonetheless valuable for the task of translation. It shows why special interests, although a minority, will often be able to protect themselves and therefore do not need heightened protection.

Farber's narrower theory of the Takings Clause is a more plausible translation of the original understanding.[407] Farber argues that the principal purpose of the Takings Clause is "horizontal equity."[408] Public choice theory shows that even in the absence of a constitutional requirement, democratic legislatures would normally compensate when they physically took property. Only the politically unprotected will not be compensated: "[I]n a world where government compensation is often available, it is unacceptable that some groups are denied compensation because of their unusual political vulnerability."[410] This principle requires compensation whenever the government physically takes property. In order to ensure that government will not strategically evade the Takings Clause, the principle must be extended to situations in which the government seeks to transfer property from one private citizen to another. For the same reason, it must also extend to "regulations that are functionally equivalent to government acquisitions."[411] *Lucas* falls within the last category. Because the government compensates when land is incorporated into national parks, and because the preservation ban challenged in *Lucas* was effectively the same as if his land had been seized for preservation purposes, Lucas should have been compensated.

Farber's approach parallels the original understanding in that both reflect a view of the Takings Clause as concerned with process failure and, at the same time, both recognize only a limited area in which majoritarian decisions will be overturned. Because of these parallels, Farber's theory provides a fairly good translation of the original understanding. Its weakness as translation is that its conception of process failure is too broad, for reasons suggested by Fischel's explanation of how special interests are able to use pluralist politics to protect their property claims. The original interpretation of the Takings Clause (under which physical takings were compensated for) closely matched the underlying end. Farber's theory embodies a looser match, since the regulations for which he would require compensation will often not be the product of process failure. *Lucas* is a prime example of this situation.

As discussed, Lucas challenged the Beachfront Management Act, which prevented him from building on his property. However, he was not alone in suffering

---

[407] Farber's theory is not originalist, although he briefly invokes the history of the clause. . . . Farber, supra note 6, at 281 & n.8 . . . .

[408] Id. at 308.

[410] Farber, supra note 6, at 206.

[411] Id. at 304.

under the Act, which affected all South Carolina beachfront landowners. . . . Lucas was part of a large (and powerful) group affected by the legislation: beach-front property owners. This is a classic example of a group well-positioned to engage in legislative logrolling. Obviously, that group lost—but that will by defi-nition occur when a takings claim is brought, since only losers will have grounds to complain. There is no evidence of process failure, and yet Farber would com-pensate Lucas. Farber would provide compensation for regulatory takings that are similar to physical takings, even though this class of regulatory takings as a whole is not one in which process failure is particularly likely.

Professor Levmore has advanced a third public choice approach to the Takings Clause, one that focuses on singling out. He argues that process failure is likely when an individual or small group of people has been singled out and that com-pensation is particularly appropriate in such situations. When a proposed statute or regulation affects a great many people, they can protect themselves through the political process, engaging in logrolling to ensure that they do not receive an unfair share of the public's burden. But the situation is very different when a pro-posed governmental action affects only a few people or, worse, a single person. Professor Levmore writes: "It is unlikely that such individuals can compete effec-tively in the political arena and it would be undesirable for them to try; the trans-action cost of individual involvement in politics is, after all, quite great."[415] For example, if the government were to take my home, in the absence of a just com-pensation clause I would be poorly positioned to go to the legislature or Congress and obtain redress. Thus, Levmore argues that takings law properly protects indi-vidual actors and small groups of actors who are affected by governmental actions but cannot effectively engage in interest group politics because they are not repeat players and because they are a tiny part of the polity.

Again, this theory, like Farber's, is an adequate translation of original intent (although it is not offered as such), and for the same reasons: It recognizes that the Takings Clause is concerned with process failure, and it limits the area in which majoritarian decisions involving property will be overturned. However, Levmore's theory represents an imperfect translation because it provides for compensation of a small group whose property interests are affected, even when a larger group would not be compensated. For example, a court will order compensation in the case of an individual whose property suffers a particularly sharp decrease in value because of airplane overflights, but not when overflights affect a larger group. In contrast, the original understanding did not involve making the individuals who were likely to suffer process failure better off than those protected by the political process. Rather, the Takings Clause was intended to put everyone who suffered the same injury on the same footing: Everyone whose property was physically taken received compensation.

Individually, the theories of Farber and Levmore do not accurately translate the original understanding of the Takings Clause. However, by synthesizing the two

---

[415] Levmore, supra note 6, at 307.

theories, one can arrive at an appropriate translation. Compensation is due when a governmental action affects only the property interests of an individual or a small group of people and when, in the absence of compensation, there would be a lack of horizontal equity (i.e., when compensation is the norm in similar circumstances). Such a theory does what the Takings Clause was initially interpreted to do; it defers to majoritarian decisionmaking in most instances but defends those most likely to be the victims of process failure.

The Supreme Court's most recent prominent takings cases can illustrate the way in which this test would operate. For reasons suggested in critiquing Farber's theory, *Lucas* would be an easy case. The challenged statute affected a large group of people that could certainly protect itself through the political process. The Court therefore should have found that there was no taking in that case.

Dolan is a closer case, but the result should have been the same. Tigard had passed a comprehensive zoning plan. When Dolan sought permission from the City Planning Commission to expand her store, the Commission conditioned its approval with standard terms previously codified in the Community Development Code and imposed on anyone who sought to expand in the Central Business District. There was no evidence that Dolan was treated differently than anyone else.

. . .

    b. *Discrete and Insular Minorities.* — Public choice theory offers one approach to process failure. However, modern legal theory also suggests that process failure is particularly likely in cases involving discrete and insular minorities. Recognition of the need for special judicial protection in view of the disadvantages faced by such groups in the political process can be traced back to footnote four of *Carolene Products*, where Justice Stone suggested that heightened scrutiny might be appropriate in "the review of statutes directed at particular religious . . . or national . . . or racial minorities."[421]

. . . [T]he Takings Clause and the claims of discrete and insular minorities intersect in one area: environmental racism, or, as it is also called, environmental justice.[423] The idea underlying the environmental racism movement is that because minority communities are not full participants in the political process, they are likely to receive more than their share of hazardous waste siting. . . .

. . . .

The limited body of empirical work now available is consistent with these theories and indicates that minority communities bear more than their share of locally undesirable land uses. . . .

Thus, empirical work and legal theories about the political process and discrete and insular minorities suggest that a translation of the original understanding of the

---

[421] United States v. Carolene Prods., 304 U.S. 144, 152-53, n.4 (1938) (citations omitted).

[423] On environmental racism, see Vicki Been, Locally Undesirable Land Uses in Minority Neighborhoods: Disproportionate Siting or Market Dynamics?, 103 Yale L.J. 1383 (1994) . . . ; Vicki Been, What's Fairness Got to Do With It? Environmental Justice and the Siting of Locally Undesirable Land Uses, 78 Cornell L. Rev. 1001 (1993) . . . ; Richard J. Lazarus, Pursuing "Environmental Justice": The Distributional Effects of Environmental Protection, 87 Nw. U. L. Rev. 787 (1993).

Takings Clause should encompass a second category of cases: environmental justice cases. Like individuals or small groups affected by governmental decisions, discrete and insular minorities are unusually likely to be the victims of process failure. One could conceivably argue for a translation under which all governmental actions that have a disparate impact on the property interests of discrete and insular minorities would be subject to heightened scrutiny under the Takings Clause. Decisions changing government benefits or taxing policies might then be reviewed under the clause. But that would not be a good translation. It would miss the limiting principle of the original understanding—the principle of general deference to majoritarian decisionmaking. Limitation of heightened Takings Clause scrutiny of governmental actions that affect discrete and insular minorities to environmental justice cases cabins the judiciary's ability to overturn majoritarian decisions, just as the initial limitation of the Takings Clause to cases of physical seizure meant that majoritarian decisions concerning property were subject to constraint only in a limited category of cases. . . .

Previously, administrative siting decisions have been challenged on equal protection grounds, with a uniform lack of success. Under the approach suggested in this Article, they should be brought instead as takings claims. The possibility of process failure permits courts to be aggressive in evaluating environmental justice claims. Because the claims of minority groups are particularly unlikely to receive a fair hearing in the majoritarian process, it falls to courts to consider individual cases, weigh public need against private harm, and determine what remedy, if any, is appropriate.

    . . . .

A modern translation of the Takings Clause must also address what standard of review courts should apply in those cases that fall within the ambit of the clause. In other words, once there has been a threshold showing that minority communities in an area are bearing a disproportionate share of locally undesirable land uses, when is a remedy appropriate? In resolving these issues, courts should apply the approach set forth in *Armstrong v. United States*[438]—an approach that Chief Justice Rehnquist, Justice Scalia, and Justice Stevens have applied in takings cases. Courts should read the Takings Clause "to bar Government from forcing some people alone to bear public burdens which, in all fairness and justice, should be borne by the public as a whole."[443] This approach puts the Court in the position that the majoritarian decisionmaker would occupy if it were not for process failure. . . .

    . . . .

    c. *Education*. — The fidelity of my model to original intent depends on strict limits on the kinds of cases that are potentially occasions for judicially mandated compensation. This model does not give courts broad discretion to award com-

---

[438] 364 U.S. 40 (1960) (holders of liens on boats and materials entitled to compensation when government seized boats and materials).

[443] Armstrong v. United States, 364 U.S. 40, 49 (1960).

pensation whenever there is political process failure. Instead, courts can award compensation only if there is political process failure in categories of cases in which such failure is most likely. As it was originally, the Takings Clause is interpreted to mandate compensation in only a limited category of cases.

At the same time, the clause, as drafted by Madison, had an educative element. Although its only literal legal effect was to require the federal government to compensate when it physically took property, the Takings Clause also stood as a statement of the principle that both the state and federal government should refrain from acting in a way that arbitrarily redistributed wealth. A translation of the original understanding should reflect this broader aim as well. Although the translated clause will empower courts to direct compensation in only a limited range of cases, it will also stand in political discourse as a statement of principle against arbitrary redistribution. Outside of a limited category of cases, then, protection of the takings principle should be entrusted to the political process, rather than to the judicial process.

Recent political developments highlight the extent to which the political process can be a forum for the resolution of takings issues. The "property rights" movement has obtained the imposition of requirements at the state and national level that would-be regulators perform takings impact analyses. The movement has also sought to require compensation for regulations that do not give rise to a judicially enforceable right to compensation. . . .

The point here is not that such statutes are needed to avoid government arbitrariness with respect to private property. That is a matter for political debate. But the point is that the statement of principle embodied in the Takings Clause—the statement that we as a people are opposed to the arbitrary redistribution of property rights—properly informs the political debate. . . .

C. *Why a Translated Takings Clause Is Superior to Current Supreme Court Takings Jurisprudence on Non-Originalist Grounds*

. . . .

1. *Modern Supreme Court Caselaw.* — Modern Supreme Court takings jurisprudence is famous for its incoherence. . . . The Supreme Court in recent years has employed a remarkable number of tests. . . .

. . . .

No unified theory underlies these various tests. Moreover, it is unclear when each of these tests should be applied and what each test means. . . .

2. *The Text.* — The most natural reading of the Takings Clause—"[N]or shall private property be taken for a public use, without just compensation"—is the one that the framers gave it. Compensation was required for physical seizure. Property is defined in its physical sense. The reading suggested in this Article is somewhat less obvious, but still makes sense of the text. Property is defined in terms of value. The government cannot take it for its own purposes unless it compensates. At the same time, the clause has a dual nature. In part, the prohibition is judicially

enforceable: Compensation is mandated for certain types of takings. In part, the clause is hortatory. But the takings principle extends to all property.

The various tests developed by the modern Court do not, in contrast, make sense of the text. All reflect a view of property as value. None directs compensation in all cases in which value is diminished. The Court has not offered a convincing textual explanation of why only some actions diminishing the value of property give rise to a compensation requirement. . . .

3. *Consistency with Larger Themes in Constitutional Law.* — Because of its confused character, current takings law fails to reflect consistent themes. In contrast, the political process theory of the Takings Clause—with its special protection for discrete and insular minorities, general deference to majoritarian will, and concern for process failure—reflects dominant themes in modern constitutional law.

. . . Thus, my approach makes interpretation of the Takings Clause consistent with broader commitments present in our constitutional structure. It defers to the political process in the types of cases where our constitutional system defers to it— those cases in which the political process generally works fairly. It does not defer to the political process in the types of cases in which our constitutional system considers it suspect.

Moreover, the idea that the clause is hortatory accords with key insights of modern constitutional theorists . . . .

. . . .

4. *Judicial Competence and Ease and Predictability of Administration.* — The model presented here also makes sense because courts are not well equipped to engage in the kind of balancing that current caselaw requires in regulatory takings claims. In a case like *Pennsylvania Coal*, the loser in a political battle comes to court, says that a government action hurt her severely, and the court weighs the harm to her from that particular governmental act against the societal benefits from that act. What this analysis misses is that interests are repeat players in the political process. That a repeat player has lost a particular game signifies relatively little. The coal companies in *Pennsylvania Coal* may have used their clout to get anti-union legislation or lower taxes. In short, if affected parties have had a realistic opportunity to enter into political deals on a range of issues, that they lose on one piece of legislation may simply indicate that this was not a particularly salient issue for them or that other issues were more salient. Because they focus on one specific governmental act, traditional balancing tests can lead to a remedy where the loss was merely the product of political give and take. They give the loser an unwarranted second bite at the apple.

In addition, current takings law is unpredictable. It is unpredictable both because of the variety of tests employed and because balancing tests are unpredictable in their results. In contrast, the tests proposed here will generate largely predictable results because they create clearly defined and limited spheres in which courts will be able to order compensation.

The translation proposed here has one weakness: It involves a departure from precedent. For example, if it were adopted, not all physical takings would give rise to a judicially enforceable right to compensation. More generally, courts would be employing new tests that reflect an attempt to recapture the original purposes of the Takings Clause, rather than building on the way the clause has evolved. Given the general dissatisfaction with takings doctrine and the advantages offered by the translation, such a departure is justified.

In addition, despite its departure from recent precedent, the proposal advanced here is consistent with a venerable tradition in takings jurisprudence. The early, narrow readings of the state and federal takings clauses reflected a notion of deference to other actors in the political process. Courts did not deny that an injury had occurred, but nonetheless concluded that, outside the very limited area of physical takings, other actors should weigh private harm against public need and decide whether compensation was appropriate. . . .

. . . .

. . . Courts consciously read the takings clauses narrowly because they believed that there was a sphere in which the legislature, rather than the courts, bore responsibility for balancing harm to the individual against advancing the commonweal. A process-based theory of the Takings Clause appropriately restores this tradition of judicial deference to majoritarian decisionmakers in those categories of cases in which those decisionmakers can be trusted to consider property claims fairly.

. . . .

CONFISCATION:
A RATIONALE OF THE LAW OF TAKINGS
William K. Jones
24 Hofstra L. Rev. 1 (1995)*

I. INTRODUCTION

. . . .

. . . This Article identifies three objectives intended to be advanced by the just compensation provision and analyzes takings problems in light of these objectives.
. . .

II. THE OBJECTIVES OF JUST COMPENSATION

The requirement of just compensation serves three purposes: (1) It alleviates insecurity among owners of private property; if their property is taken by the government, they will be compensated; (2) it provides a normative structure supportive of individual endeavor and private investment; absent the threat of confiscation, more effort will be devoted to productive undertakings and more

---

investments will be made; and (3) it imposes a measure of discipline upon those exercising governmental authority; if they require private property for a public undertaking, they must obtain public funds to pay for the property.

A. The Alleviation of Insecurity

The takings provision appears in the Bill of Rights, intended to protect individuals against the predations of the state. . . .

Owners of property are typically risk-averse. A thriving insurance industry attests to the efforts of owners to avoid risks, particularly risks of a catastrophic nature such as fires, explosions, and the like. But private insurance is unavailable to protect owners against the possibility of government confiscation. The just compensation requirement provides insurance against that risk.

. . . .

B. The Promotion of Economic Development

The prosperity of a society depends ultimately on work, savings, and investment. Without a social ethic that encourages such behavior, a society cannot hope to escape from poverty. The Constitution was written against a background of economic turmoil and stands as a commitment to economic progress. . . . Further, the institution of "property," doubly protected by the Fifth Amendment, is a critical means of mobilizing human energies to productive purposes. Accordingly, the takings provision may properly be viewed as a means of encouraging work, saving, and investment by providing security for the fruits of economic endeavors.

. . . .

Viewing the just compensation clause in the context of economic development, particular care must be taken to guard against undermining investments made in the course of such development—e.g., socially productive investments in farms, factories, mines, housing. Investments in undeveloped land may be less worthy of protection, but the potential for future development should not be ignored.

C. The Quest for Fiscal Responsibility

There is general agreement that governments should act to advance social welfare; in short, gains from government programs should exceed the losses such programs inflict. One way to advance that objective is to require that winners compensate losers. If such compensation is not possible—if losses exceed gains—then the program should not be undertaken. It impoverishes society and does not advance the general welfare. The requirement of just compensation imposes a restraint on at least some governmental inefficiencies, making projects unattractive if reimbursement of private losses is greater than expected gains to the public.

. . . .

In general, government programs should be found to require just compensation when two conditions are met: (1) gains and losses can be identified with enough specificity to say that particular persons are being saddled with disproportionately large losses—disproportionate to any gains they may expect to derive from the program at issue and disproportionate to the losses being imposed on others in the community; and (2) it is practicable as an administrative matter to fund the program from the public treasury. The absence of public funding signals the absence of fiscally responsible support for the program. By contrast, the impracticability of measuring specific gains and losses or of making appropriate collections and payments is a good reason for holding that a government program does *not* constitute a taking.

. . . .

III. PROTECTION OF POSSESSION

The just compensation requirement has been applied most consistently in protecting owners of property against physical intrusions or seizures by the government. There is less consistency in the protection afforded against other governmental actions that physically interfere with the use and enjoyment of property.

A. *Physical Intrusions on Land*

The leading case is the nineteenth century decision in *Pumpelly v. Green Bay Co.*[50] Acting under state statutes, the Green Bay Company constructed a dam that caused a river to overflow and inundate plaintiff's farm. Plaintiff sought redress under the just compensation provision of the Wisconsin Constitution, and the Supreme Court found in his favor. The Court described the flooding as one that "worked an almost complete destruction of the value of the land;"[52] it ruled that "where real estate is actually invaded by superinduced additions of water, earth, sand, or other material, or by having any artificial structure placed on it, so as to effectually destroy or impair its usefulness, it is a taking, within the meaning of the Constitution."[53]

Pumpelly advances the three purposes of the just compensation requirement. Plaintiff is awarded compensation for a substantial and unavoidable loss (the insurance objective); the farm, a productive investment, is protected against confiscation (the economic development objective); and the Green Bay Company, exercising delegated governmental responsibility, is required to account for losses associated with its enterprise (the fiscal responsibility objective).

Subsequent decisions have followed *Pumpelly* in awarding compensation to owners deprived of the use of their land by flooding or by other physical occupation attributable to the government. *United States v. Causby*[55] carried the logic a

---

[50] 80 U.S. (13 Wall.) 166 (1871).

[52] *Id.* at 177.

[53] *Id.* at 181.

[55] 328 U.S. 256, 256-259 (1946) . . . .

step further. Plaintiffs owned land on which they raised chickens; they also resided on the premises. Military aircraft from a nearby airport, passing overhead at low altitudes, caused such noise and glare that plaintiffs had to abandon their chicken farm. Further, plaintiffs' use of the property as a residence was impaired, the noise and glare resulting in sleeplessness and anxiety. The Supreme Court awarded compensation for diminution in the value of the property; the government, in its operations, had taken an "easement of flight."[56] . . .

Again, the decision comports with the purposes of the just compensation requirement. Compensation was paid for a substantial, though not a total, loss (the insurance objective); the Court recognized that the productive capacity of the land had been seriously impaired (the economic development objective); and the government, in undertaking military aviation operations, was compelled to take account of the losses inflicted on adversely affected landowners (the fiscal responsibility objective).

A similar result was reached in *Kaiser Aetna v. United States.*[58] Kuapa Pond, nonnavigable and physically separated from the adjacent bay, was developed into a private marina by the dredging of channels and by other improvements made at private expense. Fees collected from private owners paid for maintenance of the marina. The government sought to have the marina opened to all without charge. The Supreme Court found an unlawful taking, ruling that, if the government wants "a public aquatic park after petitioners have proceeded as far as they have here," it must invoke the power of eminent domain.[60] The decision protects the investment of private owners from conversion into a public facility (thereby serving the insurance and economic development objectives) and, it requires the government to pay for any "public aquatic park" it seeks to create (the fiscal responsibility objective).[61]

. . . .

More troublesome is the decision in *Loretto v. Teleprompter Manhattan CATV Corp.*[68] A New York statute required landlords to permit local cable companies to maintain cable facilities on their premises—in order to provide service to tenants—on payment of a fee to each landlord, fixed by regulation at a one-time charge of one dollar. The Supreme Court found a taking and remanded the case to determine whether the one-dollar fee was just compensation. The cable facilities were modest in size (less than two cubic feet in all); they were relatively unobtrusive (plaintiff landlord ignored them for several months); and there was no evidence that they had impaired the use of the property or diminished its value. But the Court ruled that any permanent physical occupation authorized by government is a taking even if it "has only minimal economic impact on the owner."[71]

---

[56] *Causby*, 328 U.S. at 261.

[58] 444 U.S. 164 (1979).

[60] *Id.* at 180.

[61] *Id.* at 179-80.

[68] 458 U.S. 419 (1982). . . .

[71] *Id.* at 434-35.

Clearly, the decision is not justified by any of the objectives of just compensation: there is no need to insure against a trivial loss; a nonburdensome requirement does not impede economic development; and failure to compensate for so minor an intrusion does not impugn governmental fiscal responsibility. But *Loretto* had a different end in view. The Court was seeking to establish a "bright line" for a class of takings that was readily identifiable and for which compensation could be ascertained with relative ease. To be sure, the category was overinclusive in terms of the objectives of just compensation. But is that problematic? If the intrusion at issue is trivial, then just compensation is likewise trivial. On remand in *Loretto*, the state courts limited compensation to the one-dollar fee.[73]

. . . .

B. Interference With the Use and Enjoyment of Land

. . . .

As previously noted, *United States v. Causby* awarded compensation for diminution in value caused by aircraft flying low above the plaintiff's land. But what of properties not in the flight path but adjacent to the airport? Their value is also adversely affected by the noise, fumes, and glares associated with airport operations. Most state court decisions award compensation in such instances, but the leading federal Court of Appeals decision is to the contrary. In *Batten v. United States*,[93] plaintiff property owners complained of vibrations that caused windows and dishes to rattle; loud noises that made conversations and use of the telephone, radio, and television impossible, and also interrupted sleep; and smoke that left an oily black deposit on their properties. Declines in the values of their properties ranged from 41% to 55%. In denying recovery, the Court of Appeals characterized the sound waves, shock waves, and smoke as "a neighborhood inconvenience" not actionable unless directed against particular property . . . or "unless they force the abdication of the use of space within the landowner's dominion."[94]

The *Batten* ruling is unduly restrictive. The proper approach . . . is to ask whether, if the objectionable conduct were that of a private party, it would give rise to an action in nuisance? . . .

Most government operations, including roads, schools, and post offices, do not trigger liability in the usual case because the activity, if conducted by a private party, would not be an actionable nuisance—either because the adverse impact on any one parcel of land is not sufficiently large or because an impact, though substantial, is consistent with the character of the locality (a business operation in a business district). But some government operations, such as the airport in *Batten*

---

[73] *See* Loretto v. Group W. Cable, 522 N.Y.S.2d 543, 545-46 (App. Div. 1987) (discussing proceedings on remand), *appeal denied*, 522 N.E.2d 1066 (N.Y.), *cert. denied*, 488 U.S. 827 (1988).

[93] 306 F.2d 580 (10th Cir. 1962), *cert. denied*, 371 U.S. 955 (1963).

[94] *Id.* at 585.

and government garbage and incinerator facilities, normally could not claim such immunity. . . .

The approach advocated here is consistent with the objectives of just compensation. Absent compensation, property owners are subjected to uninsurable losses of significant magnitude. (Insignificant losses would be unlikely to trigger the law of nuisance.) To permit government destruction of privately created values in homes and businesses is to discourage the work and saving and investment that created those values. Finally, as a matter of fiscal responsibility, government agencies should be compelled to reckon with severe destructions of private values and to proceed only if they are prepared to pay compensation—i.e., only where public gains exceed private losses. Practical administration is assured by restricting claims to substantial impacts peculiar to the properties of the claimants—impacts sufficient to provide standing in suits for private nuisance.

. . . .

IV. GOVERNMENT REGULATIONS AFFECTING REAL PROPERTY

The concept of "harm" plays a critical role in takings jurisprudence. Governments are privileged to abate harmful uses of property without paying compensation to the source of the harm. Yet this general rubric encompasses a varied group of cases, not all warranting the same treatment. It is useful to distinguish among: (1) uses of land that contravene general social norms not premised on the relationship of the land to surrounding terrain; (2) uses of land that are not unacceptable, but which pose problems because of their proximity to other, inharmonious uses, i.e., instances of "incompatible adjacencies;" and (3) uses of land that are normally acceptable, and not incompatible with adjacent uses, but which are viewed as posing a threat to the environment or raising similar ecological concerns.

A. Uses Contravening General Social Norms

The leading case on prevention of harm dates from the nineteenth century. *Mugler v. Kansas*[119] involved the application of a state prohibition statute to shut down two breweries. Both were constructed prior to enactment of the prohibitory legislation; and the Supreme Court apparently accepted the view that they were erected for the purpose of making beer and could not be put to any other use without severe loss of value. In rejecting a takings claim, the Court ruled that "all property in this country is held under the implied obligation that the owner's use of it shall not be injurious to the community."[121] Accordingly, a "prohibition simply upon the use of property for purposes that are declared, by valid legislation, to be injurious to the health, morals, or safety of the community, cannot, in any just sense, be deemed a taking or an appropriation for the public benefit."[122]

---

[119] 123 U.S. 623 (1887).

[121] *Id.* at 665.

[122] *Id.* at 668 . . . .

The language of the Court has broad sweep and could be viewed as subjecting all property to uncompensated destruction at the hands of the legislature. So viewed, the decision would contravene all three of the objectives of just compensation—insurance, economic development, and fiscal responsibility. The facts of the case suggest a narrower focus.

. . . .

Mugler is an example of product failure—here by reason of adverse societal norms embodied in prohibitory legislation. Every enterprise runs the risk of product failure. The risk—whether it originates in technological change, varying public tastes, or shifts in social norms—is an unavoidable part of entrepreneurial endeavor. It is not an insurable risk under any circumstances; its occurrence does not impede other efforts to market successful products; and prohibition of a product harmful to the public involves no issue of fiscal irresponsibility. Even a community without funds must have the capacity to interdict poisons, guns, explosives, and other harmful substances. Compensation is not an issue in such cases.

Social norms also affect uses internal to the property—measures designed to assure the safety of employees, tenants, patrons or other occupants. Such measures impose costs, and in some cases may make use of a particular property economically unviable. Yet compensation is uniformly denied. As long as the protective measures are of broad applicability, reflecting prevailing social norms, owners must conform to such measures or abandon the use in question. No one has a constitutional right to maintain an unsafe or unsanitary building or to demand compensation if abatement is ordered.

This point was addressed tangentially in *First English Evangelical Lutheran Church v. County of Los Angeles*.[128] An ordinance, adopted as an interim measure, prohibited any construction on land in a flood plain, precluding plaintiff from rebuilding structures swept away in an earlier flood. The California courts refused to consider a claim for damages for deprivation of use, requiring that plaintiff first obtain a judgment testing the validity of the regulation. The Supreme Court reversed, holding that the Fifth Amendment requires compensation for "'temporary' regulatory takings—those regulatory takings which are ultimately invalidated by the courts."[129] If a taking is found, the state may reconsider and repeal the objectionable measure; but it must pay for the temporary taking while the regulation was in effect.

. . . .

On remand, protection of the safety of prospective residents was one of the grounds adopted in sustaining the ordinance. Similar reasoning has been employed in upholding other restrictions on construction in flood plains and similar measures protective of public safety. . . .

In sum, normative judgments may preclude particular uses of land, without requiring compensation, in two kinds of cases: First, the norm—as in *Mugler*—may

---

[128] 482 U.S. 304 (1987).

[129] *Id.* at 310. . . .

have nothing to do with land use; the prohibition statute there at issue would be violated whether a distillery was located at a fixed site or installed in a moving railroad car. Second, the norm—as in *First English*—may be triggered by a particular land use, but it implements a principle having broad application; dangerous habitats must be vacated whether they are located in a flood plain or in an area contaminated by hazardous waste or in buildings that are structurally unsound. The common denominator is a *generality* of application of the norm, divorced from the identity or ownership of any particular parcel of land. As such, the norm reflects a risk borne by all members of society whether or not they own property.

. . . .

B. Incompatible Adjacencies: The Initial Approach

In a series of decisions dating back to the nineteenth century, the Supreme Court has sustained restrictions on the use of property based solely on the appropriateness of the use to the particular locality.

In *Fertilizing Co. v. Hyde Park*,[137] a village banished a fertilizing plant from its midst, citing offensive odors, depreciation of property values, and aesthetic affronts. The Supreme Court sustained the measure even though the fertilizing plant, when originally constructed, was situated in an area largely uninhabited; the villagers came to the plant.

In *Reinman v. City of Little Rock*,[138] a city banned the operation of a livery stable in the most densely populated area of the city, citing offensive odors and threats of disease. The Supreme Court again upheld the ban even though the stable was a lawful operation when originally instituted.

In *Hadacheck v. Sebastian*,[139] a municipal ordinance prohibited brick-making within a residential district, reducing the value of the affected property from $800,000 to $60,000. Once again, the targeted operation was there first; the residents and municipal annexation came later. The Supreme Court sustained the ordinance on the ground that brickmaking was deleterious to "the health and comfort of the community."[140] . . .

. . . Granted that the development of a community cannot be stymied by a fertilizer plant or livery stable or brickyard in its midst. But that does not respond to the issue posed by just compensation: Should the offensive use—lawful when undertaken, and lawful now if undertaken elsewhere—be banished without compensation for losses associated with irretrievable investments of the enterprise in the initially lawful location?

The answer to this question is dependent on solving an antecedent issue of private law: the problem of "coming to the nuisance." In *Fertilizing Co.* or *Reinman*

---

[137] 97 U.S. 659 (1878) . . . .
[138] 237 U.S. 171 (1915).
[139] 239 U.S. 394 (1915).
[140] *Id.* at 411.

or *Hadacheck*, an action might have been initiated by a private resident invoking the common law of nuisance. If that suit would have succeeded, clearly the challenged business would have had no right to compensation simply because the nuisance was abated by a public authority rather than a private plaintiff. In principle, these businesses *were* vulnerable to attack and abatement at the behest of private plaintiffs. While the common law is not unequivocal on this point, plaintiffs tend to prevail in cases like the ones at issue—where a use, once appropriate, has ceased to be appropriate in view of changes in the surrounding area.

. . . .

The dispositions in *Hadacheck* and earlier cases were therefore correct. The firms there involved should be viewed as having voluntarily assumed the risks of future abatement. This negates any need for insurance; risks assumed in this manner are not normally insurable. It places economic development on sound footing; potentially objectionable businesses must find suitable locations. Further, government actions challenging incompatibility are not fiscally irresponsible; they simply impose losses upon parties knowingly assuming risks.

This analysis sets the stage for *Pennsylvania Coal Co. v. Mahon*,[145] the most frequently cited opinion in the law of takings. The Coal Company acquired both the surface rights and mineral rights in substantial tracts of land. It then sold the surface rights, reserving to itself the unencumbered right to extract coal without regard to harm to the surface owner—i.e., expressly negating any duty to support the surface. In effect, the Coal Company sought to use the contractual route to respond to the problem of incompatible adjacencies: selling surface rights solely to those who would not object to its mining operations.

A state statute subsequently forbade the mining of coal that would cause subsidence under a structure used for human habitation unless the structure and the subsurface coal were under common ownership. Relying on the statute, Mahon sought to enjoin the Coal Company from mining coal under his house and endangering the structure. Local authorities also objected to the undermining of public streets, forbidden by another provision of the statute. The Supreme Court, in an opinion by Justice Holmes, held that the statute was invalid as an uncompensated taking of the Coal Company's property. . . .

. . . .

The case is much stronger if viewed from the perspective of contractual resolution of the problem of incompatible adjacencies than as one in which the state simply went "too far" in precluding the mining of coal. . . .

. . . Society seeks to encourage productive endeavors while avoiding incompatible adjacencies. One valuable means to that end is for the potential nuisance to buy up the rights of neighbors to protest against the nuisance. If at a later time that solution seems no longer to be acceptable, then the government can revise it. But the revision must be accompanied by compensation, since the initial arrangement not only had the sanction of law but was a valuable means of resolving serious future problems. . . .

---

[145] 260 U.S. 393 (1922).

The insurance objective of just compensation had some basis in *Mahon*, but the foothold was precarious. *Keystone* [*Bituminous Coal Association v. DeBenedictis*] found that the diminution in value was not so great as Holmes imagined in *Mahon* and struck a different balance, this time favoring the public's right to regulate.[157] But the contractual aspect of *Mahon* bears importantly on the objective of economic development; its disregard is a form of fiscal irresponsibility. If the state wants a larger stake in the coal mines, the path to purchase is not elusive. The *Keystone* Court gave short shrift to the contractual aspects, not recognizing (or refusing to recognize) that the contracts played a key role in defining the scope of the coal companies' property interests, which were important to economic development.

Another important decision dealing with incompatible adjacencies is *Miller v. Schoene*.[160] Plaintiffs had red cedar trees on their property. The trees were host to a fungus called cedar rust which, while harmless to the cedars, had a destructive effect on adjacent apple trees. Plaintiffs were ordered to cut down a large number of infested cedars to prevent spread of the fungus to valuable apple orchards, the order encompassing all such cedars within two miles of an apple orchard. The Supreme Court sustained the order notwithstanding the absence of compensation to the owners of the cedars.

The Court observed that the red cedar was principally ornamental, neither cultivated nor dealt in commercially on any substantial scale. By contrast, apple growing was one of the principal agricultural pursuits in the state, with millions of dollars invested. Forced to choose between the two, the state may decide upon "the destruction of one class of property in order to save another which, in the judgment of the legislature, is of greater value to the public."[161]

This seems sound. But the Court's reasoning does not explain why the owners of the cedars should be denied compensation for property destroyed in order to protect the apple orchards. . . .

Miller should be considered in light of the three objectives of just compensation. The cedars were not particularly valuable in their own right; they simply added value to the properties on which they were situated. Their destruction did not significantly diminish the values of those properties. In this context, the insurance objective of just compensation is relatively weak. Second, the trees were ornamental and indigenous to the region; their destruction did not impede or discourage economic development. Finally, while fiscal responsibility would have supported compensation (for example, by a tax on the apple orchards), the small amounts at issue may not have justified the administrative expense.

. . . .

C. Zoning as a Response to Incompatible Adjacencies

Zoning is an effort to deal with the problem of incompatible adjacencies on a comprehensive basis. It seeks to segregate, in advance of development, uses of land

---

[157] *Keystone*, 480 U.S. [470 (1987)] at 498-99 . . . .

[160] 276 U.S. 272 (1928).

[161] *Id.* at 279. The owners of the cedars were compensated for the costs of removal. *Id.* at 277.

that may be incompatible with one another. Probably the most important aspects of zoning are: (1) the separation of commercial or business districts from residential districts; and (2) the separation of apartment houses from private residences. Both elements were at issue in *Village of Euclid v. Ambler Realty Co.*,[169] the landmark Supreme Court decision upholding comprehensive zoning regulation. . . .

. . . .

The outcome reached by the Court is explicable in terms of the three objectives of just compensation. First, as to insurance, we are not now dealing with the owner of a home or a farm or a factory. We are dealing with a speculator in undeveloped land, the value of which is dependent on the course of future events. These include governmental decisions—not only on zoning, which might have been unanticipated at the time—but on the extension of infrastructure, the routing of traffic, and the imposition of clearly lawful restrictions which are protective of public health and safety. Land speculators by nature are not risk-averse. They gamble on the future, and sometimes they lose.

Second, as to economic development, it is again important that the land at issue was not improved. . . . The point is simply that the net social gain accruing from the ownership of undeveloped land is modest at most, and that no socially important losses are visited upon the owners of such land if their development plans are frustrated by the government's zoning measures. The great land lottery will continue no matter how often the government changes its course. Finally, and of particular importance, the land was not being zoned into idleness. It could be put to a productive use, though one different from the use envisaged by the owner.

As regards fiscal responsibility, the very nature of zoning precludes compensation for losses. . . . At any moment in time, some properties gain from restrictions imposed on others; at some later moment, the balance of gains and losses may shift dramatically. It is unfeasible, both at the time of initial zoning and at each subsequent revision in zoning, to reckon up the gains and losses of each owner of property and compel the winners to compensate the losers. In the long run, all may end up winners if the zoning is sound in creating an attractive and viable community, or all may lose if the zoning is irrational and unstable. The gains and losses are speculative and shifting and any effort at monetary compensation would be an administrative impossibility. . . .

. . . .

Zoning has created a welter of litigation. All of the diverse decisions cannot be explained by this (or any other) analysis. But the major trends appear to reflect the three objectives supporting the requirement of just compensation.

D. More Expansive Conceptions of Land Use Control

. . . .

Land use control has been carried to extreme lengths in ordinances concerned with preservation of historic buildings. . . .

. . . .

---

[169] 272 U.S. 365 (1926).

The issue of landmark preservation came before the Supreme Court in *Penn Central Transportation Co. v. New York City*.[203] Penn Central sought to build a fifty-five floor tower above its New York City terminal in conformity with all zoning and space requirements. The tower, once constructed, would provide Penn Central with additional annual revenues of at least $2 million. Permission to build was denied because the terminal had been designated a landmark by the City and the tower was incompatible with the historic character of the building. In lieu of the right to build, Penn Central received transferrable development rights, of uncertain value, enabling it to utilize air space above other structures in the area. A majority of the Court found no taking; a minority would have remanded to determine whether the transferrable development rights were sufficiently valuable to constitute just compensation for the taking of Penn Central's right to build the tower (its "air rights").

. . . .

. . . New York City landmarks are relatively few in number and scattered throughout the city . . . . There is no historic district to which all participants contribute and from which all derive benefits. Considered in light of the objectives of just compensation, *Penn Central* is an unsound decision.

Bearing on the insurance objective, the Court sought to minimize the financial impact of the regulation on Penn Central. On this, the dissent's position provides a better resolution: remand to determine whether the transferable development rights truly compensate Penn Central for an annual revenue loss in excess of $2 million. . . .

On economic development, the case is a major setback. Here we have a company penalized for doing the *right* thing: building a good structure. . . .

The most serious vice, however, is the fiscal irresponsibility implicit in the landmark designation measure. Some segment of society, including persons influential in city government, were persuaded that the preservation of historic landmarks was a good thing. The Court in *Penn Central* readily accepted the legitimacy of the objective. The problem, however, was that city officials, responsive to their taxpayer constituents, had not been willing to pay for the public good they had sought to obtain. So they pressed Penn Central's building into public service, paying in the bogus currency of transferable development rights. If the benefits were so great, why not pay for them in dollars or in benefits that could be evaluated in dollars? The answer, quite obviously, is that the benefits of landmark preservation were not sufficiently great to warrant the expenditure of taxpayer dollars—i.e., the public benefits, determined in a democratic process, did not exceed the private costs, determined in an eminent domain proceeding.

. . . .

In sum, *Penn Central* in its general approach is an invitation to continued confusion and obfuscation; it builds on the wrong branch of *Pennsylvania Coal*, the ad hoc inquiry into whether a regulation "goes too far." As applied to the facts before it, *Penn Central* sanctions a government deprivation that warranted compensation

---

[203] 438 U.S. 104 (1978) . . . .

under all the objectives of the just compensation requirement: insurance, economic development, and fiscal responsibility. Whatever the merits of the Penn Central structure as a historic landmark, the *Penn Central* opinion is a blight on the judicial landscape.

E. Denial of Development in the Name of the Environment

In recent years, controversies have arisen over the economic development of ecologically sensitive lands such as wetlands and coastal shores. . . .

. . . .

The issue came before the Supreme Court in *Lucas v. South Carolina Coastal Council.*[231] In 1986, Lucas paid $975,000 for two residential lots on the Isle of Palms in South Carolina. He intended to build two single family homes. In 1988, however, South Carolina enacted new legislation that barred Lucas from erecting any permanent habitable dwellings on the two parcels, a prohibition that rendered the parcels "valueless."[232] (All adjacent lots had been developed for residential purposes at the time Lucas made his purchases). Lucas did not challenge the validity of the state legislation—adopted to protect the shoreline from erosion and excessive development—but he claimed a compensable taking. The South Carolina court rejected the claim. The Supreme Court reversed, finding sufficient merit in Lucas' claim to warrant reexamination by the state courts.

The Supreme Court held that regulation constitutes a taking where it "denies all economically beneficial or productive use of land."[234] In such cases, it is unlikely that the legislature is "simply 'adjusting the benefits and burdens of economic life' in a manner that secures an 'average reciprocity of advantage' to everyone concerned."[235] . . .

. . . .

The decision in *Lucas* . . . is substantially in accord with the analysis advanced in connection with the earlier cases. The insurance objective is given weight regarding this owner since the protection of Lucas—at least as against a "total taking"—must be found in antecedent background principles of law, principles of which an owner should be apprised and subject to which he takes title to the property. The objective of economic development is implicated because the property is being zoned into idleness, although Lucas . . . had not yet built on his land. Finally, the Court's opinion insists on governmental fiscal responsibility. If the use prohibited is encompassed by antecedent background principles, then compensation is not required because nothing has been taken; the owner's title was subject to such principles from the outset. On the other hand, if the owner had clear title as related to the newly enacted prohibition, then compensation must be paid. The

---

[231] 112 S. Ct. 2886 (1992).

[232] *Id.* at 2896.

[234] *Id.* at 2893.

[235] *Id.* at 2894 (citations omitted) (quoting Penn Cent. Transp. Co. v. New York City, 438 U.S. 104, 124 (1978) and Pennsylvania Coal Co. v. Mahon, 260 U.S. 393, 415 (1922)).

Court emphasized that a "State, by *ipse dixit*, may not transform private property into public property without compensation."[250]

. . . .

F. Approving Development on Compliance with Conditions

Zoning and other land use controls are typically stated in broad prohibitory terms. But they are administered with some flexibility to permit property owners to engage in development consistent with the spirit of the controls, though possibly at variance with the letter. For example, a homeowner seeking to add a new room may exceed the bulk limitation applicable to her parcel; but a zoning agency may be persuaded to permit the construction if trees and shrubs are employed to screen the new addition. Several recent Supreme Court cases have been concerned with possible abuses of the power to impose conditions.

In *Nollan v. California Coastal Commission*,[270] permission was sought to build a beachfront house exceeding the size limitation applicable to the property. The Commission granted approval on condition that the Nollans allow bathers at nearby public beaches to traverse their private beach in walking from one public beach to another. The Supreme Court struck down the condition as an uncompensated taking because it required an easement that "utterly fails to further the end advanced as the justification for the" size restriction;[271] there was an absence of an "essential nexus."[272] . . .

. . . .

In *Dolan v. City of Tigard*,[277] the issue was revisited. Dolan wished to expand her hardware store and adjacent parking lot. The City granted a permit conditional on the dedication to the City of a strip of land to be used as a greenway and bicycle/pedestrian path. The Supreme Court ruled that, since Dolan's expanded facilities would increase both traffic and the flow of surface waters, the condition met the "essential nexus" requirement of *Nollan*. But the Court added a further requirement of "rough proportionality," i.e., "the city must make some sort of individualized determination that the required dedication is related both in nature and extent to the impact of the proposed development."[279] The dedication of the greenway was held to be unsupported because "[t]he city has never said why a public greenway, as opposed to a private one, was required in the interest of flood control."[280] (Independently of the proposed expansion, Dolan was precluded from

---

[250] 112 S. Ct. at 2901 (quoting Webb's Fabulous Pharmacies v. Beckwith, 449 U.S. 78, 86 (1911)). . . .

. . . .

[270] 483 U.S. 825 (1987) . . . .

[271] *Nollan*, 483 U.S. at 837.

[272] *Id.*

[277] 114 S. Ct. 2309 (1994).

[279] *Id.* at 2319-20.

[280] *Id.* at 2320.

developing the greenway in issue.) As to the bicycle/pedestrian path, the Court ruled that "the city has not met its burden of demonstrating that the additional number of vehicle and bicycle trips generated by the petitioner's development reasonably relate to the city's requirement for a dedication of the pedestrian/bicycle pathway easement."[281]

. . . .

In cases like *Nollan* and *Dolan*, the concern of the courts is understandable. State and local land control agencies administer regulations of broad scope that require administrative approval for almost any change of consequence. The agencies can, as a condition for approval, exact concessions from the property owner. The process results in the creation of a bogus currency (the tighter the restrictions, the greater the currency) and the land control agency can use this "currency" (their approval for desired projects) as a means of obtaining money or property from owners seeking such approval. The courts can do either of two things: (1) strike down the broad restrictions and require land control agencies to come back with more specific limitations, each of which they would have to justify; or (2) review every challenge to exacted concessions to guard against overreaching by the land control agencies. The first course of action is seemingly barred by *Euclid* and its progeny and, in any event, is almost surely impracticable. This leaves the second course, which often will require courts to make highly specific determinations in cases in which such determinations are inherently problematic for the reasons given in connection with *Nollan* and *Dolan*.

These decisions, moreover, do not address a deeper problem. If a court overturns a conditional approval, the property-owner is not necessarily a winner. The regulatory agency may decide to withhold its approval altogether. If the general regulatory standard is lawful, and if its application to the particular property is not barred by some other constraint—such as economic unviability absent approval—the agency may choose outright denial despite the prospect for a mutually acceptable settlement with conditions. The message of *Nollan* and *Dolan* could be read as "Just Say No."

Even so, the two cases share a feature that may distinguish them from more routine exactions of concessions from developers. In each, the government had a plan traversing numerous properties: an extended right of passage along California beaches in *Nollan*; an extended bicycle/pedestrian path in *Dolan*. These plans had nothing to do with development of particular properties. Had no construction occurred, the governments would have had to resort to formal condemnation proceedings in order to complete their planned passage and pathway. Development was a fortuitous occurrence that enabled the governments to expropriate land on pretexts that were disingenuous. The sole purpose of the conditions in issue was to obtain private property without making payment, the very conduct the takings clause was intended to interdict. Viewed in this light, the Supreme Court decisions are correct; but their scope is narrow.

. . . .

---

[281] *Id.* at 2321.

VII. CONCLUSION

. . . .

The general body of takings law—and the few departures in need of correction—are explicable in terms of the three objectives of just compensation: insurance, economic progress, and fiscal responsibility. With these objectives in view, the takings clause provides meaningful guidance for a vast array of very different kinds of cases. It is not necessary to resort to an amorphous standard of "fairness;" nor to continue an agnostic process of ad hoc adjudications that preclude predictability. The scope of the takings clause is rooted in history and logic; the constitutional guarantee is not a mystery beyond the comprehension of the judiciary and the legal profession.

4. Property Rights Analyzed

TAKING AND GIVING: POLICE POWER, PUBLIC VALUE, AND PRIVATE RIGHT
Gerald Torres
26 Envtl. L. 1 (1996)[*]

"So long as government action constitutes a taking *and* a giving to the same individuals in the same proportions, all is well."[1]

"Property and law are born together, and die together. Before laws were made there was no property; take away laws, and property ceases."[2]

"I cannot count upon the enjoyment of that which I regard as mine, except through the promise of the law which guarantees it to me. . . . It is only through the protection of law that I am able to inclose a field, and to give myself up to its cultivation with the sure though distant hope of harvest."[3]

---

[*]   Copyright © 1995. Reprinted by permission.

[1]   RICHARD A. EPSTEIN, TAKINGS, PRIVATE PROPERTY AND THE POWER OF EMINENT DOMAIN 211 (1985). . . .

[2]   JEREMY BENTHAM, THE THEORY OF LEGISLATION 113 (C.K. Ogden ed. & Richard Hildreth trans., 1931), *quoted in* Michael C. Blumm, *The End of Environmental Law? Libertarian Property, Natural Law, and the Just Compensation Clause in the Federal Circuit*, 25 ENVTL. L. 171, 182 (1995).

[3]   BENTHAM, *supra* note 2, at 112, *quoted in* Blumm, *supra* note 2, at 182 n.84.

I. INTRODUCTION

The quotations that begin this Lecture summarize the relationship between property as a social artifact and law. I hope that the following discussion will more fully explicate that relationship and why it is misunderstood.

. . . First, I will outline a critique of efficiency as it has functioned as the meta-narrative underlying our basic current understanding of social institutions. . . .

Second, drawing on this analysis, I will illustrate the political technique of the property rights advocates. This technique involves telling a story about property rights that personalizes and humanizes a drama in which the major characters include a big, impersonal government running out of control, and small, relatively powerless owners of private property. . . .

Third, I will review the law on these issues to reveal the sources of the discontent and to examine the extent to which the evolution of the doctrine supports the claims of the property rights advocates. . . .

II. A CRITIQUE OF EFFICIENCY

The definition of efficiency that dominates policy debate, at least at the non-specialist level, is too narrow. The definition is too narrow to the extent that a focus on Pareto-optimality[6] or Kaldor-Hicks efficiency[7] excludes other important values. These other values (like species protection or historical preservation, for example) are marginalized or excluded altogether because they cannot be assessed according to the metric that efficiency criteria require. This argument suggests that a debate over how well social institutions function has a narrative structure organized around two norms: the current distribution of wealth and revealed market-based preferences. To criticize these two norms I make two points, one obvious and the other more problematic.

First, the misnamed property rights revolution is predicated on an effort to freeze in place the existing distribution of wealth. . . .

Second, and less obvious, is the effort to hold public and private institutions to the same standard of narrow efficiency, defined provisionally here as profit maximization. . . .

These two observations lead inexorably to the normative question: What kind of society do we want? Understanding constitutional limitations on the power of the

---

[6]   A Pareto-optimal position is the state in which no possible change in position would make one party better off without making another party worse off. An action, such as a rule change or a voluntary transaction, might be described as Pareto-superior when it leaves one party better off and no one worse off. By definition, all transactions voluntarily undertaken are Pareto-superior. A Pareto-optimal state is merely the result of Pareto-superior transactions. . . .

[7]   This efficiency criterion is similar to Pareto-superiority in that it posits that the result of a transaction would leave the winners able to compensate the losers without sacrificing all of their gains. Obviously, one important difference is that Kaldor-Hicks efficiency rules are not predicated on voluntary transactions and do not require actual compensation to the losers. . . .

government to regulate private commercial behavior, especially where those regulations frustrate an economic opportunity related to real property, is central to mapping the relationship between the individual, state, and society. . . .

A constitutional order designed to ensure nothing more than an atomized citizenry can scarcely be said to provide the basis for a representative government. Yet, that is what some of the so-called property rights advocates are seeking to create. The rhetoric of these advocates indicates a willful ignorance of the social function of property: to bind us together as a society and culture, as well as to provide the basis for the maximal individual exclusion of others. To see property's exclusionary role as its principal function is to misunderstand that property rights have always created webs of responsibility between owners and nonowners. . . .

Whatever value efficiency criteria have for assessing private institutions, they do not have the same value for public institutions, but instead perform an ideological function aimed at restructuring the idea of governance. Similarly, the claim of the absolute nature of property rights is primarily a claim about the legitimacy of government to act in other than the most narrow and limited way. A decade ago, Professor Richard Epstein provided the philosophical carapace for the political fight[19] which then had the Sagebrush Rebellion as its *nom de guerre*.[20] Epstein was principally concerned with articulating the constitutional basis for controlling the problem of all majoritarian democratic systems: political domination by the majority and legislative self-dealing. He asked the questions: Has state power been captured and used for ends other than expanding total social wealth? and Is the state using the power to regulate or the power to condemn to add to its own resource base (is it appropriating the surplus of any regulatory scheme)? According to Epstein, yes to either of these questions means the state has exceeded the legitimate boundaries of its authority.

Many critical reviews of Epstein's book misunderstood its foundational importance.[23] Professor Epstein correctly identified the struggle over property rights as the grounds upon which issues of our social architecture would be fought, much in the way that the Due Process and Equal Protection Clauses provided the grounds for similar struggles a generation earlier. Epstein hinges his theory of takings on the constitutional prerequisites for a theory of limited representative government. At its core, the constitutional theory that legitimizes the government itself also protects property rights by limiting the reach of the doctrine of sovereign immunity. He would, in essence, make every governmental action subject to common-law tort

---

[19] *See* EPSTEIN, *supra* note 1, at 19.

[20] *See* R. MCGREGGOR CAWLEY, FEDERAL LAND, WESTERN ANGER: THE SAGEBRUSH REBELLION AND ENVIRONMENTAL POLITICS (1993) (examining the roots of the public lands controversy and explaining their emotional appeal); *see also* Nancie G. Marzulla, *The Property Rights Movement: How It Began and Where It Is Headed, in* LAND RIGHTS 1, 3 (Bruce Yandle ed., 1995) (capturing the history of the movement and the evolution of the Sagebrush Rebellion into the Wise Use Movement). . . .

[23] For an example of a review that noted the importance of Epstein's work, see Joseph L. Sax, *Richard Epstein, Takings, Private Property and the Power of Eminent Domain*, 53 U. CHI. L. REV. 279 (1986) (book review).

analysis and expand governmental liability to include those actions that have traditionally been considered legitimate regulatory exercises of the police power. Epstein's theory does not just modify the doctrine of sovereign immunity, his theory eliminates it. The Takings Clause, according to Epstein's view, merely enacts common-law nuisance and trespass standards into the Constitution. Because, in his theory of representative government, the state has only those rights that the people have, it is allowed to exercise the police power only to prevent harm or to arrange affairs to achieve a Pareto-superior result where the problems associated with large scale voluntary transactions make such a result unlikely. While I disagree with Epstein's conclusions, I believe that in many ways his focus is correct. I too want to concentrate on conceptions of power, value, and right and to reject the crabbed vision of social life that Epstein, the Sagebrush rebellion, and its progeny see as the future for this country.

This grass-roots movement has its academic analog. The ascendancy of the rhetoric of law and economics has led to importation of public choice and game theory into legal analysis. While that literature has contributed many important insights into the evolution of law and democratic processes, it produces an odd kind of tunnel vision when it becomes prescriptive. Part of the problem is that it adopts a particular metric, that of revealed preferences through market exchange or its methodological equivalent, that masks a range of problems when applied to non-market circumstances. Social complexity and a democratic commitment to protect the varieties of ways people value social goods require that political and social institutions designed to sustain diverse values be free to structure their normative visions in ways consistent with their own ends. Requiring that every institutional judgment conform to a specific standard produces distortions in policy to the extent that it requires the institutions of governance to mimic the institutions of the market. The institutions of the state presumably exist to effect the allocation of social goods for which there is no clear market, nor even a reasonable market substitute, and for which there is continuing contestation over the conceptions of "the good" that justifies the institution itself.

Value is a critical conception in this contest. What it is, how it is created, and how it is measured are of central importance. While the rhetoric of market value (sometimes phrased as use value or exchange value, although these terms have diverse and at times opposed pedigrees) has dominated the debate, that conception of what something is worth should not divert our attention from other struggles over things we think important. . . . Freedom, community, and neighborliness are also values; that is, we think that the particular aspects of social life summarized by those words are important and we would not sacrifice them without getting something equally important in return. Yet even here, the language of exchange should not obscure the truth that there is no objective calculus for those things, no metric or system of bargain that relieves us of the obligation to make normative judgments. As I discuss the evolution of the property rights debate, part of my argument hinges on the conception of value that has dominated the debate. This is important because the effort to impose a single evaluative criteria on the consequences of public and private action leads us to focus on the wrong questions.

The political technique used to accomplish this redefinition of value separate from values has been to tell a story about property rights. This story personalizes and humanizes the dispute over government regulations of private property by casting the story in terms of a generalized government attack on private property. The state is seen not as the insurer of private property, but its destroyer. In essence, it is a man bites dog story. The powerful are cast in the role of the victim. . . .

Despite the various technical iterations, the basic arguments of the so-called property rights advocates run this way:

1) Property ownership is tied to political power. The right to own real property is, in fact, the basic right. It undergirds all civil rights and civil liberties.

2) The Takings Clause of the Fifth Amendment to the U.S. Constitution directly limits the power of the state to expropriate private property unless those owners are compensated at the unregulated exchange value of the property.

3) Because of this limitation, the state is using regulation to achieve without compensation what the Constitution would prohibit if the government acted directly.

4) This move is a deliberate attempt to expand the power of the state at the expense of property owners and to the detriment of all citizens.

5) The regulatory zeal of the state "makes enemies of the majority of Americans"[36] and is part of the mistaken belief that the government can do things better than people can.

6) Any government action that limits development potential of real property, where that action is not aimed at preventing an immediate public harm, is a compensable taking. Compensation is required regardless of the value left in the parcel after the regulation is enacted or the reciprocal benefit conferred by the limitation.

7) The environmental motivation behind much of the regulation of private property is antihuman.

These arguments combine into a story about government that suggests the government is separated from the people and does not represent the public interest in any coherent way—especially because it makes claims in the interest of the public that we could not make against our neighbors. . . .

. . . .

III. THE CURRENT STATE OF TAKINGS JURISPRUDENCE

The assault on the proper functions of government that has been undertaken by the so-called property rights movement has not occurred in a vacuum. The legal and philosophical claims must be understood against the background of takings jurisprudence and the dominant models that have guided that type of adjudication. This Part will examine the law of takings and determine the status of contemporary takings jurisprudence and, in the process, assess the impact of the property rights

---

[36] *See* Marzulla, *supra* note 20, at 26 . . . .

movement. The property rights movement has already had a major impact on public policy discourse, but what is its impact on the law?

The basic understanding of the Takings Clause is simple. The state may not dispossess a property owner of his property unless it does so to achieve a public purpose and pays the property owner the market value of the property that the state has taken. The test that the courts apply to adjudge the constitutionality of a particular action is to inquire whether the action is justified by the police power and whether adequate compensation has been paid. That is the easy part. The hard part is where the state acts to limit the range of activities a property owner may undertake with her property, but does not actually take possession of the property. The problem is especially acute when the regulation can be shown to have diminished the exchange value of the property in some marked way.

There is no doubt that the state may regulate the uses of private property. This may be done either through the imposition of a court order resolving a private dispute or through a general legislative message designed to minimize private disputes or achieve a democratically determined public goal. The regulation is limited by the police power and, except in the case of nuisance, if the regulation eliminates all economic uses of the property, the state must typically pay compensation. But what if the regulation does not totally devalue the subject property, but merely diminishes the exchange value of the property by totally eliminating the value of one aspect of ownership? Is compensation required? The answer has typically been no, but those situations are at the heart of the property rights movement. Environmental regulations have been viewed as the principal culprit in charges of government overreaching. What is wrong with the conventional view?

Property rights advocates answer that the conventional view misunderstands both the true constitutional limitations on the exercise of the police power as well as the proper constitutional conception of the effects of state action on property rights. Their view runs roughly as follows: The Constitution requires that property be understood as a bundle of rights, each one a part of the value of the whole, but valuable in itself. When the value of any one of the rights in the bundle is eliminated the state must compensate the property owner for the loss of the value of the right regardless of the remaining value of the whole parcel. By adopting some version of the diminution of value analysis, modern takings analysis has corrupted this understanding and has led to a loss of constitutional dignity for property rights. Moreover, the state may only regulate private property if it is eliminating what would be a nuisance under common law or where the regulation produces a Pareto-optimal result based upon the extant distribution of wealth. Who is right?

One point conceded by all is that when a regulation produces "an average reciprocity of benefit," no compensation is required.[52] Even Epstein agrees with this. He would merely require a more searching and individuated inquiry and would have the reciprocal advantage analysis limited by a dollar-for-dollar balance. This is a form of the takings and givings argument. . . .

---

[52] Raymond R. Coletta, *Reciprocity of Advantage and Regulatory Takings: Toward a New Theory of Takings Jurisprudence*, 40 AM. U. L. REV. 297, 301 (1990).

In 1964, Professor Joseph Sax published an article in the *Yale Law Journal* that attempted to construct a framework for making a principled distinction among the varieties of actions that government undertakes that have a negative impact on private land value.[60] In determining which actions produce a compensable event, Sax argued that it was important to first consider the nature of the governmental action. In his analysis, the principal division between types of governmental action can be found when the government is acting in a way that merely aggrandizes its own position in relation to private actors compared to when it is arbitrating disputes between private actors. The police power is constrained by the arbitral role that the state plays. The government may act through the adjudication of individual disputes or may legislate generally, achieving the same results that would occur by the mere accumulation of the resolution of individual disputes. That this is a normative process is understood. The Takings Clause is a limitation on the police power to the extent that it prevents majority self-dealing in the guise of dispute resolution through regulation or legislation. . . . Unlike the modern advocates for limiting governmental activity through the Takings Clause, the careful analysis of decision-types asks a more sensible question about whether it is a good policy to use the uncompensated police power regulation to achieve a particular policy end.

Professor Frank Michelman, in his justly celebrated article,[66] followed a similar insight and outlined a utilitarian approach to calculating when compensation would, as a matter of policy, be required. According to Michelman, compensation is required when demoralization costs exceed efficiency gains and settlement costs.[67] . . .

This standard, when combined with the arbitral approach proposed by Sax in his 1964 article, limits the power of government in important ways. However, the limits do not arbitrarily prevent legislatures from enacting laws for the public interest. . . . The early cases that suggest that no regulation can constitute a taking seem right to this extent: the police power is not limited to securing the public from some nuisance-like harm. The Takings Clause was designed to prevent the government from localizing all of the burdens of a particular public policy. But this is a very different concern from whether the common-law boundaries of nuisance law describe the constitutional boundaries of the police power. This particular limitation on the exercise of the police power is summed up by both Professors Michelman and Sax. Where, under some theory of capture, the state is operating like a private scavenging company on behalf of the politically powerful as against the politically weak, it seems relatively easy to use the limitation of the police power to invalidate a particular action. Merely because there is some ancillary private benefit, however, is not proof of constitutional corruption and may only occasion more searching judicial inquiry. It may only be evidence of the wealth-creating aspects of regulation.

---

[60] [Joseph L.] Sax, [*Takings and the*] *Police Power*, [74 YALE L.J. 36 (1964)] . . . , at 36.

[66] Frank I. Michelman, *Property, Utility and Fairness: Comments on the Ethical Foundations of "Just Compensation" Law*, 80 HARV. L. REV. 1165 (1967).

[67] *Id.* at 1215.

The idea of partial takings, outside of the context of actual physical occupation, is quite perplexing. Because the argument for compensation is predicated upon the fact that property interests are capable of being segmented, what principle determines which loss will require compensation? . . .

. . . Are baseline common-law rules the only possible basis for making the takings determination? If so, then what of all regulation? Do we need to account for the value attributable to public action? If my property value increases because of public regulation (even assuming the limitations of the average reciprocity of advantage arguments), then shouldn't any economic loss caused by new government regulation be discounted by the corresponding value added by the existing regulations? If the change allows my neighbor to do something that diminishes the value of my property, is that just the workings of the market, or is it the result of government action? . . . *Florida Rock Industries, Inc. v. United States*,[76] a recent decision by the Federal Circuit, presents an interesting approach to these issues.

The reasoning in *Florida Rock* is deceptive because it suggests that *Lucas* decided the question of whether compensation was required. The limited holding in *Lucas* is inapposite to the dispute in *Florida Rock*. Remember that in *Lucas* the landowner purchased land without restrictions with the expectation that he would be able to use his property to the same extent as his neighbors.[78] Subsequent regulation dashed those expectations and virtually reduced the economic value of his parcel to zero. In *Florida Rock* the landowners purchased the property just before the enactment of the Clean Water Act. Before they began mining operations, however, the Army Corps of Engineers adopted regulations under section 404 of the Clean Water Act that restricted dredging and filling operations in wetlands. By the time mining operations began the landowners should have been cognizant of the restrictions on the property and should also have known that the economic use of the property for mining purposes would require a permit. To say that the permitting process reduced the value of the property is to treat the market value as though it were independent of the restrictions on all similarly situated properties. This is not a plausible construction of value, and it also elevates investment-backed expectations, the limitation created in *Penn Central*,[81] to an investment predicated upon a contingency. In *Florida Rock*, the contingency was a permit. . . . To so limit the permissible range of governmental permitting processes in this way is an argument for social paralysis and makes the public interest hostage to those who own property, rather than to the citizens who make up the polity. . . .

The reasoning in *Loveladies Harbor, Inc. v. United States*[83] is similarly flawed. In that case, the plaintiffs owned land in New Jersey that they planned to develop and sell for residential use. However, some of the land the plaintiffs aimed to develop was wetland. When the U.S. Army Corps of Engineers denied the plain-

---

[76] 18 F.3d 1560 (Fed. Cir. 1994), *cert. denied*, 115 S. Ct. 898 (1995).

[78] Lucas v. South Carolina Coastal Council, 505 U.S. 1003, 1008 (1992).

[81] Penn Central Transp. Co. v. New York City, 438 U.S. 104, 124 (1978).

[83] 28 F.3d 1171 (Fed. Cir. 1994).

tiffs a permit to develop the wetland tracts, the plaintiffs sued for compensation for the reduction in value they alleged was traceable to the permit denial. The plaintiffs claimed that the government's action constituted a taking and had effectively reduced the value of their property to zero. The trial court had found that the proposed development site was worth $2,658,000 before the Corps denied the permit and only $12,500 afterwards. This is a brutal reduction in value, but the size of the "diminution" does not resolve the question of whether compensation is required or whether the regulation is permissible.

The court held that with regard to the interest allegedly taken, the Supreme Court, in *Lucas* and its progeny, announced the test for the existence of a regulatory taking. According to the court's version of the existing jurisprudence of regulatory takings, compensation is required if three requirements are met. First, there must be proof that all economic use of the subject property was eliminated and the loss was the result of a regulatory action. The inquiry goes to the extent of the landowner's property affected by the permit denial. In the court's view, the easiest case is when the entire tract of property is affected by the regulatory action. The inquiry becomes increasingly more problematic depending upon the extent of the remaining unrestricted property. This construction of the appropriate judicial inquiry indicates that this court has fully accepted the partial taking hypothesis and asserts that the latter inquiry is whether there is a partial taking.

Second, the court looks to see if the property owner had a distinct investment-backed expectation. Third, the court must ascertain whether this investment-backed expectation was vested in the property owner as a matter of state property law and was not within the power of the state to regulate as a matter of common-law nuisance doctrine. If the court determines the answers to that set of inquiries are "yes," then compensation is required. Just compensation is then determined by the formula created in *Florida Rock*. In *Florida Rock*, the court determined that the landowner was owed the difference between the parcel's unrestricted fair market value before the permit was denied and the property's fair market value after the permit was denied. As I suggested earlier, this determination of value presumes that the property was purchased without any thought of the necessity of public approval before a particular use was made of it. Taking the court's analysis at face value would suggest that the mere existence of the regulation worked a taking. *Hodel v. Virginia Surface Mining & Reclamation Ass'n*,[97] of course, resolved that issue,[98] and economic theory suggests that the expectation value must be based on the potential realities of the market, not some imagined unregulated market for the commodity in question. Moreover, in its resolution of the "denominator" problem, the *Florida Rock* court merely looked at the economic impact of the permit denial on the regulated portion of the parcel rather than the impact on the parcel taken as a whole.

---

[97] 452 U.S. 264 (1981).

[98] *Id.* at 293-97 (holding that a mere assertion of regulatory jurisdiction by a governmental body does not constitute a regulatory taking).

Despite *Lucas*'s suggestive language, the Court has never limited the reach of the police power to the contours described by common-law nuisance. The Court has increasingly required a closer connection between the proposed regulation and the desired goal to be achieved, but that is a far cry from the limitation suggested either in *Florida Rock* or *Loveladies Harbor*. The restriction on state action in those cases creates by negative implication a theory of vested rights that gives rise to the existence of their version of the "distinct investment-backed expectation" doctrine. This analysis also creates a constitutional limitation on the exercise of the police power that is not found in the jurisprudence of the Supreme Court. It is not even a very convincing extrapolation. *Lucas* is not the only source of insight into the Supreme Court's thinking on the limitations of the police power. The Court has often suggested that the limitation is not defined abstractly in advance, but that a detailed factual inquiry is at the heart of the matter. One example is *Nollan v. California Coastal Commission*.[100] The essential nexus test developed in *Nollan* is essentially one test of the legitimacy of the police power. There the Court noted that "a use restriction may constitute a 'taking' if not reasonably necessary to the effectuation of a substantial government purpose."[101] By imposing the requirement of a close relationship between the means and the ends, the Court was reaffirming its commitment to the conditions of decision making that would prevent the kinds of democratic excesses the Takings Clause was designed to guard against.

To demonstrate the constitutional effect of the necessity of a close connection, the Supreme Court in *Dolan v. City of Tigard*[102] stressed that the obligation to demonstrate an instrumental need for the restriction would effectively eliminate the temptation to overreach. . . .

. . . .

I want to conclude this cursory discussion of the law with a brief discussion of the idea that seems so troubling to those who want to find a "principled" basis for takings decisions and who seem disgusted by the notion that the Court is acting in an *ad hoc* manner when deciding these cases. The notion can be traced back to Justice Oliver Wendell Holmes's decision in *Pennsylvania Coal v. Mahon*.[113] The approach has been criticized as allowing any eventuality to obtain. In fact, Holmes was attempting to articulate the basis for the creation of objective standards. This process is best captured by reference to the epistemology of the Pragmatists, under whose sway Holmes clearly was. That view can best be summed up as follows: "[I]nquiry is a never-ending process whose purpose is to resolve doubts generated when experience does not mesh with preconceived theory."[115] . . .

Unfortunately, the cases have not focused on the police power *simpliciter*, but rather on the "goes too far" language in *Pennsylvania Coal*. The search for what is

---

[100] 483 U.S. 825 (1987).

[101] *Id.* at 834 (quoting Penn Central Transp. Co. v. New York City, 438 U.S. 104, 127 (1978)).

[102] 114 S. Ct. 2309 (1994).

[113] 260 U.S. 393 (1922); *accord Lucas,* 505 U.S. at 1035-36 (Kennedy, J., concurring).

[115] GRANT GILMORE, THE AGES OF AMERICAN LAW 50 (1977).

"too far" has produced the diminution in value inquiry and now the partial takings arguments. Instead, the analysis, even by Holmes's admission, should have focused on that "neighborhood of principles of policy which are other than those on which the particular right is founded, and which becomes strong enough to hold their own when a certain point is reached."[121] What Holmes was describing is the way in which policy is created both logically and prudentially. He was articulating a system for recognizing when a particular position is of doubtful authority. By referring to a system of rights (and within it a system for their evolution), he was rejecting a sterile search for first principles, because he was conscious of the fact that so-called first principles are never unmediated. The way in which they are mediated (the way in which we recognize their legitimate evolution) is by constantly comparing the principle in question with the "neighboring" principles that are not in question in this case, but which describe the boundaries of the issue under consideration. Too great a deviation from the norms described by the family of principles suggests the potential illegitimacy of the deviation. Importantly, it does not foreclose that "deviation" for all time, necessarily, but cabins it when the deviation would render a system of principled restraint unstable. This approach to the problems of the extent of governmental regulatory power reveals the constellation of rights, powers, liabilities, and immunities as a dynamic system, not as the mere ordinal ranking of predetermined claims. That such a dynamic approach to analysis and adjudication leaves much undecided is not a demerit and, in fact, is an important value. To focus upon only that which is still in general social dispute is to lose sight of all that is not in dispute. Worse, such a focus ignores the general stability of the system that has protected "property rights," even if it has emerged only fitfully, and even if it has been tempered by the "neighborhood of principles," not in dispute, on which we rely.

IV. Conclusion

. . . .

The emotional pull and persuasive force of the story told by . . . property rights advocates stems not only from their ability to tell a good story, but also from the real connections the story makes to a way of life and the pressures that are making that life increasingly less tenable. Because I am a Westerner by birth and disposition, although I have lived for much of the past two decades in the Midwest, I feel a great deal of sympathy for those who make a living off the land. I have watched family farm and ranch operations struggle over the recent past, beset by the vagaries of the natural resource economy. I can appreciate the tug of those felt injustices. When one speaks to farmers, ranchers, and others in rural America, one begins to appreciate the "way of life" arguments that are pooh-poohed as mere sentimentalism by economists and some policymakers. These "way of life" arguments make sense in the context of a rural economy that is being transformed more

---

[121] . . . [Hudson County Water Co. v. McCarter], 209 U.S. [349 (1908)] at 355.

quickly than the social system can accommodate. These facts do not make the doctrinal arguments of the property rights advocates correct, but they do make the arguments and their rhetorical force more understandable.

. . . .

A Dozen Propositions on Private Property, Public Rights, and the New Takings Legislation
Carol M. Rose
53 Wash. & Lee L. Rev. 265 (1996)*

Introduction

Property rights are a hot political topic. In the last few years, the issue of regulatory "takings" of property has ceased to be merely a vastly overwritten subject in the legal academic literature. A "property rights" movement—taking aim in particular at environmental legislation—seems to have been energized by several new takings cases from the Supreme Court and, to a lesser extent, from a newly activist Court of Federal Claims.[2] "Takings" bills are debated fiercely in Congress and in statehouses all over the United States, as state and federal legislators entertain measures that confront a pattern of regulation that is said to threaten private property.[3]

Although the congressional bills deal only with federal matters, and the state measures deal with state and local regulation, most of these measures follow one of three basic strategies. First, they may require regulatory bodies or state officers to undertake assessment processes in an attempt to determine whether their actions potentially "take" the property of private parties. Second, they may attempt to redefine and expand what counts as a "taking" of property. And third, they may implicitly or explicitly narrow the defenses that regulatory bodies may raise when facing takings charges. Taken together, these measures may considerably enlarge the

---

*   © 1996. Reprinted by permission.

[2]   *See, e.g.,* Loveladies Harbor, Inc. v. United States, 21 Cl. Ct. 153, 160 (1990) (finding application of wetlands regulation to be taking), *aff'd*, 28 F.3d 1171 (Fed. Cir. 1994).

[3]   As of the fall of 1994, all state legislatures had considered, and 10 had enacted, some version of takings legislation. Robert H. Freilich & RoxAnne Doyle, *Taking Legislation: Misguided and Dangerous*, LAND USE L. & ZONING DIG., Oct. 1994, at 3, 3 & n.1. The newly elected Congress also has taken up takings legislation; the House passed the Private Property Protection Act of 1995, H.R. 925, 104th Cong., 1st Sess. (1995) [hereinafter House Property Protection Act], on March 3, 1995, and the Senate is currently considering the Omnibus Property Rights Act of 1995, S. 605, 104th Cong., 1st Sess. (1995) [hereinafter Senate Property Rights Act]. By 1995, more states had passed similar legislation, including Florida, H.R. 863, 1995 Leg., Reg. Sess. (1995) (enacted May 18, 1995), Texas, S. 14, 74th Leg., Reg. Sess. (1995) (enacted June 12, 1995), and Virginia, S. 1017, 1994-95 Leg., Reg. Sess. (1995) (enacted March 25, 1995), among others.

range of public acts that count as "takings" and, conversely, considerably contract the scope of regulatory authority.

In this article, I will address some of the issues that these acts and proposals raise, concentrating on the congressional bills because, if adopted, these federal enactments may well serve as models for subsequent state legislation.[4] But more generally, I want to clarify some of the property concepts that underlie takings jurisprudence. Because many of the proponents of takings legislation call on what they regard as the historic principles of a more property-conscious past,[5] I will concentrate on the common-law and historical legal principles relating to takings and property regulation.

Briefly, my position is that historic Anglo-American legal principles did indeed recognize the importance of private property rights, which are essential in a functioning free enterprise economy. But those principles also recognized what were called "public rights," particularly in resources that are not easily turned into private property—historically, air, water resources, and fish and wildlife stocks—because the management of such diffuse resources is also essential in a functioning economic order of free enterprise. Indeed, the essence of traditional takings law is an effort to balance private rights and public rights as they co-evolve over time. This balance is drawn principally by judicial actions, but the judiciary historically has recognized that legislatures have an important role to play, particularly in defining and protecting public rights. What is most at risk in the new takings measures is the tradition of public rights because, in their authors' anxiety to protect private rights, the measures may lose sight of the complementary character of public and private rights in any functioning property regime.

With that introduction, let me begin my Dozen Propositions—twelve observations on private property, public rights, and the new takings legislation.

Proposition 1.
 Private property rights are essential in a free-enterprise regime.

Property's importance for capitalism has been recognized at least since John Locke's famous discussion in his Second Treatise of Government,[6] a discussion on

---

[4] Takings assessment laws, the most common type among the state enactments, followed this pattern. The general model for states was Executive Order 12,630, 3 C.F.R. 554 (1988), *reprinted in* 5 U.S.C. § 601 (1994), issued late in the Reagan administration, which required federal agencies to assess the takings implications of proposed regulations. . . .

[5] *See Regulatory Takings and Property Rights: Hearings Before the Subcomm. on the Constitution of the House Comm. on the Judiciary*, 104th Cong., 1st Sess. (1995) [hereinafter *Regulatory Takings*] (statement of James W. Ely, Jr.) (arguing that American law and practice historically was solicitous of private property); *id.* (Statement of Roger J. Marzulla) (arguing that framers wished to protect property, which was under assault from environmental laws); *see also* Roger Pilon, *Property Rights, Takings, and a Free Society,* 6 HARV. J.L. PUB. POL'Y 165, 168-70 (1983) (arguing that modern restrictions on property subvert historically correct principles of private property). More recently, Pilon testified in favor of the takings legislation pending in the House of Representatives. *Regulatory Takings, supra* (statement of Roger Pilon).

[6] JOHN LOCKE, TWO TREATISES OF GOVERNMENT 290, 292-96, 299-301, 350-51 (Peter Laslett ed., student ed. 1988) (3d ed. 1698).

which both William Blackstone[7] and Jeremy Bentham[8] later elaborated. An owner must have reasonably secure expectations of continued ownership if he or she is going to expend efforts to improve resources. Similarly, reasonably secure defin-itions of property are essential to trade because trading partners must know who owns what in order for their trades to mean anything.

. . . .

Proposition 2.
Although private property rights need to be reasonably secure, their content can change with changing conditions.

Property rights in traditional law have never had fixed characteristics that apply under all conditions and for all time. Indeed, it would be undesirable and probably impossible for property rights to have such fixed definitions. . . .

A chief reason why property rights change is that they are costly to establish and maintain. At the most elementary level, it takes time, effort, and resources to put a fence around a yard. More complex systems of property rights, like copyright, require more effort and expense to establish and enforce. Because property regimes are not costless, people often do not define property rights at all until the need becomes clear; generally speaking, people do so only when resources become scarce, raising the prospect of damaging conflicts over resource use. An important way to prevent those conflicts is to define property rights.

. . . .

Grassland rights illustrate the general pattern of change in property, a pattern that responds to the benefits and costs of establishing, defining, and protecting property rights. Unrestricted open access is not a problem when resources are plen-tiful, but where congestion increases, open-access resources may deteriorate—a sit-uation often called "the tragedy of the commons."[19] People very often respond to this congestion and strife by dividing open-access resources into individual private property holdings, as some of the ranchers did on the western lands.

Proposition 3.
Some resources are candidates for public rights and management.

Private property is an important response to scarcity, congestion, and strife, but it is not always the only response or the best one. Some scarce resources require larger-scale management, even public management—a fact that has been recog-

---

[7] 2 WILLIAM BLACKSTONE, COMMENTARIES *2-*4.

[8] JEREMY BENTHAM, THE THEORY OF LEGISLATION (Principles of the Civil Code) pt. 1, chs. 7-9 (C.K. Ogden ed., 1987) (1789).

[19] This name comes from Garrett Hardin, *The Tragedy of the Commons*, 162 SCIENCE 1243 (1968). An earlier development of the idea is found in H. Scott Gordon, *The Economic Theory of a Common-Property Resource: The Fishery*, 62 J. POL. ECON. 124 (1954).

nized in the common law of property. The use of waterways, for example, has been considered a public property right since the time of the Romans and, to a lesser degree, so have fisheries.

The reason for these common or public rights relates to the costs of establishing property rights: It is more difficult to define individual property rights in some resources than others. Land is a resource in which it is relatively easy to define individual property rights. Land is fixed in location and can be visibly marked, and trespassers can be identified relatively easily—though certainly not without cost, as our modern security systems attest. . . .

The difficulty of defining and enforcing private property rights in water, wildlife, and air did not and does not now mean that these resources are not valuable but simply that they are not necessarily best treated as *individual* or *private* property rights. In traditional American law, these diffuse resources were often treated as limited common rights. . . .

Sometimes diffusely enjoyed resources were designated as "public rights." This designation reflected the fact that although a resource could not easily be privatized, it was nevertheless valuable to many people and subject to a kind of easement for public use, including passive uses such as simple enjoyment of clean air and quiet surroundings. . . .

Proposition 4.
Private land ownership often entails the use of public resources.

Private ownership, particularly land ownership, has a close connection with common and public resource uses. When people define individual property rights in land, they often use their land as the means of access to adjacent common resources, effectively "piggybacking" the use of a common resource like air or water onto their individual land ownership. This practice is not a problem so long as the common resources are relatively uncongested. As with individual property rights, there is no particular need to assert and formalize public rights in common resources, as long as the resources remain plentiful. Thus, it does not matter if one landowner disposes of small quantities of wastes in a fast-flowing stream, as long as the water can aerate and biodegrade the wastes. Similarly, no one cares much if a single landowner burns wood or coal if the amounts of smoke are small and quickly dispersed.

But where population becomes dense, these unrestricted private uses of the "commons" can become a problem. . . . That is why late nineteenth-century and early twentieth-century American law increasingly recognized rights of action for nuisance against landowners who caused undue smoke, fumes, noise, water pollution, and even loss of light and air—private nuisance in the case of nearby and specially affected owners and public nuisance in the case of the larger public or numerous members of it.

These legal developments exemplify the general pattern: Increasing congestion in common resources is a major reason for the evolution of legal definitions of property rights because greater congestion alters the costs and benefits of establishing property rights. Specifically, greater congestion makes it worth the cost and effort to define property rights more explicitly. American property law, like the law of most of the world, has always responded to increasing conditions of congestion so as to avoid strife and waste and has done so by redefining both private and public rights.

. . . .

Proposition 5.
Public rights have co-evolved with private rights.

Traditional Anglo-American law generally recognized a duty of legislatures to compensate owners when private rights were appropriated for the public benefit. At all levels of government, compensation was and continues to be the norm, for example, when land is taken for roadways. On the other hand, compensation was contingent on several defenses. For example, unless land was taken outright, compensation was generally not due when legislation imposed moderate but more or less equal burdens on large numbers of landowners. Nor was compensation due when regulation was implicitly recompensed by reciprocal benefits going to the affected landowners.

Most important, compensation was not due when regulation effectively prevented private owners from doing something to which they were not entitled. Thus traditional American law did not necessarily regard land ownership as a license for a landowner's unrestricted "piggybacked" use of adjacent diffuse resources such as water, air, or wildlife, particularly in situations in which one landowner's use could have serious effects on many other owners and persons. Such an act was considered an encroachment on the rights of others, and its restraint was not necessarily a compensable event.

Immediately neighboring landowners or other easily identifiable people might protect themselves through private trespass or nuisance law, each bringing an action in his or her own behalf. In some ways, however, the matters of more pressing concern were actions that affected the diffuse and less recognizable general public, whose collective interests might be great even though their individual interests were too minor for any of them to bring an action. These diffuse interests were the particular domain of public rights, and legislatures were widely considered their guardians. Massachusetts, for example, first as a colony and then as a state, prohibited as a "common nuisance" any unauthorized obstructions to fish passage in its rivers.[33] This law attempted to protect the then-prolific runs of anadromous shad and Atlantic salmon, widely used for foodstuffs; the legislature effectively treated these fish as public property over which it was entitled to dispose in the public's behalf. . . .

. . . .

---

[33] The statute is discussed in Commonwealth v. Ruggles, 10 Mass. 391, 393 (1813). . . .

Proposition 6.
Courts traditionally have protected evolving public rights.

Recent Supreme Court "takings" cases have shown considerable attention to the importance of historic property categories, including the traditional background concept of public nuisance, which is discussed in the 1992 case *Lucas v. South Carolina Coastal Council.*[37] As the *Lucas* Court remarked, the mere invocation of "public nuisance" is not an excuse for public appropriation of private property.[38] Indeed, it never was, but earlier courts stressed their willingness to accept reasonable legislative definitions of nuisance, which is another way of saying that they would accept reasonable legislative protections of public rights.

At least two points, however, have been insufficiently recognized in recent takings cases. First, historic American law took into account the need for changes in the protection of public rights as resources became more congested. Second, legislatures were recognized as playing a central role in making those changes.

Nuisance law was a primary protector of public rights, and nuisance law itself was at its most active stage of development in the late nineteenth century when urbanization and new technology set the stage for numerous conflicts over land uses. A part of the nuisance story was a very significant byplay between legislatures and courts.

Throughout the nineteenth century, legislatures were widely recognized as competent to define public nuisances so as to prevent private encroachments on public rights, but they also could *authorize* encroachments on public resources by private parties. And at a time of great commercial and industrial innovation, when active land uses were often regarded as beneficial to the community, uses that had been considered public nuisances indeed often *were* authorized. These authorized nuisances included legislative permission for municipalities to pollute water, for manufacturing plants to raise the dams that disrupted and depleted fish stocks, and most notoriously, for railway firms to pollute air and create noise and vibrations.

. . . .

We can now see damage from these authorized public nuisances that may not have been so obvious at the time, but even by the end of the nineteenth century, courts and legal scholarship noticed many problems. They particularly noticed problems in cases where the legislature authorized private parties, like railroad firms, to make public improvements, but where the costs seemed to fall especially heavily on certain other private persons. . . . The result was a judicial brake on the legislative authorizations that effectively "spent" public resources such as clean air, clean water, wildlife, and quiet surroundings.

How was that brake applied? Basically, it was applied through the deployment of private rights to protect larger public ones. According to courts and commentators, the legislature could authorize public nuisances but not private ones—it

---

[37] 505 U.S. 1003 (1992).

[38] Lucas v. South Carolina Coastal Council, 505 U.S. 1003, 1026 (1992).

could authorize widespread nuisances but not those that especially harmed particular individuals. . . .

. . . .

Through an evolving nuisance law, then, the later nineteenth-century courts effectively enlisted private rights to restrain legislative giveaways of the public rights in air, water, wildlife, and peace and quiet. Judicially created nuisance law required that the legislative "expenditures" of public rights at least take into account the costs to private property and at least weigh the expected benefits of public giveaways against the costs of private damage that results. . . .

. . . .

. . . [T]he earlier dynamism of court-made nuisance law appears to have gone into a period of relative quiescence after the turn of the century. It was at this time that courts ceded to legislatures—especially local legislatures, through zoning—the increasingly complex task of defining the ways that land uses might be restricted as being unusually burdensome to the neighbors or to the public at large.

For this reason, it is particularly misleading to look simply to common-law judicial definitions of nuisance as the basis for modern property rights. For almost a century now, legislators—with judicial acquiescence—have taken over the task of refining and specifying the range of acceptable landowner practices, once defined only by judicially administered trespass and nuisance law on a case-by-case basis. By comparison, judicially defined nuisance law now tends to be relatively crude and does not always reflect the greater congestion of modern life, the greater information that we now have about the effects of human activities on resources, or the more complex and nuanced remedies that legislatures can devise to moderate those effects.

. . . .

Proposition 7.
  Prior private usage gives no permanent claim against public rights.

Although property rights clearly have changed over time, there is a pattern to their change. The general pattern of the common law was to leave property usages alone and not to bother enforcing rights to the letter, so long as no conflicts arose. This pattern was efficient: Why raise a fuss when no rights or resources are endangered? And it was also a way to encourage neighborly resolutions. . . .

. . . [T]he same pattern applied to public rights. *Private* uses of *public* rights were condoned as long as no damage was threatened, but the other side of this coin was that the private owner acquired no permanent rights in the public resource. . . .

. . . .

. . . More specifically, past private usage of public resources was not necessarily an impediment to legislation that would protect public resources in the future. Thus, pigsties, brick kilns, slaughterhouses, and many other private landowners' uses were restricted as their damage to clean air and other public resources became more acute.

Proposition 8.
The province of takings law is to balance transitional compromises.

As a practical matter, when legislatures begin the transition to protecting public rights, there may be good reasons to take a cautious approach and to avoid pressing public rights to the hilt, particularly in the case of pre-existing uses. For one thing, the public authorities may be quite late in determining that particular private land uses cause damage to other persons and to public resources, or they may have suggested that these uses could continue. In the meantime, owners may have innocently sunk capital into their land uses in the expectation of being permitted to continue to consume public resources like air, water, wildlife stocks, or even peace and quiet. Halting such uses may result in the deadweight loss of expenditures that the owner has already made—deadweight in the sense that the expenditures become useless either to the owner or to anyone else.

. . . .

Takings cases traditionally have deployed several techniques to manage these competing considerations—to avoid unfairness, undue burdens, and unforeseeable losses to individual property owners while at the same time preserving the ability of legislatures to protect public rights as the need evolves over time. Like all compromises, these are messy and fraught with intellectual and even practical imperfections, but as in most other areas of life, the adjustment of property relations has a considerable element of "muddling through."[77]

. . . .

The pattern of compromise in takings cases historically has entailed inquiries that are often detailed and fact-laden. In effect, takings cases are rather like nuisance cases, but applied to governmental actions. . . .

Perhaps most important, takings jurisprudence is like nuisance law in that it can adjust to increasing congestion and new occasions for the assertions of public rights. This flexibility is evident to some degree even in recent Supreme Court cases, which have sometimes seemed particularly inattentive to the subject of public rights and the legislative role in their protection. In *Nollan v. California Coastal Commission*,[84] for example, a case that found a state coastal commission's action unconstitutional as a taking of property, Justice Scalia nevertheless recognized that the public may have a legitimate interest in protecting a view—a public resource only relatively recently recognized as such.

Proposition 9.
Recent legislative redefinitions of takings upset the balance implicit in takings jurisprudence.

Recent proposals for takings legislation purport to clean up the messiness of takings jurisprudence and clarify property rights, but in fact, many of these pro-

---

[77] *See generally* Charles E. Lindblom, *The Science of "Muddling Through"*, 19 PUB. ADMIN. REV. 79 (1959) (arguing that human capacities allow only successive limited comparisons of alternatives rather than comprehensive rational approach).

[84] 483 U.S. 825 (1987).

posals do neither. Instead, many only complexify takings questions and disrupt traditional understandings of the relationship of private and public rights.

One approach is to require an advance assessment of the takings implications of proposed regulations. State takings legislation, so far, has largely followed this model. . . . [I]f kept to a simple checklist, such ex ante assessments might help to remind regulators of important private property interests at stake without unduly hampering the regulatory process.

Considerably more complex and more problematic is the federal government's Executive Order 12,630,[88] which was an early example of the assessment approach. Unfortunately, it poses questions that are almost impossible to answer in advance. This Order requires federal agencies, in their "takings" assessments, to identify particular properties affected, their present uses, the economic impact on each, any offsetting benefits, and the duration of the adverse effects—and all this concerns only the consideration of economic impact, which by no means exhausts the Order's list.

. . . In such assessment requirements, the detailed factual inquiries of takings jurisprudence simply are shifted without being avoided, and indeed, they are shifted to a time frame in which they are less likely to yield reliable answers. At best, such overblown procedural requirements are simply wasteful and redundant, and at worst they are a kind of harassment of regulators.

Another approach attempts to define legislatively what is and what is not a regulatory taking, particularly by stating a threshold percentage of "diminution in value"—10%, 30%, etc.—beyond which an owner must be compensated. . . .

Whatever else might be said of percentage limits, they ultimately fail to clarify one of the central issues of takings jurisprudence. To posit a 10% or 20% or 30% diminution in value as a taking still does not answer the question that has always dogged the diminution in value test for regulatory takings—"percent of what?" That is, what is the underlying property to which the loss in value is compared? Even where such percentage requirements are passed, one can predict that they will generate more litigation about almost exactly the same question. Thus, on closer analysis, the percentage limits, like the assessment legislation, generally only complicate, without solving, the fact-specific inquiries that are so much a part of most takings jurisprudence.

Aside from these various "clarifying" efforts, a number of the new legislative proposals implicitly or explicitly narrow the substantive scope of public rights. One of the sharpest attacks on public rights is quite subtle. This attack is contained in what seems to be a minor adjustment to the "percent diminution" clauses in the major congressional bills, where it is stated that the percentage applies to the value of the entire property, *or to any affected part or portion*.[96] . . .

---

[88] Exec. Order No. 12,630, *supra* note 4.

[96] House Property Protection Act, *supra* note 3, § 3(a); Senate Property Rights Act, *supra* note 3, § 204(a)(2)(B)-(D).

But this seemingly innocuous phrase masks a quite radical position and would very much alter existing takings jurisprudence. Once property can be divided into "relevant" portions, any diminution can be manipulated to become a 30%, 50%, or even 100% diminution. The phrase could effectively mean that virtually *any* regulation with *any* adverse impact on an owner's parcel could become an occasion for compensation, without regard to the owner's expectations and whether they were reasonable, and without regard to the public rights that might be at stake.

. . . .

Traditional jurisprudence allowed much greater leeway to legislatures, allowing them to protect not only health and safety but also comfort, convenience, and welfare in general, whether specifically identifiable to particular properties or not. Indeed, economic logic suggests the reasons for this traditionally expansive view. If a land use causes identifiable damage to a specific property, the landowner can sue in her own behalf under private nuisance law. If a land use causes substantial health or safety hazards, the public may well be so outraged that single individuals will sue in the public's behalf or insist that public officials do so. But if a land use causes more diffuse and less identifiable damage to welfare—the thousand small cuts into clean water, fresh air, plentiful fish and wildlife and quiet surroundings—then members of the general public have only attenuated incentives to sue in their own behalf. Each person and property owner shares the problem with many others, and all may await the action of someone else. Hence, the general public, faced with diffuse and hard-to-define damage, is most in need of the legislative protection of public rights. Following this logic, legislative protection of wide and diffuse public rights traditionally has been considered a part of the police power, rather than takings of private property.

Indeed, there is a relation between standing doctrines and the police power: Private individuals may not be appropriate advocates for a broad public interest because their personal interests are slight; hence, they do not have standing. But the quid pro quo is not that broad public damage goes undefended. The quid pro quo is that the public's agents—its legislative and regulatory agencies—are entitled to protect against damage to the public. That is the traditional position of public rights.

Contrary to these historical patterns, the new proposals on takings go far beyond the constitutional protections of private ownership, even as those protections are set out in the takings jurisprudence of our recently more conservative Supreme Court. That is why this kind of legislation could seriously disrupt the balancing effort of takings jurisprudence—the balance between the protections of private rights and public rights.

Proposition 10.
Proposed legislative redefinitions of takings impair public rights and dissipate resources.

Some of the proposed takings redefinitions, if enacted, will effectively transfer public rights to private owners. They will do so by expanding the definition of a taking, by narrowing the legislature's defenses against takings charges, and by adding duplicative procedures whose costs can delay and impede legitimate legislative action. More important, they will do so without any semblance of the older justifications for legislative authorizations of encroachments on public rights—that the public good, on balance, was served by the authorization.

Quite the contrary, these transfers suggest a net social impoverishment. Like private rights, public rights have an economic justification: They maintain unified control over large-scale, common-pool resources. By cutting back on that unified control and allowing unrestricted open access to individuals, though we may chant the name of property rights, we are in effect inviting a wasteful free-for-all in common resources—the very opposite of the aim of a property regime.

. . . .

. . . A pattern of such transfers encourages disrespect for public rights and encourages private property owners to adopt an attitude of extortion and "in-your-face" about matters of known concern to the public. Property as a whole depends greatly on a civilized respect for the rights of others, including rights of the public. Citizens should expect that their legislators will avoid measures that can disrupt respect for public rights and that could instead reward persons who had no reason to expect that they could indefinitely appropriate public resources for themselves.

Proposition 11.
Legislatures nevertheless can play an important role in bringing private property concepts into the preservation of public rights.

There is no question that many of our environmental and land use laws could use improvement, both from the perspective of cost effectiveness and from the perspective of fairness to individual owners. There is a relationship between these points; legislatures that can treat other people's property as a "free good" may not have much incentive to weigh costs and benefits accurately. There are many examples: Local governments can act cavalierly in allowing—or prohibiting—land uses that primarily damage outsiders.[116] Federal laws, with their distance from specific local conditions, may be so optimistic about the efficacy of general legislation as to call for impracticable or unenforceable levels of performance, which leaves citizens confused and frustrated about their rights and duties. Environmentalists should learn a lesson from the property rights backlash that has whipped up the recent takings proposals; the cavalier treatment of private rights is very likely to have serious repercussions that ultimately can damage public rights as well.

Specific legislation to deal with these concerns can make regulation both fairer to individual citizens and more productive to the larger community. Indeed, in focusing on takings jurisprudence—which is so dominated by the judiciary—we

---

[116] For example, municipal patterns of "exclusionary zoning" often are described as efforts to foist responsibility for low-income residents on others; a good example is the famous Mt. Laurel litigation, beginning with Southern Burlington County NAACP v. Township of Mount Laurel, 336 A.2d 713, 731-34 (N.J.) (requiring city to zone for "fair share" of region's low-income housing), *cert. denied,* 423 U.S. 808 (1975). . . .

often overlook the fact that legislatures police each other in ways that can allay takings claims from the outset. For example, a number of states require that local regulation undergo a variety of planning steps, in part to improve regulatory quality, in part to give citizens an early opportunity to raise fairness concerns about land use regulation, and in part to prevent municipalities from imposing external costs on one anothers' citizens.

. . . .

Proposition 12.
Public rights are as essential to a free enterprise system as are private rights.

In a free enterprise system, public rights measure in importance beside private rights. Both kinds of rights are important because the goal of a free enterprise system, all other things being equal, is not to maximize the value of privately held resources. It is to maximize the value of *the sum of private and public resources.*

Much of the literature of the takings debate points out the dangers to private owners from uncompensated public appropriations. These dangers are real. Public appropriations can unfairly single out particular private owners to pay for public benefits, and writ large, they mean that we could impoverish ourselves as a nation by discouraging enterprise and undermining commerce. For this reason, we have constitutionalized judicial oversight of public regulation through the Takings Clause.

Handouts of public rights to private owners, however, are unfair to the public. They too can impoverish us as a nation because they decimate resources that are diffuse and difficult to turn into private property but that are still immensely valuable to the public as a whole—now and (it is to be hoped) in the future. Citizens are entitled to expect that their legislatures will safeguard public rights along with private ones and in so doing, uphold the respect for rights—including public rights—that is a necessary part of the moral infrastructure of any property regime and, indeed, of republican government itself.

Note

For further discussion of legislation and legislative proposals dealing with takings, see Mark W. Cordes, *Leapfrogging the Constitution: The Rise of State Takings Legislation,* 24 Ecology L.Q. 187 (1997); Robert C. Ellickson, *Takings Legislation: A Comment,* 20 Harv. J.L. & Pub. Pol'y 75 (1996); Frank I. Michelman, *A Skeptical View of "Property Rights" Legislation,* 6 Fordham Envtl. L.J. 409 (1995); Jerome M. Organ, *Understanding State and Federal Property Rights Legislation,* 48 Okla. L. Rev. 191 (1995). *See also* Lynda L. Butler, *The Politics of Takings: Choosing the Appropriate Decisionmaker,* 38 Wm. & Mary L. Rev. 749 (1997).

5. Solution: Now or Ever?

Ten Arguments for the Abolition of the Regulatory Takings Doctrine
J. Peter Byrne
22 Ecology L.Q. 89 (1995)[*]

INTRODUCTION

The Takings Clause of the Fifth Amendment prohibits the federal government from "taking" property for a public purpose without paying just compensation. The Supreme Court has come to interpret the clause to require that the government compensate real property owners in some unclear class of cases when regulation of the property has resulted in severe economic losses. The proposition that regulation alone, without appropriation, occupation, or use by the government, can work a taking is known as the "regulatory takings" doctrine.

The regulatory takings doctrine is a pernicious mess. It should be dispatched to whatever afterlife sustains the spirits of such deceased doctrines as constitutional review of ratemaking and measurement of "direct effects on commerce." The current rules are a hodgepodge that the Court has been unable to explain. But worse, the doctrine protects economic interests in the development of land against otherwise valid enactments of the democratic process, thereby inhibiting experimentation with new environmental initiatives. The effect the doctrine has of frustrating democratic attempts to protect the environment is reminiscent of the way judges once used the notion of substantive due process to frustrate legislative attempts to regulate the hours and conditions of work.

. . . .

I will present ten arguments why the Supreme Court should overrule *Pennsylvania Coal Co. v. Mahon*[8] and its progeny, the line of cases that established the regulatory takings doctrine. My ten arguments are heterogeneous and grounded in different traditions of constitutional interpretation. Nonetheless, the article proceeds logically: each argument builds on the previous one. In an addendum, I provide an example of a compensation statute designed to crystalize landowner expectations to promote better and less wasteful land use control.

---

[*] © 1995 by Ecology Law Quarterly. Reprinted from Ecology Law Quarterly Vol. 22, pp. 89-142, by permission.

[8] 260 U.S. 393 (1922).

I

NEITHER THE TEXT, THE INTENTION OF THE FRAMERS, NOR THE
FIRST ONE HUNDRED THIRTY YEARS OF JUDICIAL INTERPRETATION SUPPORT
APPLICATION OF THE TAKINGS CLAUSE TO REGULATION OF LAND USE

Neither the text of the Fifth Amendment nor the circumstances of its adoption suggests that its proponents had any expectation that the Takings Clause would provide an enforceable limitation on government regulation of land use. The Fifth Amendment provides that: "Private property [shall not] be taken for public use, without just compensation." . . . In short, the clause prohibits only *expropriation*; facially it says nothing about the economic effects of regulation or other government activity.

. . . .

Historical studies of the adoption of the Takings Clause confirm that the drafters intended it to reach only appropriation. A comprehensive study found that James Madison, the author of the Fifth Amendment, intended the Takings Clause "to apply only to direct physical taking of property by the federal government."[17] The drafters apparently wrote this clause because colonial and early state legislatures had regularly taken property without paying any compensation, particularly by expropriating unimproved land for roads and impressing goods for military purposes. The Takings Clause prohibited the federal government from engaging in these hotly debated practices. It did not constrain the commonplace and politically accepted regulation of land use by state and local governments.

. . . .

For more than one hundred years after the adoption of the Fifth Amendment, judicial interpretation of the Takings Clause confirmed the narrow, historically grounded interpretation. Until 1922, virtually no court found a taking when regulation restricted use but amounted neither to outright expropriation nor to permanent physical occupation. The 1887 Supreme Court decision in *Mugler v. Kansas*[24] is the paradigm case. In *Mugler*, the Court stated the broad principle that a regulatory measure passed to protect the health, safety, and welfare of the public does not effect a taking, even if it severely diminishes the value of an owner's property. *Mugler* was no sport, but instead the leading decision of a line firmly entrenched before the advent of *Pennsylvania Coal* thirty-five years later.[26]

---

[17] William M. Treanor, *The Origins and Original Significance of the Just Compensation Clause of the Fifth Amendment*, 94 YALE L.J. 694, 711 (1985). Madison actually wrote in an essay published shortly after the Bill of Rights had been adopted that now the federal government was bound by the legal command that no property "shall be taken *directly*, even for public use, without indemnification of the owner." James Madison, *Property*, *in* THE MIND OF THE FOUNDER: SOURCES OF THE POLITICAL THOUGHT OF JAMES MADISON 179, 186-88 (Marvin Meyers ed., 1981).

[24] 123 U.S. 623 (1887).

[26] *See* Hadacheck v. Sebastian, 239 U.S. 394 (1915) (upholding a law barring the operation of a brick mill in a residential area); Miller v. Schoene, 276 U.S. 272 (1928) (upholding an order to destroy diseased cedar trees to prevent infection of nearby orchards); Goldblatt v. Hempstead, 369 U.S. 590 (1962) (upholding a law effectively preventing continued operation of a quarry in a residential area).

Mugler has sometimes been said to embody a "nuisance exception" to the general rule requiring compensation when regulation is too burdensome.[27] Such an anachronistic reading misinterprets *Mugler* in at least two ways: it incorrectly limits the holding of the case to common law nuisance, and it mistakes the general rule for an exception. . . .

. . . .

II

PENNSYLVANIA COAL IS A POORLY CONSIDERED DECISION
THAT OUGHT TO BE OVERRULED

The modern doctrine of regulatory takings sprang without obvious antecedents from the decision in *Pennsylvania Coal Co. v. Mahon*. Courts and commentators have looked back to Justice Holmes' decision as the touchstone for later doctrinal development—and as the origin of the immense confusion that engulfs contemporary takings law. In fact, it is a wretched decision, inadequately explained and having no foundation in precedent.

Pennsylvania Coal held unconstitutional the Kohler Act, a Pennsylvania statute that made it unlawful to mine coal beneath the property of another in such a way as to cause the collapse of the surface. The Pennsylvania Legislature had passed the Act in the wake of technological developments in coal mining that had led to the sinking of numerous dwellings, streets, churches, and railroad lines. Pennsylvania law had long treated support as a separate estate in land, distinct from surface ownership and mineral rights. Until passage of the Kohler Act, state law had permitted mining companies to sell surface lots while retaining the legal right to extract coal.

. . . .

Given the significance of the decision, the opinion by Justice Holmes is remarkably brief. Holmes gives little guidance as to the basis for his decision. He concedes that the government must be able to diminish property values to some extent in the course of regulation without paying compensation, but simply asserts that when the diminution reaches a certain magnitude, it exceeds implied limits, requiring the government to pay compensation. He suggests that judges must determine whether an economic loss is "too great" on the basis of the particular facts of each case and in light of the gravity of the public interest served.

Holmes' opinion is seriously defective in several respects. First, he gives no hint as to why he thinks *Mugler*, its state antecedents, and numerous Supreme Court antecedents were wrong or inadequate. . . .

Second, Holmes fails to address the related question as to what constitutional values the new rule may further. All he offers is the observation that, unless the power of government to diminish economic values in property is somehow limited, "the contract and due process clauses are gone."[61] But this is plainly untrue, since

---

[27] *See* Penn Cent. Transp. Co. v. City of New York, 438 U.S. 104, 144-46 (1978) (Rehnquist, J., dissenting) (characterizing *Mugler* as a "nuisance exception to the taking guarantee").

[61] *Pennsylvania Coal*, 260 U.S. at 413.

the Takings Clause would still require compensation in cases of appropriation or permanent physical invasion.

Third, although the decision appears to turn on the magnitude of economic harm suffered by the coal company, the opinion offers little insight into how great that harm was. For example, the decision evinces no attempt to quantify the loss in dollar figures. . . .

Fourth, the opinion is woefully inadequate in its appraisal of the legislative purpose of the Kohler Act. In the first half of his opinion, Holmes eccentrically insists on treating the case as a private dispute, as if the legislation were restricted to benefitting the Mahons. . . .

. . . .

III

THE REGULATORY TAKINGS DOCTRINE IS AN
UNWORKABLE MUDDLE

The regulatory takings doctrine has generated a plethora of inconsistent and open-ended formulations that have failed to make sense of the underlying constitutional impulse. No constitutional inquiry has generated more complaints or satire. The Court itself readily admits that its doctrine lacks coherence. . . .

. . . .

The confusion about the Takings Clause doctrine stems in the first instance from Holmes' refusal to provide a formulation of when land use regulations go too far. He insisted that every case must be considered on its own "particular facts" and briefly sketched the factors that influenced his judgment. However much such reticence suggests Holmes' jurisprudential sophistication, it has nonetheless pointed a disastrous pathway for his less subtle descendents.

. . . .

The doctrinal confusion . . . is neither incidental nor temporary. It arises from the immensity of the task that the Court has set for itself in regulatory takings cases: to mark as a matter of principle when limitation of property use becomes unfair. Not only have serious philosophers differed utterly in their approaches to these questions, but the trends of adjudication have changed so often over time that observers understandably view any answers as contingent. Moreover, the Constitution itself affords no guidance, except to proscribe outright confiscation. The Court simply does not have a basis in law, history, or consensual community standards to persuasively explain why one use restriction reflects the ordinary government adjustments of conflicting interests and another violates fundamental fairness.

IV

NO OTHER COUNTRY IN THE WORLD PROVIDES
CONSTITUTIONAL OR GENERAL PROTECTION FOR
THE "DEVELOPMENT VALUE" OF LAND

Proponents of robust judicial enforcement of regulatory takings tend to equate such a constitutional rule with protection of private property *per se*. The merest glance at the laws of other countries with firm commitments to the market and to private property reveals this assertion as specious. No other nation in the world suffers under a judicial claim of constitutional authority to determine whether any land use regulation is too onerous. Whether in the common law jurisdictions, European civil law jurisdictions, or the emerging nations of Eastern Europe and Asia, the law frankly accepts the necessity of extensive government regulation of land use. Other nations award compensation to owners only according to statutory standards or in cases of outright expropriation or reversal of site-specific planning permission. The peculiar importance of constitutional judicial review in general in the United States cannot explain the uniqueness of our approach to regulatory takings.

. . . .

V

FEDERAL COURT ENFORCEMENT OF THE REGULATORY TAKINGS
DOCTRINE AGAINST THE STATES UPSETS APPROPRIATE NOTIONS
OF FEDERALISM

As adopted, the Fifth Amendment posed no problem of federalism. It prohibited the federal government from appropriating land and other resources from citizens for a public purpose without paying compensation. An extension of the Takings Clause's prohibition to permanent occupation similarly did not abridge the power of a state. However, the incorporation of the Takings Clause into the Fourteenth Amendment obviously limits the authority of the states to appropriate or permanently occupy property. This is no small constraint on the states' discretion, but does not intrude on their basic lawmaking function; expropriation does not change any legal rules but merely transfers assets to the state. However, the application of the regulatory takings doctrine to the states impairs their authority to adjust the limits of property interests created by the states themselves. Such interference by federal courts in a traditional state function suggests, at the very least, the need for a stronger justification for the exercise of national power.

. . . .

Lucas v. South Carolina Coastal Council[155] illustrates the damage that results from this judicial intrusion into state property law. *Lucas* would require compensation whenever a land use regulation deprives an owner of all economic use unless the regulation duplicates a provision of nuisance law or of some other state common law property doctrine. Such a rule reverses the majoritarian premise of every state's constitution, namely, that legislation supersedes common law rules. In no other area of law does the federal Constitution subordinate state legislation to the common law and require the former to duplicate the latter.

. . . .

---

[155] 112 S. Ct. at 2886-2926.

VI

CHANGES IN THE SCOPE OF PROPERTY INTERESTS IN LIGHT OF
EVOLVING UNDERSTANDINGS OF THE PUBLIC INTEREST ARE A
CONTINUOUS AND APPROPRIATE FEATURE OF AMERICAN LAW THAT
OUGHT NOT RAISE SPECIFIC CONSTITUTIONAL CONCERNS

Property does provide security to the owners of resources, allowing them to
profit in the future from prudent investment and conservation decisions today. This
security has permitted private gains and made possible broad public benefits, such
as the increase in aggregate material welfare and the broad diffusion of economic
decisionmaking. But property rights have continuously evolved to accord with
social conceptions of public welfare.

. . . .

Evolution in values and needs reshapes the set of interests so protected without casting doubt on the continuing commitment to the *idea of property*. The
landlord's power to evict the tenant at the end of the lease term may wane; at the
same time, the right of a celebrity to exploit her public image waxes. To the extent
that strong enforcement of the regulatory takings doctrine succeeds, ironically, it
deprives the institution of property of its strong utilitarian support.

. . . .

VII

THE RECENT CONSERVATIVE DEPARTURES IN REGULATORY TAKINGS
DOCTRINE REFLECT AN ILLEGITIMATE ATTEMPT TO EMPLOY THE
CONSTITUTION TO ROLL BACK ENVIRONMENTAL REGULATION

Expansive interpretation of the regulatory takings doctrine has become the
focal point of efforts by a school of conservative jurists and political activists to
undermine the constitutional foundations of the regulatory state. The push to protect property rights has spawned both judicial innovation and legislative campaigns.
In my view, the underlying rationale for these endeavors is unpersuasive. The judicial intervention is illegitimate, and the lobbying effort legitimate but wrong-
headed.

. . . .

Lucas may be seen in retrospect as the high water mark of constitutional property rights inflation. Justices Kennedy and Souter declined to join the opinion, and
in the subsequent case of *Concrete Pipe & Products of California Inc. v. Construction Laborers Pension Trust for Southern California,*[190] the Court returned to
its traditional reluctance to displace legislative burdens. In the recent decision of
Dolan v. City of Tigard,[192] in which the Court held that a city's requirement that an
owner dedicate a strip of land for a greenway as a condition for approval of a construction project violated the Takings Clause, a bare majority joined the Chief Jus-

---

[190] 113 S. Ct. 2264 (1993).

[192] Dolan v. City of Tigard, 114 S. Ct. 2309 (1994).

tice's opinion. Moreover, that opinion emphatically affirmed the importance of local land use regulation. Finally, President Clinton's appointees to the Court are most unlikely to find regulatory takings to be a comfortable vehicle for judicial activism.

Of more immediate concern are recent decisions of the United States Court of Appeals for the Federal Circuit and the Court of Federal Claims, where the courts have found takings in denials of permits by the Army Corps of Engineers to fill wetlands.[196] These decisions have had a peculiarly strong influence for two reasons. First, these courts were created only in 1982, and until very recently all the appointments had been nominated by Republican presidents; thus, these courts are more likely than other federal courts to be receptive to takings claims. Second, the Supreme Court's clear indications that plaintiffs can press claims (in excess of $10,000) against the federal government for regulatory takings only through actions for compensation under the Tucker Act have given the Claims Court and the Federal Circuit exclusive federal jurisdiction over such cases. Thus, decisions of these courts will be controlling *de facto* in the federal system until reviewed by the Supreme Court.

. . . .

In the executive branch, President Reagan's Executive Order No. 12,630, issued in 1988, reveals the objectives of the property rights activists.[205] The order instructs agencies to assess the effect of proposed actions on constitutionally protected property rights. Such assessments are unlikely to generate much useful guidance, given the Supreme Court's repeated insistence that takings claims can be evaluated only in concrete applications to particular properties and upon a fully developed factual record. This order would amount to no more than a bit of harmless symbolism were it not for the highly partisan account of regulatory takings doctrine that the Executive order directs agencies to apply.

. . . .

. . . [A]ctivists have now turned their efforts toward passing various species of property rights legislation. Advocating generous statutory compensation for regulatory losses is, of course, a constitutionally legitimate project, but the legislation proposed is misguided for a host of reasons. What remains most disturbing about the legislative advocacy is the asserted rationale of securing constitutionally protected property rights. Many of the bills have sought to give a legislative base to the Executive order and its bogus takings doctrine. Others go beyond the order in mandating compensation whenever legislation reduces the market value of the "affected portion" of a property by as little as 20%. Such compensation would exceed that guaranteed by the Constitution by even more than does enforcement of the current judicial takings doctrine.

. . . .

---

[196] *See* Florida Rock Indus. v. United States, 791 F.2d 893 (Fed. Cir. 1986), *cert. denied*, 479 U.S. 1053 (1987); Loveladies Harbor, Inc. v. United States, 15 Cl. Ct. 381 (1988); Ciampetti v. United States, 18 Cl. Ct. 548 (1989).

[205] Exec. Order No. 12,630, 53 Fed. Reg. 8859 (1988).

VIII

THE REGULATORY TAKINGS DOCTRINE DOES NOT
ADVANCE ECONOMIC EFFICIENCY

The mere fact that government action imposes losses on a property owner does not justify compensation on economic grounds alone. If the government puts the property to a higher value use than the private owner would, then compensating the owner reduces aggregate efficiency, *ceteris paribus*. Apart from this simple point, there seem to be two types of arguments concerning whether compensation for takings promotes efficiency. The first focuses on how compensation affects the incentives of individual landowners, asking whether compensation keeps such takings from unduly discouraging valuable investments in land. The second focuses on the legislature or other regulator, asking whether a compensation requirement curbs a tendency to pursue projects without substantial public benefit.

The incentive effects of appropriation on owners have drawn a great deal of attention.[218] Some theorists have expressed concern that uncompensated takings will discourage owners, so that they will invest too little in wealth-creating enterprises.[219] . . .

Closer examination reveals serious doubts about the incentive effects of appropriation. The risk of loss from government action resembles many other risks that investors face and mitigate through insurance, such as the threat of fire. . . .

. . . .

In today's ideological wars, the argument that a compensation requirement reins in the lust of government to transfer wealth wastefully is even more common—but is equally flawed. The argument supposes that having to pay for the losses caused by regulation will limit a legislature to those projects that actually increase overall welfare. But . . . this argument is nonsensical.[231] A legislator who supports an appropriation of property in order to satisfy some special interest should welcome the requirement of compensation because such a payoff will blunt the ferocious opposition of the property owner and those who fear similar large losses. Property owners' opposition will often be more difficult for the legislator to face than the muted concerns of taxpayers who would absorb the diffused costs of compensating the property owners. . . .

. . . .

---

[218] My understanding of these issues owes a large debt to Daniel A. Farber, *Public Choice and Just Compensation*, 9 CONST. COMMENTARY 279 (1992), a lucid critique of the literature.

[219] *Id.* at 280-81.

[231] Farber, *supra* note 218, at 292-94.

IX

ABOLITION OF THE REGULATORY TAKINGS DOCTRINE WILL
NOT LEAD TO ANY FUNDAMENTAL UNFAIRNESS
TO OWNERS OF REAL PROPERTY

Perhaps the most common justification for the regulatory takings doctrine is that fairness and justice require that some losses imposed through regulation not be borne by the owner alone but be shifted to the public at large. Preventing fundamental unfairness has sometimes been a justification for the crafting of protective constitutional doctrines from the grand generalities of the Fourteenth Amendment. But eliminating the regulatory takings doctrine will not lead to the kinds of systematic or socially divisive losses that have been thought to justify other constitutional doctrines restraining the authority of democratic majorities. The point is not that there never can, nor ever will, be regulations that impose unfair burdens on some individuals, but that there is no constitutional basis for supposing that the political process cannot adequately address such cases.

. . . .

. . . Real property ownership in the United States is very widely dispersed, and property owners have the means to be—and are—very politically active in defense of their interests. Property owners are found in all political camps and coalitions. Furthermore, legislatures cater to the concerns of property owners. Local governments, which are dependent on property taxes to finance basic services, are ever eager to promote and preserve the aggregate value of local real estate. The point immediately seems belabored: no constitutional doctrine can be predicated on a failure of the political process to properly account for the interests of property owners.

. . . .

Other constitutional rules will prevent specific types of unfairness to landowners. Singling out a particular group to bear losses raises distinct problems dealt with by other constitutional doctrines. The rule treating a permanent physical invasion as a *de facto* appropriation might protect against cases where the government seeks to press property into a public use through regulation to avoid payment of compensation. Finally, the Due Process Clause may be interpreted to strike down laws that seek intentionally to avoid these restrictions or that fail reasonably to advance the public interest.

X

THE REGULATORY TAKINGS DOCTRINE PRECLUDES
EMERGING ECOLOGICAL UNDERSTANDINGS

Accumulating scientific research and analysis and the evidence of our own experience declare that contemporary patterns of human activity, including real estate development, severely damage particular ecosystems and the global biosphere. Prophetic voices have urged for some time now that owners must develop a new land ethic that does not undermine the environment. Legal scholars and activists have begun to incorporate these data and moral visions into proposals to reshape property law to restrict owners' authority to disrupt the land's ecological integrity and to elaborate owners' duty to preserve ecosystems for their own sake and for future generations.

Regulatory takings cases nearly always involve prohibitions on schemes to develop a site for profit or pleasure, not restrictions on existing uses. In constitutionalizing an owner's right to develop his land according to the promptings of the market, the courts have promulgated a doctrine that stands in stark conceptual opposition to emerging notions of green property. Abolition of the regulatory takings doctrine will permit reformulations of property and land use law to emerge incrementally and practically from the political process. This evolution must progress lest our descendants inherit a sick, degraded planet.

. . . .

ADDENDUM: DETERMINING COMPENSATION FOR REGULATORY
LOSSES IN THE LEGISLATIVE PROCESS—THE NEED FOR
FURTHER EXAMINATION

My contention that the Constitution cannot be made to yield a principled standard for determining when compensation should be paid for regulatory loss requires some discussion of how legislation should address the compensation issue. Since I have insisted that compensation for such losses must reflect political judgments about fairness and efficiency, it seems responsible to indicate what statutory base for compensation I think appropriate. . . .

. . . .

. . . [L]egislation can provide for compensation in a way that promotes justice to landowners without precluding substantive restrictions on use to secure environmental protection. I suggest that states and the federal government adopt statutes that confer property rights upon landowners once they have received site-specific regulatory permission for a development. A statute that did this could mandate compensation for losses imposed by subsequent changes in applicable requirements for, say, three years. Not only would such a statute protect owners against frustration of justifiable reliance upon regulatory permission, but it would shape those expectations *ex ante* to promote more socially beneficial behavior by both owners and regulators. In short, such a statute would be a sensible adjustment to the ubiquity of land use regulation rather than an attempt to destroy it.

. . . .

Never Jam To-day: On the Impossibility of Takings Jurisprudence

Jeanne L. Schroeder
84 Geo. L.J. 1531 (1996)[*]

"I'm sure I'll take *you* with pleasure!" the Queen said. "Twopence a week, and jam every other day."

Alice couldn't help laughing, as she said, "I don't want you to hire *me*—and I don't care for jam."

"It's very good jam," said the Queen.

"Well, I don't want any *to-day*, at any rate."

"You couldn't have it if you *did* want it," the Queen said. "The rule is, jam to-morrow and jam yesterday—but never jam *to-day*."

"It *must* come sometimes to 'jam to-day,'" Alice objected.

"No, it can't," said the Queen. "It's jam every *other* day: to-day isn't any *other* day, you know."

"I don't understand you," said Alice. "It's dreadfully confusing!"

"That's the effect of living backwards," the Queen said kindly: "it always makes one a little giddy at first—"[1]

The jurisprudence that has developed under the takings provisions of the Fifth[2] and Fourteenth[3] Amendments to the U.S. Constitution is a top contender for the dubious title of "most incoherent area of American law." A LEXIS search will produce hundreds of recent articles attempting to reconcile, critique, or condemn Supreme Court takings jurisprudence or to justify, reinterpret, or re-imagine the underlying theory of property.

This article will, therefore, spare the reader yet another exegesis of the case law of takings. Nor will I survey the literature on takings, if for no other reason than that it is so copious that it is impracticable to do so. Nor will I take either of the two dominant analytical approaches to takings: (1) the "conservative" approach, which accepts some form of traditional property jurisprudence and then proposes how to rationalize or reconcile the case law; or (2) the "progressive" approach, which argues for a substantial reconceptualization of property concepts on the grounds that the traditional approach is incoherent and/or an intolerable barrier to beneficial government regulation.

---

[*] Reprinted with permission of the publisher, Georgetown University and Georgetown Law Journal. © 1996.

[1] Lewis Carroll, *Through the Looking Glass and What Alice Found There*, in Alice's Adventures in Wonderland and Through the Looking Glass 145, 210 (1960).

[2] The Takings Clause reads "nor shall private property be taken for public use, without just compensation." U.S. Const. amend. V.

[3] The Takings Clause of the Fifth Amendment applies to the states by incorporation under the Fourteenth Amendment. *See* Chicago B. & Q.R.R. v. Chicago, 166 U.S. 226 (1897).

What I will do is, first, defend the coherence of the notion of property, the necessary role of private property rights in the actualization of human freedom and, therefore, the importance of protecting property rights from the government. Second, I will show the impossibility of an "objective" test or algorithm for when government regulation does or does not constitute a taking. Property is not a natural right but one which can exist only in an organized society. The determination of property's boundaries can be made only through pragmatic reasoning and will always be a matter of politics. As a result, the Takings Clause cannot alone accomplish the task traditionally assigned to it of serving as the bulwark that protects private rights from oppression by the public sphere of the state.

These two viewpoints are consistent because I do not approach property analysis from any of the classical liberal schools of political philosophy and jurisprudence or from a Marxian-influenced critique associated with many critical schools of thought. I adopt a property analysis based on the political philosophy of G.W.F. Hegel. This analysis explains what classical liberalism can identify only as an embarrassing paradox: private property is not itself a natural right of man but, nevertheless, is logically necessary for man's essential freedom.

In the retroactive logic of the Hegelian dialectic in which—as the White Queen put it—we live backwards, it is logically impossible to identify the moment at which the quantitative change of a diminution of property rights becomes the qualitative change of a destruction of property rights. Therefore, at any given moment we can only see that a taking either has not yet occurred, or has always already occurred. It is always jam tomorrow or jam yesterday, but never jam today. Consequently, because we cannot rely on logic to identify the exact moment when a regulation becomes a taking, we must turn to pragmatism to adopt general standards and prophylactic rules.

I shall show, however, that this difficulty is not only consistent with, but necessary to, Hegel's conception of freedom. The failed encounter of property law seen in the dialectics of takings reflects a general failure and negativity, which lies at the heart of subjectivity and law. And yet, it is precisely this negativity which opens up room for human freedom to actualize itself by going beyond the limit. Freedom cannot be bound by a pre-existing "objective" rule; we must always leave space for subjectivity.

I. Hegelian Property

Hegelian jurisprudence is not antiliberal, but extraliberal.[6] By this I mean that Hegel did not reject the principles of classical liberalism. Rather, he started his analysis with classical liberalism, but showed that it was incomplete. He agreed with liberals that individualism, autonomy, and negative liberty are true, authentic,

---

[6]   Hegel's theory of property is set forth in G.W.F. HEGEL, ELEMENTS OF THE PHILOSOPHY OF RIGHT (Allen W. Wood ed. & H.B. Nisbet trans., 1991) [hereinafter HEGEL, PHILOSOPHY OF RIGHT]. . . .

and fundamental aspects of human nature necessary for the actualization of human freedom. He argued, however, that they are not the *only* true and authentic aspects of human nature and, therefore, cannot be the *sufficient* conditions of freedom.

For Hegel, subjectivity—the capacity to bear legal rights—can only be achieved in what psychoanalytic philosopher Jacques Lacan called the "Symbolic"—the order of law and language. By this I mean that the Hegelian subject (the legal actor) and law are mutually constituting. It is precisely the moment of the institution of law as abstract right (which includes property and contract) that is the moment of the creation of legal subjectivity as intersubjectivity. That is, to Hegel, the abstract person in the "state of nature" is not yet a "subject" in the jurisprudential sense of a being capable of bearing legal rights and being bound by legal duties. The abstract person can only achieve this capacity (subjectivity) through relationships with other legal actors (subjects) who recognize him as one of their own (hence the term "intersubjectivity"). This means that although property does not pre-exist society pursuant to natural law, neither is it the mere creature of positive law. Freedom requires property, but property and law require each other. Consequently, unlike liberalism, freedom also requires society even as it requires autonomy.

. . . .

II. The Liberal Dilemma of Takings Law

A. PROPERTY AND THE CONSTITUTION

Clearly, the Framers of the U.S. Constitution thought that private property was essential to human liberty, or they would not have given it such extraordinary protection. As Jennifer Nedelsky explains, the Takings Clause was to stand as a barrier between politics and law, between the public and the private.[62] This is why Charles Reich in the 1960s thought he could protect welfare recipients from the capriciousness of the government by redefining their entitlements as "new property."[63]

The traditional role of property as the bastion of private rights against the onslaught of the public is most consistent with the Lockean liberalism of the Federalists. If property is a, or even the, natural or fundamental right of man, and if man entered into the social contract in order to protect his natural rights, then, by definition, a government must protect private property rights to be legitimate. The jurisprudential and political problem this raises is obvious: virtually all government regulation directly or indirectly affects property.

---

[62] . . . [Jennifer] Nedelsky, [Private Property and the Limits of American Constitutionalism: The Madisonian Framework and its Legacy (1990)] . . . , at 8; *see also* Jeremy Paul, *The Hidden Structure of Takings Law*, 64 S. Cal. L. Rev. 1393, 1409 (1991) . . . .

[63] . . . Charles A. Reich, *The New Property,* 73 Yale L.J. 733 . . . (1964).

. . . .

This becomes even more problematic when one reads into the Takings Clause the Madisonian definition of property, which included not only rights with respect to material things (such as land and cattle) and intangibles (such as debts and intellectual property) but also things that fall within the philosophical concept of "objects" such as our bodies and minds (i.e., our talents, opinions, religion, speech, etc.). Richard Epstein[65] and Robert Nozick[66] are no doubt correct that, if one were to adopt this extreme version of the Libertarian view of property, only the most minimalist state could be justified.

Classical liberalism, broadly understood, is by far the dominant political philosophy in this country, but radical libertarians, who believe that virtually all government regulations constitute takings, are certainly in the minority. But to every other school of liberalism, takings jurisprudence raises a paradox. . . .

 . . . .

Inevitably, takings jurisprudence requires that we draw some line between takings and legitimate exercises of the state's police power. The need to draw lines does not, however, in and of itself make takings jurisprudence uniquely difficult. Law requires us to draw lines all the time. We typically do this through positive law—whether formally adopted by the legislature, promulgated through case law, or developed informally through custom and practice. The uniqueness arises because the Takings Clause is supposed to be the vital barrier between the public and the private. Under liberal jurisprudence, however, the usual devices of positive law would seem inept for this task precisely because the Constitution is supposed to be above politics and positive law.

The chaotic state of the case law on takings jurisprudence suggests that the Supreme Court has so far been unable to do so. Commentators love to feast upon the irrationalities and inconsistencies of the precedents, and decry either the over-solicitousness toward vested interests or inattention to fundamental rights in one or another specific decision. Few critics, however, have ventured to offer a resolution.

 . . . .

F. QUALITY

 . . . .

Hegel argues that quantity and quality are dialectically related, identical yet different. Quantitative changes are gradual; qualitative changes are sudden. Something can have more or less of a Hegelian quantity, but it either has or does not have Hegelian quality. The Hegelian concept of the identity of identity and difference, however, means that quantitative change reveals itself as always already becoming qualitative change.

---

[65] *See* RICHARD EPSTEIN, TAKINGS: PRIVATE PROPERTY AND THE POWER OF EMINENT DOMAIN (1985).

[66] Nozick recognizes a natural right of property established by appropriation (either by the owner, or by transfer from a legitimate owner). *See* ROBERT NOZICK, ANARCHY, STATE, AND UTOPIA 150-53, 174-82 (1974). . . .

This means that it is logically necessary, on the one hand, that quantitative changes eventually become qualitative changes, yet, on the other hand, there can be no fixed point at which the change occurs. This is because (by definition) the identification of a specific point of transition is to assign a quality to the transition point. This does not solve the logical problem, it just replicates it. We have just substituted a different question of qualitative differentiation.

. . . .

. . . [Q]uality is the concept of identifying things in terms of that which they are not. It is, therefore, a setting of limits; a building of fences keeping some "things" on this side, and some "things" on the other side. If, as I have just posited, we can only identify a quality in terms of what it is not, then this means that to know the true quality of a thing, we must go beyond its limit. We must climb over the fence which proscribes a quality, see what is on the other side and then look back. In this sense, Hegel believes that logic itself requires that every time we confront a limit, we must exceed the limit.

The banal witticism "rules are made to be broken" is literally true to Hegel. The Hegelian paradox is precisely that limitation and finitude create the conditions of freedom and infinity. Freedom and necessity are, therefore, dialectically related. Freedom is the lack of limits, yet it is created by limits. Freedom is to not be bound by necessity, but limits necessitate that we seek to be free. That Hegel recognizes freedom as "the beyond of the limit" as not only a logical necessity, but an ethical mandate, is evidenced by the fact that he calls the demand to surpass all limits "the ought."[115]

. . . .

G. THE MOVEMENT OF SUBLATION

1. Negation and Preservation

The common misreading of the dialectic suppresses the preserving aspect of sublation beneath its negating aspect. It forgets that at the moment the self is negated and becomes identical to the other, it still remains differentiated and separate as the self. As property becomes nonproperty, it still always retains the notion of property. Nonproperty can only be understood in terms of property—that which it is not.

. . . .

2. Potentiality and Actuality

To those who are unfamiliar with the Hegelian dialectic, the concept of sublation and the suddenness of changes in quality versus the gradualism of changes in

---

[115] *See* [G.W.F. HEGEL, HEGEL'S SCIENCE OF LOGIC (A.V. Miller trans., 1969)] . . . , at 132-33. . . .

. . . .

quantity might be hard to understand. Some are hampered by having been taught a crude caricature of the dialectic as thesis, antithesis, and synthesis whereby the internal contradistinction of thesis and antithesis are obliterated when they are replaced by synthesis. This formula is designed more as a means to discredit Karl Marx (who adopted Hegel's method) than to understand philosophy. This is how I was introduced to it in high school.

Others might be hampered by the prejudice in our society that "contradictions" (like negativity) are bad things that can and must be eliminated. Consequently, it is easy to conclude that when Hegel identifies a contradiction in the abstract right of property he is making a judgment that property is somehow incoherent or bad and in need of replacement. Nothing could be more wrong. In the Hegelian dialectic, contradiction can not be bad and it can never be destroyed. Contradiction must be resolved, but each resolution necessarily creates a new contradiction. As a result, contradiction is not only a logically necessary aspect of the world, it is precisely that aspect of the world that creates change and dynamism.

Sublation is a process by which internal contradictions of earlier concepts are resolved, but not in the sense of the suppression of difference. The German word *Aufhebung* means, paradoxically, to preserve as well as negate. . . . In sublation, the earlier stage is always preserved because it is always a necessary moment in the development of the later. . . .

Sublation (i.e., synthesis) can never destroy the differentiation between self and other (thesis and antithesis) precisely because sublation is the recognition that at one moment self and other are the same even when at another moment they are truly different. . . .

. . . .

4. Sublation as Quantum Leap

Because sublation simultaneously maintains the distinction between two concepts while creating a unity, the movement of sublation cannot be gradual. It is a change in quality, rather than quantity. The change from quantity to quality is, to use the language of modern physics, a quantum leap. . . .

. . . .

. . . [I]t is not merely empirically difficult, it is logically impossible to identify the exact moment when quantitative change becomes qualitative change—that is, when it is no longer adequate to say there is more or less of something, and we must instead conclude that there has been a change of something into something else. We are always positioned either at the point where the change (i.e., in quality) has not occurred (when, in Lacanian terminology, it is the "not yet"), or after it has occurred (when it is "always already"), but never at the point of the transition itself because there is no such point.

In the words of the White Queen, in sublation, it is always jam yesterday and jam tomorrow, but never jam to-day.

III. Takings and Freedom

A. FREEDOM

But judges are forced to act "to-day." Hegel's abstract logic is impeccable, but Hegel always refuses to give the type of pragmatic advice needed by judges. How could he? He is trying to explain the nature of freedom—if he told us what to do, we would not be free.

On the one hand, there is a logically and intuitively recognizable qualitative distinction between property and no property. Moreover, a quantitative change in how much property one has is logically distinct from a qualitative change of having property to not having property. On the other hand, a quantitative diminution of property eventually becomes a qualitative change from property to no property. This is inherent in the logical nature of the concepts of quality and quantity. The problem in takings jurisprudence is that a declaration that a taking has occurred is precisely a judgment that the change of quantity in property has passed over into a change in quality. The relationship between possibility and actuality is traumatic. Also, according to Hegel, there is no *logical* way of identifying the moment when this occurs, because it either has not yet occurred, or it has always already occurred. This problem is why pragmatism is always the necessary corollary to Hegelian idealism.

The organization of our society is in large part based on a market economy and the institution of private property, which requires that we distinguish between property and no property. Consequently, we must make a pragmatic decision as to when we will declare that the dialectical passing of quantity into quality has occurred. To Hegel, pragmatic decisions cannot be decided by logic, but only by pragmatic reasoning. This can only be done by positive law (whether in the form of custom, judicial decision, legislation or whatever). This is probably why takings cases seem so illogical and "subjective." From a Hegelian perspective, this is necessarily true.

It is also why, from a Hegelian perspective, the observation that property is both logically prior to positive law (in that it is a necessary moment in the development of subjectivity and the actualization of human freedom), yet simultaneously subject to the defining restraints of positive law, is not a troublesome logical contradiction (as it is in the classical liberalism embodied in the Constitution). Most important, it suggests that, although property is necessary for the actualization of human freedom, property is ill-suited for the role traditionally ascribed to it by liberal philosophies to "serve[ ] . . . in the office of a wall, or as a moat defensive to a house,"[136] protecting private rights from government oppression.

---

[136] WILLIAM SHAKESPEARE, KING RICHARD II act 2, sc. 1.

B. TOTALITARIANISM

Because liberalism is based on the presumption of free, self-actuating, autonomous individuals pre-existing in some hypothesized state of nature, society and the state are defined as problems. They need to be justified in light of the individual's pre-existing natural rights and liberties. As we have seen, property and the Takings Clause are traditionally seen as ways of protecting the free individual *from* the state.

In contrast, Hegel believed that the presumption of the free individual is every bit as problematic as the justification of society or government. Although Hegel contingently started his political analysis in *The Philosophy of Right* with the Kantian-liberal concept of the abstract free person (self-consciousness as free will), he argued that the very internal logic of this concept means that the person cannot actualize the potential freedom that is the essence of personhood except in the complex social relations of the family, civil society, and the state. Rights such as property are not pre-existing or natural, but are human creations. This does not, however, mean that they are unauthentic or inessential. They are logically necessary for the actualization of potential freedom.

. . . .

The point for takings law is that although society demands both individualistic property rights and some communitarian limits on property rights, there is no logical algorithm that can determine the proper balance between the two. As we have discussed, the dialectical quantum leap between property and no property is simultaneously both not yet and always already from a *logical* standpoint. Since property is not a pre-existing natural right, but a human creation (albeit a necessary one), its limits can only be determined by humans.

Citizens, therefore, must be in a state of constant diligence, watching the government so that it does not (self-defeatingly) crush human freedom. This is not merely consistent with, but required by, the Hegelian concept of actualized freedom. Freedom cannot be actualized by passively submitting to a pre-existing Symbolic order. It requires a constant positive affirmation of its existence through the exercise of subjectivity through the active creation of law.

Hegel leaves this actualization of law as abstract right to positive law (*Gesetz*). As I have said, this can only be promulgated in the civil society and state on the basis of morality and ethical life. We must also consider who should make this pragmatic decision—the executive, the legislature, the judiciary, or the "people" (through constitutional amendment)?

The specific balance of rights will, by definition, be empirical and not logical. This is because as the actualization of freedom it will have to contain a purely subjective moment. If our actions were logically predetermined, then we would not be free. It will always, therefore, have an unsatisfyingly ad hoc or arbitrary aspect to it. There is no way around this. . . . [T]he fundamental thesis of Hegel is that the human condition is a failed encounter *by definition*. But it is precisely this "failure" or incompleteness that leaves a space, an opening, through which humans can and must constantly seek to actualize our freedom and subjectivity by always exceeding our limits.

IV. BELIEVE THE IMPOSSIBLE

> Alice laughed. "There's no use trying," she said: "one *can't* believe impossible things."
> "I daresay you haven't had much practice," said the Queen. "When I was your age I always did it for half-an-hour a day. Why sometimes I've believed as many as six impossible things before breakfast . . . ."[137]

Hegelian freedom is "the ought": the ethical and logical necessity of transcending the limit. According to sublative logic, it is always already and not yet. But it is never now. We can bear the deprivation of jam today only because of memories of jam yesterday, and the self-confidence that we will win jam tomorrow. Alice saw the White Queen's paradox as the impossible and she could not believe it. The White Queen understood that it followed from "living backward"—the retroactive logic of the dialectic. Of course Alice is only a child; she sees the White Queen as befuddled. But it is precisely the White Queen's understanding of, and belief in, the impossible that makes her sovereign and free.

---

[137] CARROLL, *supra* note 1, at 238.

At Last, the Supreme Court Solves the Takings Puzzle

Douglas W. Kmiec
19 Harv. J.L. & Pub. Pol'y 147 (1995)[*]

The purpose of the Takings Clause is "to bar Government from forcing some people alone to bear public burdens which, in all fairness and justice, should be borne by the public as a whole."[1] The Takings Clause thus serves as a fulcrum upon which private property interests are balanced against the State's police power. The balance is a difficult one to maintain because both property and the police power are indeterminate concepts whose interpretations change over time and from place to place. Federalism, which traditionally has left the definition of property to state common law, and separation of powers, which serves as a check in preventing the federal judiciary from usurping functions that are better left to majoritarian legislative determination, are two structural complexities that make maintaining this balance even more difficult.

Many commentators and practitioners, ranging from property rights advocates to police power hawks, have viewed the Supreme Court's takings cases as incoherent, piecemeal, or categorical. Some of the criticism is deserved, some not. Indeed, this Article will show that with the Court's decision in *Dolan v. City of Tigard*,[3] the Court largely has solved the takings puzzle. It has calibrated the property-police power balance in a way that has not been achieved, or even acknowledged, in other areas of economic regulation. Since *Lochner*[4] and the decline of substantive economic due process, the Court has been reluctant to review economic regulations in a meaningful way. The Court has been silent whenever there is any conceivable rational basis for the regulation, and often has been silent even when there appears to be no basis that is either conceivable or rational.

. . . .

With *Nollan v. California Coastal Commission*,[7] *Lucas v. South Carolina Coastal Council*,[8] and now *Dolan*, the Court has awakened to its responsibility

---

[*]   Copyright © 1995 by the Harvard Society for Law & Public Policy, Inc. Reprinted by permission. (The article's initial footnote, which has been omitted, indicates that "[a]n earlier version of this Article will appear in" an American Bar Association book. *See* Douglas W. Kmiec, Chapter 5—*At Last, the Supreme Court Solves the Takings Puzzle, in* TAKINGS: LAND-DEVELOPMENT CONDITIONS AND REGULATORY TAKINGS AFTER *DOLAN* AND *LUCAS* 107-118 (David L. Callies ed., 1996) (© 1996 American Bar Association).)

[1]   Armstrong v. United States, 364 U.S. 40, 49 (1960).

[3]   114 S. Ct. 2309 (1994).

[4]   Lochner v. New York, 198 U.S. 45 (1905) (the much-criticized high point of economic substantive due process).

[7]   483 U.S. 825 (1987).

[8]   112 S. Ct. 2886 (1992).

under the Takings Clause to ensure the maintenance of the property-police power balance. The Court's growing recognition that an objective standard exists by which it can responsibly check the legislative process while still respecting it explains this conquering of judicial timidity. This objective standard is not a spontaneous judicial creation, as is so much of the Court's most controverted case law, but it is the product of hundreds of years of refinement, on-going evaluation, and modification. Most importantly, the standard originates primarily at the state level, and thus is consistent with the federalist structure of the republic. This standard is none other than the common law.

In particular, it is the common law of nuisance that simultaneously defines the limits of individual property rights and outlines the general scope of the police power. Relatedly, the application of the common law of nuisance is consistent with the Constitution's original understanding[10] and is aimed at stability and order, rather than social engineering. This was implicit in *Mugler v. Kansas*,[11] in which the Court explained that the use of property may be limited by the law of the land, and thus allowed the State to deny without compensation the noxious use of producing and selling liquor. In *Village of Euclid v. Ambler Realty Co.*,[12] this understanding also was the basis of the express linkage of the police power to the *sic utere* maxim.[13] For the better part of this century, however, this understanding was lost. Wholesale schemes of wealth redistribution took hold, unfettered by a judiciary that was cowed into submission by a misstated notion of judicial restraint. In the property field, the Court mustered only the weak admonition that such economic regulation should not go "too far."[14] As recently as the late 1970s, the Court did no more than speculate about a set of ad hoc factors that might limit the police power and determine the threshold of a taking.[15]

. . . .

Loretto v. Teleprompter Manhattan CATV Corp.,[16] in which the Court held that a permanent, physical occupation always is a taking, was one of the first modern takings cases to reattach the takings analysis to the common law of property. Here, the categorical protection of the right to exclude others emerged from the common law's ancient protection against trespass. . . .

---

[10] *See* Douglas W. Kmiec, *The Original Understanding of the Taking Clause is Neither Weak nor Obtuse*, 88 COLUM. L. REV. 1630 (1988).

[11] 123 U.S. 623 (1887).

[12] 272 U.S. 365, 387 (1926).

[13] The maxim *sic utere tuo ut alienum non laedas* translates to "use your own property in such a manner as not to injure that of another." Keystone Bituminous Coal Ass'n v. DeBenedictis, 480 U.S. 470, 492 (1987).

[14] Pennsylvania Coal Co. v. Mahon, 260 U.S. 393, 415 (1922) (explaining that if a regulation goes "too far" it will be recognized as a taking).

[15] *See* Penn Cent. Transp. Co. v. City of New York, 438 U.S. 104, 126-30 (1978).

[16] 458 U.S. 419 (1982).

As significant as *Loretto*'s reminder was, its practical application was limited, because not much land use regulation directly depended upon physical occupation, and so very few cases fit into *Loretto*'s bright-line rule. Thus, neither the Court nor land use players realized how directly the analytical line based on the common law of property connected the per se rule of *Loretto* with *Nollan* and its "essential nexus" test.[18] . . .

With *Nollan*, the Court returned to a sounder course, defining property and the police power in relation to a state's common law. The Court's emphasis upon a formulation requiring a regulation "substantially advancing a legitimate governmental interest," as distinct from the reasonableness or rational basis standards applied in other economic contexts and in prior cases, was the legal equivalent of a surveyor restaking parcel corners that had become hidden by overgrowth. And, of course, like neighbors who had grown accustomed to a bigger yard because of the unmarked lot line, police power hawks groused about *Nollan*'s seeming break with precedent. However, it was the intervening diminution in value cases that were the aberration from the common law balancing of private and public interests.

Although *Nollan* returned to the common law to define the limit of property and the police power, its version of a takings test was not applied easily to all situations. *Nollan*'s primary requirement that there be an essential nexus between regulatory means and ends failed to convey its important reassertion of the common law definition of property and police power, because a tight nexus between means and ends still left any nexus with a particular landowner unaddressed. . . . Land use regulators concluded that all that was required to meet the *Nollan* test was a facile matching of regulatory means and ends. . . .

Or so it mistakenly was thought. However, a critical part of the story is missing. *Lucas v. South Carolina Coastal Council*[26] is that part. . . . Calling upon the harm-benefit distinction of common law nuisance, South Carolina declared Lucas's homebuilding plans on a barrier island to be a harm. The Court partially agreed with South Carolina in 1,575,000[27] ways that the State now regrets.

Yes, said the Court in *Lucas*, the harm-benefit distinction does matter—but Justice Brennan stated in *Penn Central Transportation Co. v. City of New York* that one person's harm is another's benefit.[28] Thus, the distinction must be connected not to landowner or regulator assertion, but to the objective reality of the state's common law. To justify its regulation and refusal to pay compensation, South Carolina had

---

[18]   *See* Nollan v. California Coastal Comm'n, 483 U.S. 825, 837 (1987).

[26]   112 S. Ct. 2886 (1992).

[27]   The Court agreed with South Carolina only to the extent that it could prove that Mr. Lucas's homebuilding plans were a nuisance-like activity not part of his antecedent title. South Carolina did not make this proof on remand, but rather entered into a negotiated settlement whereby Mr. Lucas received $425,000 for each of his two lots and $725,000 in interest, attorneys' fees, and costs. South Carolina later resold Mr. Lucas's property to another developer for $785,000. *See* Douglas W. Kmiec, *Clarifying the Supreme Court's Taking Cases—An Irreverent but Otherwise Unassailable Draft Opinion in* Dolan v. City of Tigard, 71 DENV. U. L. REV. 325, 330 (1994) ("Apparently, however, it's no fun regulating if it's not for 'free'"); H. Jane Lehman, *Accord Ends Fight Over Use of Land; Property Rights Activists Gain in S.C. Case*, WASH. POST, July 17, 1993, at E1.

[28]   *See* Penn Cent. Transp. Co. v. City of New York, 438 U.S. 104, 133 n.30 (1978).

to show by antecedent inquiry that what Mr. Lucas planned to do never was part of his common law property bundle in the first place.

With this one bold stroke, the Court solved the takings puzzle. The *Lucas* decision seemingly returned the land use power to its roots as a reasonable codification of the *sic utere* principle, the law of nuisance. As Justice Sutherland predicted in *Euclid*, this principle is a "helpful clew" for determining the acceptable scope of the police power in relation to private property.[29] . . .

It is possible to argue that *Lucas* was an incomplete acknowledgment of federalism because it accepted the property definition implicit in state common law, while rejecting (or at least limiting) its redefinition by state or local legislation.[31] But this is nothing more than the recognition that under the Constitution the state police power always is bounded by private right. . . .

The *competence* of state courts in striking a proper balance between individual rights and majoritarian desire is manifest in traditional nuisance analysis, which gradually develops within a precedential system of law that invites reliance, investment, and initiative. By contrast, state legislative bodies, or their local delegates, are not limited by prior decision or enactment and are highly responsive to the shifting interests of their political constituencies. . . . No state or local legislative body can appraise fairly and balance neutrally public desire and private right. . . .

Nuisance determinations are both local and dynamic. If the aphorism "all politics are local" is correct, surely it applies to political efforts to reallocate property, which are necessarily local. A house on a barrier island susceptible to erosion and hurricane gales is not the equivalent of a house on the prairie in Kansas. So too, as the subtleties of local ecology are better understood by modern science and incorporated into local conceptions of harm, the house built yesterday may not be the equivalent of the house built today.

Some landowners may think this concession to the dynamic understanding of reality advantages the State too greatly. Yet, even with this dynamism, the fairness of looking to the state judiciary to sort out competing private and public claims is evident. The *Lucas* opinion enhances that fairness in two ways. First, *Lucas* places the burden of establishing that a landowner's use is nuisance-like on the State, which has the best means of appraisal of its regulatory interests and the greatest incentive to demonstrate any private incompatibility with them. Second, *Lucas* properly reserves some federal supervision of state nuisance determinations. Ripeness and abstention doctrines will hold these occasions to a minimum, but the fact that the Takings Clause is a *federal* assurance of property rights means that such occasions cannot be nonexistent. . . .

---

[29] . . . 272 U.S. 365, 387 (1926).

[31] In *Lucas*, the Court stated that to prevail South Carolina had to "identify background principles of nuisance *and property law* that prohibit the uses" of Mr. Lucas's homebuilding. Lucas v. South Carolina Coastal Council, 112 S. Ct. 2886, 2901-02 (1992) (emphasis added). Does the reference to "property law" beyond nuisance include state legislative limitations on use? Perhaps. Clearly, it would be circular to include the very legislative limitation under challenge. On the other hand, well-established legislative limitations in place at the time of acquisition have a better claim for being included (and thus narrowing a landowner's property law bundle), especially if they reinforce or reasonably extend a common law nuisance limitation.

Nuisance law is imprecise. However, despite this imprecision, it is clear that common law nuisance can govern the constitutional acceptability of land use regulation. The imprecision cannot be denied, because it is at the heart of the concepts of property and the police power. Neither property nor the police power is an absolute right; each evolves in context and over time. The state courts are in the best position to monitor the evolution of these two concepts, and the federal courts—by recognizing property as largely defined by an "independent source such as state law,"[40] nuisance—are in the best position to assay any takings claim that results from this evolution. This remains true whether the dispute arises out of a state or a federal regulation.

Lucas should have decided *Dolan*.[41] It did, but not as explicitly or definitively as it might have. On the surface, *Dolan* appears to extend the nexus analysis begun in *Nollan*. As the Court noted in *Nollan*, the nexus required must connect not only regulatory means and ends, but also the need for a particular regulatory imposition on a particular landowner. Complaints abound about the imprecision of the Court's "rough proportionality" language, but the Court's language is precise enough to convey two unmistakable points: the government has the burden of justifying its regulation, and the justification must be reconciled with the common law of property. The greenway dedication failed for the same reason the *Loretto* cable box failed—the right to exclude holds an important place in the common law definition of property. The bikepath dedication failed because there was no relationship between the landowner's activity and the public purpose sought to be furthered. The common law does not impose an affirmative obligation without cause.

Lucas and *Dolan* are siblings. When the takings analysis in *Dolan* is linked to the search for causation, it also is linked to the takings analysis in *Lucas* premised upon the common law definition of property. A landowner is not the proximate cause of a public land use problem, and by similar reasoning no public harm is created, by the landowner undertaking a common law use. We may want our neighbors to furnish bikepaths, beautiful buildings, or open space for an aesthetic view, and the charitable impulse may prompt individual landowners to make these welcome contributions to their communities. The rule of law, however, secures private land from public confiscation for these purposes.

Although *Dolan* and *Nollan* are rooted in the common law analysis announced in *Loretto* and made explicit in *Lucas*, these cases appear to continue an unfortunate contextual limitation. The facts of *Nollan*, *Dolan*, and *Lucas* nominally confine the Court's resolution of the takings puzzle to either property concession or total diminution in value cases. Both factors are remnants of the outdated "too far" or ad hoc approach, and both now deserve outright repudiation by the Court.

---

[40] Board of Regents v. Roth, 408 U.S. 564, 577 (1972).

[41] For a suggested alternative opinion written and published *before* the case was decided, see Kmiec, *supra* note 27 (arguing that the *Dolan* easement is compensable because it effects a total deprivation of a state-law recognized portion of the Dolans' land, and that the required dedications did not inhere in the owners' title).

There is no constitutional basis for confining the *Lucas* analysis or the derivative *Dolan* and *Nollan* nexus analysis to cases of complete value deprivation or property concession. The Court implicitly recognized this by vacating and remanding a case involving fee exaction.[43] The common law of property recognizes property in many forms, physical and monetary; specious arguments should not obscure this point. Therefore, the Court arguably was mistaken in including dicta in *Dolan* suggesting that the "rough proportionality" standard might not be applicable to general land use limitations. It is error to conclude that land concessions, fee exactions, and total deprivations differ in kind from garden variety land use restriction—they differ in degree only. Concessions, exactions, and total deprivations involve matters of diminution in value, which, unlike the common law of property, are not at the explanatory heart of the purpose of the Takings Clause.

The diminution in value formulation may forestall temporarily the Court's recognition that *Loretto*, *Nollan*, *Lucas*, and *Dolan* are all of a piece; the odd man out is *Penn Central* and its distant ancestor, *Pennsylvania Coal*. The later cases convert diminution in value, at the core of *Penn Central*, into a side issue or an early surrogate for the more searching inquiry into whether the police power has been asserted in league with, or opposition to, the common law. Even *Penn Central* recognized diminution in value as a side issue with its reference to "reasonable investment-backed" expectations. These expectations are formed largely in reference to state common law. If the Court is to find the proper denominator for the loss calculation fraction, the answer is to be found in such reasonably formed expectations.

The *Penn Central* position that landowners cannot conceptually sever their property for purposes of demonstrating regulatory loss will not hold. It should not hold because it is fundamentally at odds with the common law nature of property in which expectations often (but not always) are formed with respect to discrete aspects or segments of property. . . .

Although there is no constitutional limitation preventing the Court from removing the anti-conceptual severance or general use regulation exceptions from the Court's successful balancing of the property and the police power, there is a pragmatic one: the limited nature of judicial resources. It will take time, but several factors should help the Court meet this concern. First, the standard for a taking claim to be ripe for review is high. Second, state common law already is developing in ways that give greater identification and precision to the property segments that in proper cases should form the denominator against which to measure loss.[46] Once this happens, it is a minor step to the recognition that general use limitations can result in compensable losses every bit as much as property invasions, concessions, exactions, or total deprivations.

---

[43] *See* Ehrlich v. Culver City, 114 S. Ct. 2731 (1994). . . .

. . . .

[46] *See* DOUGLAS W. KMIEC, ZONING AND PLANNING DESKBOOK § 7.02[5][b] (1995) and cases cited therein. The Federal Circuit also has begun to outline factual circumstances in which a discrete segment may be the relevant focus of analysis. *See* Loveladies Harbor, Inc. v. United States, 28 F.3d 1171 (Fed. Cir. 1994); KMIEC, *supra*, at § 7.02[5][a].

The takings puzzle has been solved. Of course, its specific applications always will remain contentious. As with other features of our constitutional system, a "machine that would go by itself,"[47] takings analysis is subject to constant push and counterpush; so too, the destiny of the countervailing property and police power forces. *Dolan* is a modern work of genius anchored in the common sense of the ancient (yet dynamic) principle of the common law. The Supreme Court worked its way out of a judicially complacent posture that was as untenable as it was dangerous to the importance of the preservation of property to the republic. In this, the members of the present Court likely would attribute the resolution of the takings puzzle less to themselves than to those who "built better than they knew," the Framers of our Constitution.

Note

Professor Kmiec further analyzes regulatory takings in Douglas W. Kmiec, *Inserting the Last Remaining Pieces into the Takings Puzzle*, 38 Wm. & Mary L. Rev. 995 (1997).

---

[47] *See generally* MICHAEL G. KAMMEN, A MACHINE THAT WOULD GO BY ITSELF (1986).

PART IV

PARTICULAR LAND USE PROBLEMS

This part treats several vexing land use problems. Some have been touched upon previously in this anthology.

A. Discrimination

FROM JUNKYARDS TO GENTRIFICATION: EXPLICATING A RIGHT TO PROTECTIVE ZONING IN LOW-INCOME COMMUNITIES OF COLOR
Jon C. Dubin
77 Minn. L. Rev. 739 (1993)[*]

INTRODUCTION

Last year marked the seventy-fifth anniversary of comprehensive zoning[1] in the United States and the sixty-fifth anniversary of the United States Supreme Court's approval of zoning as a valid exercise of the police power in *Village of Euclid v. Ambler Realty Co.*[2] More specifically, *Euclid* upheld the general principle of using the police power to separate incompatible uses and to protect residential uses and residential environments from the pressures of growth and industrialization. Relying on analogies to nuisance doctrine, Justice Sutherland declared that "[a] nuisance may be merely a right thing in the wrong place, like a pig in the parlor instead of the barnyard."[4] Thus, the concerns over health, safety, and the general welfare that are embodied in the police power were properly extended through the device of zoning to protect single-family residences from the encroachment of commerce and industry.

---

[*] © 1993. Reprinted by permission.

[1] The New York City Board of Estimate and Apportionment passed what is generally agreed to be the first comprehensive or well-rounded zoning ordinance on July 25, 1916. . . .

[2] 272 U.S. 365 (1926). . . .

[4] *Euclid*, 272 U.S. at 388.

Prior to *Euclid*, municipalities had not only used zoning and residential district laws to segregate uses deemed undesirable but also to mandate racially segregated residential patterns. Notwithstanding judicial invalidation of many of these practices, significant segregated residential patterns remain as a legacy of discriminatory zoning and land use planning.

Although much litigation and scholarship has focused on the myriad exclusionary zoning and land use planning devices that are responsible for creating and perpetuating residential segregation, another invidious legacy of *Euclid* has gone largely unnoticed. Minority communities, which were often established as separate communities as the result of discriminatory zoning and planning devices, are then frequently deprived of the land use protection basic to Euclidean zoning principles.
. . .

Professor Rabin labeled the practice of superimposing incompatible zoning on communities of color "expulsive zoning," observing that the net effect of the practice is a piecemeal replacement of residents with the superimposed uses and their owners.[11] The imposition of incompatible zoning occurs through lower-grade zoning or zoning authorizing noxious commercial or industrial uses which undermine the quality of the residential environment and discourage continued residencies. Residents deprived of zoning protection are vulnerable to assaults on the safety, quality, and integrity of their communities ranging from dangerous and environmentally toxic hazards to more commonplace hazards, such as vile odors, loud noises, blighting appearances, and traffic congestion.

Higher-grade zoning, zoning or planning measures that induce certain higher-quality residential or other uses can produce similar incompatible and disruptive results. These higher-cost uses create market pressures that effectively price out existing low-income residents through the process of gentrification.[13] Residents subjected to incompatible upzoning face the prospect of involuntary displacement and the functional and psychological trauma of dislocation and perhaps homelessness.

This Article explores the history, development, and legal ramifications of government's failure to provide protective zoning to low-income communities of color. . . .

---

[11] *See* Yale Rabin, *Expulsive Zoning: The Inequitable Legacy of* Euclid, *in* ZONING AND THE AMERICAN DREAM 101, 101 (Charles M. Haar & Jerold S. Kayden eds., 1989).

[13] As Judge A. Leon Higginbotham explains:
Gentrification is a term used in land development to describe a trend whereby previously "underdeveloped" areas become "revitalized" as persons of relative affluence invest in homes and begin to "upgrade" the neighborhood economically. This process often causes the eviction of the less affluent residents who can no longer afford the increasingly expensive housing in their neighborhood. Gentrification is a deceptive term which masks the dire consequences that "upgrading" of neighborhoods causes when the neighborhood becomes too expensive for either rental or purchase by the less affluent residents who bear the brunt of the change.
Business Ass'n of Univ. City v. Landrieu, 660 F.2d 867, 874 n.8 (3d Cir. 1981) . . . .

I. HISTORICAL AND LEGAL BACKGROUND

A. RACIAL ZONING

Although the earliest reported case of explicit racial zoning involved San Francisco's expulsive anti-Chinese ordinance in 1890, the primary focus of early racial zoning provisions was not expulsion but exclusion and the separation of the black and white races. Shortly after the turn of the century, when legally enforced segregation approached its zenith, several southern and border cities enacted strict racial zoning ordinances designating separate residential districts for whites and blacks. Such ordinances were a response to the mass migration of southern rural blacks to the cities and to white residents' fears of racial amalgamation. Baltimore passed the first such ordinance in 1910 and within six years more than a dozen cities followed suit.

In 1917, the Supreme Court addressed the constitutionality of racial zoning in *Buchanan v. Warley* in a challenge to a Louisville, Kentucky ordinance.[21] Although the Court invalidated the Louisville ordinance, the peculiar facts of the case and the limited holding rendered the decision more a pronouncement on the primacy of property rights than a rejection of the premises underlying the enforced separation of the races.

. . . .

B. THE *EUCLID* CASE AND THE CONCEPT OF PROTECTIVE ZONING

. . . .

The Euclidean conception of protective use zoning—creating balkanized districts and categories of uses—has been widely criticized over the years as rigid, overinclusive, unsophisticated, and ill-suited to the realities of present-day urban development. Nevertheless, the Euclidean concept of using the police power to protect the quality of the residential environment from the negative by-products of incompatible uses has persevered both through zoning and through alternative, more sophisticated, land-use controls.

C. RACIAL ZONING AND PLANNING POST-*EUCLID*

By extending the police power to protective "use" zoning, the Supreme Court weakened the doctrinal underpinnings of *Buchanan*. Several localities, emboldened by *Euclid*'s liberation of the police power and responding to the continuing fear of racial amalgamation, embarked on a new round of racial zoning in open defiance of *Buchanan*. Although the Supreme Court reaffirmed *Buchanan* twice shortly after *Euclid*, it did so in unusually short *per curiam* opinions that failed to supply reasoning or moral suasion to the principled distinction between protective "use" zoning and apartheid. Thus, several localities continued to enforce racial zoning ordinances for many years thereafter.

---

[21]   245 U.S. 60 (1917).

With the eventual decline of racial zoning, numerous alternative segregative land use controls flourished. The use of racially restrictive covenants mushroomed during the 1930s and 1940s, particularly in the northern, western, and mid-western regions of the country. This practice was consistent with *Buchanan*'s limited freedom of contract rationale and initially enjoyed at least tacit Supreme Court approval.[51] Notwithstanding the Supreme Court's later extension of the state action concept to judicial enforcement of these covenants and its concomitant invalidation of the practice on equal protection grounds in 1948,[52] white property owners continued to attempt to enforce these covenants up to the early 1960s. The present day segregative consequences of this practice are manifest.

The federal government was also deeply involved in the development of discriminatory land use policies. The Federal Housing Administration (FHA) and the Veterans Administration (VA), which provided mortgage insurance to enable low, moderate, and middle-income families to obtain low- or no-down-payment mortgages, adopted policies promoting segregation in insured housing. . . .

Although the FHA adopted a policy of equal opportunity by the early 1950s, it did not even begin to address its acquiescence in the discriminatory practices of participating private lenders until 1968.[59] . . .

While the federal homeownership assistance programs promoted the creation of homogeneous white suburbs, the federal public housing program for low-income families with children facilitated the development of segregated and locationally deficient black inner city neighborhoods. From the public housing program's inception in 1937, tenants were assigned to projects on a segregated basis, with many black projects located in slums. . . .

Although Title VI of the 1964 Civil Rights Act outlawed discrimination in publicly funded programs, the Department of Housing and Urban Development (HUD) did not promulgate regulations requiring the siting of new housing in viable neighborhoods and on a non-segregated basis until 1972. This legacy of discrimination resulted in the current prevalence of separate and inferior public housing for low-income African-American families.

. . . [T]he Federal Slum Clearance and Urban Renewal Program, further exacerbated black land use inequality. Designed for the ostensibly benign purpose of eliminating urban blight, federal slum clearance uprooted and dislocated thousands of black households and then confined the displacees to segregated and inferior relocation housing. Federal highway projects produced similar results.

---

[51] *See* Corrigan v. Buckley, 271 U.S. 323, 331 (1926) (dismissing challenge of racial covenants for want of jurisdiction).

[52] *See* Shelley v. Kramer, 334 U.S. 1 (1948). . . .

[59] . . . Similarly, while the post-war VA program had adopted a policy of racial neutrality, the agency did not attempt to stop lenders whose loans it guaranteed from discriminating on the basis of race. . . .

Local governments' exclusionary zoning laws remain a significant ongoing land use planning impediment to African-American residential mobility. These zoning enactments create financial barriers to residential access virtually as effective in operation as the explicitly racial laws invalidated in *Buchanan*. Exclusionary zoning and planning techniques have been described as both "innumerable and interchangeable"[72] and include a plethora of devices that increase the cost of housing, impede the development of low-cost or subsidized housing, or preclude or discourage residential housing altogether.

Because of the historic and continuing disproportionately low income and wealth levels of African-American households, these zoning devices present seemingly insurmountable obstacles to residential access to all but a handful. Indeed, courts have recognized the racially disparate consequences of these practices.

D.   SEPARATE COMMUNITIES: UNEQUAL ZONING PROTECTION

Discriminatory zoning practices have created and perpetuated separate residential communities for African-Americans. . . .

Because government-approved, or *de jure*, segregation had its genesis in theories of white supremacy, it is not surprising that *de facto* inequality often followed separateness. . . .

"Separate" has also meant "unequal" in the land use area. Indeed, the Kentucky Supreme Court, in upholding the racial zoning ordinance at issue in *Buchanan*, specifically acknowledged that the ordinance might confine blacks to less desirable parts of the city.[84] . . .

. . . .

Inequality also followed separateness in the public housing program. . . .

Apart from land use controls that placed blacks in residentially inferior environments, governments have also engaged in practices that diminish the quality of life for the residents within African-American communities. These practices include the provision of inferior municipal services, selective use of annexation and boundary line changes to disenfranchise and deny services to black residents, inequitable relocation or non-location of important public institutions, regressive and disparate property tax assessments, encouragement of mortgage and insurance redlining, and the disproportionate displacement of African-American families through urban renewal, highway, and local redevelopment projects.

The disparate denial of protective zoning to African-American communities is another unequal vestige of segregative land use controls. While few cases have directly challenged the lack of protective zoning, numerous cases refer to the prevalence of incompatible uses and zoning in African-American residential areas.

. . .

. . . .

---

[72] RICHARD F. BABCOCK & FRED P. BOSSELMAN, EXCLUSIONARY ZONING, LAND USE REGULATION AND HOUSING IN THE 1970s 7 (1973).

[84] Harris v. City of Louisville, 177 S.W. 472, 476 (Ky. 1915), *rev'd sub nom.* Buchanan v. Warley, 245 U.S. 60 (1917).

. . . City planners deliberately displaced black residences with industrial and commercial zoning or used incompatible zoning to confine black residents to particular portions of a city.

In other cases the relatively common practice of overzoning for industrial use due to the income-generating potential of industrial development (and the wishful thinking of city planners) may have formed the impetus behind the disparate denial of protective zoning. As Professor Rabin observed in his twelve-city study of expulsive zoning, "where those grandiose [industrial development] expectations exceeded the capacity of existing vacant land, they were often superimposed on developed black residential areas."[107] . . .

. . . .

E. ZONING AND ENVIRONMENTAL RACISM

With the emerging recognition of the problem of "environmental racism," the relative powerlessness of African-American communities is often a prominent factor in zoning and siting decisions. As environmental sociologist Robert Bullard observed, "toxic dumping and the siting of locally unwanted land uses (LULUs) have followed the 'path of least resistance.'"[112] Because residents of white neighborhoods marshall substantial resources to divert LULUs somewhere else, "these LULUs usually end up in poor, powerless black communities rather than in affluent suburbs."[113] . . .

. . . .

F. ZONING AND GENTRIFICATION

Zoning that significantly increases the cost of retaining housing can be as disruptive to the residents of low-income communities of color as zoning that degrades their environment. The eventual consequence of such zoning and planning measures is the displacement of low-income residents through the process of gentrification, a process that has been labeled "suburbanization in reverse" or "reverse exclusionary zoning."[133] Gentrification has affected a significant and increasing number of African-American families. Although gentrification-induced displacement usually exacts a heavy toll on all dislocated families, African-American families priced out of their own housing must confront the additional obstacles involved in seeking affordable relocation housing in a scarce and discriminatory private housing market. These obstacles are sometimes compounded by the efforts of the new residents or "gentry" who, in the name of integration, obstruct the devel-

---

[107] Rabin, *supra* note 11, at 107. . . .

[112] ROBERT D. BULLARD, DUMPING IN DIXIE: RACE, CLASS, AND ENVIRONMENTAL QUALITY 4 (1990).

[113] *Id.* at 5, 85-86. . . .

[133] *See* Harold A. McDougall, *Gentrification: The Class Conflict over Urban Space Moves into the Courts*, 10 FORDHAM URB. L.J. 177, 180 (1982) . . . .

opment of new subsidized housing which could permit displaced residents to resettle in their old neighborhoods.

Zoning and planning measures that stimulate gentrification also have been rationalized in the name of community development. Frequently the affected communities, having been redlined for years, possess a dire need for an increased tax base, improved services, and jobs. The benefits of these government-induced private revitalization and economic development efforts often have not accrued to the original residents of the affected communities. As a result, an increasing number of low-income communities of color have challenged these measures, arguing that government has a duty to improve the neighborhoods without removing their residents.

. . . .

G. Zoning and Hispanic Communities

The historic and continuing practices of officially sanctioned zoning and land use discrimination are perhaps most pervasive and well-documented as they pertain to African-American communities. . . .

Nevertheless, other communities of color—in particular, Puerto Rican and Mexican-American communities [hereinafter hispanics]—have similarly experienced substantial governmental discrimination. Although there are no accounts of explicit racial zoning ordinances directed against these groups, racial covenants were employed extensively against hispanics in the West and Southwest. Public housing site and tenant selection and urban renewal policy have also served to confine hispanics to segregated and inferior housing.

Residential opportunities for hispanics have also been constricted by racial discrimination in the private housing market. Private market studies reveal that hispanics, particularly those who are dark-skinned, suffer substantial private housing discrimination. Because of their extreme poverty, hispanics, like African-Americans, are particularly vulnerable to exclusionary zoning and similar measures that limit residential opportunities by increasing the cost of housing.

Governments have also engaged in conduct that has diminished the quality of the residential environment within hispanic communities. This conduct includes the failure to provide adequate basic municipal services, the relocation or non-location of important public institutions, and incompatible zoning. . . . Finally, hispanic communities have also been subjected to the two modern-day land use threats discussed herein: the disparate siting of environmentally degrading uses and government-induced gentrification.

II. THE RIGHT TO PROTECTIVE ZONING

A. The Premature Demise of Municipal Services Equalization Litigation

As discussed in Part I, appropriate zoning protection is a critically important government service in determining the quality of a community's residential environment. The disparate denial of zoning protection, as with the denial of other important government services and benefits, implicates the protections of anti-discrimination and due process law.

The Fifth Circuit's decisions in *Hawkins v. Town of Shaw*[174] represent the high-water mark in judicial efforts to secure equality in the provision of municipal services for communities of color. In *Hawkins*, black residents of a Mississippi Delta town characterized by virtual one hundred percent residential segregation challenged extreme disparities in the provision of basic municipal services. Blacks occupied nearly ninety-eight percent of the homes that fronted on unpaved streets and ninety-seven percent of the homes lacking sanitary sewers. The black community was similarly deprived of surface water drainage, street lighting, water mains, and fire hydrants.

Accepting the undisputed statistical evidence of disparities in services, the district court nonetheless ruled against the plaintiffs. . . .

On appeal, Judge Tuttle's opinion for the panel's majority evinced immediate recognition of the nature and character of underserved communities such as plaintiffs' neighborhood. . . .

Although he accepted the lower court's factual finding that the gross disparities in services did not result from purposeful discrimination, Judge Tuttle provided a sweeping rejection of the district court's standard for evaluating those disparities. He reasoned that discriminatory intent or motive did not have to be directly proven, concluding that "we now firmly recognize that the arbitrary quality of thoughtlessness can be as disastrous and unfair to private rights and the public interest as the perversity of a willful scheme."[184] The plaintiffs' demonstration of the discriminatory effects of the town's municipal services practices thus established a *prima facie* violation of the Equal Protection Clause. After determining that "no compelling state interests [could] possibly justify the discriminatory *results* of Shaw's administration of municipal services,"[186] Judge Tuttle concluded that the town violated the Equal Protection Clause.

On *en banc* rehearing, the full court reaffirmed the panel's decision.[188] In its *per curiam* opinion, the majority reemphasized that it is not necessary to prove intentional discrimination under the Equal Protection Clause. . . .

. . . Four years after *Hawkins*, in *Washington v. Davis*,[191] the Supreme Court definitively and unambiguously established a discriminatory intent requirement under the Equal Protection Clause. . . . *Hawkins* was among the decisions the Court expressly disapproved.

---

[174] 437 F.2d 1286 (5th Cir. 1971), *aff'd on reh'g per curiam,* 461 F.2d 1171 (5th Cir. 1972) (en banc).

[184] *Id.* at 1292 (quoting Norwalk CORE v. Norwalk Redev. Agency, 395 F.2d 920, 931 (2d Cir. 1968)).

[186] *Id.* at 1292.

[188] Hawkins v. Town of Shaw, 461 F.2d 1171 (5th Cir. 1972) (per curiam) (en banc).

[191] 426 U.S. 229 (1976).

Since *Washington v. Davis*, race-based equalization litigation has been declared dead, or at least gravely wounded, with the suggestion that affected communities seek redress in the political arena or through resort to the common law. . . . While the difficulties inherent in systemic race discrimination litigation of any form in the 1990s cannot be overstated, there is reason to believe that the reported death of equalization litigation has been somewhat exaggerated.

B. THE FAIR HOUSING ACT

Recent amendments and judicial interpretations of Title VIII of the Civil Rights Act of 1968, commonly referred to as the Fair Housing Act,[199] provide a standard of liability for addressing municipal services disparities comparable to that enunciated in *Hawkins*. . . .

While saying little about the Act's substantive contours, the Supreme Court did mandate that the courts use "a generous construction"[202] of the Act to achieve a policy Congress considered to be of the highest priority. The primary provisions of the law prohibit discrimination in the sale or rental of housing or through conduct that otherwise makes housing unavailable, and proscribe discrimination in the terms, conditions, or privileges of the sale or rental of housing or in the services or facilities connected therewith. Lower courts applying the Supreme Court's "generous construction" mandate have extended these provisions to a range of discriminatory practices beyond the mere sale or rental of housing, including racial steering, race-based appraisal practices, redlining, exclusionary zoning and planning, public housing site selection and demolition, and discriminatory community development activities.

. . . .

Significantly, the Fair Housing Act does not require a finding of intentional discrimination to establish a violation. The Supreme Court has not directly addressed the issue, but it recently affirmed a decision of the Second Circuit applying a discriminatory impact or effects standard in *Huntington Branch NAACP v. Town of Huntington*.[214] In its *per curiam* affirmance of *Huntington*, the Supreme Court at least tacitly approved an effects standard, stating: "Without endorsing the precise analysis of the Court of Appeals, we are satisfied on this record that disparate impact was shown, and that the sole justification proffered to rebut the *prima facie*

---

[199] The current version of the Fair Housing Act is the product of two enactments: The Civil Rights Act of 1968, The Fair Housing Act, Title VIII, Pub. L. No. 90-284, 82 Stat. 73; and the Fair Housing Amendments Act of 1988, Pub. L. No. 100-430, 102 Stat. 1619. ROBERT G. SCHWEMM, HOUSING DISCRIMINATION LAW AND LITIGATION § 5.1 (1990). The act is codified as amended at 42 U.S.C. §§ 3601-3631 (1988 & Supp. I 1989, Supp. II 1990).

[202] Trafficante v. Metropolitan Life Ins. Co., 409 U.S. 205, 209-10 (1972); *see also* Havens Realty Corp. v. Coleman, 455 U.S. 363, 380 (1982); Gladstone Realtors v. Village of Bellwood, 441 U.S. 91, 93 (1978).

[214] 488 U.S. 15 (per curiam), *aff'g* 844 F.2d 926 (2d Cir. 1988).

case was inadequate."[215] In addition, there is no circuit conflict on this point, with courts in virtually every circuit having approved some version of a discriminatory effects standard under the Fair Housing Act.

. . . .

Houston v. City of Cocoa illustrates the potential value of the Fair Housing Act in addressing long term historic and present day land use inequality.[235] In highlighting the ongoing environmental intrusions stemming from the defendants' historic discriminatory incompatible zoning, the plaintiffs alleged that "heavy commercial zoning has caused: first, the intrusion of garages, auto body shops, machine shops and other uses incompatible with the homes and apartments in the neighborhood; second, the replacement of many homes by those business uses; and third, the displacement of black residents from their homes."[236] The plaintiffs claimed that the "City's long-term heavy commercial zoning of the Neighborhood has diminished the quality and safety of the area and has injured Plaintiffs by bringing loud noises, noxious odors, ugly and blighted appearances and increased traffic to a formerly peaceful and residential community."[237] In seeking a remedy for the entirety of the city's practices under the Fair Housing Act, plaintiffs alleged that the city's conduct "serve[d] to perpetuate the results of a long history of racial discrimination by the City against black residents of the neighborhood."[238]

The virtually all-black community suffered obvious adverse impacts from the city's destructive zoning and planning practices. In addition, both the incompatible commercial zoning and the gentrification-inducing rezoning resulted in increasing segregation by displacing plaintiffs from the only section of black-occupied housing on the white side of the railroad tracks, resulting potentially in the loss of one-sixth of the city's black population. In denying defendants' motion to dismiss, the district court found the contested long-term denial of protective zoning actionable under both sections 3604(a) and (b) of the Fair Housing Act.

Ultimately, the suit settled and the community obtained relief designed to remedy most of the challenged conduct and to secure a right to protective zoning for the indefinite future.[241] This relief included a protective rezoning to reflect the low-density residential character of the neighborhood, to phase out existing incompatible uses over time, and to provide inclusionary incentives for the development

---

[215] *Id.* at 18; *see* SCHWEMM, *supra* note 199, § 13.4(3)(c) (Supreme Court affirmance in *Huntington* "produced a powerful endorsement of the discriminatory effect theory"); James A. Kushner, *The Fair Housing Act Amendments of 1988: The Second Generation of Fair Housing*, 42 VAND. L. REV. 1049, 1075 (1989) (stating that *"Huntington* presents the Court's most significant tacit endorsement of the Fair Housing Act's *prima facie* effects test").

[235] Houston v. City of Cocoa, 2 Fair Housing-Fair Lending (P-H) ¶ 15,625 (M.D. Fla. Dec. 22, 1989) (order denying defendant's motion to dismiss) . . . .

[236] Complaint ¶ 80, *City of Cocoa* (No. 89-82-CIV-ORL-19).

[237] *Id.* ¶ 82.

[238] *Id.* ¶ 95. Plaintiffs also challenged both the adverse impact and segregative ultimate effects of the city's conduct. *Id.* ¶¶ 82-96.

[241] *See Settlement of Florida Zoning Case Includes Housing Rehabilitation*, 1 Fair Housing-Fair Lending (P-H) [Bulletin], May 1, 1991, ¶ 11.3 (reporting final judgment in *City of Cocoa*).

of affordable new housing in the neighborhood. The settlement also permanently enjoined any future zoning or planning action that has either the purpose or effect of involuntarily displacing the plaintiffs from the neighborhood or of "substantially undermining the quality of the residential environment."[244]

C. THE EQUAL PROTECTION CLAUSE

Under *Washington v. Davis* the complaining party's burden of proof was elevated to require a showing of intentional discrimination in cases under the Fourteenth Amendment's Equal Protection Clause, but that burden has not proven insurmountable in cases relating to municipal services, exclusionary zoning, or public housing discrimination. A year after *Washington v. Davis*, the Court addressed the application of its "new" intent standard to municipal land use issues in *Village of Arlington Heights v. Metropolitan Housing Development Corp.*[249] *Arlington Heights* demonstrated the Court's resolve to extend this more stringent standard beyond the employment discrimination context of *Washington v. Davis*. In applying this standard to land use issues, however, the Court also clarified that explicit racial classifications or "smoking gun" evidence would not be required to support a finding of intentional discrimination (at least in future cases).[250]

. . . .

The Court in *Arlington Heights* also held that a finding of discriminatory intent may be predicated on circumstantial evidence. It articulated six categories of evidence probative of discriminatory intent: first, the discriminatory impact of the defendant's decision; second, the historical background of the decision; third, the sequence of events leading up to the decision; fourth, departures from the normal procedural processes; fifth, departures from normal substantive criteria; and sixth, the legislative and administrative history of discrimination.

The Court's analysis underscored the importance of proof of discriminatory impact to a finding of intent. Although the Court reaffirmed the holding of *Washington v. Davis* that impact alone does not establish discriminatory intent, it recognized that under certain circumstances little else would be required. Demonstration of a particularly "stark" or extreme showing of disparate impact, coupled with the absence of a credible non-discriminatory explanation for the disparity, would, without more, justify finding intentional discrimination.[261]

. . . .

---

[244] Consent Decree, Parts II, V, & VI, *City of Cocoa*, No. 89-82-CIV-ORL-19. . . .

[249] 429 U.S. 252 (1977). . . .

[250] *Arlington Heights*, 429 U.S. at 264-68; *see* Lodge v. Buxton, 639 F.2d 1358, 1363 n.8 (5th Cir. 1981) (observing that one cannot expect to find a "smoking gun" in discrimination cases), *aff'd*, 458 U.S. 613 (1982). On the merits of the *Arlington Heights* case, the Supreme Court determined that plaintiffs failed to prove intentional discrimination, even though the record contained at least two types of circumstantial evidence identified by the Court as probative of discriminatory intent. *Arlington Heights*, 429 U.S. at 269-71.

[261] *Id.* at 266.

The federal courts' broad remedial power to redress constitutional violations also provides an approach for remedying the continuing effects of historic land use discrimination. In language that is now commonplace in remedial decrees, the Supreme Court has charged the lower courts with "not merely the power but the duty to render a decree which will so far as possible eliminate the discriminatory effects of the past as well as bar like discrimination in the future."[274] The sweeping language of several decrees equalizing municipal services which apply the Court's remedial mandate furnish a firm basis for securing a right to equality of zoning protection.

D. THE THIRTEENTH AMENDMENT

The Thirteenth Amendment arguably provides an alternative constitutional basis for addressing land use discrimination. In *City of Memphis v. Greene*,[277] the Supreme Court left open the question of whether section 1 of the Thirteenth Amendment applies to "badges and incidents of slavery" or merely to the institution of slavery and involuntary servitude.[278] The lower courts have provided some support for the broader proposition. Whether or not section 1 reaches "badges and incidents," legislation enacted pursuant to section 2 of the Thirteenth Amendment, such as 42 U.S.C. § 1982, does.

Under a "badges and incidents" approach, a long-term, pervasive, or significantly disruptive practice of land use discrimination should be actionable. . . .

E. THE POLICE POWER—SUBSTANTIVE DUE PROCESS

Low-income communities of color that are unable to secure land use equity through anti-discrimination law might find limited solace in the substantive due process limits on the police power. As a general matter, the judicial standards governing the substantive review of police power enactments mandate extreme deference to municipal objectives. There are, however, circumstances under which a city's damaging zoning or planning conduct justifies greater skepticism. For example, the use of incompatible zoning to depress land values and decrease the cost of government acquisition warrants no similar deference to the asserted municipal objectives.

Furthermore, *Euclid* demonstrates that the Court recognizes the importance of protecting residential communities and the residential environment from the negative by-products of industrialization and commercial development. Thus, the Court in *Euclid* found that it is manifestly within the general welfare to protect res-

---

[274] Louisiana v. United States, 380 U.S. 145, 154 (1965) . . . .

[277] 451 U.S. 100 (1981).

[278] *Id.* at 125-26.

idential communities from the dangers and degradations of blighting or disruptive uses. Conversely, police power enactments that substantially undermine these basic Euclidean principles by authorizing the intrusion of such uses should, at a minimum, be subject to a diminished presumption of validity.

Additionally, the state courts' emerging heightened recognition of governments' police power responsibilities to plan for the housing needs of low- and moderate-income families provides further support for a right to protective zoning in low-income communities. The leading manifestations of this trend at the state level are the New Jersey Supreme Court's decisions in *Mt. Laurel I*[294] and *Mt. Laurel II*.[295] In *Mt. Laurel I*, the New Jersey Supreme Court invalidated a township's zoning provisions that had erected virtually insurmountable barriers to residential access for low- and moderate-income families.[296] Finding these "parochial" devices violative of the general welfare, the court imposed affirmative responsibilities on the township and other developing municipalities to employ land use regulations that provide a realistic opportunity for meeting a "fair share" of the region's present and prospective low- and moderate-income housing needs.[297]

Frustrated with the slow pace of compliance with this mandate, the court in *Mt. Laurel II* broadened municipalities' obligations by requiring their performance of affirmative inclusionary measures to ensure the provision of low- and moderate-income housing.[298] Significantly, the court also extended these affirmative obligations to developed municipalities and, in so doing, provided a principle for addressing land use inequality in low-income communities through the substantive review of land use controls. It noted that "the State controls the use of land, all of the land. In exercising that control it cannot favor rich over poor. It cannot legislatively set aside dilapidated housing in urban ghettos for the poor and decent housing elsewhere for everyone else."[299] The court recognized that a municipality's "zoning power is no more abused by keeping out the region's poor than by forcing out the resident poor."[300]

It remains to be seen whether the New Jersey Supreme Court's expansive interpretation of the substantive limits on the police power will be widely followed in other states. Nevertheless, the *Mt. Laurel II* approach provides further support for a right to land use regulation designed to improve the quality of the residential

---

[294] 336 A.2d 713 (N.J.), *cert. denied*, 423 U.S. 808 (1975).

[295] 456 A.2d 390 (N.J. 1987).

[296] *Mt. Laurel I*, 336 A.2d at 729-34. The township's practices included substantial overzoning for industrial uses, costly minimum lot size and house size requirements, and the exclusion of multi-family housing. *Id.* at 718-24.

[297] *Id.* at 732-33.

[298] *Mt. Laurel II*, 456 A.2d at 442-52.

[299] *Id.* at 415.

[300] *Id.* at 418. . . .

environment and avert involuntary displacement in low-income communities of color.[301]

CONCLUSION

The persistence of stark patterns of residential segregation in the 1990s serves as a reminder of this country's legacy of systematic discrimination in land use policy. At the same time, new and insidious forms of land use assaults—ranging from the disparate siting of toxic waste facilities to the stimulation of foreseeable race-based gentrification—pose unprecedented risks to the survival and integrity of low-income communities of color. Both new and recycled legal approaches offer the potential for reinvigorating community improvement and equalization litigation efforts to remedy historic and modern-day land use inequalities. These and other nonlitigation efforts are necessary to provide long overdue fulfillment of the congressional promise of a suitable living environment for all American families[302] and to return Justice Sutherland's proverbial pig from the "hood" to the barnyard once and for all.

Note

For an assessment of the impact of the *Mount Laurel* opinions, see John M. Payne, *Norman Williams, Exclusionary Zoning, and the* Mount Laurel *Doctrine: Making the Theory Fit the Facts*, 20 Vt. L. Rev. 665 (1996). Land use innovations, such as mandatory set-asides and density bonuses, designed to address the housing problems identified in the *Mount Laurel* decisions have precipitated considerable analysis. *See, e.g.,* Lawrence Berger, *Inclusionary Zoning Devices as Takings: The Legacy of the Mount Laurel Cases*, 70 Neb. L. Rev. 186 (1991); Andrew G. Dietderich, *An Egalitarian's Market: The Economics of Inclusionary Zoning Reclaimed*, 24 Fordham Urb. L.J. 23 (1996).

---

[301] For discussion of the potential applications of *Mt. Laurel II* to zoning and land use issues within developed municipalities' low-income communities see Steve Dobkin et al., *Zoning for the General Welfare: A Constitutional Weapon for Lower-Income Tenants*, 13 N.Y.U. REV. OF L. & SOC. CHANGE 911, 917-24 (1984-85); Harold McDougall, Mount Laurel II *and the Revitalizing City*, 15 RUTGERS L.J. 667 (1984); Peter W. Salsich, Jr., *Displacement and Urban Reinvestment: A* Mount Laurel *Perspective*, 53 U. CIN. L. REV. 333, 361-79 (1984).

[302] *See* 42 U.S.C. § 1441 (1988).

B. Exactions

"EXIT" AS A CONSTRAINT ON LAND USE EXACTIONS: RETHINKING THE UNCONSTITUTIONAL CONDITIONS DOCTRINE
Vicki Been
91 Colum. L. Rev. 473 (1991)[*]

INTRODUCTION

In one of its most recent plunges into the murky waters of the takings clause, the Supreme Court held that the California Coastal Commission violated the fifth amendment by conditioning a building permit for beachfront property on the owners' dedication of an easement allowing the public to walk on the portion of the property nearest the ocean.[1] The Nollans, who had an option to buy the property conditioned upon their promise to build a house on the lot, challenged the "exaction" of public access on the ground that it constituted an uncompensated taking. The Nollans' attack invoked the unconstitutional conditions doctrine,[3] which holds that even if the government is not constitutionally required to grant a particular privilege or benefit, once it offers that benefit, it may not condition the offer upon the recipient's surrender or waiver of a constitutional right.[4]

The Supreme Court considered it beyond question that if the Nollans had not applied for the building permit the Coastal Commission could not have taken an easement from them without paying just compensation. The Court assumed that the Coastal Commission had the right to prohibit the Nollans from building if the new house would have harmed the public interest by blocking the public's view of the

---

[*] This article originally appeared at 91 Colum. L. Rev. 473 (1991). Reprinted by permission.

[1] Nollan v. California Coastal Comm'n, 483 U.S. 825 (1987). The Nollans' claim was based on the fifth amendment as incorporated through the fourteenth amendment.

[3] Although the parties did not mention the unconstitutional conditions doctrine by name, the central issue in the case was framed as an unconstitutional conditions question: "to what extent, and under what circumstances, [may] an owner . . . be required by the state to give away real property without compensation as a condition of receiving approval to make some use of his land." Appellants' Jurisdictional Statement at 14, Nollan v. California Coastal Comm'n, 483 U.S. 825 (1987) (No. 86-133) . . . .

[4] Epstein, Unconstitutional Conditions, State Power, and the Limits of Consent, 102 Harv. L. Rev. 4, 6-7 (1988); Hale, Unconstitutional Conditions and Constitutional Rights, 35 Colum. L. Rev. 321, 321 (1935); Sullivan, Unconstitutional Conditions, 102 Harv. L. Rev. 1413, 1415 (1989).

ocean. The question, therefore, was whether an exaction that would be unconstitutional standing alone could become constitutional if imposed as a condition to the grant of a building permit.

The *Nollan* Court initially seemed to reject the basic reasoning of the unconstitutional conditions doctrine, adopting instead the doctrine's converse, "the greater-with-the-lesser argument": "the Commission's assumed [greater] power to forbid construction of the house in order to protect the public's view of the beach must surely include the [lesser] power to condition construction upon some concession by the owner, even a concession of property rights, that serves the same end."[8] Justice Scalia, writing for the majority, explained that it therefore would be constitutional for the Commission to impose conditions upon building that would protect the public's ability to see the ocean, such as a "requirement that the Nollans provide a viewing spot on their property for passersby" to use to look out at the ocean.[9]

The Court quickly backtracked, however, to the unconstitutional conditions doctrine: "[t]he evident constitutional propriety disappears . . . if the condition substituted for the prohibition utterly fails to further the end advanced as the justification for the prohibition."[10] Unless the condition imposed "serves the same governmental purpose as the development ban"[11] and indeed "substantially advance[s]"[12] the legitimate state interest that the prohibition on construction sought to achieve, Justice Scalia wrote, the "building restriction is not a valid regulation of land use but 'an out-and-out plan of extortion.'"[13]

The *Nollan* Court's concern that land use regulators will "extort" property owners has its roots in the allegations of coercion and illicit motive that long have animated judicial and academic debate about exactions and more generally, about the unconstitutional conditions doctrine. Even if valid in the context of other conditioned benefits, that concern seems somewhat odd in the context of land use exactions. Just as the law generally assumes that the judiciary need not, indeed should not, closely supervise the terms of bargains when the conduct of the parties is adequately constrained by market forces, the law tends to reflect the assumption that if the government *qua* regulator must compete for the opportunity to regulate, market forces will suffice to constrain the government from overreaching. The best known example is the law of corporate charters, in which competition among the states is regarded as protecting corporations seeking government charters from overregulation or overreaching by any one state. Other areas of the law, such as banking regulation and the regulation of harmful business activities, also tend to rely on competitive governmental "markets" to prevent overregulation.

---

[8] *Nollan*, 483 U.S. at 836.

[9] Id.

[10] Id. at 837.

[11] Id.

[12] Id. at 834 & n.3, 841.

[13] Id. at 837 (quoting J.E.D. Assocs. v. Atkinson, 121 N.H. 581, 584, 432 A.2d 12, 14-15 (1981)).

A primary source of discipline in the market is, to use Albert O. Hirschman's paradigm, the availability of exit—the opportunity a dissatisfied person has to refuse to buy a firm's products or services, to withdraw from an organization, or to move from the jurisdiction.[18] Before advocating extensive judicial scrutiny of exactions, therefore, scholars should examine the exit options available to property developers who are unhappy with the conditions upon which a local government has offered a land use permit, and evaluate whether those protections render heightened judicial scrutiny such as the *Nollan* nexus test unnecessary or inadvisable.

Indeed, one would expect that those who generally advocate reliance upon market forces would be especially reluctant to call for close judicial supervision of local governments' exactions practices unless market forces were shown to be inadequate to constrain government behavior. But the proponents of judicial limits upon exactions, including those law and economics scholars who generally distrust interference with private market transactions, have been curiously silent about the protections the market might offer property owners. . . .

The purpose of this Article is to fill that gap by analyzing whether competition in the market for development is sufficient to constrain local governments from overregulating or overcharging through development exactions, and therefore renders unnecessary the judicial scrutiny associated with the unconstitutional conditions doctrine. . . .

I. LAND USE EXACTIONS: A BRIEF OVERVIEW

Exactions require that developers provide, or pay for, some public facility or other amenity as a condition for receiving permission for a land use that the local government could otherwise prohibit. Exactions are an outgrowth of the centuries-old practice of levying "special assessments" upon real property to pay for public improvements, such as paved streets, that provide a direct and special benefit to the property. In the 1920s and 1930s, widespread bankruptcies and delinquencies on special assessments, which typically were levied after an improvement was installed, left many local governments unable to recoup the costs of public improvements. Communities then sought ways of shifting the initial costs of improvements, and hence the risk of failure, to the private subdivider. Initially, local governments required *on-site dedications*: the community demanded that a developer dedicate land within the subdivision on which the community could construct streets, sidewalks, utilities, and other such facilities. Alternatively, the local government required the developer to construct and dedicate these facilities to the community. Communities initially required dedications only for such basic facilities as streets and sidewalks, but many communities eventually demanded that develop-

---

[18] A. Hirschman, Exit, Voice, and Loyalty (1970). Hirschman pointed out that a person dissatisfied with the status quo has two primary responses: exit and voice. One uses the voice option by attempting "to change, rather than to escape from, an objectionable state of affairs" through complaints to the management, public protests, lobbying for legislative or regulatory action, or other means of political participation. Id. at 30. . . .

ers dedicate land within the subdivision for schools, fire and police stations, and parks or open space.

Land or facilities within a subdivision were not always ideally suited to meet a particular need, so local governments began to impose *off-site dedications*, which required developers to dedicate land or facilities not located within the subdivision. They also began to charge *fees-in-lieu-of-dedication*, giving developers the option of contributing money to the community rather than dedicating land or facilities.

Because fees-in-lieu-of-dedication typically could be applied only to subdivisions, many local governments implemented broader *impact fees*, which assess developers for the costs that the development will impose upon the government's capital budget for public services. Impact fees can be levied upon apartment buildings or other residential dwellings that are not located in a subdivision, as well as upon office, commercial, and industrial developments.

Linkages are a hybrid of impact fees and off-site dedications. Linkage programs condition approval of certain central city developments (usually commercial or office space) upon the developer's provision of facilities or services for which the development will create a need, or that the development will displace. These programs have been adopted in a variety of cities for such needs as low-income housing, mass transit facilities, day care services, and job-training and employment opportunities. *Set-asides* or *inclusionary zoning programs* are similar in concept to linkages, but are addressed specifically to the need for low- and moderate-income housing. They require a developer to make a certain percentage of the units within a development available at prices affordable to residents with low and moderate incomes, or to pay in-lieu-of contributions to an affordable housing fund.

The practice of imposing exactions is fairly widespread, although exactions are most common in communities in growth areas. Local governments impose exactions either according to a nondiscretionary, predetermined schedule, or through case-by-case negotiations. Nondiscretionary exactions may be a set amount per square foot or per unit, or may be calculated based upon mathematical formulas that attempt to measure the precise impact that the development will have on particular public services. Studies of municipalities' exactions reveal a wide variation in prices. . . .

The main reason municipalities impose exactions upon development is, of course, to shift to the developer the costs of the public infrastructure that the development requires. But exactions serve a variety of other purposes as well. First, by forcing the developer and its customers to assume or share in the costs of infrastructure, exactions induce a more efficient use of the infrastructure. Second, exactions serve to mitigate the negative effects a development may have on a neighborhood, such as increased traffic congestion, noise, and environmental degradation. In serving this purpose, exactions again encourage efficiency by forcing the developer and its customers to internalize the full costs of the harms that the development causes.

Third, exactions serve as growth enablers: in areas that are growing so rapidly that the government cannot provide public facilities fast enough, exactions allow growth that might otherwise be stalled by growth control measures. Or, in areas in which a particular development, or growth in general, is controversial, a local government that favors a project may use exactions to counter or "buy off" opposition. Fourth, a local government may use exactions to try to discourage all growth, or to prevent certain kinds of development, such as low- and moderate-income housing, in order to preserve the exclusiveness of a community or to preserve its fiscal position.

Finally, exactions may be used either to redistribute wealth from the developer or its customers to others, or to prevent the developer from appropriating wealth created by the activities of the local government. A community may impose exactions as a means of capturing part of the developer's profit. Or, in some markets, a community may adopt exactions in order to inflate the price of existing housing and thereby allow the current residents to profit at the expense of newcomers. On the other hand, a community may use exactions to recapture from the developer part of the value added to land by improvements financed by the community.

II. LAND USE EXACTIONS AND THE EVILS OF CONDITIONED BENEFITS

The first step in determining whether market forces might be a more appropriate constraint upon bargains between local governments and developers than the unconstitutional conditions doctrine is to analyze the ways in which exactions may threaten constitutional values. Because exactions are a form of conditioned government benefit, no different in structure from the conditioned government largess at issue in the typical unconstitutional conditions problem, the threat exactions pose is best approached by examining the general theories jurists and scholars have posited for deciding when a citizen's agreement to accept a conditioned benefit should be unenforceable.

Five theories have held the most prominence. The extortion theory argues that conditioned benefits are unconstitutional when the condition is imposed for an illegitimate purpose. The coercion theory asserts that a recipient's "agreement" to waive or forego constitutional rights in exchange for a government benefit is unenforceable when the recipient has no "real" choice but to agree to the condition, or when the government acts improperly in putting the recipient to the choice. The inalienability theory holds that such an agreement is unenforceable when the constitutional right at stake is one that cannot be waived or bartered. Professor Sullivan recently advanced a fourth theory: that conditioned benefits should be subject to strict scrutiny whenever they result in better treatment for the recipients of conditioned benefits regarding matters (such as religion) on which the government is supposed to be neutral; when they have the effect of relegating to a separate caste those people whose dependence upon the state makes them especially vulnerable to the government's conditioned offers; or when they redistribute power between the government and rightholders.[67] Finally, Professor Epstein has advanced the the-

---

[67] See Sullivan, Unconstitutional Conditions and the Distribution of Liberty, 26 San Diego L. Rev. 327, 330-32 (1989); Sullivan, supra note 4, at 1489-99. . . .

ory that conditioned benefits should be unconstitutional when they reflect bargaining failures:[68] when the offer of the conditioned benefit has the effect of redistributing wealth among citizens; when citizens confronted with the offer face collective action problems; or when the government has a monopoly over the benefit it offers.

The following sections examine what each of these theories would identify as the danger posed by land use exactions. Each points in the same direction: the risk of exactions is that they will lead the government to overcharge or overregulate property developers.

. . . .

F. *Dangers of Exactions: Overcharging and Overregulation*

A distillation of the various theories that seek to explain the unconstitutional conditions doctrine reveals that land use exactions pose two dangers: exactions allow municipalities to redistribute wealth by charging the developer more than the costs of the harm that the development is causing, and transferring that overcharge to others; and exactions may encourage the government to overregulate in order to give itself a way of raising money or other benefits. The dangers are related, in the sense that overregulation is nothing more than charging a price for what should be free, and thereby redistributing wealth. But overregulation has consequences beyond redistribution. Unnecessarily stringent regulation may prevent development that would have been socially beneficial. Further, the sales or trades that overregulation makes possible eventually may lead to underregulation: municipalities will become so dependent upon exactions as a way to balance their budgets without the political difficulties of tax increases that they will sell development too cheaply and thereby provide insufficient protection against the harms that development may impose upon a community.

This Article addresses the problems of redistribution and of regulation that is so stringent that it prevents the socially optimal level of development. I save the problem of underregulation for another day, for several reasons. First, viewing the problem as one of unconstitutional conditions naturally leads to a focus upon the developer, not the public, because it is the developer that invokes the unconstitutional conditions doctrine to get out of what it perceives to be a bad deal. If neighbors or other members of the public believe that the government got the bad end of the bargain by selling an exemption too cheaply, their legal remedy will be to challenge the exemption. Unless those other legal challenges are shown to be inadequate remedies for underregulation caused by exactions, we need not resort to the unconstitutional conditions doctrine to protect the interests of neighbors or of the public. Second, municipalities have long been criticized as being much too prone to grant variances, rezonings, and special exceptions, even when exactions are not

---

[68]   See Epstein, supra note 4, at 15-28. . . .

at issue. The courts have attempted to constrain such grants by scrutinizing exemptions closely and by imposing procedural safeguards for those affected by exemptions, and by requiring that exemptions be consistent with an overall plan. Accordingly, any effort to protect the public from the underenforcement of land use regulations must look not only at exactions, but at the whole scheme of exemptions, and at the various means by which local governments' discretion to grant exemptions is controlled. Finally, none of the "solutions" that have been offered for the dangers posed by land use exactions, such as *Nollan*'s nexus text, makes sense as an effort to control underregulation; the "solutions" seem to be aimed instead at limiting government's opportunity to overregulate. This Article tries to meet those tests on their own terms.

III. COMPETITION AS A CONSTRAINT UPON GOVERNMENTS

According to the theory of competitive federalism, competition among governments will constrain governments from overcharging or overregulating. The sections that follow first examine that theory, then analyze whether local governments face competitive pressures in their role as land use regulators.

A. *The Political Theory of Competitive Federalism*

Competition in the market for goods and services restrains the self-interested pursuit of profit by placing control of prices beyond the reach of any individual producer. In a perfectly competitive market, there are so many producers that each is a "price taker," unable to affect the price of a commodity because it supplies only a small fraction of that commodity. If a producer seeks to raise the price, consumers will buy elsewhere; each producer accordingly takes the market price as a given. In a monopolistic market, on the other hand, the producer or seller is a "price maker," able to dictate or influence the price of the commodity because it supplies all or nearly all of the commodity available.

Just as competition among producers of products and services constrains greed, the theory of competitive federalism postulates that competition among and within governments and between a government and private parties serves as a significant constraint upon the behavior of the politicians and bureaucrats who make up the government. The theory has its roots in an argument advanced by political economist Charles Tiebout[157] in response to the claim of Paul Samuelson and Richard Musgrave that there is no mechanism by which local governments can accurately ascertain the amount of public goods[158] that they should supply to satisfy the preferences of consumer-voters.[159]

---

[157] See Tiebout, A Pure Theory of Local Expenditures, 64 J. Pol. Econ. 416, 424 (1956).

[158] . . . See Samuelson, The Pure Theory of Public Expenditure, 36 Rev. Econ. & Statistics 387, 388-89 (1954).

. . . .

[159] See Musgrave, The Voluntary Exchange Theory of Public Economy, 52 Q.J. Econ. 213, 213-17 (1939); Samuelson, supra note 158, at 388-89.

Tiebout asserted that a decentralized governmental system in which there are many local governments will act like a market to force consumers to reveal their preferences for public services. Just as consumers shop for goods in the private market, consumers will "shop" for a particular level and combination of public goods and "buy" by moving to the community that offers the preferred package. Tiebout argued that because consumers will thus "vote with their feet," it is at least conceptually possible that municipalities will provide services efficiently because municipalities will compete for residents by trying to offer a desirable package of services at the lowest cost. Tiebout's argument led to the insight that just as producers of products and services in the private market are constrained by the ability of consumers to "exit," local governments are constrained by the opportunity citizens have to "exit" in response to governmental policies.

B. *The Influence of Competitive Federalism*

Several bodies of law reflect the theory of competitive federalism by assuming that the disciplining and limiting effect of interjurisdictional competition is sufficient to constrain state and local governments from overreaching in their dealings with individual citizens and corporations. The most prominent example is corporate law, in which competition among states for corporate charters is widely accepted as preventing overregulation by government. . . .

. . . .

C. *Competitive Federalism and Land Use Exactions*

A community faces competition from several sources when it imposes exactions. First, the community must compete with other jurisdictions if it wants to encourage development because a developer dissatisfied with a community's exactions policy can take the project to another jurisdiction that offers better terms. In some parts of the country, the municipality must compete not only with existing neighboring jurisdictions, but also with potential new jurisdictions because a developer can seek to have its site incorporated as a new jurisdiction.

Second, the community must compete with its own electorate. In many jurisdictions, a developer can bypass the local government and go directly to the voters, seeking approval of the project through an initiative measure, or asking the voters to veto the local government's adverse policy through a referendum. . . .

Third, the community must compete with higher levels of government. States unwilling to lose a project to other states may strong-arm towns that balk at accepting a developer's terms or may impose limits upon local governments' abilities to block development or levy exactions. Or the federal government may step in, offering to allow development on land that it owns.

Finally, a community must contend with competition from the private sector because a developer can invest the money it would spend on a development project in some other capital-seeking enterprise. Or the developer may shift its investment to development projects such as commercial or industrial buildings that typically are subject to fewer exactions than housing development.

A state or local government accordingly faces competitive pressures not only from other governments at the same level, but from other levels of government and from private or nongovernmental forces. If a municipality uses exactions to over-regulate or overcharge, the developer will take, or threaten to take, its capital elsewhere: from the overreaching community to another community, from the residential market most often affected by exactions to the commercial market, or from the building market to other forms of investment. Under the theory of competitive federalism, and more generally, the principles of free market economics, the unconstitutional conditions doctrine therefore should not be necessary to constrain local governments from overreaching through exactions.

D. *Do Municipalities Compete in the Pricing of Exactions?*

Data about how municipalities actually price their exactions would be the best evidence whether competition constrains their exactions policies. Direct evidence is quite limited, but it points in the direction of a competitive market. First, impact fees tend to be much lower than the actual cost of providing infrastructure, indicating that some pressure prevents municipalities from overcharging and may even cause municipalities to undercharge. . . .

In addition, anecdotal evidence indicates that municipalities compete for development in establishing their exactions policies. Cities woo developers by promising a favorable development climate. . . .

Additional data about the nature of the competitive pressures municipalities face in bargaining with developers can be derived from evidence that local governments compete for new businesses and residents. If a local government hopes to win new business or industry, it must, of course, offer a development (or developable land) suitable for the office or plant. In addition, the local government must offer housing for the business' workers. Research on industrial location has shown that issues relating to the quality of life a site will offer a firm's managers and employees, such as the quality of the neighborhood and the quality of housing available, significantly affect a firm's location decision. Indeed, firms increasingly consider whether appropriate housing will be made available to their workers when they negotiate with local governments over location incentives. To compete for business and industry, therefore, communities must compete for both industrial and office development and housing development. Similarly, if a local government hopes to attract additional residents, it must be able to offer those residents a place to live, and therefore must seek to attract housing development. Accordingly, the next two subsections examine in greater detail whether communities compete for business and residents.

1. *Competition for Industry and Business.*—Competition among state and local governments for business and industry is so intense and pervasive that it has been referred to as the "Second War Between the States."[188] State and local governments

---

[188] The Second War Between the States, Bus. Wk., May 17, 1976, at 92; War Among the States for Jobs and Business Becomes Ever Fiercer, Wall St. J., Feb. 14, 1983, at 1, col. 6; Sunbelt vs. Frostbelt: A Second Civil War?, Sat. Rev., April 15, 1978, at 28; The War Between the States (Public Broadcasting System, MacNeil-Lehrer Report No. 1950, Mar. 18, 1983) . . . .

offer a wide variety of incentives to attract businesses to their jurisdictions, such as exemptions from or abatements of property, income, and sales taxes, industrial bond financing, government-sponsored recruitment and training of employees, direct loans for plant construction, provision of developed sites or industrial parks, below-market sales or outright grants of land, infrastructure improvements, loosening of regulatory restrictions, and home mortgage subsidies for employees. . . .

2. *Competition for Residents.*—Evidence whether communities compete for residents primarily stems from the efforts of scores of economists and political scientists to test the accuracy of Tiebout's theory that citizens' opportunities to "vote with their feet" will result in the efficient provision of public goods by local governments. Those studies provide substantial proof that local jurisdictions do compete for residents.

. . . .

In summary, then, data about the extent to which differences in public service expenditures and taxes are capitalized into house values, data about the relationship between migration patterns and fiscal characteristics of communities, and data about the increasing homogeneity of communities all support the proposition that consumers consider a community's public service and tax packages when they choose where to live. Given the availability of numerous communities from which to choose and differences between the public service and tax packages that communities offer, the fact that consumers shop for a public service and tax package is strong evidence supporting the core Tiebout proposition that jurisdictions compete for residents by attempting to offer desirable public service/tax packages. Municipal leaders often cite competition from nearby communities as the justification for their inability to raise taxes or decrease public services. The empirical evidence indicates that such competition is indeed a reality.

IV. Is the Market Sufficiently Competitive to Regulate Exactions?

The evidence that municipalities compete for businesses and residents, and for the developments to house those businesses and residents, does not address the ultimate, quantitative question: is the market *sufficiently* competitive to render judicial constraints upon exactions unnecessary? . . .

. . . .

A. *Imperfections in the Market for Development*

The model of perfect competition requires that there be a large number of producers, offering a homogeneous product to perfectly informed consumers, in a market in which other producers are free to enter, and there is no collusion among producers. Like most markets, the land use market falls far short of that ideal. . . . [D]evelopers are not freely mobile; it is costly to "shop" among municipalities because a developer must locate sites in each municipality, engage in preliminary negotiations over the price of the sites, conduct soil tests and gather the other data needed to assess the sites' suitability for the project, and perhaps commission preliminary sketches of the project that the developer envisions.

Nor is the product homogeneous. Local governments differ not only in their exactions policies, but also in their taxes, infrastructure, public services, transportation networks, scenic views, access to beaches and other recreational sites, cultural opportunities, status, and proximity to employment centers. Differences among communities mean that when a developer tries to shop among jurisdictions, the developer will have to make trade-offs between a community's exactions policy and its strengths and weaknesses in dozens of other areas.

The differentiation among the products makes it unlikely that developers will have perfect information about the exactions policies of each competing community. Because communities vary in a myriad of ways, no development project will have exactly the same impact in two different towns. Differences in surrounding uses and in the physical characteristics of alternative sites may mean, for example, that a project that would destroy wetlands in one town would pose no threat to wetlands in the next town, but would overload that town's mass transit system. Comparing exactions is therefore difficult and costly and the comparison is likely to be incomplete or otherwise flawed.

Finally, although in most urban areas there are a large number of communities that might compete for development, some communities seek to limit or stop growth and thus cannot be considered active competitors at all. Other communities cannot be considered as active competitors because they do not behave as rational economic actors: they choose to maximize something other than the aggregate wealth of their residents (such as the wealth of a politically powerful subset of residents); or they fail to respond to competitive pressures in a timely and effective manner because they are constrained by political processes. . . .

It is important, however, to keep those imperfections in perspective. While there are costs to shopping among jurisdictions, and it is not always easy to compare the exactions policies of different jurisdictions, many exactions are fairly easy to predict because they are imposed through formulas or established standards. Even if a developer is unable to predict exactly what kind of exactions will be imposed for the project and how much those exactions will cost, the developer will be able to assess the town's general reputation regarding exactions policies. Comparative information also may be available in the form of surveys.

Although communities differ in many respects from the economically rational actors that traditional market models envision, in many if not most communities, the goal of pursuing growth is shared by enough of the community's various interest groups to ensure that the city will compete for an increased tax base. In addition, even communities that are not currently active competitors serve as a constraint upon their neighbors because they may reenter the competition at any time.

. . . .

. . . In sum, while the market for development permits suffers many frictions, those imperfections hardly are insurmountable.

B. *The Special Charter Era*

The exactions market does suffer many more imperfections than the market for corporate charters that currently serves as the prototype for the theory of competitive federalism. . . .

    . . . .

. . . In sum, even when the market for corporate charters suffered many of the kinds of frictions that characterize today's market for development permits, history reveals that competition served as a serious constraint upon overregulation.

C. *When Exit Will Not Be a Sufficient Alternative to Regulation*

Competition could not serve to constrain the states in one segment of the special charter market: for small corporations already operating within a state, the costs of exit gave a state room to rent-seek. Although the corporation could move its operation to another state, it would be costly to do so, so the state could exact a price up to those costs for a charter. Two similar situations occur in the development market. First, a landowner who owned land within a jurisdiction before the community began imposing exactions does not have a mobile asset and cannot exit if the community attempts to overcharge through exactions. Second, a homeowner who is bargaining directly with the municipality may stand in the same position as the corporation that had its plant within the state in the special charter era. Even a family that has few emotional ties to a community will have to incur moving costs in order to exit the community; a municipality can attempt to exact an amount up to those moving costs. Many families also would suffer psychological costs if they moved, and thus could be made to pay a substantial exaction before they would leave the community.

In the first situation, whether the landowner actually will be subject to exploitation will depend upon whether the landowner will bear the full cost or incidence of any exactions. Three parties (or any combination of the three) can bear an exaction: the developer (or the developer's suppliers, such as the building construction trade) by taking reduced profits; the landowner by taking less for the land; or the consumers of the project, either by paying higher prices or rents or by accepting lower quality.

The empirical evidence regarding who actually bears the costs of exactions is relatively sparse. Many scholars have assumed or theorized that the full costs of exactions usually will be passed on to the buyer. Others have argued that the costs generally will be passed back to the landowner. Both extremes are unlikely because the incidence of exactions will depend upon the nature of the supply and demand in the market, as well as the structure of the local building industry. The consumer will be willing to absorb the full costs of the exaction when demand for housing is relatively inelastic (insensitive to price increases or decreases) and the supply of housing or land is relatively elastic (sensitive to changes in price). In other words, consumers are likely to bear the cost of the exaction when there are no other communities in which they can find the package of housing and community characteristics that they desire because one community has some unique locational feature that makes it more attractive than all the surrounding communities. But if there are substitutes for the community that imposes exactions, the consumer will refuse to absorb the cost of the exaction and will buy in a substitute community instead.

On the other hand, the landowner will be willing to absorb the full costs of the exaction only when demand for the land is relatively elastic (price increases result in a disproportionate reduction in demand) and the supply is relatively inelastic (decreases in the price of land have little effect on the supply of land). As long as there are uses for the land that would not be subject to exactions, the landowner need not absorb the exaction. If, for example, exactions are applied to housing development but not to office buildings, and the land is appropriate for both uses, the housing developer will have to bid against the office developer, and will thereby be constrained in its ability to pass the exaction back to the landowner.

In the more usual case, in which neither the housing market nor the broader market for land is perfectly competitive, the incidence of the exaction is likely to be shared by the parties. As long as the developer is likely to share some portion of the burden, it will have an incentive to bargain the price of the exaction down as far as possible. The property owner will be the indirect beneficiary of the developer's exit power because the competition for development will constrain the local government from overcharging the developer, who will then have no overcharges to pass back to the landowner.

Even when the developer's assessment of supply and demand might suggest that the developer will be able to pass all the costs of an exaction back to the landowner, a prudent developer would nevertheless seek to bargain the cost of the exaction down as far as possible. The elasticity of the supply of land depends, of course, upon landowner behavior. Landowners appear to have an artificially high "reservation" price—the amount below which they will not sell the land—because they do not accurately assess the time value of money, and because holding costs for undeveloped land often are quite low. The reservation price also may be affected by life-cycle factors: the landowner may sell at a particular time because she is ready to retire from farming, rather than because the land has reached a particular value. Because the behavior of the landowner will be difficult to predict, the developer again will be inclined to use its bargaining power with the community to attempt to avoid the cost of an exaction. Even though the landowner has an immobile asset, then, she will be protected against municipal overcharging through the bargaining of the developer.

In the second situation in which competition may not adequately constrain communities' imposition of exactions—the situation of the homeowner who is asked to pay an exaction because she wants to renovate or expand her house—such indirect protection does not exist. In reality, however, few jurisdictions impose such exactions and as long as a majority of a jurisdiction's voters realize that they might be affected by such a policy, a jurisdiction is unlikely to impose exactions on renovations or expansions. While exit does not protect a current homeowner, then, other protections such as the political process may be sufficient to render judicial scrutiny unnecessary. If judicial intervention is necessary, the law of exactions might profitably look to contract doctrines that seek to police changes in the terms of a relationship in which one party has significant leverage over the second by virtue of the costs the second would have to bear to object to the exercise of power. The homeowner's situation is directly analogous, for example, to that of a member of a condominium or cooperative association who is subject to increased fees or rule changes by the cooperative or condominium board. The situation of the homeowner also is similar to that of parties to relational contracts and franchise arrangements. Those bodies of law may provide a more satisfactory approach to the problem of community overreaching than the nexus test.

Conclusion

In any imperfectly competitive market, there are costs to relying on competition to regulate contractual relationships. But there are disadvantages as well in permitting the judiciary to police those relationships. Indeed, the unconstitutional conditions doctrine, in the form of the *Nollan* nexus test or the similar forms of heightened judicial scrutiny that Professors Epstein, Sullivan, and others propose, is quite costly. First, it will prevent local governments from spending exactions for something other than a remedy for the harm at issue, even when that course would be most efficient. It may be that there is no practical way to remedy a particular harm if the development is allowed; if building a high-rise will cast a shadow over a large portion of Central Park, for example, there may be no technologically feasible way to have both a high-rise and a sunny park. Or the remedy for the harm may be more costly than the value of preventing the harm; Justice Scalia's idea of a viewing spot on property that blocks visual access to the ocean may strike the municipality as unworkable because the cost of maintaining the viewing spot, enforcing the public's right to use the spot, and resolving disputes that may arise over such access may be higher than the value the public receives. A community then can quite justifiably seek a "second best" solution: a benefit that substitutes or makes up for the harm for which there is no feasible or cost-effective solution. That the municipality accepts a substitute remedy in those circumstances does not signal that the municipality was overregulating; it shows instead that the municipality acts rationally by trying to maximize the benefits that its citizens will receive in payment for the harm they must suffer. But the nexus test prevents substitute remedies.

The nexus text also raises the possibility that judges will substitute their value judgments for the judgments of the legislature under the guise of assessing the closeness of the fit between an exaction and the purposes for which development might have been denied. The calculation of harms caused by a development, and the allocation of costs among new developments, or between new residents and existing residents, is fraught with complexities for which judges enjoy no special competence. Those calculations, as well as the judge's initial determination of the legislature's purposes, leave plenty of room for a judge to substitute her notion of the public good for that of the legislature. Finally, the nexus requirement has the cost of chilling local governments' creative attempts to resolve the pressing prob-

lem of harmonizing demands for economic development with the goals of preserving the environment and improving the quality of life within the community.

In light of those costs, it is essential to examine other means of policing local
governments' exactions policies. Because our legal system usually relies upon the
principles of the free market, market forces are a prime candidate for an alternative
to judicial scrutiny. The evidence that the forces of competition may serve to constrain local governments from overregulating and overcharging through exactions
is at least sufficient to require that those who call for heightened scrutiny justify their
departure from the ideology of the free market. It will be interesting indeed to hear
why the market forces deemed adequate to protect poor women seeking abortions,
and workers seeking government employment from unjust conditioned benefits
suddenly just won't do when the government makes an offer to a developer.

Notes

1. Consider the Supreme Court's opinion in Dolan v. City of Tigard, 512
U.S. 374 (1994), vis-à-vis Professor Been's analysis.

2. For discussion of the constitutional limits on exactions, see Robert H.
Freilich & David W. Bushek, *Thou Shall Not Take Title Without Adequate
Planning: The Takings Equation After* Dolan v. City of Tigard, 27 Urb. Law.
187 (1995); Gideon Kanner, *Tennis Anyone? How California Judges Made
Land Ransom and Art Censorship Legal*, 25 Real Est. L.J. 214 (1997);
Nancy E. Stroud & Susan L. Trevarthen, *Defensible Exactions After* Nollan
v. California Coastal Commission *and* Dolan v. City of Tigard, 25 Stetson
L. Rev. 719 (1996).

C. Transferable Development Rights

The Future of Transferable Development Rights in the Supreme Court

Linda A. Malone
73 Ky. L.J. 759 (1985)[*]

Introduction

Despite growing utilization of transferable development rights (TDRs) to insulate land use measures from taking challenges, the Supreme Court has yet to address the issue of whether TDRs can salvage government regulation that would otherwise constitute a taking of private property without just compensation. The saving grace of TDRs is that they may permit an owner of property that has been restrictively zoned to recoup any economic loss on the restricted property by selling the property's severed development rights to receiving properties authorized for increased density of development.[2] In theory at least, the use of TDRs precludes taking clause objections. Restricted landowners cannot claim that the restrictive zoning has deprived them of the economic value of the restricted property, since any economic loss can be compensated through sale of the TDRs. In this way, TDRs have proven to be useful as a tool for preservation of properties—such as farmland, landmarks, historic sites and open space—which are threatened by approaching development.

The growing popularity of using TDRs as a farmland and historic site preservation device makes it quite likely that the Supreme Court soon will find it necessary to face the constitutional issues that TDRs pose. A likely factual scenario for the Court would be as follows: A landowner owns two or more contiguous parcels of property in an area of growing development, and the land has been zoned for commercial or residential use. One of the parcels of property is undeveloped—that is, the property has no commercial development and little or no residential devel-

---

[*]   © 1985. Reprinted by permission.

[2]   For an analysis of the mechanics of various TDR schemes, see Merriam, *Making TDR Work*, 56 N.C.L. Rev. 77 (1978); Torres, *Helping Farmers and Saving Farmland*, 37 Okla. L. Rev. 31, 38-45 (1984).

A preservation technique related to the transfer of development rights is the technique of purchase of development rights. In such a program the development rights are purchased by a local planning agency to hold in abeyance indefinitely (in what has been referred to as "land banking") or until a decision is made to release them for further development. E. Roberts, The Law and the Preservation of Agricultural Land 76-77 (1982). . . .

    . . . .

opment—and, in that state of undevelopment, the property provides agricultural, aesthetic or ecological benefit to the rapidly developing community. The county zoning board then rezones the landowner's property so that the undeveloped parcel must remain undeveloped, but the landowner's other contiguous parcels of property are to retain the same density of development as under the prior zoning ordinances. To compensate for the restrictions on the undeveloped parcel, the county zoning ordinances provide that the parcel's unused development rights may be transferred: (a) to the owner's other contiguous and noncontiguous property or (b) to other designated, contiguous or noncontiguous lots under different ownership. The landowner subsequently submits a development plan for the undeveloped parcel to the zoning board, but the board disapproves the plan in accordance with the newly passed ordinances. The landowner then files suit in state court claiming damages for inverse condemnation and seeks a declaratory judgment that the ordinances have effectuated a taking of property without just compensation.

Assuming for purposes of the hypothetical that the restrictions imposed on the undeveloped parcel deprive it of all or almost all of its economic value, a court faced with a challenge to the validity of the ordinance could take any one of several approaches. First, the court could compare the value of *all* of the landowner's contiguous property to the value of the TDRs and conclude that the restrictions on the one parcel do not constitute a taking because they do not sufficiently deprive the landowner of the economic return on the property as a whole. In reaching such a conclusion, the court might even take into consideration the owner's noncontiguous property on which the TDRs might be used. Secondly, the court could focus only upon the economic detriment to the restricted parcel, and conclude that the conferral of the TDRs salvages the constitutionality of the ordinance from a taking challenge even if the ordinance would otherwise be a taking of the restricted parcel. Alternatively, again focusing only on the restricted parcel, the court could find, without considering the value of the TDRs, that there had been a taking. The court then would have to determine whether the TDRs satisfy the constitutional requisites for just compensation.

The foregoing hypothetical would raise two as yet unresolved issues of fundamental importance to every TDR scheme: (1) What is the appropriate unit of property in relation to which a taking is to be evaluated? and (2) Is the value of TDRs relevant to whether a taking has occurred or relevant only to whether just compensation has been provided once a taking has been found?

A TDR scheme poses unique problems in defining the unit of property which is allegedly being taken. In the usual zoning situation, the unit or units of property for taking purposes will be determined to a large extent by the challenged action of the zoning authority. If the parcels are separately rezoned and/or treated as separate parcels by the zoning authority, the reviewing court is more likely to determine the taking issue separately with regard to each parcel, even if the landowner is claiming that both parcels have been taken. If the landowner claims that only one of the contiguous parcels is being taken, however, the courts differ as to whether to consider the effect on the landowner's contiguous property as a whole or on the restricted parcel only.

The TDR situation is further complicated by the fact that the restricted parcel is economically and administratively linked to the receiving area for the TDRs, which may be contiguous or noncontiguous parcels and which may be under the same or different ownership from that of the restricted parcel. In evaluating the economic effect of the zoning on the landowner's "property," should contiguous non-receiving parcels under the same ownership be part of the property? Further, should contiguous and/or noncontiguous receiving parcels under the same ownership be part of the property?

Another question is whether the value of the TDRs should be relevant initially in determining whether a taking has occurred, or if it should be relevant only in deciding whether just compensation has been provided if a taking is otherwise found. TDRs defy easy categorization as either regulation or compensation. TDRs' hybrid character is reflected in the disagreement within the Supreme Court as to which of the two prongs of the taking test triggers consideration of TDRs. Compounding this disagreement, it appears that the Court is now less inclined than in the past to look at the landowner's economic situation as a whole in evaluating whether a taking has occurred. The focus may no longer be on how many "sticks" out of the bundle of rights known as property have been taken, but on which one or ones have been taken. Therefore, both the owner's vestigial rights following the governmental action and the extensiveness of the landowner's other property are less important to the analysis of taking. Instead, the result is concentration on the "nature" of the right invaded and its economic value to the landowner. Under the emerging view, the deprivation of one property right alone is more likely to result in a taking if that property right is economically significant, but the requisite degree of significance has yet to be delineated. Thus far, the right to exclude others for competitive advantage has been of sufficient economic significance that its deprivation has twice been held by the Court to constitute a taking. These cases cause one to wonder if the right to develop can be far behind.

. . . .

I. PENN CENTRAL AND ITS PROGENY

In 1978 the Supreme Court upheld the application to the Grand Central Terminal of New York City's Landmarks Preservation Law, rejecting in the process claims that this application of the law had taken the owners' property without just compensation and had arbitrarily deprived them of their property without due process of law.[15] To alleviate the economic burden placed on landmark owners, the preservation law permitted affected owners to transfer their unusable development rights in the landmark site to other proximate lots. The *Penn Central* decision triggered an optimistic flurry of innovative zoning techniques that frequently employed the transferability of development rights to provide greater insulation against taking challenges. But *Penn Central* actually posited relatively limited reassurance for

---

[15] *See* 438 U.S. 104.

such zoning, and lower courts have had to grapple with the Court's repeated admission that taking challenges entail essentially ad hoc, factual inquiries.

Without reaching the issue of whether a TDR could be just compensation, the Court in *Penn Central* did suggest that the availability of a TDR might be of some significance in determining whether a taking has occurred. . . .

. . . .

. . . In reaching its holding, the Court addressed only briefly the relevance of the TDRs to the taking issue:

> [T]o the extent appellants have been denied the right to build above the Terminal, it is not literally accurate to say that they have been denied *all* use of even those pre-existing air rights. Their ability to use these rights has not been abrogated; they are made transferable to at least eight parcels in the vicinity of the Terminal, one or two of which have been found suitable for the construction of new office buildings. Although appellants and others have argued that New York City's transferable development-rights program is far from ideal, the New York courts here supportably found that, at least in the case of the Terminal, the rights afforded are valuable. While these rights may well not have constituted "just compensation" if a "taking" had occurred, the rights nevertheless undoubtedly mitigate whatever financial burdens the law has imposed on appellants and, for that reason, are to be taken into account in considering the impact of regulation.[30]

Having concluded that there was not a taking, the Court had no need to address the issue of whether the TDRs would have provided "just compensation" had a taking occurred.

Although the majority seemed more inclined to consider the value of TDRs in relation to the taking issue, Justice Rehnquist in his dissent, joined by Chief Justice Burger and Justice Stevens, took a different approach. Justice Rehnquist concluded that the landmark preservation ordinance had taken Penn Central property by restricting use of the property's air rights. . . .

Nevertheless, Rehnquist would have remanded the case to the New York Court of Appeals "for a determination of whether TDRs constitute a 'full and perfect equivalent for the property taken'."[35] As to whether the TDRs are a "full and perfect equivalent for the property taken,"[36] he considered as negative factors the severely limited area to which transfer was permitted, the complex procedures required to obtain a transfer permit, the uncertain and contingent market value of the TDRs, and the failure of the TDRs to reflect the value lost. As a factor favoring the TDRs as just compensation, Rehnquist acknowledged that Penn Central had been offered "substantial amounts" for its TDRs.[38]

---

[30] *Id.* at 137 (footnote omitted).

[35] *Id.* at 152 (Rehnquist, J., dissenting) (quoting Monongahela Navigation Co. v. United States, 148 U.S. 312, 326 (1893)).

[36] *Id.* at 151-52 (Rehnquist, J., dissenting).

[38] *See id.* at 151-52 (Rehnquist, J., dissenting).

After *Penn Central* there followed a series of cases in which the character of the interference with the property right was outcome-determinative of the taking issue. In *Kaiser Aetna v. United States*,[39] the Corps of Engineers claimed the government had a navigational servitude on what had been a private lagoon, which the owners had connected to the Pacific Ocean, with Corps approval, in order to build an exclusive marina-based community. Writing for the majority, Justice Rehnquist stated that the Court would decide the taking issue by examining "the economic impact of the regulation, its interference with reasonable investment backed expectations, and the character of the governmental action."[41] The Court rejected the government's claim that a navigational servitude existed. Finding that public access would result in an actual physical invasion of private property by the government, Justice Rehnquist stated that impairment of the property owners' right to exclude others would frustrate the owners' reasonable investment-backed expectations and, therefore, constitute a taking.

In contrast, in *PruneYard Shopping Center v. Robins*,[44] the Court upheld a state constitutional requirement that shopping center owners permit individuals to exercise their free speech and petition rights in the shopping center despite the owners' argument that they were being deprived of their property without compensation. In *PruneYard*, as in *Kaiser Aetna*, the character of the governmental action was a physical invasion of private property. Justice Rehnquist, again speaking for the Court, suggested that deprivation of a right to exclude others by its very nature is more likely to constitute a taking. In *PruneYard*, however, the Court refused to find the physical invasion to be dispositive because, not surprisingly, there was no showing that the right to *exclude* others was important to the economic value of the shopping center.

The Court's emphasis on the character of the governmental interference reached its peak in *Loretto v. Teleprompter Manhattan CATV Corp.*[49] In an opinion by Justice Marshall, from which Justices Blackmun, Brennan and White dissented, the physical invasion resulting from a television cable installed on an apartment owner's roof, as authorized under New York law, was held to constitute a taking of the apartment owner's property without compensation. Despite the minimal interference by the cable in the owner's enjoyment of his property, the Court held the physical invasion to be a "per se" taking of private property. Thus, the character of the governmental action has become, not merely a factor, but the only factor in finding a taking when the governmental action is a physical invasion of property.

This series of physical intrusion cases provides little direct guidance as to the direction the Court will take after *Penn Central* in evaluating TDR techniques. . . .

---

[39] 444 U.S. 164 (1979).

[41] *Id.* at 175.

[44] 447 U.S. 74 (1980).

[49] 458 U.S. 419 (1982).

Rehnquist's approach, and the approach generally taken in *Kaiser Aetna* and the cases which followed, is to first determine which of the so-called "bundle of sticks" constituting property has been taken (for example, the right to exclude others), and then to determine how important that "stick" is to the use or economic value of the property. If that property right is of an as yet unspecified level of significance to the economic value or use of the property, then its deprivation alone may constitute a taking.

In contrast, the *Penn Central* majority would be more inclined to examine the entire bundle of sticks, (for example, the full fee interest or all the landowner's contiguous property) and refuse to find a taking unless some significant number of sticks had been destroyed by the governmental action. The implications for any land use regulation that severely restricts development cannot be ignored. Following Justice Rehnquist's approach, the denial of a right to develop one's property could be important to the economic value of the property for the landowner. Thus, the deprivation of a single important property right, one stick in the bundle, could be a taking. Under the approach of the *Penn Central* majority, deprivation of one property right alone would rarely constitute a taking. The landowner would still have use of all the property rights other than the right to develop, and the only question would be whether the economic value of the property as a whole had been destroyed. In sum, under Justice Rehnquist's approach the nature of the property right taken becomes more important than what property rights remain.

Although the majority and the dissenters were unable to agree in *Penn Central* on the extent of economic deprivation necessary to constitute a taking, the Court was able to agree on some general guidelines in the recent case of *Ruckelshaus v. Monsanto Company*.[55] In *Monsanto*, the Court determined that under Missouri law trade secrets were property for purposes of the fifth amendment's taking clause. In addition to disclosing some of the data to the public pursuant to the provisions of the Federal Insecticide, Fungicide, and Rodenticide Act (FIFRA),[57] the Environmental Protection Agency (EPA) had utilized trade secret information submitted to it for pesticide registration by Monsanto, a pesticide manufacturer, in order to evaluate other pesticide manufacturers' applications for registration.

On behalf of a unanimous Court Justice Blackmun stated that whether a governmental action has gone beyond "regulation" to a "taking" depends upon " 'the character of the governmental action, its economic impact, and its interference with reasonable investment backed expectations,' "[60] a test first formulated in *Penn Central*. The *Penn Central* Court focused only on the last factor as being so "overwhelming" under the facts of that case as to be dispositive of the taking question.[61]

---

[55] 104 S. Ct. 2862 (1984).

[57] 7 U.S.C § 136 (1982).

[60] *Id.* at 2875 (quoting PruneYard Shopping Center v. Robbins, 447 U.S. at 83).

[61] *See* Penn Central Transp. Co. v. City of New York, 438 U.S. at 124.

According to the *Monsanto* Court, the explicit governmental guarantee of confidentiality in the 1972 amendments to FIFRA was the basis for Monsanto's reasonable investment-backed expectation. The EPA's disclosure and utilization of the data deprived Monsanto of its "right to exclude others [which] is central to the very definition of the property interest" in a trade secret.[63] The essential economic value of the property right lay in the competitive advantage—an advantage destroyed by disclosure of the data; consequently, the remaining uses of the data were "irrelevant to the determination of the economic impact" of the EPA's action on Monsanto's property right.[64] For the first time in a case not involving a physical invasion, the Court found that the importance of the property interest invaded outweighed consideration of any remaining rights in the property.

II. THE MOST LIKELY SCENARIO FOR
THE COURT: OPEN SPACE ZONING AND TDRS

A. *Judicial Dodgeball and TDRs*

In three cases, *Agins v. City of Tiburon*,[65] *San Diego Gas & Electric Co. v. City of San Diego*,[66] and *Aptos Seascape Corp. v. County of Santa Cruz*,[67] the Court skirted taking claims in which TDRs played pivotal roles. In each case, zoning to preserve open space was tempered by conferral of TDRs on the open space lots. The likelihood of such a case appearing before the Court has increased in light of several decisions invalidating open space zoning on constitutional grounds.[68]
. . . .

B. *Defining the Unit of "Property" in Relation to TDRs*

Agins, San Diego Gas, and *Aptos Seascape* indicate that the hypothetical posed in the introduction to this Article is destined to reach the Supreme Court. When it does, the unanswered questions from *Penn Central* will have to be addressed: (1) What is the appropriate property unit? and (2) Are TDRs relevant to the taking determination or to the just compensation determination? . . .
. . . .

The inherent difficulty caused by TDR schemes in attempting to characterize the zoning authority's treatment of separate parcels is that the use of TDRs inextricably links together several parcels of property which may or may not be con-

---

[63] [104 S. Ct.] . . . at 2878.

[64] *Id.* . . .

[65] 447 U.S. 255 (1980).

[66] 450 U.S. 621 (1981).

[67] 188 Cal. Rptr. 191 (Ct. App. 1982), *appeal dismissed,* 104 S. Ct. 53 (1983).

[68] *See, e.g.,* Sheerr v. Township of Evesham, 445 A.2d 46 (N.J. Super. Ct. Law Div. 1982); Morris County Land Improvement Co. v. Township of Parsippany-Troy Hills, 193 A.2d 232 (N.J. 1963); Lemp v. Town Board of Islip, 394 N.Y.S.2d 517 (App. Div. 1977).

tiguous or under the same ownership. By their very nature, TDRs coordinate densities between separate parcels of property, thus in a sense making such parcels a unit for planning purposes.

Penn Central triggered the dilemma of definition, but did nothing to resolve it. Its broad suggestion that " 'taking' jurisprudence does not divide a single parcel into discrete segments"[113] is easily circumscribed by the facts of the case . . . . The Court's reasoning in this context was addressed to Penn Central's argument that the property in question was air rights, which in turn was a segment of a single parcel—the city tax block designated as the landmark site. *Penn Central* is perhaps more instructive for what it did not do: It did not define the property to encompass other contiguous or noncontiguous property owned by Penn Central to which the development rights could be transferred.

. . . .

In short, *Penn Central* poses no immediate barriers to TDR land planning techniques that impose severe restrictions on a single parcel of property in a planning area. The opinion on its face supports looking at the restricted parcel in conjunction with the value of the TDRs to determine the extent of economic interference. Even if the ordinance were to deprive the landowner of all reasonable return on the property, therefore, it is conceivable that the TDRs might redeem the ordinance from a taking perspective. Moreover, in its underlying receptiveness to a broad-based economic analysis of the impact of the regulation, *Penn Central* leaves open the economically sound possibility that the regulatory impact could be determined with reference to all of the landowner's contiguous property that functions as an economic unit in response to the regulation. Under either analysis, a taking is unlikely to occur unless the landowner is deprived of all or almost all of the defined property's reasonable use and the TDRs fail to have a reasonable, ascertainable value. However, if *Kaiser Aetna, PruneYard* and *Monsanto* are seen as a reformulation of taking jurisprudence along the lines of the *Penn Central* dissent, the property right, not the property unit, is determinative of a taking challenge. If the right itself is central to the *type* of property at issue, its deprivation may be enough to constitute a taking, without regard to any remaining uses, to other economically related property, or to the availability of TDRs. Given *Monsanto*'s recent emphasis on loss of profit potential, deprivation of the right to develop property stands a better chance of protection under the taking clause. With TDRs relegated to the issue of just compensation, zoning prohibitions against any development may not withstand a taking challenge under this approach.

C. The Second Issue: Are TDRs a Panacea for a Taking, or (Un)just Compensation?

Transferable development rights can be viewed as a hybrid of the police power and eminent domain, a synthesis of regulation and compensation. By granting TDRs, has the zoning authority avoided a taking or has it obviated the issue by providing remuneration for lost rights? In *Penn Central*, Justice Brennan assumed that

---

[113] Penn Cent. Transp. Co. v. City of New York, 438 U.S. at 130.

the value of the TDRs was relevant to determining whether a taking had occurred; Justice Rehnquist found a taking without reference to the TDRs and would have remanded for a determination of their value as just compensation. Neither Justice explained his underlying assumption as to the relevance of the TDRs to the two-part inquiry of "taking" and "just compensation." The question is certainly not academic. TDRs appear much less likely to be an effective barrier to a taking challenge under the rubric of just compensation than under the multifactor concept of "reasonable use." Although much has been written on regulatory schemes which may best insure the economic viability of TDRs,[129] the fact remains that even the most carefully tailored TDR scheme provides no direct monetary compensation and depends upon market factors beyond a zoning authority's control. The Supreme Court's analysis in *Agins* and *San Diego* demonstrates that nonmonetary remedies for a taking will be closely scrutinized.

. . . .

In *Monsanto, PruneYard, Kaiser Aetna* and *Penn Central,* the Court has stated that three factors are relevant to a taking: "the character of the governmental action, its economic impact, and its interference with reasonable investment-backed expectations."[160] Any evaluation of the economic impact of the regulation is necessarily incomplete without inclusion of the value of TDRs in the taking computation. Whatever might be the economic wisdom or lack thereof in excluding the value of postregulation vestigial rights from the economic tally, it is unjustifiably myopic to exclude the economic value of TDRs that relate directly to the economic value of the specific property right allegedly being taken. For example, even if the Rehnquist approach would exclude the economic value of remaining uses of the restricted property (e.g., recreational, agricultural) from the economic impact computation, why exclude the market value of TDRs in relation to the economic loss which the TDRs are designed to offset?

With reference to the relatively unexplored element of "interference with reasonable investment-backed expectations," the Court will be confronted with a traditional zoning analysis. Under such analysis, absent perhaps some governmental action which reasonably induced good faith reliance either on a right to continued development as in *Kaiser Aetna* or on utilization of profit potential as existed in *Monsanto,* there are no vested rights to develop based on reliance on any preexisting zoning scheme. Whether as a general rule there exists a reasonable investment-backed expectation of some development, no matter how minimal, remains to be seen. Implicit in the concept of land use regulation is the premise that property rights are not absolute. Of all the so-called property rights, a right to develop one's property is the most likely source of conflict and, concomitantly, the right most likely to necessitate compromise. It is no longer reasonable to expect one's

---

[129] *See, e.g.,* Delaney, Kominers & Gordon, *TDR Redux: A Second Generation of Practical Legal Courses,* 15 URB. LAW. 593 (1983); Richman & Kendeg, *Transfer Development Rights—A Pragmatic View,* 9 URB. LAW. 571 (1977).

[160] Ruckelshaus v. Monsanto Co., 104 S. Ct. at 2874 (quoting 447 U.S. at 83).

property rights to extend "from the center usque ad coelum."[164] A theory of taking jurisprudence which reinstates the right to develop as fundamental or paramount fails to reflect the modern realities of land use regulation or the expectations of the property owner.

From a legal perspective, the better analysis is to consider TDRs in relation to both the taking issue and the just compensation issue. In a regulatory taking two related constitutional challenges may be made—deprivation of due process and taking without just compensation. The second challenge consists of two distinct components—"taking" and "just compensation." Relegating TDRs to the just compensation evaluation leads to an anomalous result. The question common to both challenges—whether the landowner may still make a reasonable return on the property—would include consideration of the TDRs' value under the due process analysis but not under a taking analysis. For purposes of due process analysis there is only a one-part inquiry—whether there is a reasonable return—to which the value of TDRs is either relevant or irrelevant. There is no second inquiry under which the TDRs may be considered. To totally exclude the value of TDRs from a due process analysis appears unjustifiable, yet inclusion of this value would result in a more expansive due process analysis of economic impact than permitted under the taking clause.

Justice Rehnquist's criticism of Justice Brennan's approach remains: If a taking is judged by the diminution in value of the property as a whole, what is the appropriate property unit in any given case? . . .

. . . [I]t is perhaps time that the Supreme Court disengage itself from "ad hoc factual" inquiries where property, rather than personal, rights are involved. . . . Greater deference to the planning agency's findings as to the appropriate unit of property would serve the interests of judicial economy, yet judicial review of the ultimate issue of whether a taking had occurred would be preserved. Moreover, regardless of whether TDRs are held to be relevant to the taking or to the just compensation issue, the Court will at some point find itself obligated under its present scope of review to ascertain the economic value of TDRs in a limitless range of economic situations. When that occurs, deference to the local planning agency's expertise should be effected through reviewing facts under the traditional substantial evidence standard.

Conclusion

The Court appears to be moving toward a taking jurisprudence which would elevate certain select property rights, and potentially the "right to develop," above other rights and above the needs of the community. This approach invites conflict between standards for a taking violation and those for a due process violation. It focuses on the nature of the property right, rather than on the true economic impact of the regulation and the public policy concerns for preservation. Although the countervailing "diminution in value" approach necessitates some definition of

---

[164] Hay v. Cahoes Co., 2 N.Y. 159 (1849).

the property taken, such factual matters may best be left, under either approach, to the expertise of the local planning agency. Regardless of which approach prevails, at some point the Court will find itself confronted with a complex evaluation of the economic value of TDRs. It is difficult to posit a question which calls more for judicial deference to the expertise of the local planning agency.

TDRs are an innovative advance in preservation techniques. When well planned and implemented, TDRs promise an equitable distribution of the costs of preservation among all of those who would benefit from it. Farmland, landmarks and scenic open areas are "public goods" like clean air and clean water; without regulation of the allocation of preservation costs, these costs will not fall proportionally on all those who benefit from preservation. If TDRs do not fit neatly into our traditional concepts of police power versus eminent domain, regulation versus compensation, the fault may not lie with TDRs as much as with the traditional concepts. Land use is indeed one of the areas, like medicine and technology, in which innovation has rendered many legal precepts inadequate or obsolete. There is a need for greater flexibility in taking jurisprudence, and this need can be met through increased deference to the difficult economic and administrative findings made by local planning agencies. The present approach of the Court toward a hierarchy of property rights suggests there will be less flexibility and, accordingly, less of a future for innovative land use planning.

Notes

1. In Suitum v. Tahoe Regional Planning Agency, 117 S. Ct. 1659 (1997), the Supreme Court considered a regulatory takings action that involved transferable development rights. The Court found that the landowner's claim passed the "final decision" part of the ripeness test, but noted: "[W]e do not decide, whether or not these TDRs may be considered in deciding the issue of whether there has been a taking in this case, as opposed to the issue of whether just compensation has been afforded for such a taking." *Id.* at 1662. Three Justices (O'Connor, Scalia, and Thomas), however, opined in a concurring opinion authored by Justice Scalia that the TDRs in question have no bearing on a takings inquiry and are germane only to the compensation question. *Id.* at 1671-1672.

2. Although the Supreme Court has yet to address fully the transferable development rights issues touched upon in *Penn Central*, the Court has decided a number of takings cases since Professor Malone's article appeared. What impact do these decisions have on analysis of the role of transferable development rights in takings controversies?

D. Historic Preservation

THE CURRENT STATUS OF HISTORICAL PRESERVATION LAW IN REGULATORY TAKINGS JURISPRUDENCE: HAS THE *LUCAS* "MISSILE" DISMANTLED PRESERVATION PROGRAMS?

Marilyn Phelan
6 Fordham Envtl. L.J. 785 (1995)[*]

INTRODUCTION

The Supreme Court's current liberal construction of the Fifth Amendment's Takings Clause is grounded in more than a century of rulings in which the Court often has judged governmental regulation inflicting a burden or harm on private property to be a compensable taking. Yet, to date, the Supreme Court has not formulated an explicit rule to determine the precise point at which governmental regulation becomes a "taking." The dissenting Justices in the Supreme Court's recent decision in *Lucas v. South Carolina Coastal Council*[1] maintained that the Court drafted a new regulatory takings doctrine when it ruled that total regulatory takings require compensation. If, indeed, the Supreme Court has charted a new course in applying the Takings Clause to governmental regulation, the proponents of historical preservation must assess how the new principles relate to preservation laws. However, given the recent decisions of the Supreme Court, which reveal the diversity among members of the Court over the proper application of the Takings Clause to governmental regulation, the position of historical preservation regulation in regulatory takings jurisprudence is confusing at best.

. . . .

This Article addresses the conflict between governmental regulation to preserve cultural, architectural, or historical aspects of property and the Takings Clause. . . .

---

[*] © 1995. Reprinted by permission.
[1] 112 S. Ct. 2886 (1992).

I. A HISTORY OF THE TAKINGS CLAUSE FROM A SUPREME COURT PERSPECTIVE

. . . .

. . . [T]he Court in *Penn Central Transportation Co. v. New York City*,[82] reviewed, for the first and only time, the application of the Takings Clause to historical preservation laws.

. . . .

In *Penn Central*, the Supreme Court ruled that New York's landmarks law was not a "taking" when its application had the effect of precluding the Penn Central Transportation Company from building a skyscraper atop Grand Central Terminal. The Court decided that a determination of what constitutes a taking is "essentially" an "ad hoc, factual inquir[y]," but pointed out several factors "that have particular significance."[90]

One important factor the Court listed was "character of the governmental action."[91] The Court also declared that a " 'taking' may more readily be found when interference with property can be characterized as a physical invasion by government."[92] The Court cited the economic impact of the regulation on the property owner and "particularly, the extent to which the regulation has interfered with distinct investment-backed expectations," as relevant considerations.[93] The Court resolved the "fairness" issue by concluding that the New York law did not "interfere in any way with the present uses of the Terminal."[94] The Court decided that designation of the Terminal as a landmark "not only permits but contemplates that [its owners] may continue to use the property precisely as it has been used for the past 65 years."[95] The Court reasoned there was no taking because restrictions on use of the property were "substantially related to the promotion of the general welfare."[96]

. . . .

II. ARE HISTORICAL PRESERVATION LAWS A "TAKING?"[204]

Beginning at the turn of the century, Congress and the states began to realize that many historically significant properties in the United States were in jeopardy,

---

[82] 438 U.S. 104 (1978).

[90] *Id.* [at 124.]

[91] *Id.*

[92] *Id.*

[93] *Id.*

[94] *Id.* at 136.

[95] *Id.*

[96] *Id.* at 138. The Court concluded that the restrictions permitted "reasonable beneficial use" of the landmark and also afforded property owners opportunities "further to enhance not only the Terminal site property but also other properties." *Id.*

[204] Some of the summary material of historical preservation laws was taken from MARILYN PHELAN, MUSEUM LAW, A GUIDE FOR OFFICERS, DIRECTORS AND COUNSEL (1994), and MARILYN PHELAN, NONPROFIT ENTERPRISES §§ 16:07 to :08.50, 16:20 to :21 (1985).

and that many others had already been destroyed without considering their historical or cultural value. However, efforts to preserve and to protect archaeological and anthropological resources were initially ineffectual because of their limited scope. At that time, there was little, if any, governmental regulation of the use of private property. Thus, courts were not required to determine applicability of the Takings Clause to preservation regulations.

The later impetus to enact legislation to preserve historical treasures within domestic boundaries was precipitated by two concerns.[205] One was the "recognition that . . . large numbers of historic structures, landmarks, and areas ha[d] been destroyed without adequate consideration of either the values represented therein or the possibility of preserving the destroyed properties for use in economically productive ways."[206]

The second concern was the "widely shared belief that structures with special historic, cultural, or architectural significance enhance the quality of life for all."[207] The enactment of historical preservation statutes eventually resulted from a recognition that historical treasures not only "represent the lessons of the past and embody precious features of our heritage, they serve as examples of quality for today."[208]

The first congressional attempt to save historic treasures within the United States was its enactment of the Antiquities Act of 1906.[209] The Act provides penalties for destroying or damaging any historic ruins on public lands. The Antiquities Act was limited in its application, however, because it subjected persons to penalties for the appropriation of a "ruin," "monument," or "object of antiquity," terms which the Act did not define.

The Antiquities Act became more effective when Congress enacted the Historic Sites Act in 1935.[213] The Historic Sites Act declared it a national policy "to preserve for public use historic sites, buildings, and objects of national significance for the inspiration and benefit of the people of the United States."[214] The Secretary of the Interior was given the power to contract, and to enter into cooperative agreements with the states, municipal subdivisions, and private organizations and individuals, to protect, preserve, maintain, or operate historic structures and sites connected with a public use. Thus, as late as the 1930s, historical preservation laws were directed toward preserving historical structures on public property; such laws did not restrict a citizen's use of private, historical properties.

---

[205] Penn Cent. Transp. Co. v. New York City, 438 U.S. 104, 108-09 (1978).

[206] *Id.* at 108.

[207] *Id.*

[208] *Id.*

[209] An Act for the Preservation of American Antiquities, Pub. L. No. 59-209, §§ 1-4, 34 Stat. 225 (codified as amended at 16 U.S.C. §§ 431-433 (1988 & Supp. V 1993)).

[213] An Act to Provide for the Preservation of Historic American Sites, Buildings, Objects, and Antiquities of National Significance, and for Other Purposes, Pub. L. No. 74-292, §§ 1-7, 49 Stat. 666 (codified as amended at 16 U.S.C. §§ 461-467 (1988)).

[214] 16 U.S.C. § 461.

In 1939, a court first ruled that a government could "take" private historical property and preserve it for the "public good." In *Barnidge v. United States*,[216] the Eighth Circuit held that the Secretary of the Interior could institute condemnation proceedings to acquire private property that the Secretary determined to possess exceptional value as a historical site. Regulation of the "use" of such property followed.

In 1949, the National Trust for Historic Preservation in the United States (the "National Trust") was chartered as a private, nonprofit organization.[217] The National Trust was established "to receive donations of sites, buildings, and objects significant in United States history and culture, [and] to preserve and administer them for the public benefit."[218] Recently, the Supreme Court of Illinois ruled that the National Trust had standing to maintain actions in courts to prevent the destruction or alteration of buildings with national historic significance.[219]

For the most part, governmental regulation of the use of private properties that have historical value began with the National Historic Preservation Act,[220] which was enacted in 1966. The Act provides for the maintenance and expansion of "a National Register of Historic Places composed of districts, sites, buildings, structures, and objects significant in United States history, architecture, archaeology, and culture."[221] In 1980, the Act was amended to provide better guidance for the National Historic Preservation Program at the federal, state, and local levels. At that time, Congress asserted that a partnership had developed between the federal government, the several states, and the private sector to protect the nation's historic resources.

Most historical preservation is accomplished through the states in cooperation with the federal government. In the past two decades, numerous state preservation programs have been initiated, and each state has established some form of a state preservation agency. But an impediment to state historic preservation is the concern that once a structure is designated as having historic significance, it may not be altered or destroyed. For example, in *Penn Central Transportation Co. v. New York City*,[224] the owner of Grand Central Terminal wanted to demolish a portion of the terminal building and construct an office tower above it. The terminal, one of New York City's most famous buildings, had been designated a "landmark" pursuant to city law. When New York City refused to grant permission, Penn Central brought a lawsuit alleging that the designation restricted the use of property and diminished

---

[216] 101 F.2d 295 (8th Cir. 1939).

[217] An Act to Further the Policy Enunciated in the Historic Sites Act (49 Stat. 666) and to Facilitate Public Participation in the Preservation of Sites, Buildings, and Objects of National Significance or Interest and Providing a National Trust for Historic Preservation, Pub. L. No. 81-408, 63 Stat. 927 (codified as amended at 16 U.S.C. §§ 468-468d (1988)).

[218] 16 U.S.C. § 468.

[219] Landmarks Preservation Council v. City of Chicago, 531 N.E.2d 9 (Ill. 1988). . . .

[220] 16 U.S.C. §§ 470 to 470w-6 (1988 & Supp. V 1993).

[221] 16 U.S.C. § 470a(1)(A). . . .

[224] 438 U.S. 104 (1978).

its value, thus constituting a "taking." The Supreme Court did not find a taking, likening New York's Landmarks Preservation Law to zoning regulations that are "substantially related to the promotion of the general welfare."[226] Thus, the Court held that the diminution in property value caused by application of the preservation law to the owner's property did not constitute a taking.

. . . .

Since the Supreme Court's decision in *Penn Central*, lower courts have cited that decision as authority that no taking occurs when historical preservation laws restrict the use of privately-owned historical properties. . . .

III. Determining Whether Preservation Regulations Constitute Compensable Takings

In essence, the issue currently before preservation planners is whether they can continue to rely upon *Penn Central* to resist compensation to private interests when preservation laws substantially limit the use of landmark property. If the Supreme Court has tipped the balancing test scales in favor of private interests, then some preservation regulation, which previously did not require payment to landowners, may now transgress the constitutional limitations imposed by the Takings Clause. Owners who have sought, or who have accepted without objection, designation of their property as a landmark may have waived any takings claims relating to restrictions on the use or modification of their properties. It can hardly be said that these owners have been singled out unfairly. Furthermore, a general and comprehensive preservation program, which affects all property owners in a certain historical district equally and does not target individual properties, is less likely to constitute a taking of the property interests of the individual owners. However, if a preservation regulation totally destroys any future economic or beneficial use of historical properties, the Supreme Court would undoubtedly rule that such regulation amounts to a taking. . . .

. . . An intelligible takings inquiry must ask whether the extent of the interference is so exacting as to constitute a compensable taking in light of the owner's alternative uses for the property. In *Dolan v. City of Tigard*,[251] the Supreme Court ruled that local governments and officials must make an "individualized determination" that a governmental exaction through permit or similar conditions is "related both in nature and extent to the impact" of the condition and that there be a "rough proportionality" between any burden placed on private property and the "benefit" to the public through the exaction.[252] There is a question whether the majority opinion in *Dolan* would also apply to some, or all, forms of government regulation. In addressing this possibility, perhaps local governments and officials should make such an "individualized determination" respecting the nature and

---

[226] *Id.* at 138.

[251] 114 S. Ct. 2309 (1994).

[252] *Id.* at 2319-20. The burden for making such a determination is on the government. *Id.* at 2320 n.8. . . .

extent of restrictions placed upon private property through preservation regulation, and should consider that a substantial diminution in value of historical property through restrictions on its use may now require compensation to the owner. Clearly, the Court's ruling in *Penn Central*, that a destruction of one "strand" of an owner's otherwise full "bundle" of rights is not a taking, may no longer be valid in light of the Court's more recent decision in *Lucas*.

. . . .

CONCLUSION

While there remains a lack of clarity in the Supreme Court's application of the Takings Clause to governmental regulation of private property, historical preservationists can discern some principles to serve as guidelines when they embark on preservation programs. It is clear that, unless private property was already subject to preservation restrictions when it was acquired, any physical invasion of private property through preservation regulation, whether temporary or permanent, must now be compensated. But, it would seem that comprehensive nondiscriminatory preservation programs, which do not "specifically or disproportionately burden"[258] a landowner, would continue to be, like zoning regulations, "facially constitutional."[259] Still, in applying preservation restrictions to the "use" of private property, governmental officials should quantify, through some form of mathematical calculation, the extent of the burden on private property. If the burden is substantial, planners should consider compensation.

The new constitutional limitations placed upon land-use planners by recent Supreme Court rulings will unquestionably "lessen the freedom and flexibility"[260] historical preservationists experienced in the past. But perhaps preservationists may find some redeeming value in the current posture of the Supreme Court. When governmental officials become more willing to assess the cost of governmental regulation to private interests, some of the fear associated with having private property designated as a historical landmark may be abated. If the present concern in some circles about the burden placed upon private property through preservation regulation is alleviated, private interests may be more inclined to join the government in its efforts to preserve historical treasures. Thus, rather than dismantling historical preservation programs, the *Lucas* missile could ultimately improve and enhance the movement.

---

[258] *See* Carter v. Helmsley-Spear, Inc., 861 F. Supp. 303, 327 (S.D.N.Y. 1994).

[259] *See* Agins v. City of Tiburon, 447 U.S. 225 (1980). . . .

. . . .

[260] *See* First English Evangelical Lutheran Church v. County of Los Angeles, 482 U.S. 304 (1987) . . . .

Note

For another analysis of historic preservation measures, see John Nivala, *The Future for Our Past: Preserving Landmark Preservation*, 5 N.Y.U. Envtl. L.J. 83 (1996). Freedom of religion may become an issue whenever a structure owned by a religious organization is identified for historic preservation. *See* City of Boerne v. Flores, 117 S. Ct. 2157 (1997) (declaring Religious Freedom Restoration Act of 1993 unconstitutional in case where building permit for church expansion was refused on basis of ordinance establishing historic district); Alan C. Weinstein, *The Myth of Ministry vs. Mortar: A Legal and Policy Analysis of Landmark Designation of Religious Institutions*, 65 Temple L. Rev. 91 (1992) (discussing scope of First Amendment's Establishment and Free Exercise Clauses in historic preservation setting).

E. Activity at State Level

THE QUIET REVOLUTION REVISITED:
A QUARTER CENTURY OF PROGRESS
David L. Callies
26 Urb. Law. 197 (1994)*

I. Introduction

NEARLY TWENTY-FIVE YEARS AGO, *The Quiet Revolution in Land Use Control*[1] reported a shift in governmental regulation of land use from local governments back to the states. . . . *Quiet Revolution* illustrated the ways in which selected states exercised their fundamental police powers to regulate the use of land to implement state and regional policies. In virtually every such state, the exercise of such regulatory authority superseded or replaced local land-use regulations of the typical zoning and development control variety. The states acted because of the relative lack of planning at the local level, together with a disregard of the regional and statewide implications of such unplanned local land-use decision making. *Quiet Revolution* concluded that:

1. The concept of land had changed from a commodity only to both a resource and a commodity;
2. States were attempting to address truly statewide and regional issues rather than merely create another layer of land development control;
3. Nevertheless, duplication was rampant and a permit explosion resulted because few states made changes in local zoning enabling laws per se;
4   There was increased emphasis on planning and the relationship between local and state land-use controls and planning;
5. The new regulations renewed interest in the extent to which land-use controls raised constitutional "takings" problems; and
6. The new laws introduced and focused upon the importance of a state agency to implement the statewide and regional land-use controls.

Since those conclusions, much has transpired. Local zoning has not withered away (nor did we anticipate that it would). There has been precious little permit

---

[1]   FRED BOSSELMAN & DAVID CALLIES, THE QUIET REVOLUTION IN LAND USE CONTROL, Council on Environmental Quality (1971). . . .

simplification. Growth management has become the accepted rubric, embracing both state and local land-use development and regulatory reform. The environmental decade of the 1970s continued unabated into the 1980s (though in a somewhat different form). A series of U.S. Supreme Court land-use decisions in the late 1980s and early 1990s rekindled interest in the famous Holmes decision in *Pennsylvania Coal Co. v. Mahon*,[13] which held for the first time that a regulation which goes "too far" is a constitutionally protected taking of property—an issue which most state courts had explained away in dealing with challenges to "revolutionary" new land-use regulations. Lastly, several more states have adopted regional or statewide land-use control regimes either to protect resources of more than local concern or to manage growth which promises to have more than local impact.

What follows is a selective survey—a backward glance—of what has happened to the "quiet revolution" in the last two categories: which states have joined the revolution, and how state courts have treated the "revolutionary" laws when challenged.

II. The Continuous Revolution in Land-Use Control

A. *Hawaii, Where "It All Began"*

Hawaii was both prototype and inspiration for *Quiet Revolution*. Its then decade-old Land-Use Law[16] classified all the land in the state into four districts—urban, rural, agriculture, and conservation—and left boundary "amendments" to an appointed state Land-Use Commission upon petition by interested parties. Reviewed every five years under a statutory mandate, the present boundary division and district allocation results in less than five percent of the state's land area in the county-controlled urban district. Virtually all of the remainder is more or less evenly divided between agriculture (where the state Land-Use Commission (LUC) unevenly shares district regulatory authority with the counties) and conservation (where the state's Department of Land and Natural Resources, through its governing Board of Land and Natural Resources, or BLNR, controls the use of land absolutely). No significant urban development is permitted in either of these last two districts, though agricultural "subdivisions" on half-acre lots are permitted on certain agricultural lands if both the LUC and the county agree. While bills to amend the Land-Use Law emerge every few years, none have so far made much impact on the basic structure of the land-use regulatory system which it embodies. Nor has litigation over the boundary amendment (redistricting) authority of the LUC or the Act itself ever reached the courts.

More critical is the drafting and implementation in 1979 of Act 100, the Hawaii State Plan.[20] Virtually the only state plan which is enacted *tout ensemble* as

---

[13] 260 U.S. 393 (1922).

[16] HAW. REV. STAT. § 205 (1985).

[20] HAW. REV. STAT. § 226 (1985).

a statute, the plan requires state agencies such as the LUC and BLNR to conform their decisions and other land-related actions to a series of goals, policies, and objectives contained in the statute, and to use as guidelines eleven subject-specific "functional" plans (which average about thirty pages each). Language requiring counties also to conform their plans and land-use regulations to these state plans was largely stripped from Act 100 in 1984 and, together with the dilution of key definitions such as "conform" and "guidelines," results in a state plan the terms of which make compliance fairly easy. . . .

Despite the comparative weakness of the planning conformity requirements in the revised Act 100, the Hawaii Supreme Court recently declared, in ringing terms, that plans and planning are the keystone supporting the entire land-use regulatory program in Hawaii. In *Lum Yip Kee v. City and County of Honolulu*,[24] the court responded to a challenge to a city council "downzoning" by holding that all zoning in Honolulu must conform to detailed county development plans formulated with "input" from state and county agencies as well as the general public. . . . On balance, then, Hawaii appears to have continued to expand its part in the quiet revolution, and its courts have been broadly sympathetic.

B. *Vermont and Statewide Planning*

In 1971, Vermont, another of the original "revolutionary" states, was notable for its Environmental Board and Environmental Commissions which subjected certain land development decisions to regional review, appealable to a state agency. While contemplating a series of statewide plans, Act 250 actually produced only a preliminary classification system of marginal significance.[26]

Vermont became serious about statewide planning in 1988 with the passage of Act 200.[27] Establishing twelve statewide substantive planning goals to which each level of government is to conform, local governments' municipal plans are supposedly subject to review and confirmation by regional planning commissions, as consistent with the aforementioned goals. While mandatory conformance to these goals (but not mandatory planning) was stripped from Act 200 by the Vermont legislature in 1989, nevertheless there are advantages to being "confirmed" by a regional planning commission as conforming to the state goals: no state affordable housing review, assured compatibility of state agency plans (which must, under Act 200, be consistent with the aforementioned goals) with municipal plans, authority to levy impact fees on new developments, and eligibility for certain state funds.

---

[24] 767 P.2d 815 (Haw. 1989). For extensive commentary on this and other recent land-use and environmental law cases from Hawaii, see David L. Callies, et al., *The Lum Court, Land Use, and the Environment: A Survey of Hawai'i Case Law 1983 to 1991*, 14 U. Haw. L. Rev. 119 (1992).

[26] Vt. Stat. Ann. tit. 10, § 6001 (1984) . . . .

[27] Vt. Stat. Ann. tit. 24, § 4301 (1992).

C. *Maine: A Step Backward?*

Maine's site location law was also chronicled as a bellwether state in *Quiet Revolution*. Indeed, its 1988 Comprehensive Planning and Land Management Act mandated the preparation of local government comprehensive plans conforming to ten growth management goals, and provided substantial funding to implement the Act together with such incentives as (like Vermont) the power to impose impact fees.[31] Unfortunately, the Act fell victim to 1991 budget reductions, eliminating not only funding for the Act's implementation, but the entire Comprehensive Planning Office, as well as the mandatory planning elements of the Act. Some funds were allocated to the Department of Economic and Community Development in 1992 to continue the process, and a municipality which chooses to prepare a comprehensive plan must follow the aforementioned state standards.

D. *Florida and Concurrency*

Florida was not a "revolutionary" state in 1970, but it has certainly made up for it in the intervening quarter century. While concern over protecting critical environmental areas, together with the need to control large developments, provides strong impetus for Florida's program, the huge population gains in the 1970s and 1980s probably provided more.

Commencing with the Environmental Land and Water Management Act in 1972,[34] Florida began its foray into statewide land-use controls by protecting areas of critical state concern through state designation and regulating developments of regional impact through regional and statewide oversight by means of an appeal (from local government designation) process. So far, four areas of critical state concern have been designated: Big Cyprus, Green Swamp, the Florida Keys, and Apalachicola Bay.

. . . .

Then, in the mid-1980s, Florida adopted its tripartite planning system and concurrency. The product of a second Environmental Land Management Study (ELMS) Committee, the Florida State and Regional Planning Act of 1984[41] mandated the preparation of a state comprehensive plan and the preparation and adoption of regional plans by each of Florida's eleven planning regions, each to be consistent with the state comprehensive plan. Amendments to the Act in 1985[42] required each local government to prepare and adopt local plans consistent with both regional and state plans, and to implement such local plans through local land development regulations and development orders. The amendments also provided for state financial sanctions against local governments which failed to adopt consistent local plans, and established broad standing requirements for citizens to chal-

---

[31] ME. REV. STAT. ANN. tit. 30-A, § 4301 (1993).

[34] FLA. STAT. ANN. § 380.012-10 (1972).

[41] FLA. STAT. ch. 186.001-.911 (Supp. 1984).

[42] FLA. STAT. ch. 163.3161-3215 (Supp. 1986).

lenge inconsistent (with local plans) local land-use regulations and development orders. Thus, land-use controls at the local level must ultimately be consistent with state and regional planning goals through the planning consistency process. . . .

Moreover, the 1985 amendments to the Act require the local formulation of a program for providing infrastructure (need and location of public facilities, as well as their projected costs) and forbid the granting of any land development permits unless public facilities will be concurrently available to meet the needs generated by that development. . . .

   . . . .

E. *Georgia Plans*

The largest state east of the Mississippi, Georgia, also commenced serious efforts at state planning and growth management after watching its population more than double between 1940 and 1986, with one-third of that population growth (1.25 million people) occurring since 1970. Often described as a "top-down" approach to statewide land-use controls, Georgia passed a startlingly comprehensive state-regional-local planning consistency program in the late 1980s, . . . the Georgia Planning Act of 1989.[50]

The Georgia Planning Act closely resembles the conceptual framework of Florida's legislation in several respects, but without some of Florida's mandatory features. . . .

Thus, like Florida, Georgia local governments—at least those thus "persuaded" to participate—must conform land-use regulations to local comprehensive plans which must, in turn, conform to regional and state plans. . . .

F. *Oregon: Planning as Process*

Oregon is perhaps the paradigm conformance state. Just as the legislature passed the basic legislation (in 1973) establishing its statewide land-use system, the Oregon courts startled the country by establishing that local plans took precedence over local zoning, and that any conflicts between them were to be resolved in favor of the plans.[53] Established by the 1973 legislation,[54] a Land Conservation and Development Commission (LCDC) adopts and enforces nineteen statewide planning goals, to which local plans (and, after the aforementioned court cases, local land-use controls) must conform. The goals are adopted after a complex publication and hearing process.

---

[50] GA. CODE ANN. § 50-8-1 (1990). . . .

[53] Fasano v. Board of County Comm'rs, 507 P.2d 23 (Or. 1973), and Baker v. City of Milwaukee, 533 P.2d 772 (Or. 1975).

[54] OR. REV. STAT. § 197.040 (1991).

A 1977 amendment to the statute provides an administrative process by which the LCDC "acknowledges" that Oregon's local government land-use plans are in conformance with the state goals.[56] . . .

Acknowledgment results in local plans and regulations, as well as state goals as the basis for land development in a city or county. Moreover, state agencies are also bound by both the goals and duly acknowledged local plans and implementing regulations. . . .

Perhaps the most unique aspect of Oregon's process and conformance-oriented state land-use system is the creation of a special administrative court to hear and decide most local land-use controversies besides those dealing with goal compliance as discussed above. Established in 1979, the Land-Use Board of Appeals (LUBA) has the power to review all land-use decisions of local governments, state agencies, or special districts, whether legislative or quasijudicial in nature. This effectively shifts most land-use cases to LUBA from the judiciary as a "court of first impression."

G. *New Jersey: Fragmented Purposes, Fragmented Plans*

The roots of New Jersey's statewide planning effort are different from most of the "revolutionary" states. In the mid-1980s, two disparate and seemingly unrelated events ultimately produced the New Jersey State Planning Act of 1985:[62] the New Jersey Supreme Court rendered its famous landmark fair housing decision, *Southern Burlington County NAACP v. Township of Mount Laurel*,[63] which required adherence to a 1980 State Development Plan Guide, and an incoming governor promptly abolished the state's Division of State and Regional Planning which had prepared the guide. What followed was an attempt to take back from the state supreme court (which had lamented the lack of legislative action and maintained that it acted only after legislative dereliction) the initiative over allocation of affordable housing, coupled with urban growth pressures resulting from the state's location (between New York and Philadelphia). Moreover, New Jersey is the only "revolutionary" state of its size to have dealt with its principal critical areas—the Pinelands and the Hackensack Meadowlands—by separate legislation, producing separate land-use plans and regulations administered by separate governmental agencies.

The 1985 Act is long on rhetoric but short on implementation. The resulting 1989 State Plan establishes statewide goals and objectives for land use, housing, economic development, transportation, natural resource conservation, agriculture, farmland retention, recreation, urban and suburban redevelopment, historic preservation, public facilities and services, and intergovernmental coordination. It further divides the state into seven tiers for purposes of deciding where to encourage growth, redevelopment, and resource preservation. . . .

---

[56] OR. REV. STAT. § 197.250 (1991).

[62] N.J. STAT. ANN. § 52:18A-196 (1993).

[63] 456 A.2d 390 (N.J. 1983).

But until 1992 the only means of implementation was by a process called "cross-acceptance": the comparing of planning policies among governmental levels in order to attain compatibility between local, county, and state plans.[66] Originally envisioned to take a few months, it has instead taken several years. . . . Finally in late 1992, state regulations (issued by the State Planning Commission) to provide for state certification of local plans for consistency with the State Plan may well result in strengthened plan implementation, because zoning in New Jersey must, by statute, be consistent with local master plans, at least with respect to housing and land use.

H. *Washington: More Than an Oregon Clone?*

Apparently reacting to the effects of rapid urbanization on their "Northwest" way of life, the Washington legislature passed the latest in "revolutionary" state land-use laws in 1990 and 1991, both entitled Growth Management Acts.[71] The centerpiece of the legislation is the requirement that all counties with urban growth problems (those with populations over 50,000, or with a ten to twenty percent growth rate) must prepare comprehensive plans with certain mandatory elements: land use, housing, capital facilities, utilities, rural lands, and transportation. Moreover, each such county's plan must reflect a cooperative effort with each unit of local government in that county's jurisdiction, and each mandatory element must be consistent with the other elements in the plan as well as with the plans of each city or county sharing a common border or regional problem. In such counties (indeed, in all counties which have a plan), all land-use regulations must be in conformance with such plans.

    . . . .

I. *Rhode Island*

The Rhode Island statewide land-use control system also utilizes strict conformance between compulsory local plans and state planning goals. These are embodied in the Comprehensive Planning and Land Use Regulation Act and the State Comprehensive Plan Appeals Board Act.[81] The former lists ten state goals with which local government comprehensive plans (including implementing programs) must be consistent. Among these are protection of natural resources, open space, recreational, cultural and historic resources, development of affordable housing, economic development, and the compatibility of growth with the natural characteristics of the land. The local plans must also be consistent with a range of regional goals, including public facilities financing for transportation, recreation, and the like.

The state director of the Division of Planning reviews local plans for consistency with the state act as described above. A local government can appeal a non-

---

[66] N.J. Stat. Ann. §§ 52:18A-202b (1993).

[71] Wash. Rev. Code § 36.70A.10 (1992).

[81] R.I. Gen. Laws § 45-22.2-1 (1991).

consistent determination to a Comprehensive Plan Appeals Board appointed by the governor. In the event that the local comprehensive plan is inconsistent, the director prepares, and the Appeals Board adopts, a comprehensive plan for the recalcitrant local government. . . .

J. *Maryland: The Latest Revolutionary State*

The Maryland Economic Growth, Resource Protection, and Planning Act of 1992[88] requires all local governments to conform to a series of "visions" set out in the Act and lists a number of required local plan elements, among them: a land-use element, a public facilities element, a transportation element, a mineral resources element, a critical areas element, and a streamlined development applications review in designated growth areas. Particularly, if a local government fails to adopt the latter, state standards instead apply.

III. Conclusion: Came the Revolution . . . ?

While several other states have begun to wrestle with growth management, resource protection, and statewide land-use controls through the appointment of commissions and task forces and the drafting of bills, the foregoing represent the major advances in the quiet revolution over the past quarter century. It may very well be true that it is too early to declare the revolution complete, as some commentators have suggested, but if one concentrates only on those states wrestling with growth and/or trying to protect scarce natural and/or cultural resources, the trend is unmistakable. Moreover, the "revolutionary" laws have so far been broadly supported by state courts.

These new "revolutionary" state programs have more in common besides judicial acceptance. Virtually every one is based upon a state plan, though they vary in length and complexity from pages of detailed (and often ultimately inconsistent) goals, criteria, and implementing actions to a few well-chosen standards. Also, most of the new systems either require comprehensive land and facilities planning at the local government level in accordance with state standards, or require those local governments that choose to plan to meet those standards. For the most part, the states offer incentives for local governments to engage in such comprehensive planning. About half go further and impose sanctions for noncomplying local governments. All require a measure of conformance between the state and the local plans, and most specifically require that local land development regulations and permits conform to the state-approved local plan, thereby ensuring a degree of consistency with state plan elements as well. A few jurisdictions are experimenting with direct "concurrency" between public facilities planning and implementation and local land-use permitting, though none appear to have gone so far as Florida.

---

[88] 1992 Md. Laws 437 . . . .

Finally, approval of a local plan by a state agency usually results in a measure of local control over state decisions in that local jurisdiction.

Since protection of natural areas and resources was a primary goal of the original revolution, it is not surprising that most of the new state programs explicitly provide for the protection of such values, whether or not formally called areas of critical state concern. Some states have added historical and cultural values to the list of protected areas. In order to oversee these and other "revolutionary" programs, many of the states have created new state and regional agencies for the purpose. Some—like Oregon—have created "land courts" to hear and decide disputes arising under the new programs.

In sum, state plans and the relationship of local plans and implementing regulations continue to be a hallmark of the revolution. So does the creation of new state agencies. On balance, state courts continue to be supportive, although the continued libertarian and property rights focus of the present U.S. Supreme Court may render some of that support meaningless. Permit simplification continues by and large to elude revolutionary remedy, and there is yet no clear answer on how best to provide public facilities to serve new development.

F. Growth Management

ADEQUATE PUBLIC FACILITIES REQUIREMENTS: REFLECTIONS ON FLORIDA'S CONCURRENCY SYSTEM FOR MANAGING GROWTH

Thomas G. Pelham
19 F.S.U. L. Rev. 973 (1992)[*]

I. INTRODUCTION

Florida's concurrency system is our nation's most ambitious experiment in growth management for several reasons. First, it integrates local capital improvements programming with the local land development regulatory process. The integration of these two historically distinct processes is embodied in the concurrency requirement, which provides that adequate public facilities shall be available concurrent with development. Second, this system is the first attempt to implement the concurrency concept on a statewide basis, a truly monumental task considering that Florida is the fourth largest and one of our fastest growing states. Third, this system is being implemented as part of a state, regional, and local planning process that has made Florida the uncontested leader of the ongoing national movement to reform traditional local development regulatory systems. . . .

II. OVERVIEW

The use of capital improvements controls as tools to manage growth in rapidly urbanizing areas has increased dramatically in the past two decades. These controls establish a connection between a local government's capital improvements activities and the local land planning and regulatory process. At the planning level, local capital improvements planning and programming are integrated with the local comprehensive planning process. At the regulatory level, development approvals for individual projects are linked to the provision or availability of certain public facilities or services.

The growing popularity of capital improvements controls is primarily the result of two related trends. First, local officials and planners have increasingly recognized the critical relationship between local government capital improvement activities and the development process. . . .

Second, the judiciary has become more receptive to the use of capital improvement controls to manage growth. . . .

Among the capital improvements controls devised by local governments, perhaps the most popular is the adequate public facilities requirement. This requirement makes the issuance of development approvals contingent on the availability of adequate public facilities. In some states, like Florida, the requirement is phrased in terms of ensuring that facilities are available "concurrent" with development or the impacts of development, hence the "concurrency requirement." The terms "concurrency," "concurrency requirement," and "adequate public facilities requirement" are used interchangeably in this Article to refer to the legal mandate that development approval be conditioned on the provision of public facilities and services.

Until recently, the enactment of adequate public facilities requirements was primarily a local government phenomenon. Following the judicial sanction of these requirements in New York in 1972 in the landmark case of *Golden v. Planning Board of Ramapo*,[7] local adequate public facilities ordinances proliferated throughout the nation, particularly in high growth areas. For example, a recent survey revealed that thirty percent of California's cities have adopted an adequate public facilities requirement, making it the most commonly used local growth management technique in that state.

Enacted pursuant to home rule powers, traditional state zoning enabling legislation, or in some instances through the initiative and referendum process, these local regulations vary widely in stated purpose, scope, and detail and the extent to which they are linked to a comprehensive planning framework. . . .

. . . .

State governments have begun to take a more active role in this arena, not only to authorize local adequate public facilities requirements, but to establish guidelines for their adoption and implementation. In the *Ramapo* case the New York Court of Appeals held that zoning controls that linked the timing of development to the availability of public facilities were within the ambit of that state's traditional zoning enabling legislation. Nevertheless, following the *Ramapo* decision, several states, to remove any doubt about this issue, amended their zoning enabling acts to expressly authorize their local governments to impose such requirements. Recently, two states—Florida and Washington—moved beyond permissive enabling legislation and mandated their local governments to adopt and implement concurrency systems pursuant to state guidelines.

In 1985 Florida became the first state to adopt mandatory concurrency legislation; it included the mandate in its landmark growth management legislation, which establishes a state, regional, and local planning process. This legislation expresses the intent "that public facilities and services needed to support development shall be available *concurrent* with the impacts of such development."[23] To

---

[7]   285 N.E.2d 291 (N.Y.), *appeal dismissed*, 409 U.S. 1003 (1972).

[23]   FLA. STAT. § 163.3177(10)(h) (1991) (emphasis added).

meet this requirement, each of Florida's local governments must adopt a local comprehensive plan containing a capital improvements element identifying and providing for the public facilities needed to accommodate projected growth and establishing minimum level-of-service (LOS) standards for those facilities. Local governments also must adopt implementing land development regulations that prohibit issuance of a development permit that would result in a reduction of the LOS below the established standards.

In 1990 Washington became the second state to impose the concurrency requirement on its local governments.[26] Although the Washington system is not as comprehensive as Florida's, it does link the concurrency requirement to a mandatory local planning process. . . .

Other state and local governments are likely to consider adoption of adequate public facility requirements. Several states are engaged in planning processes or special programs that may culminate in the adoption of statewide concurrency systems. Consequently, the early experiences of states such as Florida merit serious attention and study.

. . . .

III. THE ADEQUATE PUBLIC FACILITIES REQUIREMENT: ORIGINS, PURPOSES, AND CONCERNS

The adequate public facilities or concurrency requirement is a growth management tool for ensuring the availability of adequate public facilities and services to accommodate development. It seeks to coordinate the timing of development with capital improvements planning by providing for the delivery of necessary facilities simultaneously with, or within a reasonable time of, the permitting or occupation of new development. It attempts to ensure the adequacy of the facilities and services by setting minimum performance standards or measures for each facility or service category. The linchpin of the requirement is a prohibition against the issuance of a development permit unless the requisite facilities and services will be available within the prescribed time and will be adequate as measured by the established standards. However, the purpose of the requirement is not to impose a moratorium on development. Rather, it seeks to avoid the necessity for moratoria by ensuring that public facilities are available when needed.

Concurrency is a fundamentally sensible but frequently controversial concept. Driving the concurrency requirement is a "pay as we grow" public policy that development should not be permitted unless simultaneous financial commitments are also made to provide the public facilities and services necessary to serve the development. This policy's logic is difficult to refute. Nevertheless, concurrency evokes considerable controversy. The land development industry is likely to protest any application of a concurrency requirement because it controls the timing of development, a factor which traditionally has been left to the private sector and the

---

[26]   1990 Wash. Legis. Serv. 1375 (West).

dictates of a free market economy. The requirement also raises the specter of building moratoria because of inadequate facilities unless developers pay to upgrade inadequate infrastructure. Even among some strong proponents of land use controls, a concurrency requirement may engender considerable suspicion and criticism if it appears to be an exclusionary device or thinly disguised no-growth scheme, neglects other equally important planning goals such as affordable housing, or if it is imposed arbitrarily without the benefit of advance study and planning and the existence of adequate infrastructure funding systems.

Given the controversial nature of the concurrency concept, judicial challenges to local governments' efforts to implement the requirement are inevitable. The challengers are likely to characterize the requirement as an illegitimate means of halting growth and development, restricting private property rights, and unfairly shifting the cost of providing public facilities to the development industry. If the concurrency concept and its origins are not understood, or if the purposes of a particular concurrency system are either not clearly articulated or are suspect, a reviewing court may be persuaded by such characterizations. Accordingly, in designing, implementing, and evaluating concurrency systems, it is important to understand the origins and purposes of the adequate public facilities requirement and the concerns that land use planners and commentators, affected interests, and the courts may have about its implementation.

. . . .

Public concern for the funding and delivery of infrastructure to accommodate growth became increasingly evident during the development of subdivision controls over the last several decades. Initially, subdivision controls consisted of simple platting requirements designed to make it easier to buy and sell land. After rampant land subdivision and speculation produced millions of vacant platted lots lacking basic public facilities and services, state and local governments expanded their subdivision regulations in the 1920s and '30s to address infrastructure needs. . . .

The financial pressures of providing infrastructure intensified with the rapid suburbanization of American cities following World War II. As local governments struggled to provide facilities and services to sprawling developments, they searched for ways to make new development pay for itself. Local governments began to amend their subdivision regulations to require developers to dedicate land or make monetary contributions to finance a wide range of subdivision improvements, including onsite and offsite street improvements and park and school sites. From this practice evolved impact fee systems for requiring developers to pay a pro rata share of the cost of a range of public facilities needed to accommodate new development. As a result of judicial challenges, the law of subdivision exactions and impact fees was developed by state courts to uphold the validity of these requirements so long as certain conditions were met. . . .

Another significant phase in the evolution of both American land use controls generally and capital improvements controls specifically began in the 1950s and '60s. Historically, the adoption of a separate comprehensive plan was not a legal prerequisite to the exercise of zoning and other land use regulations. However, many land use planners and commentators long advocated such a requirement. . . .

Inspired by such advocacy, a number of states in the 1960s and '70s enacted legislation requiring that local land use regulations be consistent with a separately prepared and adopted comprehensive plan. The local comprehensive plan was to become the vehicle for integrating capital improvements planning with land use planning.

In the 1960s and '70s a few local governments also began developing timing and sequential development controls. By linking zoning and subdivision regulations with the capital improvements elements of local comprehensive plans, these controls sought to coordinate the granting of new development approvals with the planned provision of adequate public facilities. . . .

. . . .

Placed in historical context, the Florida concurrency requirement is a logical outgrowth of the zoning, subdivision, and planning controls that have evolved over the last five or six decades. It is a growth management tool that builds upon earlier efforts to ensure the availability of adequate public facilities to accommodate new development. Conceptually, the concurrency requirement is a neutral growth management tool; it neither encourages nor discourages growth, but it simply commands that development be accompanied by the provision of adequate public facilities. But like other land use controls, concurrency can be designed or manipulated to achieve a variety of purposes, some laudable and some suspect. Thus, while the concurrency requirement itself is not revolutionary, it is important to understand the purposes for which it is being imposed and the concerns that it engenders.

As noted earlier, *Ramapo*[76] is the seminal decision establishing the legality of adequate public facilities requirements. In *Ramapo* the New York Court of Appeals reviewed the first comprehensive system for coordinating the timing and phasing of development with the provision of public facilities, discussed a number of concerns raised about the purposes and effects of such systems, and rejected statutory and constitutional attacks on the Ramapo system. Therefore, it is worthwhile to revisit in detail both the Ramapo approach and the rationale of the court's decision.

The Ramapo system was built on a comprehensive planning foundation. Following a study of the community's existing land uses, public facilities, economic base, housing needs, and projected growth, the Town adopted a master plan. To implement the master plan, it also adopted a comprehensive zoning ordinance and both a short-term and a long-term capital improvements program. The short-term program consisted of a capital budget providing for the development of facilities identified in the master plan during the initial six-year period. The long-term capital improvements program provided for the location and timing of the development of facilities specified in the master plan during the subsequent twelve-year period. Collectively, the two plans specified the capital improvements needed for maximum development of the town over an eighteen-year period consistent with the adopted master plan.

---

[76] 285 N.E.2d 291 (N.Y.), *appeal dismissed*, 409 U.S. 1003 (1972).

In order to coordinate residential development with the Town's ability to provide public facilities under its adopted capital improvements programs, the Town amended its subdivision ordinance to prohibit residential subdivision approval in the unincorporated areas of the Town unless the developer first secured a special permit. Issuance of a special permit was made contingent on the availability of five public facilities or services: sanitary sewer; drainage; parks or recreation, including public schools; roads; and firehouses. The availability of the facilities and services was measured by a point system based on a sliding scale of values assigned to the specific facilities. No permit would be issued unless fifteen points were accumulated, but a developer was permitted to earn points and accelerate the date of subdivision approval by providing the facilities. At least one single-family residential dwelling was permitted on each tract of land, and provisions for vested rights, variances, and reduced property tax assessments were included to avoid unreasonable restrictions. As described by the court, the system provided "an over-all program of orderly growth and adequate facilities through a sequential development policy commensurate with progressing availability and capacity of public facilities."[87]

Individual local landowners who had been denied subdivision approval and the county builders association contended that the Town was not authorized to adopt the amendments to its subdivision ordinance and also challenged both the purposes and the alleged effects of the amendments. First, they alleged that the regulation of population growth through timing and phasing controls was not authorized by the state's zoning enabling act. Second, they contended that the Ramapo scheme did not advance legitimate zoning purposes. Third, they argued that the ordinance, by restricting development for up to eighteen years, diminished the value of property to such an extent that it prevented any profitable or beneficial use of the landowners' property. Accordingly, the alleged effect of the ordinance was so confiscatory as to constitute a deprivation of property without due process of law and a taking of property without just compensation.

The court rejected the *ultra vires* argument based on its interpretation of the New York zoning enabling act and its understanding of the purposes of the Ramapo ordinance. . . .

Similarly, the court easily disposed of the attacks on the system's purposes. . . .

. . . According the Ramapo scheme the traditional "presumption of validity"[106] and refusing "to substitute its judgment as to the plan's over-all effectiveness" for that of the local legislature,[107] the court easily concluded that Ramapo's system of timing and sequential development controls was a reasonable means of achieving its legitimate public purposes.

The court almost summarily rejected the contention that the Ramapo system constituted an unlawful taking of the plaintiffs' property. After citing its own prior ruling that a regulation which *permanently* precludes all reasonable use of property

---

[87] *Id.* [at 296.]

[106] *Id.* at 301. . . .

[107] *Id.* . . .

is a taking, the court concluded that the Ramapo restrictions, while "substantial in nature and duration,"[110] were only "temporary," even if they remained in effect for the eighteen-year life of the program.[111] Moreover, based on the assumption that the Town would fully and timely implement its capital improvements program, and noting the various savings provisions in the Ramapo system, the court observed that landowners would be able to make reasonable use of their property within the fixed eighteen-year period. Accordingly, the court held that the ordinance did not violate either the federal or state constitutions.

Despite the New York court's validation of the Ramapo plan, many land use lawyers, planners, and commentators have expressed a variety of concerns about inappropriate purposes and undesirable effects of such systems. . . .

Perhaps the most forceful criticism of the Ramapo plan and its progeny is that they are vehicles for exclusion. Left to their own devices, local governments have engaged in various exclusionary schemes. Some have sought to exclude population generally through limited or no-growth schemes. Others have attempted to exclude discrete segments of the population such as racial or minority groups or particular uses such as low-income housing. Still others have engaged in fiscal zoning practices to maximize the local tax base through the promotion of commercial and industrial uses and the exclusion of residential uses that do not pay for themselves. Critics of the Ramapo plan have suggested that it contained all of these elements. . . .

Ostensibly, the *Ramapo* majority did not take lightly the contention that the municipality's plan cloaked exclusionary purposes. Quoting from a famous Pennsylvania exclusionary zoning case, the court stated: "[Z]oning is a means by which a government body can plan for the future—it may not be used as a means to deny the future."[123] Accordingly, the court warned that it would not tolerate any local exclusionary efforts to avoid the burdens of growth and that communities must "confront the challenge of population growth with open doors."[124] However, impressed by the Town's comprehensive planning efforts, its commitments to provide public facilities, and its provision for low-income housing, the court concluded that the Ramapo plan was an attempt "to maximize growth by the efficient use of land" and therefore assimilated rather than excluded population.[125] Because of its highly deferential posture, the court did not closely scrutinize the Ramapo plan's particulars, which were inconsistent with either the maximization of growth or the efficient use of land.

. . . .

---

[110] *Ramapo*, 285 N.E.2d at 304.

[111] *Id.* at 303.

[123] Golden v. Planning Bd. of Ramapo, 285 N.E.2d 291, 301 (N.Y.), *appeal dismissed*, 409 U.S. 1003 (1972) (quoting National Land & Inv. Co. v. Kohn, 215 A.2d 597, 610 (Pa. 1965), which invalidated a four-acre minimum lot size requirement as exclusionary).

[124] *Ramapo*, 285 N.E.2d at 302.

[125] *Id.*

A second major concern relates to the perceived need for a broader geographic perspective in land use planning. The propensity of local governments to pursue their own parochial and selfish interests at the expense of their neighbors and region has been widely noted and criticized. Some critics have contended that Ramapo-type controls would further encourage those tendencies and that local governments should not be allowed to impose them without state supervision or a requirement that it be in accordance with state and regional planning goals and policies. . . . The *Ramapo* majority also recognized the broader geographical dimensions of urban problems, the failure of local governments to effectively address and solve those problems, and the need for a regional or statewide planning process. Nevertheless, accurately observing that "the power to zone under current law is vested in local municipalities, and we are constrained to resolve the issues accordingly," the majority declined to invalidate the Ramapo ordinance "in the wistful hope" that the various reform movements "will soon bear fruit."[139] Based upon its construction of the New York zoning enabling act, the court held that the Town was empowered to adopt the Ramapo plan, which it characterized as "a first practical step toward controlled growth achieved without forsaking broader social purposes."[140]

. . . .

Another criticism of the Ramapo plan was that it promoted and programmed urban sprawl. This criticism is ironic because the Ramapo system was adopted "for the alleged purpose of eliminating premature subdivision and urban sprawl."[148] But as some critics have pointed out, while the system discouraged the "leapfrog" variety of sprawl by requiring sequential development patterns, it perpetuated the continuing spread of low-density residential sprawl because it failed to alter the underlying spatial pattern of large-lot, single-family zoning. . . . Given the traditional presumption of validity that it afforded the Ramapo ordinance, the court was not inclined to second-guess the overall effectiveness of the Ramapo system and appeared to accept at face value the Town's contention that the purpose of the plan was to control urban sprawl. Nevertheless, given the Ramapo plan's almost total embrace of low-density residential zoning, the criticism that the plan promoted urban sprawl is a valid one.

Perhaps the most fundamental question raised about Ramapo-type plans is the nature of the local government's obligation to provide the requisite facilities. If development permission is contingent upon the availability of public facilities, the local government can effectively stop growth simply by failing to provide the necessary infrastructure. . . . The *Ramapo* court repeatedly refers to the Town's "obligation" to provide the facilities and its "commitment" in its adopted comprehensive plan to the construction of capital improvements. Impliedly, the court recognized a legal obligation on the part of the Town to provide the facilities necessary to gain

---

[139] *Ramapo*, 285 N.E.2d at 299-300.

[140] *Id.* at 301.

[148] *Ramapo*, 285 N.E.2d at 295.

development approval under the Ramapo system. The court also acknowledged the potential impact on the landowner or developer if the Town defaulted in its obligation or commitment. However, the court noted that in resolving a challenge to the facial validity of the Ramapo ordinance, it "must assume not only the Town's good faith, but its assiduous adherence to the program's scheduled implementation."[156] In the event the Town later defaulted in its obligation to provide the facilities, the court observed that an aggrieved landowner could bring an action to declare the ordinance unconstitutional as applied to his property or to have the restrictions removed from the property. The court did not mention the possibility of an action to compel the Town to provide the facilities or whether an action for damages would be available because of the Town's breach of its obligation.

The issue of local government's obligation takes on added significance when one considers Ramapo's rather dismal performance in implementing its six-year capital improvements program. Following the adoption of the Ramapo plan in 1969, the Town deferred major portions of its 1971 capital budget, did not even adopt capital budgets for 1972 and 1973, and significantly altered its 1974 budget. Perhaps not coincidentally, the number of dwelling units approved during each of the first five years of the plan was almost fifty percent less than the annual rate before adoption of the plan. In view of this record, perhaps a court reviewing a Ramapo-type plan should carefully scrutinize and analyze the financial feasibility of the local capital improvements program rather than assume a local government's good faith, as did the *Ramapo* court?

Closely related to the issue of the local government's obligation is the criticism that such controls can unfairly shift the burden of providing public facilities from the local government to the landowner. If a local government fails to provide the facilities necessary to obtain development approval, the developer or landowner may be forced to finance or provide the facilities, assuming this is an economically feasible option. . . .

Finally, the concern raised most frequently by the development community is that Ramapo-type systems unlawfully restrict private property rights. Not surprisingly, this was a major contention of the plaintiffs in the *Ramapo* case. Although the New York Court of Appeals rejected these contentions and the United States Supreme Court denied review of *Ramapo*, the decision hardly presents an insurmountable barrier for takings claims against other adequate public facilities requirements. . . .

Numerous commentators have criticized the *Ramapo* decision for being too deferential in its review of the Ramapo system. Undoubtedly, the traditional presumption of validity and low level of scrutiny afforded the Ramapo ordinance by the court obscured legitimate concerns about its purposes and effects. But there is more to this story than excessive judicial restraint. The court was demonstrably impressed by the Town's planning efforts. After describing in detail the Town's planning activities, including its adopted master plan and capital improvements pro-

---

[156] *Id.* at 299 n.7.

grams, the court repeatedly used these activities to buttress its disposition of the various issues. . . . The obvious moral of the *Ramapo* story is that a comprehensive plan will alleviate many judicial concerns.

. . . .

IV. The Florida Concurrency System

. . . .

Florida established a state and regional planning process and strengthened its local planning legislation in the 1980s. . . .

Florida's concurrency system is implemented within and as an integral part of this comprehensive planning process. Because the concurrency requirement intrudes sharply, visibly, and controversially into the land use regulatory process by threatening the denial of development permits, it tends to overshadow other important components of the larger planning system of which it is a part. In evaluating Florida's concurrency system, however, it is essential to understand and consider the underlying state, regional, and local planning system that supports it. Like its Ramapo precursor, the Florida concurrency system has a strong local comprehensive planning foundation, but it also encompasses state and regional issues and addresses many of the other concerns raised about Ramapo-type systems. Unlike the Ramapo plan, a locally inspired initiative applicable only to undeveloped areas, the Florida system is state-driven and applies to all areas. Pursuant to state guidelines, every local government must adopt a concurrency system that applies to both developed and undeveloped areas. These new variations on an old theme create challenging implementation problems and some potentially thorny legal issues.

A. The Comprehensive Planning Framework

Florida has created a pyramidal planning hierarchy. At the top of the hierarchy is the State Comprehensive Plan, at middle level are comprehensive regional policy plans, and at the foundation are local comprehensive plans. The three planning levels are integrated through consistency requirements. The goals and policies of the State Comprehensive Plan must be implemented through the regional policy plans that are consistent with the state plan and through local plans that are consistent with both the state and regional plans. Local comprehensive plans must be implemented through land development regulations and development orders that are consistent with the local plan.

1. State and Regional Issues

The cry of the Ramapo critics for a state and regional planning system has been heeded in Florida. A state and regional perspective is injected into the local planning process in three important ways. First, local comprehensive plans must be consistent with both the state and the applicable regional policy plan. Second, local comprehensive plans must satisfy statutory intergovernmental coordination requirements to ensure that extraterritorial issues are adequately addressed. Third, the Florida Department of Community Affairs (DCA) must review and approve local plans for consistency with the state and regional plans and compliance with the intergovernmental coordination and other state requirements.

. . . .

2. The Local Comprehensive Plan

As in the Ramapo plan, implementation of Florida's concurrency requirement is linked to a local comprehensive planning process. Before imposition of the concurrency requirement, a local government must confront and resolve the basic issues of growth and development, infrastructure needs and costs, and existing and projected revenue sources. The vehicle for addressing these threshold issues is the local comprehensive plan, which must be reviewed by DCA pursuant to the agency's minimum criteria rule[200] for compliance with state law.

. . . .

3. Accommodating Growth in Well-Balanced Communities

The Ramapo plan sought to maximize commercial and low-density residential development to the exclusion of other land uses, despite the Town's alleged goal of "a balanced cohesive community" and its disavowal of exclusionary motives.[219] This strategy would not be acceptable under Florida's growth management laws. The express philosophy of this state's local planning Act is that local governments must accommodate growth in well-balanced communities.

. . . .

4. Planning and Programming Capital Improvements

One of the most impressive features of Florida's local comprehensive planning system is a strong capital improvements planning and programming requirement. Local governments cannot impose the concurrency requirement until a program for providing infrastructure has been formulated and adopted as a component of the local comprehensive plan. This program must describe how, when, and where the local government will provide infrastructure to serve development allowed under the comprehensive plan. . . .

. . . .

5. Providing Affordable Housing

As the criticisms of the Ramapo plan illustrate, growth management systems are frequently alleged to be exclusionary in purpose or effect, especially with

---

[200] FLA. ADMIN. CODE ANN. ch. 9J-5 (1991).

[219] Golden v. Planning Bd. of Ramapo, 285 N.E.2d 291, 295, 302 (N.Y.), *appeal dismissed,* 409 U.S. 1003 (1972).

regard to low-income groups. This problem has been considered and addressed in Florida. Recognizing the importance of housing and the possibility that growth management systems may be used for exclusionary purposes, Florida's comprehensive planning laws emphasize the provision of affordable housing for all income groups. . . .

6. Preventing Urban Sprawl

A central policy of Florida's growth management laws is the discouragement of urban sprawl. The State Comprehensive Plan contains numerous goals and policies designed to prevent sprawling development patterns. Several of these goals and policies relate directly to the coordination of land development and the provision of public facilities. . . .

. . . .

B. The Concurrency Requirement

Florida's concurrency requirement is an integral part of the state's comprehensive planning legislation. However, the statutory concurrency provisions offer little practical guidance for its actual implementation and application. Consequently, the regulatory parameters of the requirement have been largely developed through DCA's administrative rulemaking and local plan compliance review processes, albeit with considerable consultation with the Florida Legislature. . . .

1. The Statutory and Rule Bases of the Requirement

Although the term "concurrency" did not appear in either the State Comprehensive Plan or the local planning legislation enacted in 1985, these two acts together established the statutory foundation for Florida's concurrency system. In addition to establishing the comprehensive planning framework discussed in the previous section, the 1985 legislation enunciated the basic principle of concurrency. . . .

. . . .

2. The Public Facilities Subject to Concurrency

The Florida Legislature has not satisfactorily dealt with the issue of which public facilities should be subject to the concurrency requirement. Neither the 1985 Act nor the original chapter 9J-5 expressly defines the public facilities which are subject to the concurrency requirement. . . .

. . . .

3. The Standards for Measuring the Adequacy and Availability of Public Facilities

The capital improvements element of a local comprehensive plan must establish "[s]tandards to ensure the *availability* of public facilities and the *adequacy* of those facilities including acceptable levels of service."[280] The Legislature defined "availability," but, unfortunately, included no definition of adequacy and provided no guidance for establishing standards for measuring it other than a requirement that it must be measured in terms of LOS standards. Consequently, DCA and local governments have been compelled to develop standards through the administrative rulemaking and plan compliance review processes.

. . . .

4. The Special Case of Transportation

For numerous reasons, transportation has been the most difficult facility category to subject to effective concurrency management. A large portion of Florida's existing infrastructure deficiencies relate to transportation facilities; the state already has many miles of backlogged roads. Transportation facilities are much costlier and take significantly more time to construct than do the other public facilities. Local governments are not able to internalize traffic impacts in their communities because they cannot control access to roads that cross jurisdictional boundaries. . . .

DCA has recognized some of these problems by giving local governments much greater flexibility in dealing with transportation concurrency in their local plans. For example, recognizing the undesirability of traffic-related moratoria and the fact that traffic congestion, while it may be inconvenient, does not affect public health and safety to the same degree as inadequate water, sewer, and drainage facilities, DCA has found in compliance local plans that allow continuing development on backlogged systems while the local government eliminates existing deficiencies over a ten-, twelve-, or fifteen-year period. . . .

. . . .

5. The Governmental Obligation to Provide Adequate Public Facilities

The 1985 Act does not expressly impose upon local governments a duty to provide the facilities necessary to comply with the concurrency requirement. However, this obligation is implicit in the relevant provisions of the Act and chapter 9J-5. . . .

. . . .

---

[280] Fla. Stat. § 163.3177(3)(a)3. (1991) (emphasis added).

6. Paying for Infrastructure

The obligation to provide adequate public facilities cannot be satisfied without adequate revenue. As the Ramapo experience illustrates, a local government's ability to fund its capital improvements program is critical to the success of adequate public facilities requirements, or at least those that are intended to accommodate rather than exclude growth. Consequently, if a state legislature mandates that local governments impose and enforce a concurrency requirement, it has a corresponding obligation to ensure that adequate revenue is available to local governments. Florida has not yet satisfactorily fulfilled this responsibility.

. . . .

7. The Relationship Between Concurrency and Other State Planning Goals and Policies

The State Comprehensive Plan contains a broad range of state planning goals and related policies. Encompassing social, economic, environmental, and physical land planning concerns, the twenty-seven goals are of equal weight and status. The state plan does not rank or give preferred status to any of the planning goals, including those relating to concurrency. Obviously, these goals may conflict when applied to particular programs and situations. Consequently, the 1985 Legislature envisioned a balancing process for applying the various goals: "The plan shall be construed and applied as a whole, and no specific goal or policy in the plan shall be construed or applied in isolation from the other goals and policies in the plan."[332]

. . . .

8. The Local System for Monitoring and Enforcing Concurrency

How does Florida enforce the concurrency requirement? Essentially, the State relies on the good faith of local governments and citizen actions to ensure that development permits will not be issued unless adequate public facilities will be available. Each local government must adopt a concurrency management system to monitor and enforce LOS standards. . . .

Ultimately, however, if a local government does not meet its obligation, enforcement of the Florida concurrency requirement is left to citizen action. . . .

V. OF BROKEN COMMITMENTS, MORATORIA, AND TAKING CLAIMS: THE NEED FOR AN EFFECTIVE LANDOWNER'S REMEDY

Florida's growth management laws address many of the concerns raised by landowners and others about the Ramapo adequate public facilities requirement. If properly implemented, the state, regional, and local comprehensive planning

---

[332] FLA. STAT. § 187.101(3) (1991).

processes ensure that Florida's local governments cannot use their concurrency systems for exclusionary purposes and that they must plan for and accommodate growth with due consideration for state and regional concerns. Nevertheless, concurrency systems will still impinge on private property rights, especially if adequate public facilities are not available to satisfy the concurrency requirement. Consequently, constitutional challenges to local concurrency systems based on the Due Process, Equal Protection, and Taking Clauses are inevitable. These constitutional claims are likely to disappoint landowners in most cases.

. . . .

Given the breadth of the public welfare concept and the deferential standard of judicial review, successful due process and equal protection claims against concurrency systems are likely to be a rare occurrence. . . .

Taking claims are more complicated than due process-equal protection cases and are equally problematic for landowner relief. . . .

. . . . In *First English Evangelical Lutheran Church v. County of Los Angeles*,[363] the [Supreme] Court reaffirmed that a land use regulation may go so far as to effectuate a taking and recognized the concept of temporary regulatory takings. Even more important, the Court held that if a regulation does rise to the level of a taking, invalidation of the ordinance is not a sufficient remedy, although it does render the taking a temporary—rather than a permanent—deprivation of property rights. The Just Compensation Clause of the Fifth Amendment, as made applicable to the states by the Fourteenth Amendment, requires compensation "for the period during which the taking was effective."[365] Significantly, however, the Court did not modify its previously enunciated taking tests or decide whether the regulation in question constituted a taking. Furthermore, it held that preliminary activities leading up to adoption of a regulation do not constitute a taking and expressly refrained from addressing issues arising from "normal delays in obtaining building permits, changes in zoning ordinances, variances, and the like which are not before us."[367]

. . . .

First English does not stand for the proposition that a temporary delay in the right to develop property automatically constitutes a temporary taking. As mentioned above, the Court in *First English* did not modify its previously adopted tests for determining the taking issue. Under those tests, courts have frequently held that a temporary, as opposed to a permanent, restriction on the use of property does not constitute a taking. Recall that the *Ramapo* court determined that a restriction on development of up to as much as eighteen years was temporary and therefore not a taking. Further, on remand in the *First English* case, the California Court of Appeal held that the interim regulation prohibiting construction in the flood plain did not constitute a taking even though it had been in effect for eight years.[380]

---

[363] 482 U.S. 304 (1987).

[365] *Id.* at 321.

[367] *Id.* at 321.

[380] 258 Cal. Rptr. 893, 906 (Cal. Ct. App. 1989).

According to the California court, *First English* does not convert "moratoriums and other interim land use restrictions into unconstitutional 'temporary takings' requiring compensation unless, perhaps, if these interim measures are unreasonable in purpose, duration or scope."[381] Some commentators interpret *Keystone Bituminous Coal Ass'n v. DeBenedictis*,[382] decided the same year as *First English* . . . , to mean that deprivation of present use will not necessarily constitute a taking if future use remains.[383] Arguably, then, when temporary restrictions are involved, the appropriate question should be whether there will be "a reasonable use of property measured over a reasonable period of time."[384] Consequently, the temporary taking doctrine of *First English* will probably afford much less relief from temporary, concurrency-induced moratoria than it might appear to offer at first glance.

. . . .

. . . Consider . . . the situation, as in *Ramapo*, where land in urban fringe or rural areas is not programmed to receive the public facilities and services necessary to satisfy concurrency immediately or even in the foreseeable future. Suppose, for example, that pursuant to its state-approved local comprehensive plan, which is designed to curtail urban sprawl, a local government decides not to provide public facilities—under either its short-term or long-term capital improvements plan—to support urban type development on land outside its designated urban services area. Finding it financially unfeasible to provide all of the facilities and services necessary to satisfy concurrency, a landowner who desires to develop outside the urban services area brings suit to invalidate the concurrency requirement or compel the local government to provide the necessary facilities and services. Will the landowner win?

Assuming the local plan and its application are otherwise reasonable and defensible, the concurrency requirement should withstand such attacks. The *Ramapo* decision itself is persuasive authority for the validity of this planning strategy, especially if the local plan permits the landowner to meet concurrency by providing the necessary facilities. . . .

Under a properly devised local comprehensive plan, courts may reject constitutional challenges even if the local plan does not permit the landowner to obtain development approval by providing its own facilities. *Construction Industry Ass'n v. City of Petaluma*[394] involved such a growth management plan. The Petaluma plan imposed an annual limit of 500 residential units that could be constructed in housing projects of more than four units. These 500 units were to be allocated in accordance with a point system based on the availability of public facilities and services and other land use criteria that allowed the City to deny development approval even when facilities and services were available. Especially relevant to the

---

[381] *Id.*

[382] 480 U.S. 470 (1987).

[383] *See, e.g.,* Linda Bozung & Deborah J. Alessi, *Recent Developments in Environmental Preservation and the Rights of Property Owners,* 20 URB. LAW. 969, 1017 (1988). . . .

[384] Bozung & Alessi, *supra* note 383, at 1017.

[394] 522 F.2d 897 (9th Cir. 1975), *cert. denied,* 424 U.S. 934 (1976).

hypothetical situation posed here, the plan also established an urban service area beyond which the City would not provide services for at least fifteen years. Unlike the Ramapo plan, the Petaluma plan contained no guarantee of ultimate development approval within a definite time period and designated areas in which the City would provide no services at all. Nevertheless, the court, in rejecting due process and other constitutional attacks on the plan, held that the City's planning goals of preserving its "small town character" and avoiding "the social and environmental problems caused by an uncontrolled growth rate" were legitimate police power objectives.[397] Under this rationale, as long as the landowner is allowed any reasonable use, whether present or future, the local plan may be able to prohibit the use of private systems pending future governmental provision of public facilities and services.

. . . .

Because of Florida's growth management requirements, especially the concurrency requirement, a local comprehensive plan imposes substantial restrictions on the use of property. As the foregoing discussion indicates, except in truly egregious cases, constitutional attacks on these restrictions will bring little relief for landowners, in part because of the comprehensive plan that imposes the restrictions. It would be both ironic and unfair if a local government that uses its comprehensive plan as a shield against constitutional challenges to concurrency restrictions could also avoid any liability or accountability for failing to fulfill the very funding commitments on which its plan is based. Invalidation of the concurrency restriction, as some courts have suggested, is not a desirable remedy because it would defeat the public purposes for which the concurrency requirement is imposed. Thus, should not the landowner be allowed to enforce the local government's statutory obligation to provide the facilities and services in accordance with its adopted local plan, even though the governmental breach of the obligation has not risen to the level of a constitutional violation?

. . . .

The courts that have considered the possibility of such actions usually have avoided the issue or reacted with caution. . . .

. . . .

Florida courts should recognize a landowner's cause of action for injunctive relief, and for damages where appropriate, to enforce local plan commitments to provide the facilities and services necessary to satisfy concurrency. A landowner can compel issuance of a development order that is consistent with the local plan. Similarly, the landowner should be entitled to compel provision of facilities and services for an otherwise permissible development that may be unreasonably delayed for concurrency reasons because of the local government's failure to deliver the facilities in accordance with its plan. . . .

. . . .

---

[397] 522 F.2d at 906-09. The court stated that while "the Plan may frustrate some legitimate regional housing needs, the Plan is not arbitrary or unreasonable." *Id.* at 908.

VI. Conclusions and Recommendations

The adequate public facilities requirement is becoming the most popular land use control in rapidly growing urban areas. A technique for controlling the timing and sequencing of development through the coordinated use of local government's fiscal and police powers, the requirement prohibits the granting of development approvals unless adequate public facilities are available to accommodate the development. . . .

In 1972 the adequate public facilities requirement was judicially sanctioned in the landmark case of *Golden v. Planning Board of Ramapo*. The New York Court of Appeals upheld Ramapo's plan for coordinating development approval with the availability of adequate public facilities and rejected contentions that the Ramapo system was exclusionary, indifferent to regional concerns, and unduly restrictive of private property rights. Critics claimed the plan was an exclusionary, fiscal zoning device that promoted commercial uses at the expense of low- and moderate-income housing, perpetuated existing patterns of low-density residential sprawl, and unfairly shifted the burden of providing public facilities to the private sector. In retrospect, the critics also should have questioned the financial feasibility of the plan.

Florida's growth management laws establish state guidelines to ensure that local governments adequately address the criticisms and concerns raised about the use of adequate public facilities requirements. . . .

Nevertheless, Florida's state-mandated concurrency system still has imperfections resulting from the Legislature's failure to consider and address a number of fundamental issues. . . .

. . . .

The most glaring defect in the Florida concurrency system is the Legislature's failure to resolve the issue of infrastructure funding. As the Ramapo experience demonstrates, concurrency requirements cannot be implemented without adequate revenue for local capital improvement programs, on which legitimate adequate public facilities requirements must be based. . . .

. . . .

Despite its flaws and some early difficulties in implementation, the Florida concurrency system is an impressive achievement in both scope and design. With little experience from other states to guide them, Florida and its local governments are putting in place the plans and regulations designed to ensure that the state grows in a financially responsible manner. In a state accustomed to "building now and paying later," the new concurrency system has engendered much controversy. . . .

Now the question is whether Florida government, both state and local, can sustain the political will necessary to implement, fund, and enforce the concurrency system it has created. In other words, will Florida's commitment to its grand experiment be equal to the grand ambition that launched it? . . .

Note

For other perspectives on growth management, see James A. Kushner, *Growth Management and the City*, 12 Yale L. & Pol'y Rev. 68 (1994); Charles L. Siemon, *Successful Growth Management Techniques: Observations from the Monkey Cage*, 29 Urb. Law. 233 (1997).

William L Evans